When A Theological Shift Changed a Nation

Mark R. Kreitzer

When A Theological Shift Changed a Nation

A Kuyperian Analysis of *Church and Society 1990*, and a Way Forward for South Africa

PETER LANG

New York · Berlin · Bruxelles · Chennai · Lausanne · Oxford

Library of Congress Cataloging-in-Publication Data

Names: Kreitzer, Mark R., author.
Title: When a theological shift changed a nation : a Kuyperian analysis of
church and society 1990, and a way forward for South Africa / Mark R.
Kreitzer.
Description: New York : Peter Lang, [2024] | Includes bibliographical
references and index. | Summary: "The volume critically analyzes the
crucial paradigm shift in the Dutch Reformed Church of South Africa
(DRC) away from both apartheid theology and classic Reformed theology.
It provides a hope-filled way forward to restore a sound Trinitarian,
covenantal, and sola scriptura theological foundation for a truly
renewed Southern Africa"— Provided by publisher.
Identifiers: LCCN 2024034418 (print) | LCCN 2024034419 (ebook) |
ISBN 9781433197338 | ISBN 9781433197345 (ebook) | ISBN 9781433197352 (epub)
Subjects: LCSH: Nederduitse Gereformeerde Sendingkerk in
Suid-Afrika—History. | Belhar confession. | Christian sociology—South
Africa—History. | Christian sociology—Reformed Church—History of
doctrines. | South Africa—Church history.
Classification: LCC BX9623.A4 K74 2024 (print) | LCC BX9623.A4 (ebook) |
DDC 284/.268—dc23/eng/20240911
LC record available at https://lccn.loc.gov/2024034418
LC ebook record available at https://lccn.loc.gov/2024034419
DOI 10.3726/b22212

Bibliographic information published by the Deutsche Nationalbibliothek.
The German National Library lists this publication in the German
National Bibliography; detailed bibliographic data is available
on the Internet at http://dnb.d-nb.de.

Cover design by Peter Lang Group AG

ISBN 9781433197338 (hardback)
ISBN 9781433197345 (ebook)
ISBN 9781433197352 (epub)
DOI 10.3726/b22212

© 2024 Peter Lang Group AG, Lausanne
Published by Peter Lang Publishing Inc., New York, USA

info@peterlang.com - www.peterlang.com

All rights reserved.

All parts of this publication are protected by copyright.
Any utilization outside the strict limits of the copyright law, without the permission of the
publisher, is forbidden and liable to prosecution.
This applies in particular to reproductions, translations, microfilming, and storage and
processing in electronic retrieval systems.

This publication has been peer reviewed.

To
my godly and beautiful wife
Nancy Carol

FOREWORD

On the surface, *Church and Society*'s (C&S) paradigm shift in social theology seems to desire to maintain faithfulness to a classic Reformational, culture-transforming worldview. However, its new paradigm adopted a futurist eschatology, cut off from God's creation, and an individual-based social-ethical system that is not found in the classic worldview that the Dutch Reformed Church established in Southern African throughout its first three and a quarter centuries there.

Still the DRC's paradigm shift in theology and in social theology did significantly facilitate massive changes in the South African nation-state at least beginning in the 1994 election that brought former prisoner, Nelson Mandela, into the President's mansion in Pretoria. The DRC borrowed its new paradigm from contemporary theologies which are similar to those of the Radical Reformation in the two respects I mention above. Like modern futurist theologies, the DRC's C&S' reflects a church-centered ecclesiology and a vison for the future that also cuts itself off from the creation and the Creator's design-norms such as the male-female binary and created languages. This opened a way to experiment with something radically new, presciently termed "the Rainbow Nation." Furthermore, like modern theologies a non-covenantal and non-Trinitarian dualistic philosophy deeply influenced C&S. This concept was

viii FOREWORD

what British Imperial Field Marshall and South African Prime Minister, Jan Smuts, coined and termed as "holism." It shared with medieval, neo-orthodox, and Radical Reformation theologies several philosophical presuppositions that are not common with classic continental Reformed theology but are shared with collectivist ideologies.

In addition, C&S rejects the classic Dutch Reformed definition of biblical infallibility (or "inerrancy") and the Heidelberg Catechism's view of justice based on biblical law. Instead, it adopts a humanist philosophy of rights based on the United Nations man-made, humanistic norms. The result is a covert radicalism seeking more-or-less to realize a postulated future, holistic kingdom but in contemporary social structures.

In summary, I analyze both the classic DRC covenantal perspective based on biblical wisdom and norms alongside of the philosophical presuppositions that C&S shared with the above-mentioned dualist theologies. I conclude that the two cannot be fused or syncretized, as C&S attempted, without much social and theological instability.

In this volume, like C&S, I reject apartheid as evil. However, unlike C&S did, I still acknowledge a covenantal worldview founded on the infallible Word, literal creation design-norms, and a long-term optimistic hope. This alternative social theology allows for self-determining yet also (con)federated ethno-linguistically based culture-groups to exist under God in both church and civil spheres. In other words, I propose an ideal of visible structures of unity that is church and civil unity, modeled on the Trinity in which true unity and real diversity must exist together in balance. This biblical alternative also provides for social compassion and impartial justice for all, including aliens and the poor. This is actually a renewal and rebuilding of Abraham Kuyper's vision for a Christianized social order with additional insights from Scripture that would rightly reject color-based discriminatory legislation. In addition, I propose mandatory biblical norms for evaluating whether ethno-linguistically based churches make or break the unity of Christ' Body in the new covenant.

Last, I contrast two models for transforming culture: The updated classic, Reformational model that I mentioned above and a neo-Radical model advocated by neo-orthodox theology and Theologies of Hope. I conclude that the DRC has embarked on the step-by-step process of falling away from a biblical view of the relationship of social systems to Scripture and church, that more or less were formerly based on the Protestant-Reformed view of Scripture. It is an anti-Reformational paradigm shift that transformed the New South Africa in 1994 but can be rectified over time. Realistically, it will take decades to rebuild and to overhaul the present constitutional order in a post New South Africa. But the Lord of heaven and earth mandated his people in every geographic area of the world to be both salt and light but also to actively build the biblical ideal of equal standards of liberty and justice for all. These biblical standards can and must be renewed in a refreshed social order in Southern Africa that respects creation design, biblical infallibility and norms, Trinitarian unity, and a long-term realistic hope both for this present age into which our Lord has broken-in and in the age to come. But this vision is not merely for Southern Africa but also for every imperially defined nation-state throughout the earth that will one day or another experience the long-term results of Spirit taught and empowered renewal in every area of life. This is the way forward!

CONTENTS

Foreword		vii
List of Tables		xiii
Acknowledgments		xv
List of Abbreviations		xvii
1	A Bird's Eye Overview of the Paradigm Shift	1
2	A Ground-Level View of the Historical Background	13
3	The Trinitarian Principle as Key	37
4	The Trinitarian Principle Applied: Reformers and C&S Differ on Ethno-Churches	61
5	The Scripture Alone Principle and the DRC	93
6	Applying the Scripture Alone Principle to C&S	105
7	The Creation Restoration Principle and C&S	125

8	The Creation Restoration Principle Applied to C&S	151
9	The Covenant Principle and Peopleness in Scripture	171
10	Covenant and Peopleness Applied to C&S	203
11	Whole Bible Principle: Moses, Law, and Culture	229
12	Applying the Whole Bible Principle to C&S	245
13	The Whole Bible Principle: C&S and Social Antinomian Tendencies	271
14	Summary and a New Way Forward	291
	Bibliography	303
	Index	321

LIST OF TABLES

Table 1. Presuppositions of Covenantal vs. Radical Reformations   173
Table 2. Two Models for Culture Transformation   293

ACKNOWLEDGMENTS

Thank you, Nancy, my most precious wife of 30 years for encouraging me to finish this work, which is a second volume of what will be, Lord willing, a three-volume series using South Africa as the context for discovering cross-culturally valid principles for culture transformation.

Lastly, I want to thank my parents, the late Robert and Eleanor Kreitzer of Nixa, Missouri for their patient love during the original writing of this work, for their generous subsidizing my two trips to South Africa for research, and of our living costs during this time.

LIST OF ABBREVIATIONS

ANC-SACP	African National Congress, South African Communist Party (alliance)
BC	Belgic Confession
C&S	*Church and Society (1990)*
CCN	Council of Churches of Namibia
CRC	Christian Reformed Church (USA)
DRC	Dutch Reformed Church (equivalent to the DRC)
GKN	*Gereformeerde Kerken van die Nederlanden*
GSC	General Synodical Commission
HC	Heidelberg Catechism
HKSA	*Hervormde Kerk van Suid-Afrika*
HRLS	*Human Relations in the Light of Scripture*
ICT	Institute for Contextual Theology
ICWE	International Congress of World Evangelization
KLAS-WK	Kommissie vir Leer- en Aktuele Sake (Wes-Kaap) [Commission for Doctrine and Contemporary Affairs (Western Cape Regional Synod)]
LWF	Lutheran World Federation
DRC	*Nederduitse Gereformeerde Kerk*

LIST OF ABBREVIATIONS

NGSK	*Nederduitse Gereformeerde Sending Kerk*
REC	Reformed Ecumenical Council (present name of RES)
RES	Reformed Ecumenical Synod
S&S	*Skrifgesag en Skrifgebruik: Beleidstuk van die Nederduitse Gereformeerde Kerk, soos Goedgedeur deur die Algemene Sinode,* 1986 [The Authority and Use of Scripture: Policy Document of the DRC, Approved by the General Synod, 1986]
SACC	South African Council of Churches
UNISA	University of South Africa
WARC	World Alliance of Reformed Churches
WCF	Westminster Confession of Faith
WCRC	World Communion of Reformed Churches
WLC	Westminster Larger Catechism
WCC	World Council of Churches

· 1 ·

A BIRD'S EYE OVERVIEW OF THE
PARADIGM SHIFT

A Short Synopsis

During the last six decades, theologians of virtually every branch of the world-wide church have critiqued Afrikaner, Dutch Reformed social theology.[1] Especially pointed was the international church's criticism of Afrikaner "apartheid" missiology. How could the DRC reach the ethnic other in Africa while participating in a blatantly divisive policy of separate denominations for each race group.[2] Partially in response to this criticism, the 1974 General Synod of the Dutch Reformed Church of South Africa (DRC) [*Nederduitse Gereformeerde Kerk van Suid-Afrika*] produced a definitive response. This largest Afrikaner, Reformed church in the Republic of South Africa (RSA) defended their

---

1 Two examples, John De Gruchy and Steve de Gruchy, *Church Struggle in South Africa: 25th Anniversary Edition* [Church Struggle], 3rd ed. (Minneapolis: Fortress, 2005); J. A. Loubser, *The Apartheid Bible: A Critical Review of Racial Theology in South Africa* [Apartheid Bible] (Cape Town: Maskew, Miller, Longman, 1987).

2 See J. C. Adonis, *Die Afgebreekte Skeidsmuur weer Opgebou. Die Verstrengeling van die Sending Beleid van die Nederduitse Gereformeerde Kerk in Suid-Afrika met die Praktyk en Ideologie van die Apartheid in Historiese Perspektief* [The Broken-Down Dividing Wall Rebuilt: The Inter-twining of the Mission Policy of the DRC in South Africa with the Practice and Ideology of Apartheid in Historical Perspective] [Broken-Down Wall] (Amsterdam: Rodopi, 1982).

2   WHEN A THEOLOGICAL SHIFT CHANGED A NATION

doctrine of apartheid for distinct ethnic and racial groups in a carefully written document entitled *Human Relations and the South African Scene in the Light of Scripture* (HRLS). The English translation covered up its more provocative Afrikaans title, which can literally be translated as *Race, People [Volk], and the Relationship of Peoples [Volkere] in the Light of the Scripture*. The DRC developed their doctrine defending apartheid over decades and made their apex defense of it in HRLS in the mid-1970s. It was not only their last official defense but also a careful yet deeply syncretistic biblical and theological defense of a Kuyperian-influenced doctrine of the relationship of the church to society.[3]

The attack upon the teaching exemplified by the HRLS document, however, intensified. The World Alliance of Reformed Churches (WARC), the then Reformed Ecumenical Synod (RES) (now merged with the WARC and renamed WCRC), the Lutheran World Federation (LWF), the South African Council of Churches (SACC), and the World Council of Churches (WCC) all put increasing pressure on the DRC to abandon their doctrine of how Scripture applies to the transformation of society and urged them to rejoin the world theological consensus.[4]

Many churches associated with the World Council of Churches declared that all theological justification of social or group separation in church and society was evil. They declared: "Apartheid is a heresy," the title of a very important volume edited by English South Africans Charles Villa-Vicencio and John De Gruchy, both them at the time senior academic theologians at the University of Cape Town (UCT), South Africa.[5] The vision of the WCC, its South African affiliate, the South African Council of Churches, and related institutions, such as the radical leftist, Institute for Contextual Theology (ICT), was to establish a sign of the kingdom of God in South Africa by creating the opposite of the apartheid order: a nonsexist, non-racist, non-classist and ultimately a non-homophobic, democratic state and a unified church built on the same presuppositions.[6]

---

3 Loubser, *Apartheid Bible*; P. J. Strauss, "Abraham Kuyper, Apartheid and the Reformed Church in South Africa in their support of Apartheid," *Theological Forum* XXIII (March 1995): 4–27.

4 De Gruchy, *Church Struggle*.

5 John De Gruchy and Charles Villa-Vicencio, eds., *Apartheid Is a Heresy* [Apartheid Heresy] (Cape Town: David Phillip; Guildford, England: Lutterworth, 1983).

6 See Pauline Webb, ed., *A Long Struggle: The Involvement of the World Council of Churches in South Africa* [Long Struggle] (Geneva: WCC Publications, World Council of Churches, 1994).

Under great domestic and international pressure, the DRC General Synod decided in 1982 that HRLS "should be completely revised."[7] Instead of a revision that reworked non-biblical elements, the appointed commission actually wrote a new document: *Church and Society: A Testimony of the Dutch Reformed Church (Ned Geref Kerk)*. The General Synod adopted it in 1986. In time for the 1990 General Synod, the original document with three chapters was further revised, slightly condensed into two chapters, and reprinted as *Church and Society* 1990 (C&S 1990 or simply C&S, with the section number).[8] The first doctrinal chapter is entitled "Basic Scriptural Principles" and includes discussions on biblical authority, hermeneutics, and kingdom focus; the church; and "the church and group relationships." The second chapter, "Some Practical Implications," discusses, among other things, the various spheres of life that include the relationship of the DRC to the Afrikaner people (*volk*); to political models, to civil government and society, to "marriage in a multicultural society"; and to education.[9]

Afrikaner theologian Johann Kinghorn reports that C&S had the seeds within it of a major paradigm shift even though it shifted "from a purely ideological position [on apartheid] to a pragmatic, ideological position."[10] He was quite prescient as subsequent history developed. C&S reflected the emerging majority consensus within the DRC, which rejected the older, Kuyperian-based apartheid theology but was not yet ready to make a clean break with apartheid practice in all its ramifications.

In the years between the writing of HRLS (1974) and the adoption of C&S (1986), a rapid and virtually unnoticed paradigm shift in the theology taught in the DRC's seminaries had gained ascendancy among the ministers of the DRC. This shift, begun at least in the mid to late 1960s and accelerating rapidly in the 1970s and early 1980s, reflected the growing influence of the theology of Karl Barth mediated through Reformed, Dutch theologians such

---

7   General Synodical Commission, *Church and Society: A Testimony Approved by the Synod of the Dutch Reformed Church as Translated from the Original Afrikaans Manuscript. October 1986* [C&S 1986] (Bloemfontein: Pro Christo, 1987), 1.

8   General Synodical Commission, *Church and Society 1990: A Testimony of the Dutch Reformed Church (Ned Geref Kerk) as Translated from the Original Afrikaans Manuscript. Approved By the General Synod of The Dutch Reformed Church. October 1990* [C&S] (Bloemfontein: General Synodical Commission), 1991.

9   C&S, n.p.

10 Johann Kinghorn, "On the Theology of Church and Society in the DRC [Theology of C&S]," *Journal of Theology for Southern Africa* 70 (1990a): 29.

as G. C. Berkouwer and H. Ridderbos.[11] This Barthian theology is much in evidence in both *Church and Society* 1986 and the revised 1990 edition. I will deal mostly with C&S, 1990 in this volume except where noted.

Using the late Adrio König (1936–2022) as an example, important Dutch Theologian Hendrikus Berkhof also acknowledges this theological paradigm shift. Interestingly enough, though König was an initiator "among those theologians in South Africa who [attempted] . . . to break away from a traditional fundamentalist approach to the Bible" under the influence of Barth, in his later life he was called a "conservative" and helped lead a moderate evangelical renewal movement in the DRC.[12]

Importance of the Paradigm Shift

The social theological paradigm shift that *Church and Society* (1986 and 1990) introduced included a model for social and cultural transformation. This includes an implicit—sometimes explicit—goal to overturn the former social structures. This goal desires, first of all, to remove the socially divisive apartheid societal structures. Secondly, it desires to replace the old structures with new, more equalitarian, democratic structures. These new inclusive social structures emphasize the collective whole of South African humanity over any separate, exclusive part of that humanity, such as sex, gender, race, tribe or ethno-cultural group. Social unity, thus, is seen as of primary importance. Social diversity possesses merely a descriptive, secondary importance as a means of serving unity. Unity is, consequently, a goal of far greater eschatological importance than any social diversity, which ultimately are divisive.

If this description of the paradigm shift is indeed correct, the new paradigm is much more akin to ideological worldviews postulating the correctness of holism. Social holism has a logical corollary: the primary goodness of social collectivism as a foundational presupposition of social thought. This new ideological paradigm would then be similar, though in a moderated form,

---

11 J. J. F. Durand, "Church and State in South Africa: Karl Barth vs. Abraham Kuyper," in *On Reading Karl Barth in South Africa*, ed. Charles Villa-Vicencio (Grand Rapids: Eerdmans 1988), 122.

12 Hendrikus Berkhof, foreword to *Here Am I*, by Adrio König (London: Marshall Morgan & Scott; Grand Rapids: Eerdmans, 1982), viii. See also, Gerdrie van der Merwe, "Aktueel, In Memory: Adrio König," *Die Kerkbode*, July 25, 2022, https://kerkbode.christians. co.za/2022/07/25/gerekende-akademikus-en-teoloog-vir-almal-sterf/.

to the social theology and resulting missiology adopted by World Council of Churches (WCC) circles.[13]

This same type of "new mission," according to pioneering Fuller School of World Mission missiologists Donald McGavran and Arthur Glasser, was slowly being introduced into evangelical missiology through the holistic mission movement, starting about the same time as the paradigm shift was accelerating in South Africa.[14] This new direction of South African Dutch Reformed social theology, then, still serves the evangelical and Reformed communities worldwide as an important experiment from which to observe, learn, and be warned. This has become especially relevant because the DRC in South Africa rapidly shifted over the last 50 years toward a more ecumenically oriented theology. They first abandoned Herman Bavinck and Abraham Kuyper's doctrine of Scripture and then apartheid theology, which was a perversion of Kuyper's position. Then, the DRC began ordaining women elders and pastors in 1986 at the same Synod that brought C&S's first edition. Now the DRC authorizes the ordination of LGBTQ+-oriented clergy (2015), rescinded in 2016 but enforced by a Pretoria High Court's ruling (2019), to which the DRC acquiesced. In doing so, it took a decidedly non-Reformed, Erastian-like position of the superiority of the State over the Church.[15]

---

13 The concept of a paradigm shift comes from the philosophy of science through the work of Thomas Kuhn (Thomas S. Kuhn, *The Structure of Scientific Revolutions: 50th Anniversary Edition*, 4th ed. [Chicago: University of Chicago Press, 2012]; see David Bosch, *Transforming Mission: Paradigm Shifts in Theology of Mission*, 20th Anniversary ed. American Society of Missiology Series, No. 16 [Transforming] [Maryknoll, NY: Orbis, 2011] for discussion of use in missiological and social theological research).

14 See (1) William J. Larkin, Jr., *Culture and Biblical Hermeneutics: Interpreting and Applying The Authoritative Word in a Relativistic Age* (Eugene, OR: Wipf and Stock, 2003); (2) Arthur Glasser and Donald McGavran, *Contemporary Theologies of Mission* (Grand Rapids: Baker, 1983).

15 See (1) Luiz de Barros, "Dutch Reformed Church Agrees (Again) to Allow Same-Sex Unions," October 9, 2019, http://www.Mambaonline.com; (2) Lodewyk Sutton and Walter Sutton, "The Legal Consequences of Decisions Made without Complying with Procedures Prescribed in the Church Order with Respect to the Decisions by the General Synod of the Dutch Reformed Church [Regsgevolge volgens die *Gaum*-saak vir Nienakoming van Kerkordelike Prosedures ten opsigte van Besluite deur Die Algemene Sinode van die Nederduitse Gereformeerde Kerk]," *Sabinet: African Journals*, November 4, 2019, https://hdl.handle.net/10520/EJC-192d0dd06b, https://journals.co.za/doi/abs/10.10520/EJC-192d0dd06b.

Five Evaluation Criteria and Underlying Presuppositions

In this volume I seek to develop a Reformation-based yet cross-culturally valid paradigm for a social theology that can be used as a standard of evaluation for the Dutch Reformed Church's C&S documents (1986, 1990). My goal is to revitalize classic Reformational principles both to encourage and to facilitate the body of Christ's subtle "leavening" as well as its overt action in transforming all earthly ethno-culture-groups of earth according to these biblical principles. This is just as our Lord mandated in his most widely quoted version of the Great Commission: Disciple all peoples while teaching them to do all that he mandates (Mt 28:18–20). Last, I've designed my conclusion, in part then, to summarize and synthesize into a complete culture transformation paradigm. I pray it would significantly serve the whole Christ-following community throughout the earth. As our King's bride, she has been discussing this theme of culture transformation in the field of missiology and social theology since at least the social gospel movement begun about the late 1880s up to the present in the social justice movement. However, arguably, the discussion dates even centuries earlier within the European-oriented and then British Isle-oriented Reformed social transformation discussions, if not even before then.

Further, I will evaluate the DRC's paradigm shift in social theology against a composite yet still classic Reformed standard to detect if the DRC, by means of C&S, is actually moving away from its Reformed heritage. My conclusion, to provide a spoiler, is that the DRC has actually moved toward and now adopted many of the social theological presuppositions used by the World Council of Churches and the South African Council of Churches. In actual fact, the DRC has wholesale adopted another syncretistic, ideologically influenced social theology. In its move away from syncretistic apartheid theology, it has adopted an even more lethal alternative, while passing over other more biblical and Reformational visions.

Five Evaluation Criteria. More specifically, I seek to evaluate the DRC's paradigm shifting, social theology from a five-fold perspective, developed for this book (and the dissertation that it is based upon).[16] This five-fold perspective includes the following classic Reformed world and life view presuppositions:

---

16 I have rearranged, reconceptualized, and renamed the five presuppositions originally gleaned from Gary North and David Chilton. See (1) Gary North and David Chilton, "Apologetics and Strategy," in *Tactics of Christian Resistance*, 100–41 (Tyler, TX: Geneva Divinity School Press, 1983); (2) Gary North, "Publisher's Preface," in *Days of Vengeance,*

(1) The Trinitarian Principle: The Trinity serves as an interpretative key to all of life.

(2) Scripture Alone Principle: Scripture is infallible and without error and thus serves as the foundational framework and sometimes even as a broad blueprint for Christ-followers to transform culture according to the standards of Christ's kingdom.

(3) The Creation Restoration Principle: A long-term optimistic and ultimately victorious view of the future that gives hope to the body of Christ to persevere in this already-but-not-yet age before the Second Coming.

(4) The Covenant Principle: Covenantal models bind together distinct yet foundational family, church and civil governments under the Lordship of King Jesus.

(5) The Whole Scripture Principle: The whole Bible must impact all areas and spheres of life. In other words, both tables of the Decalogue are to impact family, church and civil governments.

Five Assumptions behind the Five Criteria. First, the presupposition that the doctrine of the covenant and the kingdom are two sides of one coin is biblically valid. This two-sided presupposition serves as a key unifying theme throughout Scripture, according to, for example, Presbyterian scholar, O. Palmer Robertson. The covenantal relationship is comprehensive, involving all of life. The covenant-kingdom relationship is between mankind as the administrative deputy or governor of God (technically termed "vicegerent") and God as the only proper, sovereign Lord (suzerain) of his kingdom. It unites into one perspective: (1) the cultural mandate of the original creation covenant with (2) the redemptive, covenantal mandate of our reigning, mediatorial king, Jesus. The so-called Cultural Mandate of Genesis 1:26–8 and the Lord's "Great Commission Mandate" are two administrations of the single covenantal plan of our Father.[17] Robertson further describes this relationship aptly as a "total life-involvement," which is explicit within "the [divine-human] covenant relationship." Entrance into "God's present kingdom," furthermore, only occurs "by repentance and faith, which requires the preaching of the gospel."

---

by David Chilton (Tyler, TX: Institute for Christian Economics, 1987a); (3) Gary North, *Millennialism and Social Theory* (Tyler, TX: Institute for Christian Economics, 1990a).

17 O. Palmer Robertson, *The Christ of the Covenants* [Covenants] (Phillipsburg, NJ: P&R, 2017), 83.

8 WHEN A THEOLOGICAL SHIFT CHANGED A NATION

Despite much contrary popular teaching, however, this "gospel" is not merely directed to the salvation of individuals, who then must be gathered into congregations, waiting the Second Coming. Instead, the biblical good news is inseparably connected to our resurrected Lord's presently comprehensive and growing kingdom that will never be perfected until King Jesus destroys his last enemy in the Resurrection. Consequently, the Gospel that is true and authentic to our Lord's teaching inseparably involves discipling men and women in "all the peoples/nations" to guard and apply every one of the commands of Christ beginning in the first chapter of Genesis (Mt 28:18–20).[18]

Necessary, then, to that discipling process is prayer to awaken in disciples a growing awareness of their responsibilities under Christ's lordship to all of God's creation, not merely people. Redeemed humanity, remade in God's image, must fulfill—even surpass—that which God originally determined for the first man and his wife to be and do. In such a manner, the mandate to preach the gospel and the mandate to form a culture glorifying to God merge with one another into a single all-encompassing plan of action.[19]

In summary, as the late Calvin College theologian Gordon Spykman writes: "By sovereign design, the Garden was destined to become a City."[20] The Fall into sin was only a temporary obstacle to that ultimate goal. But the gracious redemption in Christ has overcome and will continue to destroy every obstacle sin erected against it until death finally is destroyed. Paul writes: "Where sin increased, grace increased all the more" (Ro 5:20 NIV) so that "he must reign until he put all his enemies under his feet. And the last enemy to be destroyed is death" at the Resurrection (1 Cor 15:25–6 NIV). Or as a slight modification of the Authorized Version puts it: "Therefore as by the trespass of one [man, God's] *judgment came* upon all [mankind resulting in] condemnation; even so by the [completed] righteousness of one [man] *the free gift came* upon all [mankind] unto justification of life" (Rom 5:18, AV modified by author). Our Lord reverses in his finished work, which is now steadily being applied over the whole world of tribes, peoples, and languages, everything that

---

18 Robertson, *Covenants*, 83.

19 Robertson 2017, 83.

20 Gordon Spykman, *Reformational Theology: A New Paradigm for Doing Dogmatics.* [Reformational] (Grand Rapids: Eerdmans, 1992), 256. See also (1) Gregory Beale, "Introduction," in *The Temple and the Church's Mission: A Biblical Theology of the Dwelling Place of God (New Studies in Biblical Theology)* (Downers Grove, IL: IVP Academic, 2004); (2) Gregory Beale and Mitchell Kim, *God Dwells Among Us: A Biblical Theology of the Temple*, Essential Studies in Biblical Theology (Downers Grove, IL: IVP, 2021).

A BIRD'S EYE OVERVIEW OF THE PARADIGM SHIFT 9

God cursed because of Adam's one defiant act against his rightful King. God brought his comprehensive curse upon the whole creation, which was under Adam's dominion (e.g., Rom 8:18–21). The Second Adam's one completed work of righteousness, on the other hand, brings an all-encompassing healing and blessing because he bore the curse for his people. This blessing grows from a mustard seed size to a tree under which all the animals and birds find their rest, an OT picture of the world-encompassing scope of our Lord's kingdom at the End.

The second presupposition I am making is that God's covenant and kingdom both provide an essential guide to the purpose and meaning of the original creation design. Gordon Spykman, terms this rather awkwardly but accurately as the "bi-unitary index to the meaning of the creation." In other words, both covenant and kingdom begin and end together as they serve to help transform the Garden into a glorious world-encompassing City. Or again, in Spykman's technical sense, both are "alike in their depth of meaning and coterminous in their cosmic scope." The concept of covenant connotes an "abiding *charter*," whereas the concept of kingdom implies the idea of an "on going *program*." Thus "kingdom may ... be conceived of as covenant looking forward with gathering momentum toward its final fulfillment."[21]

Covenant and kingdom as "interchangeable realities" have a common origin in the Creator, cover the same terrain, and "involve the same people."[22] Therefore, at the beginning of the creation, mankind was covenanted into the kingdom of the triune God who reigns over all things in heaven and earth (Ps 103:17–22). As a result, our Triune God's "royal authority ... proclaims his covenantal claim on his creatures."[23] Mankind and all creatures are responsible to thank, trust, and obey the Creator (Ro 1:18–30) ultimately "in Christ" the Last Adam (1 Cor 15:45). God designed covenant and kingdom to be inexorably connected to his redemption in King Jesus of Nazareth.

The historic Reformed emphasis upon an all-encompassing covenantal kingdom and a necessary redemption that extends as far as the creation was affected by the Fall (Ro 8:18–22), is much more than individualistic dogmas. These transforming teachings of Scripture cannot be reduced to merely saving individuals. That inevitably leads God's people into a "dualist worldview, structured along nature-creation/grace-covenant lines."[24] In other words, our

21 Spykman, *Reformational*, 258.
22 Spykman, *Reformational*, 258.
23 Spykman, *Reformational*, 258.
24 Spykman, *Reformational*, 261.

Lord is not so much interested in the physical world of creation as in saving individuals by grace. Both actually are true. The Second Adam heals the curse Adam brought upon the whole earth, including the animal world, and upon humankind in Christ.

Third, I presuppose yet also argue extensively for each of the five presuppositions I list above. Each are biblically valid and each is found in the Calvinist-Reformed fathers and foundational confessions, though not necessarily with all of the contemporary development, emphasis, and application.

Fourth, as I demonstrated in assumptions one and two, the growth and ultimate victory of the Kingdom of God, in King Jesus, is the goal of the mission of God. It is the task he designed for all mankind from the beginning. His ultimate passion is that the "earth would be filled with the glory of the LORD as the waters cover the seas" (Hab 2:14; Is 11:9; Nm 14:21). Indeed, our Lord shall reign until he makes his enemies a footstool under his feet (see 1 Cor 15:22–8; Eph 1:10 NIV). The last enemy to be destroyed is death itself only at the resurrection. Our Lord is step-by-step crushing all his other enemies before the end of the present age. This gives us both a present and future hope to engage in his comprehensive mission.

Fifth, God created the three basic governments, family, ecclesial, and civil, to be social structural means of glorifying the Creator.[25] Hence, though the people in them may be unregenerate or regenerate, the structures in themselves are in themselves good because God created them. Everything created by God is good, Paul states (1 Ti 4:1–7). The laws and norms governing them can become twisted to serve Christ's enemy, but they can also be untwisted, healed in other words "redeemed" by our Lord's regenerated citizens. The result of Christ's comprehensive redemption, then, is that all three governments can be included in the Kingdom of God and Christ (e.g., Pss 2, 110; Ps 138:4; Rv 21:24). The eternal goal, purpose and meaning of these institutions revolve around outshining God's glory into the surrounding moral darkness, both demonic and human (see Mt 4:15–17; Is 9:1; Eph 2:6, 3:10–11). All societal groups must, therefore, center around his glorious majesty!

---

25 Albert M. Wolters, *Creation Regained: Biblical Basics for a Reformational Worldview* [Regained] (Grand Rapids: Eerdmans, 2005).

Definitions of Key Terms

1. *General or Universal Equity.* Whole Bible ethics develop principles of evenhanded justice and neighbor love call "equity" or "general equity." These principles are based upon God's character and creation design, found in every judicial law. They alone define both impartial justice (social and legal-system ethics) and loving righteousness (individual and interpersonal ethics) yet do not destroy God created boundaries found, for example, in the Ten Commandments.[26]
2. *Holism.* A word coined by South African Prime Minister, Jan Smuts. It emphasizes that particulars are evolving into wholes, which are above, apart from, and more important than any separate part. Philosophically, holism is similar to Platonism and aspects of Hegelianism.[27]
3. *Social Theology.* The outworking of theology into the various social spheres, defining their content, boundaries, and interrelationships. Social theology thus includes the sub-discipline of social ethics. As such, social theology is defined here as a branch of theology that deals with the conversion and transformation of culture.
4. *Wholism.* In contrast to holism, "wholism" is a concept that reality must not be seen in terms of a dualism between matter and form, nature and grace, form and freedom, good and eternal spirit, or transitory and carnal flesh. All things are not evolving into every greater, boundary-dissolving unities, until everything loses its individual distinctiveness in the unity of the All. Instead, all of life, both body and spirit, physical and spiritual, nature and grace, are good in themselves because they are created by the Word. Both can be instruments of evil when controlled by the "devil who holds them captive to do his will" (2 Ti 2:26; Eph 2:1–2) or instruments of righteousness when they are ruled by the Holy Spirit (Rom 6:12–14).

---

26 I recommend: (1) Walter Kaiser, Jr., *Toward Old Testament Ethics* [OT Ethics] (Grand Rapids: Zondervan/Academie Books, 1991); (2) Walter Kaiser, Jr., *The Uses of the Old Testament in the New* [OT in New] (Eugene, OR: Wipf and Stock, 2001).

27 See, e.g.: (1) Jan Christiaan Smuts, *Holism and Evolution* [Holism] (Cape Town: N & S Press, 1935/1987); (2) Piet Beukes, *The Holistic Smuts: A Study in Personality* [Holistic Smuts] (Cape Town: Human and Rousseau, 1989).

· 2 ·

A GROUND-LEVEL VIEW OF THE HISTORICAL BACKGROUND

Introduction

To understand the nation-changing effect that the DRC made in the 1980s and early 1990s, I will discuss the relationship between the former General Synod decision, HRLS and the C&S in its two iterations (1986, 1990). The ecumenical and political world put tremendous internal and external pressure upon the DRC to abandon their former apartheid-supporting document Human Relations in the Light of Scripture (HRLS). This pressure greatly facilitated the DRC's movement toward consensus-building with their own creation of a so-called colored church, the Dutch Reformed Mission Church, and its *Belhar Confession*, which in turn led to reintegration with the world conciliar movement (e.g., the WARC and the WCC).

Several Background Factors

Several background factors influenced the DRC's decision to adopt *Church and Society* in the watershed synod of 1986. Of these factors, interestingly enough, apartheid social theology developed historically from missiological roots. These include the desire to reach the indigenous peoples of Southern Africa, yet also

14   WHEN A THEOLOGICAL SHIFT CHANGED A NATION

the desire not to assimilate into their cultures but to maintain a distinct, separateness (apartness or in Afrikaans, "apartheid").

Historical Development of Apartheid Social Theology

Dutch Reformed apartheid social theology did not reach the zenith of its development until the 1974 General Synod of the DRC, which approved HRLS (Afrikaans: *Ras, Volk en Nasie en Volkereverhouding in die Lig van die Skrif*), sometimes also called the report of the Landman Commission in the literature. The literal translation is *Race, [Afrikaner] People and [South African] Nation and Relationships between Peoples in the Light of Scripture*. HRLS primarily focused on the relationship between the Afrikaner volk, and the various ethno-racial groups in the South African society. The document was released to the world with the English title *Human Relations in the Light of Scripture* (HRLS) and gave a qualified approval of separate or parallel development (apartheid) (HRLS 13.6–7).

In response to severe worldwide criticism of this justification of a "separating" social theology, the 1982 General Synod mandated that a commission revise and update the 1974 document, HRLS. The commission consisted of both of some missiologists but mostly theologians, including Carel Boshoff (Professor of Missiology at the University of Pretoria [U.P.]), J. Heyns (Prof. of Dogmatics: U.P.), and P. A. Verhoef (Prof. of Old Testament: University of Stellenbosch). The decision to revise HRLS came several years too late to stop the severe ecumenical reaction to that General Synod's official apartheid theology, moderated as it was. For example, HRLS was "the document that was responsible in large part for the action taken by the WARC [World Alliance of Reformed Churches] in 1982 against the DRC," as University of Cape Town Liberation Theologian Charles Villa-Vicencio stated.[1] *Church and Society*, adopted in 1986, was the DRC's official response to the criticism of HRLS. C&S commissioner Prof. Carel Boshoff wrote an insider's perspective of the revision process of HRLS. He titled his work *Church and Society in Personal Perspective [Kerk en Samelewing in Oëskou]*. Boshoff was the President of the elite exclusive Afrikaner *Broederbond* (League of Brothers) and later founded an exclusive Afrikaner village named Orania along the Orange River just across the border from the Orange Free State province. It still exists to this day and is growing.

---

1 Charles Villa-Vicencio, "Report from a Safe Synod," *Reformed Journal* 36 (November 1986), 9.

A GROUND-LEVEL VIEW OF THE HISTORICAL BACKGROUND   15

In this work, Prof. Carel Boshoff described the context in which HRLS was revised and C&S was produced as one of increasing ecumenical criticism of the DRC. First was the accusation that the DRC was a "false church because it has violated the unity of the church" through the policy of planting "separate daughter churches." Second, he wrote, the DRC was "accused of heresy because it made a theology of apartheid and with it raised irreconcilability [of races and peoples] to a basic [scriptural] principle." Both were profoundly disturbing for the emerging new consensus in the DRC.[2]

Missiological Background of HRLS and C&S

Missiology is the department of study in mostly historically Christian institutes of tertiary education that involves integrating biblical-theological insights with those of the social sciences such as social anthropology, linguistics, and sociology. With that as my professional backdrop, I can put HRLS and its revision, C&S, in a proper missiological and historical contexts. HRLS was a fairly comprehensive apologia for the DRC's mission strategy of separate denominations for each so-called "racial" groups: White, Asian, Colored, and African (also called "Black" or "Bantu"). It also provided a summary of the "theological apology for the philosophical concept of the diversity of nations." This apology then attempts "to state the theological case for ethnicity as the root order of humanity and thus also the root order for socio-political as well as ecclesiastical structures."[3]

Historical Development of DRC's Missiology. HRLS was the crystallization of a long process of missiological and theological reflection. The process actually began in the early colonial days when the largely Dutch Reformed colonists in the Dutch colony, the Cape of Good Hope, under the influence of faulty views of the doctrine of the covenant, began to see themselves as exclusively Christian.[4] Afrikaners, it seems, were influenced from the beginning by a Calvinistic

---

2 Carel W. H. Boshoff, *Kerk en Samelewing in Oënskou: Kommentaar en Kritiek* [Church and Society in Review: Commentary and Critique] (Pretoria: Suid-Afrikaanse Calvinistiese Uitgewersmaatskappy Beperk, 1987), 6.

3 Johann Kinghorn, "The Theology of Separate Equality: A Critical Outline of the DRC's Position on Apartheid," in *Christianity amidst Apartheid*, ed. M. Prozesky, 57–80 (New York: St. Martin's Press, 1990b), 27.

4 Jonathan N. Gerstner, *The Thousand Generation Covenant: Dutch Reformed Covenant Theology and Group Identity in Colonial South Africa, 1652–1814* (Leiden: Brill), Gerstner describes this early process in great detail.

   See my review, Mark R. Kreitzer, "Review of *The Thousand Generation Covenant: Dutch Reformed Covenant Theology and Group Identity in Colonial South Africa, 1652–1814*," by

16 WHEN A THEOLOGICAL SHIFT CHANGED A NATION

covenantal model leading to an exclusivist, "us" versus "them" worldview. The natives, on the other hand, were virtually non-convertible *kaffirs*, an Arabic term borrowed from Muslim slaves, meaning "infidel" or "heathen," but still used, though now illegally in the New South Africa, as the Afrikaans derogatory term for African background RSA citizens.

Missiology professor, J. C. Adonis, described the development of the separate mission church for Afrikaans-speaking "Cape Coloreds." These were a relatively diverse group of people who descended from the intermarriage and cohabitation of European and the Khoisan groups that inhabited the area of original European settlement. Genetically the Khoi Khoi and the San (Bushmen) groups were possibly some of the first inhabitants of the African continent, who had been pushed ever southward by the rapidly expanding Nguni people-groups that came from the Great Lakes region of East Africa.

Adonis described an ecclesiastical process that began in 1858 that ended in the division into European and "Colored" Reformed denominations. At that time, the General Synod of the Dutch Reformed Church in the Cape decided to allow the separation of in the Lord's Supper of these intermarried parishioners, speaking a distinct Afrikaans dialect from the "Dutch," who spoke a distinct Dutch dialect increasingly called "Afrikaans." This process culminated in the founding of the Dutch Reformed Mission Church (*NG Sending Kerk*) in 1881 for these brown "Dutch" speakers.[5] The Synod correctly saw the two ethnies as distinct, but contrary to biblical principle decided to hold two distinct times and/or places for the Lord's Supper. This was a crucial step into syncretizing "race" or "color" with distinctive ethnic identity.

By 1935 the policy of separate churches for distinct peoples had been solidified and shaped into a solid missiological doctrine adopted by the Federal Council of the Dutch Reformed Church, the forerunner of the presently uniting family of Dutch Reformed Churches. It was this missiological principle of supposedly self-governing denominations for each type of color group that was "used for more than merely a yardstick for missionary activities." It was "put into use in the judging of political ideas including, naturally, the question of [social-political] apartheid."[6]

Jonathan Gerstner, in *Contra Mundum: A Reformed Cultural Review* 13 (Fall 1994): 64–8. Notice also, D. Akenson's *God's Peoples: Covenant and Land in South Africa, Israel, and Ulster* (Ithaca: Cornell University Press, 1992) documents this covenantal view extensively.

5 Adonis, *The Broken Down Wall*.

6 See documentation in Johann Kinghorn, *The Growth of a Theology—from Mission Policy to a Theology of Diversity* (*Die Groei van 'n Teologie—van Sendingbeleid tot Verskeidenheidsteologie*),

A GROUND-LEVEL VIEW OF THE HISTORICAL BACKGROUND 17

Summary of Missiological Background. HRLS was the apex of the Euro-South African, DRC's theological evolution supporting the planting indigenous, self-governing daughter churches for each broadly sketched "racial" group based more or less on color and other external phenotypical features such as hair type. After its adoption, HRLS' opponents' primary goal was to introduce what they considered to be a more Christian substitute: A unification policy emphasizing one united Reformed denomination for Southern Africa. Adonis, for one, summarizes the reasons for this goal. First, the older DRC mission policy was "synonymous with the 'apartheid policy.'" Second, the relationship between the churches should no longer be one of mother to daughter but a relationship between mature sister churches. Therefore, the DRC should cease to control the younger churches as immature daughters but should be in relationship with them "in all circumstances as equally worthy of the status of *the* church."[7]

The implication, according to Adonis, is that if there is indeed only one church of Christ according to the Scripture, and if all younger churches equally possess the status of "the church," then there should be in fact as well as theory only one church institution belonging to Christ. Consequently, there is no justification at all for the concept of mission churches or mother-daughter church relations in any geographically demarcated nation-state nor ultimately for the whole earth. Christ, therefore, mandates that the DRC and its "daughters" unite into one structure with the churches they planted. This is not only Prof. Adonis' proposal but also that of his denomination's *Belhar Confession.*

This conclusion seemed to have been a quite understandable reaction to the DRC's policy of racially dividing the universal Community of Christ the King using a fully developed color-based, apartheid missiology. However, I hasten to add ironically, that most other sectors of the world church following the Second World War reacted in reacted in almost the opposite direction. In those years of anti-colonial and liberation sentiment, these churches planted overseas by mainline denominations usually desired structural independence along with equal status from the mother churches, because they wanted the right to control their own theological, linguistic, cultural and financial direction under God.[8] However, one huge distinction between the two cases existed. The

---

in *Die NG Kerk en Apartheid* [The DRC and Apartheid], ed. Johann Kinghorn (Johannesburg: Macmillan, 1986b), 87.

7 Adonis, *The Broken Down Wall*, 207; emphasis in original.

8 See classic work by Peter Beyerhaus, *The Responsible Church and the Foreign Mission* (London: World Dominion, 1964).

mother and the daughter churches existed side-by-side in the same country in RSA. For the rest of the world, structural unification with the planting church seemed rarely, if ever, was an issue except in cases of close geographic proximity such as in Southern Africa. Most Younger Churches, as they were termed at the time, were content to merely join world ecumenical organizations.

Interestingly enough, several Dutch theologians and missiologists such as J. C. Hoekendijk and J. Verkuyl, strongly reacted after WWII against the National Socialist racial supremacy horrors. Using that revulsion, they actively opposed independent ethno-churches in South Africa and other settler contexts on principle, because the claimed that all such separation sinfully divides the one Church of Christ. Several of their Afrikaans-speaking followers, such as J. C. Adonis and David Bosch, substantially agreed.[9] These two groups and their Ecumenical allies in the World Council of Churches, in turn, vehemently rejected theologians and missiologists from the Fuller School of World Mission in Pasadena, California that emphasized planting indigenous churches in every one of the thousands of ethno-linguistic based "people-groups" of earth. Key examples are Ralph Winter, Donald McGavran and C. Peter Wagner. They lumped this group of what came to be known as the Church Growth School of missiology with the German idealist group of theological missiologists from a generation earlier, such as Gustaf Warneck and Bruno Gutmann. In lumping the Germans with the Americans, the natural next connection was to group both with Afrikaner apartheid theology and its related theory of Christian missions, rejecting all three groups as heretical and divisive because they divided the unity of Christ's single Church.

Furthermore, the Ecumenical and anti-apartheid missiologists emphasized that all racial and the ethno-cultural distinctiveness in church planting and church structure is actually building upon the divisions of the fallen first creation and not upon the totally new nature of the Christ's new creation. In Christ and his new creation realities, no racial or ethnic ("no Jew or Greek"), social class ("no slave or free"), and no sex or gender-based ("no male and female") distinctions exist (e.g., Gal 3:28). Consequently, any theology, missiology, or denomination that does not build on the unities of the eschaton,

---

9 See, e.g.: (1) Johannes Hoekendijk "Church and People in German Missiology" (DTh diss., Rijksuniversiteit of Utrecht, 1948); (2) Johannes Verkuyl, *Break Down the Walls: A Christian Cry for Racial Justice* [Break Down], ed. and trans. Lewis B. Smedes (Grand Rapids: Eerdmans, 1973); (3) Johannes Verkuyl, *Contemporary Missiology: An Introduction* [Missiology] (Grand Rapids: Eerdmans, 1978); (4) Adonis, *The Broken Down Wall*; (5) David Bosch, *Transforming.*

A GROUND-LEVEL VIEW OF THE HISTORICAL BACKGROUND 19

the New Creation, are schismatic and evil. This critique, as I will show, is crucial for understanding the DRC of South Africa's crucial paradigm shift that changed the nation.

These critics claimed, therefore, that any emphasis upon the created uniqueness of the ethno-linguistically distinctive people-groups of the earth is exclusivist and divisive. Their interpretation of Christ's gospel, they would claim on the other hand, was and is fully inclusivist, including LGBTQ+ individuals as well. They conclude that no people-group has any New Testament authority to express their uniqueness within the universal church by means of ethno-linguistically distinct self-governing, self-financing, self-propagating, and self-theologizing ethno-church structures.[10]

The Dutch Reformed Mission Church's (DRMC) controversial *Belhar Confession* and the WARC decision on apartheid as heresy, supported their more inclusivist perspective based on the theology of Karl Barth. Ironically, I would add, Afrikaner inclusivist critics of HRLS such as David Bosch rarely discussed which language and culture will dominate in a unified institution or whether there should be a new culture and a common unifying language. Unfortunately, throughout history powerful imperial languages always dominate such contexts such as, for example, Mandarin in Tibet and what dissidents term East Turkestan, Russian in the old Russian empire, Spanish and Portuguese in Latin America, and other important European languages such as French, and most importantly for South Africa English, in the remnants of their African empires.

In summary, instead of divisive, creation-based structures, inclusivist theologians and missiologists taught then and still teach that the church is one "new fellowship [that] . . . transcends every limit imposed by family, clan, tribe, ethnic group, nation, and culture. This new people is a seed of the new humanity."[11] This one church is the harbinger of one new world, the Kingdom of God. Therefore, the church should express its culture transcending newness (1) by unifying all ethnic branches into one universal structure in which (2) the church and mission distinctions cease to exist, and (3) social divisions should be leveled as much as is possible. This is the ideal of the world ecumenical movement represented by the WCC and WARC and now by the uniting Dutch Reformed denominations in the Republic of South Africa.

---

10 See, e.g., Bosch, *Transforming.*
11 Verkuyl, *Missiology,* 107.

Evolutionary Development of DRC Social Theology

International Ecumenical Pressure to Abandon Apartheid Social Theology

The international and internal pressure put on the DRC to modify their social theological doctrine of separate denominations for each race (color) group had been massive and very painful. After the WCC sponsored conference at Cottesloe, a suburb of Johannesburg, the DRC resigned from that organization because they saw the growing gale looming against their racial separation policy. A. H. Lückhoff's account, entitled *Cottesloe*, carefully documents the conference and the surrounding events.[12] The DRC leadership who had attended the conference accepted the joint conference resolution criticizing certain aspects of apartheid. Ironically, the resolution "was largely based on the preparatory documents [the DRC leaders themselves] . . . had produced for the consultation."[13] However, all the DRC regional synods, under political pressure from the National Party and its constituency, rejected the document. This led to incrementally increasing ecumenical pressure upon the church from all parts of the world.

After the Cottesloe conference, various sources in the international and South African ecumenical movement as well as several internal DRC sources published documents that were critical of apartheid social theology (including its missiology). The tempo of negative criticism increased in 1974 after the approval of HRLS or *The Report of the Landman Commission* named after W. A. Landman, who was the chairman of the Commission that wrote HRLS.

The Institute for Social Ethics of the Swiss Federation of Protestant Churches published an important example of an ecumenical critique of HRLS' social theology by Daniel Von Allman.[14] He is especially critical of the interpretative principles used in the HRLS as it read the Bible. He claimed that in spite of careful denial that the Bible can be used as a handbook for sociology or ethnology, the HRLS does indeed use the quasi-ethnological concepts of race

---

12 Lückhoff, A. H., *Cottesloe* (Cape Town: Tafelberg, 1978).

13 De Gruchy 1966, 66.

14 Daniel von Allman, *Theology—Advocate or Critic of Apartheid: A Critical Study of the "Landman Report" [HRLS] (1974) of the Dutch Reformed Church [South Africa]* [Advocate or Critic] (Berne: Swiss Federation of Protestant Churches, 1977).

A GROUND-LEVEL VIEW OF THE HISTORICAL BACKGROUND 21

and *volk* (people-group) as the, to paraphrase the German, interpretive grids or controlling themes through which the Scripture should be read.[15]

Von Allman is certainly correct in stating that extra-biblical criteria should not be used as the glasses through which to read Scripture. He correctly asserted that HRLS justifies the separate existence of volk-groups and makes this the guiding theme in developing a scriptural doctrine of inter-ethnic relations. While certainly a very relevant motif, its focus is too narrow to develop a comprehensive social-ethical doctrine. At least, the multitude of passages in the Pentateuch speaking of the just treatment of the permanent resident alien (*ger*) needed to be considered, as well as a correct understanding of the redemptive-historical development of the people of God in the new covenant. These were seriously neglected. (Actually, I published a much-needed correction on this topic in 2008 entitled, *The Concept of Ethnicity in the Bible: A Theological Analysis*).[16]

To its credit, HRLS tried to take seriously the biblical material on ethnicity, which C&S refused to do. That was commendable because all Scripture is God-breathed (God-created) and applicable to all of life (e.g., 2 Ti 3:16–17; Rom 15:4; 1 Cor 10:6, 11). However, HRLS' shortcoming was, at critical points in the argument, equating ethnic identity with race. Race at the time in RSA meant using darker skin-color, kinky hair, and other external measures as crudely demeaning, ethno-racial demarcation indicators. That identification is nowhere to be found in the biblical material analyzed by the study but seems to have been derived from the racial prejudice of the well-documented Afrikaner ideological history and culture. HRLS at this point was what clearly seemed to be an immoral syncretism between a self-serving folk-ideology and sound biblical material—"a 'Contextual' Theology Gone Wrong."[17]

In answer to the critical studies by the ecumenical movement of HRLS, the DRC released official replies of its own. The purpose was usually to defend the practice of apartheid, not the biblical exegesis nor interpretative principles upon which the church tried to support apartheid theology and missiology. For

---

15 Von Allman, *Advocate or Critic*, 5.

16 Mark R. Kreitzer, *The Concept of Ethnicity in the Bible: A Theological Analysis* [The Concept of Ethnicity] (Lewiston, NY: Mellen, 2008).

17 See (1) J. A. Loubser, "Apartheid Theology: A 'Contextual' Theology Gone Wrong?" *Journal of Church and State* 38, no. 2 (1996): 321–37; (2) Schalk Gerber, "On the Political Theology of Apartheid: A Philosophical Investigation," *Social Dynamics: A Journal of African Studies* 48, no. 3 (2022), 442–56; (3) Gwashi Freddy Manavhela, *Theological Justification of Apartheid in South African Churches: Did Churches in South Africa Justify Apartheid?* (London: Lambert Academic Publishing, 2012).

example, *A Plea for Understanding: A Reply to the Reformed Church in America*, by DRC Stated Clerk, W. A. Landman, carefully documented some genuine misinformation and distortions in the criticism of apartheid. His attempt to fend off criticism tried to show how much the South African government was actually doing for the "Bantu," the collective racial-ethnic term the South African regime used in their justification for their "apartness" policies. He defended apartheid by claiming that according to the doctrine of separate development whites would only dominate others in the so-called white areas, actually very inaccurate. Non-whites, he claimed, were analogous to foreign guest workers there, albeit under white "guidance" for a very long period of time.[18]

Landman, in my perspective, lacked a scriptural evaluation of apartheid's despotic and paternalistic guardianship based on the love that God commanded his people to demonstrably show the ethnic alien living in their midst. Scripture bases this firmly upon the ground of "neighbor love" (Lv 19:18; compare the near context 19:33–4). Consequently, Landman justified many genuine elements of injustice and oppression. Afrikaners needed much more compassion and sensitivity to the feelings of genuine injustice because of their own real experience of genocidal oppression by British imperialism in the Anglo-Boer War (1898–1902), in which the Afrikaner lost perhaps one-third of their population, primarily women and children.[19] Ironically, their social context was parallel to the context of the law in Leviticus: "When an alien resides with you in your land, you must not oppress him. You will regard the alien who resides with you as the native-born among you. You are to love him as yourself, for you were aliens in the land of Egypt; I am the LORD your God" (Lv 19:33–4).

The Afrikaners' perception of themselves as citizens of the land and having been serfs of the British imperial regime should have sensitized them to their own enserfment of the "Bantu" (see Ex 23:9; Dt 5:15, 15:15, 24:18, 22). For example, according to African American free market economics writer, Professor Walter Williams and other scholars, the former South African homelands had less economic freedom until the mid-eighties than the eastern bloc countries had under the mercantilist, state socialism of the Russian-Soviet empire. The apartheid system's paternalism and lack of legal impartiality was a direct violation of impartial biblical justice: "The same laws and regulations will apply both to you and to the alien living among you" (Nm 15:16; see Nm 15:29;

---

18 W. A. Landman, *A Plea for Understanding: A Reply to the Reformed Church in America* [Plea] (Cape Town: Nederduitse Gereformeerde Kerk-Uitgewers, 1967), 135.

19 Irving Hexham, *The Irony of Apartheid: The Struggle for National Independence of Afrikaner Calvinism against British Imperialism* (New York: Edwin Mellen Press, 1981).

Lv 19:15, 33–4; 24:22; Dt 1:16–17; Rom 2:5–11; 1 Tm 5:21; Jas 2:9). The same was documented by Libertarian economics authors, Leon Louw and Francis Kendall in *After Apartheid: The Solution for South Africa*. They did not merely bemoan the lack of economic freedom for the "homelands" of South Africa but give a positive solution based on the Swiss model of a confederation of many cantons. This excellent beginning for a true solution was never considered. It should be in the post New South Africa, whenever that day comes.[20]

Internal DRC Dissent after Adoption of HRLS

1982 marked the decision by the DRC General Assembly to revise HRLS. DRC church history professor P. J. Strauss wrote that HRLS had been the victory of an older generation of Afrikaner scholars, who had studied under Abraham Kuyper at his Free University of Amsterdam: This report was a "culmination of a Kuyperian support of apartheid [with]in the DRC."[21] After the publication of the HRLS document, "particularly at the non-official level the debate on the role of the church in society was stimulated. The church's standpoints were increasingly questioned."[22] As already discussed, the theological consensus in the DRC was rapidly breaking up under the leadership of the newer generation of scholars no longer influenced by Dutch theologian Abraham Kuyper, but that of the neo-orthodox Swiss theologian Karl Barth. Barth was a key internationalist-oriented, neo-Marxian leader of the German theological resistance to the movement termed "German Christians," who unconditionally supported National Socialist, Adolf Hitler, based upon a race-based, natural theology. For those younger Afrikaner theologians trained in under Barth and his colleagues, that European context was uncomfortably similar to their own homeland.

The decade of the seventies, with its long and divisive debate, was closed on Reformation Day (October 31, 1980) when "eight professors from [the

---

20 See (1) Walter Williams, *South Africa's War against Capitalism* [War against Capitalism] (New York: Praeger, 1989; Cape Town: Juta, 1990); (2) Leon Louw and Frances Kendall, *After Apartheid: The Solution for South Africa*, 3rd ed. (Bisho, Ciskei: Amagi, 1989), https://www.sahistory.org.za/archive/after-apartheid-solution-south-africa-leon-louw-and-frances-kendall-foreword-clem-sunter.

21 P. J. Strauss, "Abraham Kuyper, Apartheid and the Reformed Church in South Africa in their Support of Apartheid," *Theological Forum* XXIII (March 1995): 22.

22 Pieter G. J. Meiring, "The Churches' Contribution to Change in South Africa [Contribution]," in *Change in South Africa*, ed. D. J. Van Vuuren, N. E. Wiehahn, J. A. Lombard, and N. J. Rhoodie (Durban: Butterworths, 1983).

24 WHEN A THEOLOGICAL SHIFT CHANGED A NATION

prestigious Universities of] Stellenbosch and Pretoria (six of them lecturers at the two [DRC] theological faculties) participated" in the publication of a mildly critical *Reformation Day Testimony* urging the DRC to change its social theological justification for apartheid.[23] As the eighties dawned, the DRC was shaken by several book-length internal documents that were critical of apartheid social theology and the dogmatic theories under-girding it.

First appeared an Afrikaans collection of essays titled in English translation, *Storm Compass: In the Search of a True Direction in the South African Context of the Eighties* [Storm-Kompas].[24] The editors were two prominent DRC missiologists, Nico J. Smith, Professor of Missiology and Pieter G. J. Meiring, later, Professor of Missiology at the University of Pretoria. Both came out of what I call the pietist, Andrew Murray missions wing of the DRC that expressed great concern for mission and positive witness among the indigenous African population. The other editor was an ecumenicist, F. E. O'Brien Geldenhuys, then head of the DRC's department of ecumenical affairs This demonstrated a budding ecumenical and pietist-missional coalition against the Apartheid system. *Storm-Kompas* [Storm-Compass] consisted of articles written by well-respected church bureaucrats and professors and was a cannon-shot across the bow of the DRC. These men rejected the isolationist social theology of the church and its infallibilist Kuyperian view of Scripture. They were in favor of reunification with the world ecumenical movement with its espoused justice mission to our one world. The book was a harbinger of the strong resistance building in the church against apartheid theology.

The next volley was the "Open Letter" (*Ope Brief*) eventually signed by 148 influential pastors and individuals in the DRC. The subsequent volume commenting on it elicited much discussion. It was edited by very well-known and respected Afrikaner, Barthian-oriented theologians, David Bosch and Adrio König, as well as DRC pastor Willem Nicol.[25] The volume is again dominated by younger Barthian-influenced, non-Kuyperian scholars educated in the 1960s and 1970s who have rejected Kuyper's doctrine of creation ordinances as well as his doctrine of an inerrant Scripture. None of them seemed

---

23 Meiring, *Contribution*, 309.

24 Nico Smith and others, *Storm Compass: In the Search of a True Direction in the South African Context of the* Eighties [Storm-Kompas: Opstelle op Soek na 'n Suiwer Koers in die Suid-Afrikaanse Konteks van die Jare Tagtig] [Storm-Compass] (Kaapstad [Cape Town]: Tafelberg, 1981).

25 David J. Bosch, Adrio König, and Willem Nicol, *Perspektief op die Ope Brief* [Perspectives on the Open letter] (Cape Town: Human & Rousseau, 1982).

A GROUND-LEVEL VIEW OF THE HISTORICAL BACKGROUND   25

to be members of the Afrikaner ruling elite, but were internationally influential outsiders to those elite governing circles.

Third, F. E. O'Brien Geldenhuys, the newly retired and still influential director of the DRC's ecumenical affairs department in the 1970s, wrote a commentary on the development of the DRC's social theology in 1982.[26] One key implication Geldenhuys makes is that the inerrantist, Kuyperian scholars were the developers of apartheid theology. In rejecting the Kuyperian support for apartheid, Geldenhuys also himself rejects the Kuyperian doctrine of Scripture and of creation design structures as well.

These documents illustrate the internal pressure upon the DRC to revise their apartheid-affirming document, *Human Relations in the Light of Scripture*, which they did in 1986 with the approval of *Church and Society*. That began the rapid paradigm shift from the classic and, to be honest, syncretistic Kuyperianized apartheid social theology and mission theory to ecumenical theology via the mediating theology of Karl Barth.

Ecumenical Movement Declares DRC Social Theology Heretical

In the meantime, the inter-church and intra-church conflict over HRLS social theology, both within southern Africa and in the international arena, had been growing increasingly painful. This was especially true even for the designers and proponents of the C&S document who seemed to genuinely believe that this document would "would satisfy the conditions" which the more radically oriented World Alliance of Reformed Churches (WARC) and the moderate, more evangelically oriented Reformed Ecumenical Synod (RES) "had set for the re-entry of the . . . [DRC] into ecumenical relations."[27]

The Lutheran World Federation (LWF) at its June 1977 meeting in Tanzania and the WARC (1982) had earlier taken a strong initiative in the theological war against the HRLS' justification of apartheid by officially proclaiming, "Apartheid is a heresy."[28] Apartheid, they declared, was a violation of their mutual confessions of faith, a *status confessionis*. In other words, every aspect of apartheid in all of its ecclesiastical, ideological, social, and civil aspects, along with its theological justification, outrages the very essence of the gospel of

---

26 F. E. O'Brien Geldenhuys, *In die Stroomversnellings* [In the Rapids] (Cape Town: Tafelberg, 1982).

27 Kinghorn, *Theology of C&S*, 22.

28 See De Gruchy and Villa-Vicencio, *Apartheid Heresy*.

26   WHEN A THEOLOGICAL SHIFT CHANGED A NATION

reconciliation. The two ecumenical bodies, therefore, declared the South African situation to be one necessitating the confession of a theology stressing the unity of humankind over any apartheid ethnic or racial separationist ideology.

A *status confessionis* context, they believed, had arrived, that is a "situation had arisen within the . . . [South African church] requiring the [universal] church to confess its faith anew against an ideology that was subverting the gospel and its proclamation."[29] The quote actually refers to Karl Barth and Dietrich Bonhoeffer's decision to see Nazism as such a confession-demanding situation or context. Later John De Gruchy shows how the world churches saw the South African situation as an analog of Nazi-dominated Germany in the 1930s. Many other denominations in South Africa and the world followed, including the largest groups of Reformed denominations in the West. These included a then moderately evangelical Reformed Ecumenical Synod, the rapidly radicalizing Reformed Churches in the Netherlands (*Gereformeerde Kerken in Nederland*), the Reformed Alliance in Germany (*Reformierte Bund*), the Christian Reformed Church in America (now the Christian Reformed Church of North America [CRCNA]), the Protestant Churches in Germany (*Evangelische Kirche in Deutschland*) and the Federation of Protestant Churches in Switzerland.[30]

This movement included the ecumenically oriented United Church of Canada. Its publication entitled *Apartheid is a Heresy* summarized what many other churches in the world conciliar movements believed. Some but not all aspects of this statement deeply concerned me at that time and still do as a Reformed evangelical because I believed it was as syncretistic as was the earlier apartheid theological syncretism, a concern I will unpack in future chapters.

> The Bible reveals that God's intention for all creation and for all humankind is harmony, peace, unity, friendship, justice and righteousness. Human beings are created in the image of God and in Christ all cultural, racial, sexual and other differences are *rendered void* (Galatians 3:23 [*sic*, 3:28]). Apartheid denies not only these biblical truths but also denies the central act of reconciliation in Christian faith—the life, death, and resurrection of Jesus Christ. Apartheid maintains that human beings are fundamentally irreconcilable—a flat contradiction to the life and ministry of Jesus and to the heart of the Christian message.[31]

29 John De Gruchy, *Liberating Reformed Theology: A South African Contribution to an Ecumenical Debate* [Liberating] (Grand Rapids: Eerdmans and Cape Town: David Philip, 1991a), 210. See also, De Gruchy and Villa-Vicencio, *Apartheid Heresy*.

30 Meiring, *Contribution*, 313–14.

31 Ann Naylor, *Apartheid Is a Heresy* (Toronto: South African Education Project, United Church of Canada, n.d.), 4; emphasis added.

Furthermore, I wholeheartedly agreed then with the first two points of the World Alliance of Reformed Churches' (WARC) suspension of the membership of the DRC and conditions for readmission. I was equivocal on the second half of the third point about dismantling the total political system, because, as I will share in coming chapters, the most just solution would have granted independence to fully, and generously consolidated ethnic-territories of *at least* KwaZulu-Natal, the old Transkei-Ciskei-Border Xhosa heartland, and a greatly enlarged Bophuthatswana, perhaps confederated with Botswana.

In addition, the WARC provided three conditions for readmission: (1) "Black Christians are [to be] no longer excluded from holy communion;" (2) "Concrete support in word and deed is given to those who suffer under the system of apartheid ('separate development');" (3) "Unequivocal synod resolutions are [to be] made which reject apartheid and commit the Church to dismantling this system in both church and politics."[32] In short, the WARC was requiring the DRC to agree with their declaration that the total system of petty discrimination *and* the grand land-partitionist vision is sin because "apartheid is a sin" and the "theological justification of it . . . is a theological heresy" without any equivocation.[33]

DRMC Develops the *Belhar Confession*

In direct response to LWF and the WARC declarations, the synod of the DRC's largest mission church, the so-called colored DRMC (NG Sending Kerk or NGSK), presented the *Belhar Confession* in 1982 to the DRMC's General Synod.[34] It was officially approved the same year (1986) as was C&S by the mother church, the DRC. It was to be a fourth confessional statement binding the ministers and officers of the church alongside of and on equal par with the Three Forms of Unity. The Belhar Confession adopted the WARC and LWF's perspective that apartheid in all of its manifestations is so evil and heretical that a *status confessionis* situation existed.[35]

---

32 Páraic Réamonn, ed., *Farewell to Apartheid? Church relations in South Africa. The WARC consultation in South Africa March 1–5, 1993. Koinonia Centre. Judith's Pearl, Johannesburg* [Farewell to Apartheid] (Geneva: World Alliance of Reformed Churches, 1994), 83.

33 Heideman, Eugene P., "Old Confessions and New Testimony," *Reformed Journal* 38 (1988): 7. See review of ecumenical struggle to declare as heresy sins against *orthopraxis*: Neville Richardson, "Apartheid, Heresy, and the Church in South Africa," *The Journal of Religious Ethics* 14 (Spring 1986): 1–21.

34 G. D. Cloete and D. J. Smit, *A Moment of Truth: The Confession of the Dutch Reformed Mission Church, 1982* [Moment of Truth] (Grand Rapids: Eerdmans, 1984).

35 De Gruchy, *Liberating*, 214; Cloete and Smit, *Moment of Truth*.

28   WHEN A THEOLOGICAL SHIFT CHANGED A NATION

John De Gruchy was quite candid about the Belhar Confession. It "connect[s] Reformed and Liberation Theology," reinterpreting "the confession of Jesus Christ from the liberatory perspective of a commitment to the poor." Ethnically or racially separated denominations break the unity of the church in its mission to the world. The confession "affirms the true nature of the church's unity and mission: a confession of Jesus as Lord and a commitment to the struggle for God's justice in the world."[36]

De Gruchy clearly saw the implications of the Belhar Confession's emphasis upon structural unity of the church in the struggle against social injustice, racism, and poverty. The church context and the social-political situation are parallel, he claimed. The poignant critique by the chairman of the Council of the *Evangelischen Kirche in Deutschland* [Protestant-Lutheran Churches of Germany] [EKD], Bishop Martin Kruse, who in his official capacity accused the C&S of making "belonging to the [Afrikaner] volk and the [Afrikaans language] . . . a stronger bond than the baptism with the living water of divine grace"[37] Here as I will point out more in a future chapter, I believe he prioritizes unity over diversity instead of seeing the equal priority, the equal ultimacy of unity and diversity at the same time as in the Trinity.

John De Gruchy similarly claimed, "If black and white are baptized into the same Christ they are part of the same church, privileged to share in the same Eucharist, and this means that there can *no longer be any theological grounds for segregation in society*." He continues later by stating with crystal clarity that a correct appreciation of the meaning of the sacrament of baptism "not only undermines apartheid in the church; it should also *undermine apartheid in society*; and all other forms of oppression as Paul indicates in Galatians 3:27–8. For baptism is a sign of human solidarity redeemed in Christ."[38]

Here the ideal of the church is the ideal for society, the social order. This means ultimately, that no ground at all exists for partitioning multilingual, multiethnic countries. It would instead approve only a one-world government based on individuals and that uniformity not multiformity (diversity) is the universal ideal. Instead, Abraham Kuyper was correct as the older Afrikaner leaders averred, yet, I must emphasize again, *without their color-based racialism*. True unity and real ethno-covenantal diversity can exist in balance as in the Trinity. But I am anticipating again.

36   De Gruchy, *Liberating*, 214–15.
37   Martin Kruse, "Duitse Kerke se Mening oor 'Kerk en Samelewing' [German Churches' Opinion on 'Church and Society']," *Kerkbode* [Church Messenger] (December 16, 1988): 9.
38   John De Gruchy, *Liberating*, 215–16; emphasis added.

A GROUND-LEVEL VIEW OF THE HISTORICAL BACKGROUND 29

Instead, according to Anglo-South African, Professor De Gruchy and German churchman Martin Kruse, all those who confess the unity of believers in the Church, which is sacramentalized in water baptism, must stand with God, who himself stands "against injustice and with the wronged," as the DRMC's Belhar Confession states. Consequently, to know God is to side with him *and all others* who struggle against racism and any other structures causing poverty and social divisions. As we shall see, taking the option to side exclusively with the poor and oppressed is a syncretistic, neo-Marxian-based theme that liberation theology took up and emphasized. Our Creator and God *is* genuinely with the poor and oppressed and has *real* compassion upon them (e.g., Ps 103:6). However, he is actually only siding with those who humble themselves and solely trust him for life and justice as he defines justice in the whole of Scripture. These, then, are those, who we shall see, are actively take their place among the poor *coram Deo*, before God's face (Ps 34:6). This is true whether they are actually rich or poor. The wealthy can be genuinely generous like Abraham (Gn 15:1), to whom the Lord said, "I am your shield, your exceedingly great reward." However, both poor and rich must truly be trusting and dependent, even while generously living among the unjustly oppressed poor like the Hebrew slaves in Egypt (see, e.g., Ps 37; 1 Pt 2:23).

The October 1994 DRC General Synod decided to take steps to join the Uniting Reformed Church (*Verenigende Gereformeerde Kerk*) and to unite with its new syncretistic social theology. This uniting church is made up of the Dutch Reformed Mission Church (NGSK) (the so-called colored, Afrikaans-speaking denomination) and the Dutch Reformed Church in Africa (DRCA) (primarily Nguni and Sotho-speaking Afro-ethnics). Both have accepted the Belhar Confession. To join this new church, the DRC would need to receive as one of their fundamental confessional statements, the Belhar Confession as well. The reason is that accepting Belhar and joining the Uniting Reformed Church were the key prerequisites for rejoining the world reformed movement and the ecumenical World Council of Churches (WCC). By 2023 this has not yet occurred.

As preparation for this step, the October 1990 DRC General Synod declared that Belhar is "not in itself contradictory to" the DRC's doctrinal standard, which are the Three Forms of Unity (the *Heidelberg Catechism* (1563), the *Belgic Confession* (1566) and the *Canons of Dordt* (1619)), and that Belhar "need not bring any distance between the churches."[39] At that general time

---

39 See *Kerkbode* [DRC Church Messenger], November 1, 1991.

30 WHEN A THEOLOGICAL SHIFT CHANGED A NATION

frame, the well-respected, DRC ruling elder and UNISA theologian Adrio König wrote a persuasive *Kerkbode* [Church Messenger] article that was entitled: "Belhar—Uniting or Dividing Factor?" He demonstrated at several crucial points "a large agreement" between Belhar and *Church and Society* (1990). He noted, first, that Belhar and C&S "confess that faith in Jesus Christ is the only prerequisite for membership in the [institutional] church and that heredity or any other human or social factor may not be a co-determining [factor of such membership]." Second, König wrote that there is also a "remarkable agreement in the passage in which the Belhar Confession and *Church and Society* confess the unity of the church." Last, he stated that both documents claim that "in the Bible, God places diversity in the service of unity (1 Cor 12).["][40] In other words, both refused to "absolutize" diversity, that is put diversity on an equal par with unity as equally ultimate and important. As we shall see, this is a crucial, and I contend, a devastating surrender to syncretism in both documents.

In addition to mentioning that there are "many more such striking agreements between the two documents," he cites two more crucially important ones. Fourth, the two documents agree that God is "in a special way the God of the destitute, the poor, and the wronged and that he calls his Church to follow him in this" (Belhar Confession). König cites several passages in the 1986 and 1990 editions of C&S which are very similar. Fifth, both documents "show agreement in the statements about apartheid." König then summarizes: "There are no theological objections to accepting it in the future as a[n equal] confession."[41]

Public Law Professor Nico Horn of the University of Namibia and Stellenbosch University in the Western Cape Province of the new South Africa reports almost three decades later in 2011 that "the majority of the pastors and congregations of the DRC are not in favour of accepting Belhar as a confession." The Uniting Reformed Church in South Africa (URCSA) "refuses to compromise on the issue. In their understanding it is an important landmark in the struggle against a heresy" that of apartheid alone. However, at least in 2011 the *Belhar Confession* could still not be used, for example, to invite the LGBTQ+ movement into the fold as people similarly oppressed. This is exactly what one of the authors of that confessional document, Dr. Allan Boesak advocated, claiming in 2011 that it was the logical concomitant of the *Belhar Confession*: "The Belhar, he said, was never meant to be just an anti-apartheid

---

40 Adrio König, "*Belhar—Verenigende of Verdelende Faktor?* [Belhar—Uniting or Dividing Factor?] [Belhar]," *Kerkbode* 1995, 7.

41 König, *Belhar*, 7.

document, but a document against discrimination of all kinds."[42] This would include, as we shall see more completely, any discrimination against the LGBTQ+ community (and any other human from any marginalized group whatsoever, it seems).

DRC Leadership Desires to Rejoin the World Conciliar Movement

As Johann Kinghorn stated above, many church officials and several professors of theology, missiology and ecumenics at DRC seminaries had been very vocal in the need to abandon apartheid social theology, unify the DRC with the younger churches of southern Africa, and rejoin the world ecumenical movement (WARC, REC, and the WCC/SACC). The theologians and pastors who supported social apartheid had virtually lost control of the church by the 1986 General Synod, leading to dissension and schism, as already discussed. However, to re-enter the ecumenical fold, the church needed to convince the denominations related to the World Council Churches that DRC Synod Policy documents met the conditions for re-entry. This the emerging majority of theologians in the DRC were willing to do. Notwithstanding the movement toward reconciliation with the ecumenically minded groups within DRC circles, the WCC-oriented South African Council of Churches had been continually pressuring the DRC to unequivocally repudiate the complete system of apartheid as well as the theology that justified it.

Consequently, even in 1992 the SACC still denied even observer status in the council to the DRC because the SACC "believe[d] that the white church has not done enough to repudiate apartheid." The SACC severely criticized even C&S 1990, which included a paragraph moderating the DRC condemnation of apartheid. That paragraph reads as follows: "It would also be unreasonable to brand as wrong and bad everything which took place within the political structure of apartheid and to deny the positive developments achieved in various fields."[43]

---

42 (1) Nico Horn, "The Belhar Confession—29 years on," *Niederduitse Gereformeerde Teologiese Tydskrif* [NGTT], 54/3–4 (September–December 2013): 8, https:// hdl.handle. net/10520/EJC146118; (2) Alan Boesak, *Black and Reformed: Apartheid, Calvinism, and the Calvinist Tradition* (Eugene, OR: Wipf and Stock, 2015); (3) CRCNA, "World News: Allan Boesak Quits Church Posts over Homosexuality Policy, Belhar," *The Banner*, January 18, 2011, https://www.thebanner.org/news/2011/01/world-news-allan-boesak-quits-chu rch-posts-over-homosexuality-policy-belhar.

43 Christian Century, "Membership denied," *Christian Century* 109 (June 3–10, 1992): 579.

32   WHEN A THEOLOGICAL SHIFT CHANGED A NATION

In response to this ecumenical pressure, the DRC delegation *unreservedly* relented to the ecumenical consensus identified themselves at the Reformed Ecumenical Synod in Athens (June 1992) with the following: "*Apartheid* is an oppressive political system that is unacceptable in the light of Scriptures. All our churches condemn *apartheid* unequivocally in all its ideological, politico-economic and religious manifestations as essentially and fundamentally a sin."[44]

Did C&S Actually Abandon HRLS' Social Theology?

Some scholars such as Charles Villa-Vicencio and Johann Kinghorn believed that *Church and Society* only made cosmetic changes. C&S (1986), University of Cape Town Theologian Villa-Vicencio claims, was merely a move "toward a more moderate stance on the points that made the DRC most unpalatable to the ecumenical church." *Church and Society* still emphasized Afrikaner interests and security above everyone else.[45] On the other hand, some such as Dutch-American scholar Paul Schrotenboer and Afrikaner Theologian J. Loubser interpreted the document as actually abandoning the previous report and its justification of apartheid.[46]

However, according to a group of die-hard protesters within the DRC who issued a manifesto in 1987 entitled *Faith and Protest* (*Geloof en Protes*), it was indeed a radical break with the past at least in principle.[47] They foresaw, correctly I believe, that C&S completely abandoned racial separation in principle and surreptitiously accepted its corollary, an ethnically and racially unified church in a unified, pluralistic state. They complained that C&S explained "away 'race' (a creation fact)—a Kuyperian construct—for the sake

---

44 Réamonn, *Farewell to Apartheid*, 34.

45 Villa-Vicencio, *Safe Synod*, 9; Johann Kinghorn, *'n Tuiste vir Almal: 'n Sosiaal-teologiese Studie oor 'n Gesamentlike Demokrasie in Suid-Afrika* [A Home for Everyone: A Social Theological Study on a Common Democracy in South Africa] [Home for Everyone], with a foreword by Bernard Lategan (Stellenbosch, South Africa: Sentrum vir Kontekstuele hermeneutiek, Universiteit van Stellenbosch, 1990c).

46 Paul G. Schrotenboer, "Turning the Tide?" *The Reformed Journal* (January 1987): 1ff; Loubser, *Apartheid Bible*.

47 Voortsettingskomitee, *Geloof en Protes: 'n Antwoord Namens Beswaarde Lidmate op Sekere Aspekte van "Kerk en Samelewing"* [Faith and Protest: An Answer in the Name of Dissenting Members to Various Aspects of "Church and Society"] [Faith and Protest] (Pretoria: N.P.: Die Voortsettingskomitee, 1987).

A GROUND-LEVEL VIEW OF THE HISTORICAL BACKGROUND   33

of a borderless human community (and a multiracial, unitary state)" similar to that advocated by the World Council of Churches.[48]

The difference of opinion between the critics from the exclusivist and inclusivist points of view seems to have come about because different sections of the C&S document are emphasized by each group. The inclusivist critics appeared to be mostly responding to the paragraphs in the moderate application section of C&S, with little reference to the logical outworking of the more radical paragraphs in the second, norm-giving "Scriptural Principle" sections, which deny that Scripture has any bearing upon the racial issue at all. The die-hard Afrikaner nationalist critics of the C&S, on the other hand, seemed to focus most of their attention on the implications of the more socially and theologically radical paragraphs of the normative section(s) of C&S (1986).

Interestingly enough in the midst of virtually rejecting the whole of the 1986 Synod's decision, the radical inclusivist Anglo-South African critic Charles Villa-Vicencio makes a crucial admission. In his article, "Report from a Safe Synod," he claims that "many of the cardinal theological principles found in the report are acceptable and pleasing [from his inclusivist perspective]. But they are irreparably compromised when they are put to the hermeneutical service of the prevailing political dispensation [in the practical sections]."[49] From Villa-Vicencio's perspective, the privileges and prejudices of the white Afrikaner oppressor class are coddled to in the practical sections. This compromised the radical, social structure overturning principles in the normative section.

His colleague at the University of Cape Town, Theologian John De Gruchy sums up the gradual but rapidly progressing paradigm shift at that time. The DRC was beginning to rapidly converge with the ecumenical South African Council of Churches' (SACC) social theology. From 1986 up to the World Council of Churches' (WCC) sponsored Rustenburg, RSA conference in 1990 the movement was breathtakingly rapid from both an insiders' and outsiders' perspective.[50] As an Afrikaans-speaking American, I personally lived there and experienced it at that time (1983–92). This conference was virtually a repeat of the earlier WCC-sponsored Cottesloe conference in the early 1960s, but much more favorable for change this time around.

The cannon shots across the bow of the DRC and the ecumenical and social-political artillery bombardment against apartheid had accomplished

---

48 Die Voortsettingskomitee, *Faith and Protest*, 29.
49 Villa-Vicencio, *Safe Synod*, 10.
50 De Gruchy and De Gruchy, *Church Struggle*.

34 WHEN A THEOLOGICAL SHIFT CHANGED A NATION

their goal over the preceding twenty years of theological and real political war against the regime and their ecclesial supporters. The old guard was devastated mostly by death, and the new generation influenced by modernity and post-modern theology took up the mantle of rapid change. This time it occurred in the midst of a rapidly developing process in which both the internal DRC and National Party dominated civil government's pressure was exactly the opposite of that which occurred after the original conference in 1960. The WCC's Rustenburg conference was held just after the DRC General Synod that approved the revised, second edition of C&S (1990).

As it did in the first ecumenical Cottesloe conference, the DRC leadership again fully participated in the conference. This time, however, they signed the following confession:

> We confess our own sin and acknowledge our heretical part in the policy of apartheid which had led to such extreme suffering for so many of our land. We denounce apartheid in its intention, its implementation and its consequences as an evil policy. The practice and defense of apartheid as though it were biblically and theologically legitimated was an act of disobedience to God, a denial of the gospel of Jesus Christ and a sin against our unity in the Holy Spirit.[51]

Pieter Potgieter, then Moderator of the General Synod, stated that "on this one issue all agreed, the unequivocal rejection of apartheid."[52]

Conclusion

In retrospect, even such a longtime apartheid critic as UNISA missiologist J. J. (Dons) Kritzinger could admit by 1994 that even C&S (1986) "was a radical break with the previous efforts to base racial policies on scripture."[53] DRC pastor and apartheid critic, J. A. Loubser, agreed. Concerning the original edition of C&S (1986), he claimed: "In general one can thus say that the DRC has finally closed its 'apartheid bible.'"[54] This was a bit premature, but C&S

---

51 Philip Potter, "The Task Ahead," in *A Long Struggle: The Involvement of the World Council of Churches in South Africa*, ed. Pauline Webb (Geneva: WCC Publications, World Council of Churches, 1994), 123–4.

52 Louw Alberts and Frank Chikane, ed., *Road to Rustenburg: The Church Looking Forward to a New South Africa* (Cape Town: Struik Christian Books, 1991), 92, 100.

53 J. J. (Dons) Kritzinger, "The Witness of the Reformed Churches in South Africa: A Certain Past and an Uncertain Future," *International Review of Mission* LXXXIII, no. 328 (January 1994): 181.

54 Loubser, *Apartheid Bible*, 114.

A GROUND-LEVEL VIEW OF THE HISTORICAL BACKGROUND   35

had been, as its critics asserted, an *evolving transitional document.* This policy statement definitely helped move the church—and very possibly through it the former civil government dominated by DRC members—away from the separating, apartheid social theology and toward a reunion with the world theological and social consensus—a totally new social theological paradigm.

There exists at present, a virtual consensus that a theological paradigm shift took place and has been implemented in the DRC theology over the past five decades (1970–2023). By 1993 at the WARC consultation in Johannesburg, Beyers Naudé a dissident Afrikaner DRC theologian much respected in world ecumenical circles, summarized what has occurred in the decade since 1982: "Since 1986, a fundamental shift (sometimes not clearly visible or acknowledged) has taken place within the DRC regarding the issue of *apartheid*. The DRC has stated that apartheid is a sin and the theological justification of *apartheid* is a heresy."[55] The response of the official DRC delegation at that 1993 consultation revealed the absolute rejection of all forms of apartheid social theology and its related mission theory (missiology): "We want to assure this consultation that the DRC is committed to the unity of the DRC family. We agree with the statement that this is the acid test whether the DRC has finally distanced itself from the racism of *apartheid* and we are willing to be part of this process." This comprehensive rejection of *apartheid* lock stock and barrel led the delegation to plea with the WARC: "We hope that these answers will satisfy the consultation . . . and that it will be possible for WARC to restore this church as a full member of the Alliance."[56]

This paradigm shift was fueled by a preliminary and more fundamental shift in the theory of Scripture interpretation (hermeneutics). The late, theologically progressive Professor Ferdinand Deist, at the time head of the department of Ancient Near Eastern Studies at the prestigious University of Stellenbosch, summarized the changes in the science of biblical research in the DRC. In South Africa his field of research had gone through dramatic changes from the early 1970s to the early 1990s, Deist wrote. It was a "confusing time" especially for the lay members of the DRC because their trusted leaders had made a "one hundred and eighty degree reversal in the church's opinion on what the Bible has to say about the South African social, political and economic scene [social

---

55 Beyers Naudé, "Support in Word and Deed," in *Farewell to Apartheid? Church Relations in South Africa. The WARC Consultation in South Africa March 1–5, 1993. Koinonia Centre. Judith's Pearl, Johannesburg,* ed. Páraic Réamonn (Geneva: World Alliance of Reformed Churches, 1994), 73.

56 Réamonn, *Farewell to Apartheid,* 77.

36   WHEN A THEOLOGICAL SHIFT CHANGED A NATION

theology]." "Many laymen, were shocked," he continued, "that the Bible now suddenly says *precisely the opposite as what it has always said*."[57]

This foundational paradigm shift I will discuss in Chapter 5: The Scripture Alone Principle and the DRC. However, first and of principial importance is to understand the Trinitarian Principle as Key, which is the central foundational principle to discern the country-changing paradigm shift that *Church and Society* (1986 and 1990) activated.[58]

---

57   Ferdinand Deist, *Ervaring, Rede en Metode in Skrifuitleg* [Experience, Reason, and Methodology in Scripture Exposition] [Experience] (Pretoria: Raad vir Geesteswetenskaplike Navorsing, 1994), iii; emphasis added.

58   For ecumenical opinion of the period during the writing of C&S 1990, see: (1) De Gruchy and Villa-Vicencio, *Apartheid Heresy*; (2) Hennie Serfontein, *Apartheid, Change and the NG Kerk* (Johannesburg: Taurus, 1982); (3) Johann Kinghorn, *Die NG Kerk en Apartheid* [The DRC and Apartheid] (Johannesburg: Macmillan, 1986a); (4) W. Weisse and C. Anthonissen, eds., *Maintaining Apartheid or Promoting Change? The Role of the Dutch Reformed Church in a Phase of Increasing Conflict in South Africa* (New York: Waxman Münster, 2004).

For Radical Reformation opinion (Mennonite and those allied with the perspective): (1) Gabriel M. Setiloane and Ivan H. M. Peden, eds., *Pangs of Growth: A Dialogue on Church Growth in Southern Africa* (Braamfontein, Johannesburg: Skotaville, 1988); (2) Wilbert R. Shenk, ed., *Exploring Church Growth* (Grand Rapids: Eerdmans, 1983).

For recent DRC opinion, see, e.g., (1) T. D. Moodie, "Confessing Responsibility for the Evils of Apartheid: The Dutch Reformed Church in the 1980s," *South African Historical Journal* 72, no. 4 (2020): 627–50. https://doi.org/10.1080/02582473.2020.1839542; (2) Louis R. Van der Riet and Cobus G. J. Van Wyngaard, "The Other Side of Whiteness: The Dutch Reformed Church and the Search for a Theology of Racial Reconciliation in the Afterlife of Apartheid," *Stellenbosch Theological Journal* 7, no. 1 (2021): 1–25. Overview of the changes in the DRC from 1986 to 2019 General Synod.

· 3 ·

THE TRINITARIAN PRINCIPLE AS KEY

Is C&S Philosophically Anti-Trinitarian?

The Trinity serves as an interpretative key to all of life because the Triune God is the only, independent, everlasting Living One, who was, is, and is to come (Rev 4:8, 1:8). This God is the sole, independent Creator of all other dependent reality in heaven and earth. Consequently, the basis for all correct biblical thinking is the foundational presupposition that unity is as equally ultimate as diversity. The principle of equal ultimacy is valid both within the Godhead and within the creation that he made to reflect his triune glory. The late Kuyperian Professor F. J. M. Potgieter, 1990 DRC General Synod Moderator Pieter Potgieter's father, correctly terms this the "Trinitarian key" to biblical hermeneutics.[1]

Cornelius A. Van Til and others such as Colin Gunton have argued, contrary to C&S, that the ontological Trinity is foundational to explaining everything else, as we will see, and this includes more than hermeneutics.[2] All

---

1   F. J. M. Potgieter, *Kerk en Samelewing—'n Wesenskou* [Church and Society—A Look at its Essence] [C&S Essence] (Cape Town: NG Kerk-Uitgewers, 1990).

2   See (1) Colin Gunton, *The One, the Three and the Many: God, Creation and the Culture of Modernity.* The 1992 Bampton Lectures (Cambridge: Cambridge University Press, 1993); (2) Rousas J. Rushdoony, The *One and the Many, The: Studies in the Philosophy of Order and*

human knowledge "rests upon the ontological Trinity as its presupposition," its inescapable transcendent foundation. The simple reason is that, according to Scripture, the Triune God created everything to reflect his glory through Christ in the Spirit.[3] This involves more than mere "spiritual" or "religious" knowledge a point very relevant to C&S. There is no bifurcation or dualism between spiritual/religious and empirical science as both depend upon the Word of the Creator, now incarnate and who upholds all things by the word of his power (Col 1:17, 2:2–3; Heb 1:3). This the Kuyperian, early Free University of Amsterdam school of apologetics and philosophy correctly averred. The authors of C&S either possibly ignored this foundation as irrelevant or perhaps never even heard about it in their European graduate schools. Again, Van Til explains, "True scientific certainty, no less than true religious certainty, must be based upon the presupposition of the ontological trinity."[4] The ontological Trinity is the final reference point required for interpreting all phenomena, as I have shown in a relevant article, entitled: "Toward a Biblical Philosophy of Science." The triune God created all facts and providentially controls all facts. Without the biblical given, there is no knowledge whatsoever.[5] Pushing this out of one's mind and out of a collective culture's mind, leads to the step-by-step degeneration of such a culture as Paul so distressingly demonstrated in Romans 1:18–32. In short, Trinitarian theism is the only sound foundation of everything in the created universe both visible and invisible.

The most vital question, then, that I wish to address is whether *Church and Society* relativizes true diversity and makes the principle of unity more important and of a better moral quality than true diversity. In other words, is C&S philosophically anti-Trinitarian, that is to say, covertly Modalist or Unitarian in the actual outworking of its doctrines of the nature of the community of Christ, its mission to the nations, and its social theology?

C&S Claims Diversity Must Not Affect Undivided Unity. Although ethno-linguistic and other aspects of the God-created human diversity have a certain role to play within the unity of the church, C&S states that this

---

Ultimacy [One and Many] (Vallecito, CA: Chalcedon/Ross House, 2009); (3) For a brief introduction, see R. J. Rushdoony, "The One and Many Problem—The Contribution of Van Til," in *Jerusalem and Athens: Critical Discussions on the Philosophy and Apologetics of Cornelius Van Til*, ed. E. R. Geehan (Philipsburg, NJ: Presbyterian and Reformed, 2023), 339–48.

3 C. A. Van Til, *Introduction to Systematic Theology*, 2nd ed. (Phillipsburg, NJ: P&R, 2007), 59.

4 C. A. Van Til, *Common Grace and the Gospel*, 2nd ed. (Phillipsburg, NJ: P&R, 2007), 64.

5 See Mark R. Kreitzer, "Toward a Biblical Philosophy of Science," *Christianity and Society: The Biannual Journal of the Kuyper Foundation* XVII, no. 2 (Winter 2007): 6–19.

diversity may not touch true unity, which seems then to be primary. For example, particularity, that is "geographical factors, social conditions, etc., can also be a factor in meeting specific [ministry] needs [*bedieningsbehoeftes*]." However, "the ministry must be structured in such a way as to enrich the unity of the church and to promote the fellowship of people."[6] A little later, C&S states the church is a kerygmatic (proclamation), Word-bound fellowship.[7] This kerygma-centeredness of the church contrasts with the creation-word and Scripture-word balance in Reformed theology. This is an indication of Barthian influence. Karl Barth denied any universal creation-word.

One implication is that "with a view to the effective ministry of the Word and in order to minister to the needs of various linguistic and cultural groups, allowance may be made for the church to be indigenous."[8] Because there is no appeal to divine creational design, however, by implication this implicitly denies any sub-branch of the whole universal Community of Christ to be self-governing both linguistically and pragmatically ("practical problems") even if gathered in wider confederal structures, which I would recommend. It must, like the Roman Church, be submitted to wider, necessarily top-down ecclesial structure. If my conclusion seems tenuous, the further discussion to come will demonstrate this adequately, I believe. "The New Testament," C&S adds in the 1990 edition, "is realistic in its handling of the practical problems arising from specific needs of various people" (Note here no reference to the creation design information from the Old Testament that the earlier HRLS document added and which C&S specifically says cannot be used in the NT Community).

This is an attempt in its context to correct and ameliorate the stark, almost Maricon distinction between the Old and New Testament in the 1986 document. Notice also while reading the quote below how the DRC Synod added this positive paragraph in the 1990 edition to replace the more negative emphasis in C&S 1986, which read simply: "Such practical considerations in ministering to people must, however, never obscure or endanger the unity of the Church."[9] The 1990 edition attempts to ground linguistic diversity on the Pentecost miracle rather that the Babel miracle in which God created the various proto-languages of earth. The HRLS document bases linguistic diversity on divine creation, but C&S bases pragmatic considerations of linguistic

6 C&S, 32.
7 C&S, 32–3.
8 C&S, 38.
9 C&S 1986, 32.

40   WHEN A THEOLOGICAL SHIFT CHANGED A NATION

diversity on Pentecost, while never denying the point that "the unity of the Church" is always primary. Diversity is merely "understood from the pastoral perspective" and "effective ministry" viewpoint, but not from the creational perspective that HRLS appealed to. Yet still, all "ministry must be structured . . . as to enrich the unity of the church." Unity has logical priority over diversity, instead, as in the Trinitarian Principle, neither unity nor diversity is prior but both are "equally ultimate" and important.

> The New Testament is realistic in its handling of the practical problems arising from specific needs of various people. The language miracle of Pentecost, for instance, must be understood from the pastoral perspective. What is relevant here, is that each listener heard of the great deeds of God in his own language. Therefore, what is of importance is the effective ministry of the Word. The same motive is also apparent when Paul states that for the Jews he became a Jew and all things to all men for the sake of the Gospel. Geographical factors, social conditions, etc., can also be a factor in meeting specific needs. The ministry must be structured in such a way as to enrich the unity of the church and to promote the fellowship of people.[10]

C&S Claims the Primacy of Unity over Diversity. The logical conclusion of the above examples is that C&S makes unity primary over any diversity. I will provide three examples.

The first example seems somewhat ambiguous at first. Unity is primarily made visible through love, it states. However, disunity among churches of the same confession, *without qualification*, is termed a sin. This sin, implicitly is the sin of "apartheid," which would become explicit as the 1990s developed as we saw in the second chapter. Would this exclude, to use a North American example, the separate Korean classis in the Christian Reformed Church or the non-geographically bound Korean-speaking Presbytery in the Presbyterian Church in America (PCA)? It seems so. C&S reads: **"This means** . . . that this unity becomes primarily visible in mutual love; . . . that Christians may never be content with disunity." "Disunity" translates *verskeurdheid* in Afrikaans, a word that carries a much more negative connotation than English "disunity." "Verskeurdheid" implies "something torn apart." The document continues, "disunity among the churches, especially among those with the same confession," is always evil and believers "must acknowledge and confess it as a sin; . . . that the church bears the responsibility, in so far as it is practically possible, to experience and make visible its unity with all believers."[11] "Practically" is added in English, but the Afrikaans reads: *"sover dit moontlik is"* (as far is it is possible).

10 C&S, 32.
11 C&S, 84–6.

THE TRINITARIAN PRINCIPLE AS KEY   41

In other words, the ancient Western Churches' ideology that led often but not always to practice was correct. This included Roman Catholic, Anglican, Lutheran, and Reformed Churches practice that one parish church must exist for all within a geographical area with ecclesial Latin used in the Roman churches and a princely imposed languages often for the Reformed. Certainly, C&S 1990 adds, practical contingencies must be considered "as far as is possible." Interestingly enough, even the later Reformed Synod of Dort's Church Order (1618–19) allowed for linguistic diversity between the Walloons (French) and the Dutch in its Church Order at congregation, classis (presbytery), and *linguistic* ("particular") synod levels with the added advice that the ministers and elders should gather monthly to promote "good unity and correspondence":

> 51. Since two languages are spoken in the Netherlands, it is considered advisable that the churches using the Dutch and Walloon languages have their own consistories, classical meetings, and particular synods.
>
> 52. Nevertheless it is advisable that in the cities where the aforesaid Walloon churches are found some ministers and elders of both sides should gather every month in order to promote good unity and correspondence with one another and as much as possible to support one another with advice according to need.[12]

However, C&S 1990 is not this specific, deliberately so it seems, because this would have kept them out of the world ecumenical consensus that demanded an absolute break with all aspects of apartheid including congregations, classes and synods based on language. This inevitably opens wide the door for an imperially imposed language to become slowly dominant. Ironically in South Africa, that language now is English and the Anglicization process can speed ahead as it has been for about two hundred years since British annexation of the Cape and later of Orange Free State and the Transvaal Republics. Despite the legal resistance of the Afrikaners during the apartheid decades the process now is again proceeding apace.

Also of interest to note, that this policy was not necessarily the Orthodox practice which still allows for distinguishable indigenous denominations with their own ethno-national Patriarch, for example, the Russian, Bulgarian, and Romanian Patriarchs. All of these autochthonous (self-governing indigenous) Churches find unity as they are bound together as equals in brotherly

---

12 Richard R. De Ridder, ed., *The Church Orders of the Sixteenth Century Reformed Churches of the Netherlands Together with Their Social, Political, and Ecclesiastical Context*, trans. Richard R. DeRidder. Translated from C. Hoijer, *Oude Kerkordeningen der Nederlandsche Gemeente (1563–1638)* (Zalt-Bommel: Joh. Noman en Zoon, n.d.).

42 WHEN A THEOLOGICAL SHIFT CHANGED A NATION

fellowship by confession and under the presidency of the Ecumenical Patriarch of Constantinople (now Istanbul).

A second example is C&S 1990, 81 that explains more in-depth the document's development of the primacy of unity over and above any diversity in its discussion of individual gifts and the unity of the church. This substantiates further my point that made in the first example, that C&S seems to relativize true diversity and makes it secondary and of a lesser quality than the primary good of unity. Section 81 states: "Diversity must not be seen as a threat to the church's unity, but as enriching it and as an opportunity for mutual service to the extent that each member has received his own gift of grace." It then adds point 2.9.3: "**The church has the responsibility to confess its profound, inviolable unity in Christ and to experience and make this unity visible in this broken and divided world.**"[13]

The intention here seems quite noble. The Church of Christ must make its unity structurally visible in a world cursed "in this broken and divided world." I agree wholeheartedly if by these divisions C&S mean divisions "caused by sin." Furthermore it continued, a true church of Christ in a specific nation-state must never be subservient to the diversities of what I interpret it to mean ethno-national identity.[14] The church is not "in the service of specific nations,"[15] but it is the "church of Christ,"[16] an independent sphere under God. Therefore, the Church of Christ in the New Testament is not semi-Erastian, serving under the "nation and chiefly . . . function[ing] to grant religious sanction to that nation's values, ideals and ambitions."[17] Indeed, it is also certainly true that no one ought to be righteously turned away, who desires to hear the word.[18] I agree wholeheartedly.

However, in appealing to the body and members figure of speech used especially in Paul's Letters, C&S seems to make an exegetical error. In the context of the passage referred to, 1 Corinthians 12, Paul is discussing the diverse gifts of individuals within the local face-to-face community, the local assembly-community (*plaaslike gemeente*). No valid conclusion should be drawn from the relationship of unity and diversity of individuals in the local congregation and then be applied to the problem of ethnic diversity in the universal

---

13   C&S, 81; bold in the original.
14   C&S, 117.
15   C&S, 120.
16   C&S, 117.
17   C&S, 117.
18   C&S, 67.

church or to an ethno-linguistically diverse Christian community in a country with imperially imposed boundaries such as Nigeria, Kenya, or South Africa— actually all of Africa including Ethiopia with its Amharic imperialist heritage.

To do so would violate what the clause cited above stated: The Church in its visible manifestation must not be "in the service of specific nations," and it must not be serving under the "nation and chiefly . . . function[ing] to grant religious sanction to that nation's values, ideals and ambitions." The Church of our Lord is in the service of the most holy Imperial Majesty, King Jesus of Nazareth, who will establish his one nation and kingdom in every language of the whole geographic expanse of the earth: One kingdom, all ethno-nations. His community must not be subservient to any nation's ethnic nor to an ethnocidal (i.e., anti-tribal) goals that support and give "religious sanction" to a rainbow nation-state's homogenizing "values, ideals and ambitions." This applies both to the Afrikaner-led apartheid state with a complicit Anglo-South African minority as well as to the New South Africa's ANC/Xhosa-dominated nation-state with its implicit and sometimes explicit Anglicization goals supported by a complicit Zulu ethno-nation.

Yet at the same time, the visible unity of Christ's one worshiping community can proclaim and consider real ethno-linguistic diversity and even loudly proclaim the Scripture's truth that our God has directly or providentially created each language group and placed them on a specific geographical place to seek and to serve their one God in Christ Jesus the Lord. True unity and real diversity are not dialectical opposites in the Godhead nor should be made to be so in any just human sphere of life, to use a Kuyperian turn of phrase. God hates both homogenizing imperialism, destroying his created diversity as well as idolatrous ethno-nationalism, destroying real confederal unity.

Therefore, no just and biblical conclusion should be drawn from this following passage in C&S that declared unity primary and all-inclusive and diversity subservient. "Unity includes [embraces] diversity." However, biblical unity does not merely embrace or include diversity but also diversity includes unity within all-defining concept of the Trinity. Deny the real diversity of God and one becomes a Unitarian or a Modalist. Deny the true unity of God and one becomes a polytheist. Indeed, just the opposite conclusion is demanded in Christ's body and in his Kingdom. Each person is unique, separate, and apart as an individual. God has "divided" to him a gift different and unique from all others. This is a true and definite diversity that stands on its own but not without the unity of the whole body in Christ, who is the head. In Christ's

44   WHEN A THEOLOGICAL SHIFT CHANGED A NATION

kingdom, the unity never destroys true ethno-linguistic diversity nor does that real diversity destroy the Spirit's bond of unity.

True diversity does not necessarily destroy unity nor does it serve it as secondary as C&S seemed to imply: "In the New Testament all differences and diversities among believers are regarded as subservient to this unity in the Triune God."[19] On the contrary, true diversity is as primary as unity. Both are equally good and equally ultimate in the church. *Both serve one another* and must be held in balance as it exists within the Triune Godhead. Primary diversity works together with true unity so that both are preserved.

As a consequence, the former DRC, as an Afrikaner ethno-church (*volkskerk*), did not necessarily commit injustice and oppressive sin simply because it stood ethno-linguistically and culturally distinct from other churches and, with its own indigenous leaders, is adapted to a specific ethno-cultural group. However, this can only be true to the Gospel if each language group is in visible confederal structures such as in the Synod of Dort's Church Order or perhaps as more faintly exemplified in the communion of Orthodox Churches. The centralized Roman model is not biblical and is not the ideal for which the ecclesial, civil, and familial spheres need to emulate. That model with one Emperor, one Church, one State, and in the West one language is antithetical to the biblical model as we shall see more completely in future chapters.

Further, only when "apartness" violates God's specific command to love the alien does it become sinful and oppressive evil as was the apartheid system. In other words in the churches of our Lord, sinful "apartness" occurs when there are services and sacraments closed to some believers and a rejection of mutual discipline in an ecumenical synod. Sinful evil also occurs when about 87% of the population is forced to live in 13% of the land even if some that land was the most fertile in the country.

The third and last example is when C&S stated that "under the Old Testament dispensation the emphasis was strongly on the separateness of God's people."[20] This means that the church was mono-ethnic. Now, however, it continued, the new covenant "dispensation" of the church there is "even less" restriction "to one nation or location. It includes people of all nations from the whole world, who through faith in Jesus Christ have become members of the true people of God." In other words the implication seems to be that believers now are seen as individuals not members of ethno-linguistic clans, tribes,

---

19   C&S, 75; see C&S, 120.
20   C&S, 64.

THE TRINITARIAN PRINCIPLE AS KEY   45

peoples, languages and nations: "All believers from among all peoples become members of the one people of God."[21]

Ethno-linguistic, sex, and social-economic status are ultimately done away with: "Amid and despite all the differences between Jew and non-Jew, Greek and non-Greek, male and female, slave and freeman, the New Testament knows but one church." Now individuals are melded together, it seems: "These people are the one unique nation of God, the one bride of Jesus Christ, the one temple of the Holy Spirit. In the New Testament all differences and diversities among believers are regarded as subservient to this unity in the triune God.[22]"

In addition, in contending for a unified denomination in one imperially defined nation-state (RSA), C&S rightly complains that "contextualisation [sometimes] results in the establishment of separate closed people's or cultural churches which exclude believers of other communities."[23] It need not do so if both unity and diversity are held in balance. C&S did show a noble intention to reject "closed" churches that forbid other ethnic groups and racial groups from attending an indigenous or "people's church." However, this can be accomplished using the Trinitarian principle and the specific commands in both testaments that regulate inter-ethnic relations as Chapter 11 discusses ("The Whole Bible Principle: Moses, Law, and Culture").[24] Sadly, however, C&S denies that these principles exist: "God's Word contains no direct prescription regarding the regulation of relationships among peoples."

C&S, actually claims that in the New Testament, ethnic distinction based upon God-created linguistic difference is less important and merely useful to or of service to ("subservient to") the unity of the one people of God. On this inclusivist assumption no one can be excluded ever at all including LGBTQ+ people as the DRC has now been "forced" by South African courts to accept and it has acquiesced to without any official remonstrance.[25] Granted, it is absolutely true that the new covenant church of God, fulfilling the Abrahamic covenant, is not now limited to one people (Gn 12:1–3; Pss 22, 96; Rom 4; Gal 3). However, does the move from the Old Testament to the New Testament entail a metaphysical paradigm shift from divided and exclusive ethnicity (the Hebrew people) to a homogenized-unified and inclusive non-ethnicity (i.e., from the group and the family to the individual stripped of all group identity)

21 C&S, 65.
22 C&S, 74–5.
23 C&S, 122.
24 C&S, 123.
25 C&S, 75; C&S, 120.

46 WHEN A THEOLOGICAL SHIFT CHANGED A NATION

as C&S seemed to imply?[26] The exact opposite is true. As I will discuss more completely later, the biblical paradigm shift entails a movement away from mono-ethnicity (Israel) to multi-ethnicity ("all the peoples"; see, e.g., Is 19:23–5). God's one people (unity) is now made up of many peoples (true diversity). This "people" does not consist of mere individuals extracted out of the various peoples, melted together into one new identity, "a third race." Instead, it results in all peoples, in their ethnic bonds (*volksverband*), moving into the one Abrahamic blessing and one Kingdom of Abraham's "Seed" Jesus: "all the families of the peoples" will be blessed in that seed (Gn 12:3, Rom 4, Gal 3).

C&S Made Church Unity Prior to Any Ecclesial Diversity. C&S 116–22 (completely cited below) seemed to make the church as the sphere of unity something prior to and completely distinct from any created diversities. The church as a prophetic institution must be "in" (indigenous and contextualized) and yet, in a certain sense, "above" all nations and peoples. This seems conceptually close to the ecclesiocentric, medieval Roman doctrine with its nature-grace distinction, making the church a sphere above the specificities of nature. Further, if this is true, the HRLS writers and supporters as ethnic and sphere sovereignty theologians were correct in calling this aspect of C&S out of conformity with some aspects of the Dutch Reformed doctrine of the Church.

As I cite these paragraphs, however, I readily admit that there is much good in them concerning indigenization and not subordinating the church to national interest as I mentioned above. However, the subtle subordinating of diversity to unity in a nature-grace dialectic is what, I believe, is at issue in this passage:

3.2 The relationship between church, nation and nations
3.2.1 By virtue of its universality or catholic nature the church is a church for the nations

The activity of the church has a close relationship with real human life. Through the proclamation of the Gospel to the nations, the church of Christ is formed from believers of different nations. Thereby the church in different countries and within different national and cultural communities will display characteristics which are typical of those communities. This indigenizing of the church is a positive sign that the Gospel has taken root at [sic] local level and within a specific community, that is to say, that it has become "contextualized."

3.2 Church and nation may not be identified as one

Through the ages the contextualisation of the Gospel owing to many factors, amongst others, those of a geographical and political nature, resulted in the establishment of people's churches or state churches in various countries. Side by side

---

26 See, e.g., C&S, 119.

THE TRINITARIAN PRINCIPLE AS KEY

with the positive fruits that the christianisation of culture and public life brought about, there were also negative fruits in so far as church and nation were identified with each other, these people's churches to a great extent forfeited their true nature as a faith fellowship. Therefore it must be maintained that the indigenization of the Gospel must never mean that church and nation become so interrelated that the church loses its character as a confessional church and becomes an exclusive church of a particular nation, which serves that nation and chiefly has the function to grant religious sanction to that nation's values, ideals and ambitions.

This means

  * that membership of the church is not determined by birthright, lineage and culture;
  * that God does not make his covenant with people on a national basis.

3.2.3 The church's prophetic task with regard to the nation

The church is not indifferent with regard to the diversity of nations, but it is also not in the service of specific nations. The church is in fact not the church of the nation, but the church of Christ, and therefore the church for the nation and for all peoples.

The church has the calling and freedom to give guidance, to admonish, to call to repentance and to combat the sins of the people and nations in the name of the Lord. The preservation of its identity as the church of Christ is absolutely essential for . . . [its biblical tasks].

3.2.4 In the structuring of the church, provision may be made for linguistic and cultural differences related to the diversity of peoples, but then in such a way that the *church's unity is not jeopardised, but served.*

The necessity of contextualising and indigenising the Gospel and the pastoral needs interwoven therewith, means that in a country in which more than one cultural and national community dwell together, provision may be made in the structuring of the church for specific needs which are brought about by language and cultural differences. The universal or catholic nature of the church is particularly expressed therein. In the light of what Scripture teaches about the nature and unity of the church, however, it may not be done to *the detriment of the unity of the church* or the communion of the saints over all boundaries of language and cultural communities. That happens when contextualisation results in the establishment of separate closed people's or cultural churches [volks- of kultuurkerke] which exclude believers of other communities.[27]

Diversity Finds Its Reality Only in Unity's Embrace. The implication of the above is that the institutional church must be one structure and also to be truly contextualized. This, however, will not allow for a completely contextualized church that does not take into consideration the unity of the universal body of Christ. This is certainly correct. However, C&S unequivocally states that contextualized diversity finds its *reality* only within the encompassing

---

27 C&S, 116–22; bold in original, italics added.

48   WHEN A THEOLOGICAL SHIFT CHANGED A NATION

embrace of unity. Unity is logically prior. The 1986 Synod stated with this bold header: "**2.9.2 This unity does not obliterate the diversity among God's people, but encompasses it.**" If the foundational presupposition had truly been Trinitarian, it could have added: This diversity does not obliterate the unity but constitutes it. But it did not do so and continued: "The diversity in the church of the New Testament is always a diversity within unity."

Notice the emphasis upon the "New Testament." Could this be a subtle, almost dispensational movement away from the DRC's heritage of whole Bible-based, covenant theology? That classic confessional theology could have claimed exactly the same with the caveat that the Old Testament focuses more on the one distinctive nation of Israel, whereas the NT focuses more on all peoples and nations. C&S then immediately continued: "This is clearly evident in the image of the church as the one body of Christ, consisting of many parts. It is precisely, and only, because they belong to the one body that the diversity of members can be of service and a blessing to each other."[28] Certainly this is accurate if the word "only" were dropped and if the context of a single community in the city of Corinth. To be more biblical and I might add covenantal, the reverse should have been added: *This is clearly evident in the image of the universal Church as constituted of one unifying head who is Christ and his many members. It is precisely, and only, because Christ is the Head that they are united into one body that serves and blesses each other.* This demonstrates the equal importance and ultimacy of diversity and unity, unity and diversity in the community of Christ.

In addition, can one generalize from the local almost certainly all Greek speaking Corinthian church to the universal Church? I think not. The Old Testament covenant view of the coming ministry of the Christ and his new covenant, emphasized *also* that all clans, peoples, and ethno-nations would be blessed in Abraham's Seed (e.g., Gn 12:3 [clans/families], 18:8 [ethno-nations]; Pss 22:27, 96:7). This prophesied universal incoming of all ethnies into the kingdom, body, and Universal Church of King Jesus is also a strong NT emphasis as well as I've demonstrated in *The Concept of Ethnicity in the Bible: A Theological Analysis.*[29]

Observe next how both the 1990 more radical description of the relationship of unity and diversity: Diversity within the unity ("*verskeidenheid binne die eenheid*") and the concept of unity "encompass[ing]" diversity come dangerously close to a key pantheistic New Age description of the relationship of

28 C&S, 79.
29 Kreitzer, *The Concept of Ethnicity.*

unity and diversity: diversity-in-unity or unity-in-diversity. In saying this, no claim is being made that C&S is New Age. That would be irresponsible. However, the conclusion could be drawn that C&S shares a concept of the relationship of unity to diversity that is gaining a considerable following in Western culture as it more and more prioritizes the collective whole over the individual unity whether that unit is the individual or a distinct ethno-linguistic group. Afrikaner Jan Smuts was a South African Oxford philosopher, scholar, Boer General and British General, South African Prime Minister, and WWII British Field Marshall. He coined the term "holism" in his book *Holism and Evolution* to describe this priority of ever-evolving unity in the social order.[30] Smuts was one of the key authors of the United Nations Charter and was what is colloquially termed today, a globalist. He taught like Neoplatonism and ancient pantheist Brahmanism did that the goal of diversity was for humanity to evolve while returning back to a simple, non-diverse One. Piet Beukes, one of Smut's biographers, demonstrated that Smuts even considered himself to be a pantheist in *The Holistic Smuts*.[31]

Lastly, it is significant that C&S (1990) removes key references to ethno-linguistic diversity in the creation. This certainly must imply that the Synod wanted to remove any vestige of so-called "natural theology" as it is defined by followers of Karl Barth as I mentioned in Chapter 2 were dominating the leadership of the DRC at that time. Removing the reference implies that in the unique, new creation—that is, the church—such created diversity is indeed being overcome because it is divisive of unity instead of being on the level of equal ultimacy with unity. That this is implied is virtually certain when one remembers two things. First, the DRC leadership rejected the traditional justification of male-only leadership as I will discuss in a coming chapter. Second, the General Synod 1990, the same Synod that authorized the return to world conciliar movements also mandated that women should be ordained into all ecclesiastical offices using among other texts, Galatians 3:28, taken out of context.

In summary, then, diversity is not of the same importance and of equal ultimacy as unity. As we have seen, this *implicitly* and *quite subtilty* rejects classic Trinitarian teaching by welcoming some sort of unitarian Sabellianism or modalistic Monarchianism.

---

30 Smuts, *Holism*.
31 Beukes, *Holistic Smuts*; Smuts, *Holism*.

Is C&S Infected with Unconscious Holism?

Next in importance, after having established that C&S prioritizes unity, is the following question: Does C&S read into the Scriptures a Smuts-ian like, holistic definition of good and evil? The answer, again it seems, is a qualified yes.

Does C&S Consider Division less than the Perfect? In several paragraphs, the words "divided" (*verskeurdheid*), which I mention previously connotes "torn," "torn apart in pieces," with the further nuance of "divided," or "fragmented"[32] and "broken" (*gebroke*) are used. The last term is an ambiguous word meaning either (1) ruined [*stukkend*] or (2) torn apart, broken in two, divided. It is a normal description in Reformed circles to describe the ruin sin caused the world. However, these with other similar terms seem to unconsciously indicate that a key problem in the world, and even in "reality" itself, is its dividedness, that is, its fragmented nature but not its rebellion against God. The assumption would seem to be that nature is foundationally chaotic. Upon this presupposition, the Holy Spirit working through the Church will bring health and holistic welfare springing from a return to primal unity.

If this is true, then the implication is that diversity, which is part and parcel of divided data of this world, is evil, or at least not perfect, and certainly not primary. Clearly, however, this preunderstanding confuses all "division" with "sinful division" and "ruined and sinful" with "broken in two, divided, sinful and evil apartness." Consequently, all "apartness" is simply "evil" therefore all forms of "apartheid" is evil and heretical as the world ecumenical community declared it to be without *any* nuance at all. This I deny by simply noting that the partitioning of the United States and later Canada, Australia and New Zealand can be seen as morally good. Could the same be true for most African countries, whose borders were imperialistically defined? I believe so.

Again, two examples will be sufficient. Example one is most important. Under the bold heading of "**The church is a missionary fellowship**," C&S reads: "[This means] . . . that the exemplary conduct, love, understanding and service of the church and of believers is a powerful means for demonstrating the Gospel's power against all opposition in this fragmented [*verskeurde*], unjust and distrustful world."[33]

An implication seems to be that the good (i.e., unity) must be sought after by removing the fragmented, torn and diverse world *from the church*, which in its essence is one in spirit—small letter deliberate. The close connection with

---

32 See C&S, 71, 72, 81 as good examples.
33 C&S 45, 49.

THE TRINITARIAN PRINCIPLE AS KEY

"unjust" and "distrustful" adds to the impression that such "fragmentation" of ecclesial oneness is indeed always evil and hence heretical.

I must then next ask: If this truly a statement of what the world is like in essence does it not deny the meaning of the result of a time-space Fall of Adam? Furthermore, when being "sinful and broken" is inherent in the world, it has definite philosophical ramifications for both the nature of the Godhead but also that of created nature.

If "sinful and broken" is indeed inherent in the created world, then, it is clearly not in any way biblically accurate according to classical Reformed hermeneutics, which the pre-1980 DRC scholars at least nominally held to. According to sound deduction from the DRC's Three Forms of Unity (*Belgic Confession*, *Heidelberg Catechism*, and *The Canons of Dort*), even after the Fall of Adam, the first man, this world did not lose all its created unities. For example, gendered humankind everywhere is indeed binary and every person knows that to be true by observation and the sense of right and wrong written upon every human's heart (Rom 1:18–21, 24–7, 2:14–16). The human duo-sexual family is universal even in its polygamous and polyandrous distortions.

Furthermore, the truthful meaning of one language can be translated *and* understood across every culture, otherwise our Lord would never have originally mandated his Jewish people with the Great Commission to disciple every other ethno-linguistic group of earth with his single gospel message. Meaning is built on commonly observed creational universals even after Adam's rebellion. It has never been created by hermetically sealed linguistic and cultural communities to be actually incommensurable cross-culturally as, some postmodernity infected DRC scholars might have averred at the time of C&S 1986 and 1990. According to the Three Forms of Unity, the Fall of Adam was not mythological but historical truth. It twisted creational design but not beyond recognition. Even a severely mentally handicapped human girl or boy, for example, is still fully human and could produce even brilliant offspring.

Consequently, if creation is inherently "fragmented, unjust and distrustful," there never ever could have been meaningful communication at all, and especially not in a written and infallible revelation. In addition, this world now partakes of both good creational unities and diversities have become broken and fragmented by *sin*, which by definition in Scripture and Confession is defined by rebellion against the Creator's norms and creation designs. If it be said, then, that sin fragmented everything, this is not accurate. Sin has polluted everything but did not fragmented everything *in essence*. The redemption of Christ, the Second Adam, and his gift of grace heals everything that Adam and his biological children, twisted, perverted, bent out of shape.

This means simply it is not in itself heretical and sinful that a linguistic community can develop self-determination in both ecclesial and civil government spheres as it does in the nuclear family sphere. The only necessary caveat I must add is a major if. If within such a self-determining sphere, a practiced and enforced consensus develops that all humans are created in the image of God and that the single law of God in conscience or in Scripture is the *only* standard by which every individual should be judged in just courts of law. In addition, that consensus must revel in the truth of the Gospel that Jesus died to redeem all tribes, peoples, and languages, who have equal value, dignity, and significance. In other words to do *the opposite* of what legal apartheid affirmed. There must be a single law for those considered aliens and citizens under the one God, one Lord, one Spirit, one justice based upon the single Creator's character and his creational design-norms. The DRC of South Africa failed to develop this consensus before the country-changing C&S and still fails after it. But more on this topic in upcoming chapters.

Therefore, it seems that, subtly, C&S equivocally connects words connoting ecclesial and social "diversity" with negative words so that the total meaning signified is that social divisions are something that are inherently evil. These divisions "tear up" (*verskeur*) something good, healthy and whole. The missionary model, the words this section began with, is ultimately an imperialistic model. In an attempt to deconstruct the divisive and oppressive, apartheid-imperial colonialism, it replaces it with an ultimately the unifying globalist imperialism of English. For communication to take place in an imperial area, normally a "unifying" imperial language is enforced upon the whole. A case in point is the formerly Gallic-Celtic speaking province of Rome. It now speaks a Latin-derived language, which was imperially imposed upon them before the Franks, a Germanic tribe from the north, invaded. That Romance language is called French after the Franks, but has only a small Germanic influence. The same applies to Ireland, Scotland, Cornwall, and Wales. All are dominated by English. Would not a better approach be to decolonize the political and ecclesial decolonializers with the Gospel that supports the "Trinitarian Principle as the Key"?

This leads to a second similar example: "**2.8 The church is a window to God's imminent new world.**"[34] It is of great interest to observe that the literal

---

34 C&S, 72.

meaning of the following and third sentences is: "[To make] something of the future visible [now]" ["*iets van die toekoms sigbaar maak*"] in the church. This means, "the church may not rest in its own brokenness" ["*die kerk mag nie in sy eie gebrokenheid berus nie*"]. Again, "brokenness" implies in the context, divided and damaged by not being an undivided whole. But the further connotation, considering the last example, is that a denomination that has spun off at least four other racial and linguistic daughter Churches is inherently broken and must be reunited into one single institution. This is beginning to become visible even now in the Uniting Reformed Church in Southern Africa, attempting to meld the predominately Afrikaans and English-speaking colored DRMC with the multi-lingual "black" Dutch Reformed Church in Africa.

This was an attempt to heal the division of the Dutch Reformed Church planted by the Dutch colonialists in 1652. Later as mixed race came into the faith, these "colored" individuals were all placed into the Dutch Reformed Mission Church irrespective of whether they spoke Dutch-Afrikaans or even English. When what was termed "blacks" began streaming into the Reformed faith primarily through the efforts of Afrikaner missionaries, they were given the new denomination called the Dutch Reformed Church in Africa irrespective if they spoke Tswana, Zulu, Xhosa, Sotho or one of the several other indigenous languages. Later, a much smaller group of people from the Indian subcontinent, termed "Indians" were placed into a new denomination, the Reformed Church in Africa. A small congregation in the Johannesburg area with fraternal relationships with the DRC, called the Andrew Murray Church, spoke English and ministered to Jews. This was the only truly linguistic-based "denomination"—it was only one congregation—as all the others were devised based upon the illogical and highly offensive apartheid racial distinctions.

After speaking about the "window to God's new world," supposedly racially and non-ethno-linguistically based, it seems, C&S explains: "As God's new creation, and as the sphere of the Holy Spirit's operation, the church must in all its activities provide a glimpse of the future." The certain implication of this new future is that "the divisions within the church" which are now present in apartheid South Africa "must not be accepted as normal. In the church, love must triumph over enmity and hate, the truth over falsehood, unity over division, reconciliation and peace over violence and confrontation." This leads directly to the conclusion: "Only in this way will the church be a true church, and prove to be a credible window to the future of our Lord Jesus Christ."[35]

---

35 C&S, 72.

54 WHEN A THEOLOGICAL SHIFT CHANGED A NATION

Here again the word "brokenness" [gebrokenheid] seems to be used as a synonym for "separated," and "divided" (*geskei, verdeel*). It is then coupled with "enmity and hate," "falsehood," "division," "violence and confrontation." The connotation, again, is that the DRC as it now exists as an independent, indigenous church for "white" Afrikaners (which did not even attempt to incorporate brown or a small handful of black Afrikaners or even acknowledge their existence) is reflecting an old, "sinful, broken, passing [away] world" (*sondige, gebroke, verbygaande wêreld*) as it is termed in other sections of the document.[36] This is sinful world is a world of hate, lies, violence, confrontation *as well as* division, torn-apartness, and broken-dividedness. Observe once again the subtle word-play that combines the concept of sin in the above phrases with words and concepts that may have behind them various created social divisions. These are, for example, ethno-linguistic identities such as Sotho and Zulu, and the two sexes and resulting genders. Once again, a negative connotation in connected to such created social group diversities. (I will discuss this more in-depth in a coming chapter).

C&S teaches that the DRC instead of reflecting sin and division must reflect a coming new world of a unified humanity—"one new humanity in Christ,"[37] as another section states. In this new world, unifying love, non-divisive reconciliation, and warm and accepting inclusive truth must conquer violent and confrontational division, that is social divisions.

If this interpretation is accurate, then C&S was accepting a myth, yet without yet welcoming all its logical conclusions. Some of the logical conclusions of the myth the General Synod began to welcome appeared a mere two to three decades later when the General Synod acquiesced to such anti-biblical practices as gay ordination and marriage. This myth has been common to Western Civilization since at least Plato, the Gnostics, medieval mystics, Anabaptist millenarian visionaries, and socialist Utopians. One form of this myth teaches that the ideal world is a unified and loving communal whole. All share in the communal property so all have enough. There is no inequality—no mine and yours, no hierarchy—especially not between male and female, no privatized families as all men and women live in total community and all children are the possession of the "village," that is the whole of the group.

This myth led many, such as Thomas Müntzer and Jan van Lyden, to preach and live out in practice the concept of communal property and wives. According to another form of the myth, the Fall and hence evil came with

36 C&S, 24, 25, 26.
37 C&S, 25.

THE TRINITARIAN PRINCIPLE AS KEY   55

social distinction and hierarchy, one man above another, private property and private wives.

The answer to Adam's fall, in the myth's doctrine of "redemption" (soteriology), is either to return to an idealized, holistic past (repristination) or move forward to a totally new and different future (futurism). Both forms of the myth believe history is moving toward a non-discriminating, non-ethnic, nonsexist, non-creedal (no creed above another), non-ageist, non-classist, non-homophobic unitary society. Influential Sussex University History Professor, Norman Cohn, and others have described this as a return to "The Egalitarian State of Nature."[38]

Subtle Derogation of Created Diversity

In this connection it is interesting to note that C&S couples all the words concerned with diversity in the church, both those with negative and relatively neutral connotations,[39] with the concept sin. As a result, C&S usually contends without qualification that all division is sin and that God's will is unity, implying an undivided unity with no room for ethno-linguistic groups having distinct congregations, classes, and synods even if conjoined with (con)federal, overarching fellowships. Consequently, in coupling words concerning any sort of division in the church with the words "sin" and "sinful," C&S leaves the reader, deliberately or not, with certain negative impressions of indigenous self-governing, self-financing, self-propagating, and especially not self-theologizing ethno-linguistically founded communities of Christ-followers (denominations). It implies that any and all division, distinction, particularity, or unique identity in the one body of Christ is at least imperfect, perhaps even evil. There are several examples.

Example One. After speaking about the spiritual and eternal oneness of the church, C&S states the following: **"This means . . . that it is the will of God that the deeper spiritual unity of his church must be experienced concretely**

---

38 See, e.g.: (1) Norman Cohn, "The Egalitarian State of Nature," chapter 10 in *The Pursuit of the Millennium: Revolutionary Millenarians and Mystical Anarchists of the Middle Ages* [Pursuit] (London: Paladin, 1970), 187–271; (2) see also Cohn, *Pursuit*, chapters 11–13, "The Egalitarian Millennium (i, ii, iii)"; (3) Eric Voegelin, *Science, Politics, and Gnosticism: Two Essays* [Gnosticism] (Washington, DC: Regnery Gateway, 1990).

39 For example, a word describing church dividedness in emotionally neutral terms is "diversity" (*verskeidenheid*). Words with a negative connotation concerning church division are literally translated as "torn," "torn apart," "torn up" (*verskeur, verskeurdheid*). Words describing division in moderately negative terms: "divided," "dividedness" (*verdeeld, verdeeldheid*).

56 WHEN A THEOLOGICAL SHIFT CHANGED A NATION

and must be maintained in the midst of all diversity." This non-divided "spiritual unity" is correctly seen as a gift in union with Christ: "Although this unity is given in Christ, it can be denied and obscured through the sin of division [*verdeeldheid*] and disunity [*verskeurdheid*]. Because Christ is not divided, the church may also not be divided."[40]

The document at this point appeals to the rebuke Paul gave to the Corinthians for their divisions in the church (1 Cor 1:10–13). However, this is an illicit appeal. In the close context, Paul is speaking about ethical divisions, that is, divisions created by sins such as quarreling (1 Cor 1:11, 3:3), jealousy (1 Cor 3:3) and pride in human wisdom instead of God's wisdom (1 Cor 1:18–20). Paul is not speaking here about the divinely created sex divisions such as those between male and female, young and old, truth and falsehood, and various ethno-cultural groups. Social class division, often brought into the picture at this point, is not as absolute as the created distinction between male and female. However, when sin and genuine oppression are removed from the equation, still some will have more ability to make money than others because of family values learned in the socialization process or because of God-created gifting. These are merely examples of learned ad created abilities that leads to social class divisions and ethically must not be leveled. Consequently, C&S does not give any exegetical evidence needed to transfer the rebuke about ethical divisions onto social structural issues.

Example Two. Shortly after the above, C&S continues with the concept that diversity only finds its being within unity.[41] The implication again seems to be that all "natural" or better, created distinctions, are merely givens, "clearly evident." Consequently, the context does not consider them to equally ultimate with unity and hence, it tends to make these natural or created distinction a cause the evil of divisiveness [*verskeurdheid*]: "The diversity in the church of the New Testament is always a diversity within unity . . .. **This means** . . . that the diversity which according to the Bible is clearly evident in the church, must not be used as a pretext for disunity [*verskeurdheid*] in the church."[42] By implication, then, natural distinctions cannot be used to support ethno-linguistically based indigenous church nor, I must add, any discrimination between male and female in ecclesial offices of ruling elder, deacon, and ministers of the Word and Sacrament. This same almost Gnostic philosophical presupposition will be later used by DRC radicals in the twenty-first century

40 C&S, 78.
41 C&S, 80.
42 C&S, 79, 80.

THE TRINITARIAN PRINCIPLE AS KEY

and earlier to justify the full admission of gay and lesbian pastors to ecclesial office. These fully valuable human dignified by their Creator with equal value, importance and dignity are still excluded in Scripture and the DRC's classic Scripture-bound tradition because these identities are based on sin, which only the Gospel can heal as Paul explicitly states: "Such were some of you."

> Do you not know that the unrighteous will not inherit the kingdom of God? Do not be deceived; neither the sexually immoral, nor idolaters, nor adulterers, nor [both submissive and dominant male][43] homosexuals, nor thieves, nor the greedy, nor those habitually drunk, nor verbal abusers, nor swindlers, will inherit the kingdom of God. Such were some of you; but you were washed, but you were sanctified, but you were justified in the name of the Lord Jesus Christ and in the Spirit of our God. (1 Cor 6:10–11 NASB 2020)

Now in the light of the General Synod's 1994 decision to seek some sort of structural, visible unity with all the Reformed churches in South Africa, this passage definitely means that the then present system of independent color/race-based churches united by confession and councils at General Assembly level is sinful, divisive and evil. Hence, by extension, it seems that no attempt to justify any sort of self-governing ethno-church (volkskerk) is righteous. Indeed this seems to be one purpose of the document.

Having said this, I must here affirm my unequivocal and complete rejection of color-bound restrictions on church membership or office. Color is only tangentially related to created and providentially created ethno-linguistic identities. The apartheid legislation used color in immensely hurtful and oppressive ways with absolutely no biblical basis. After all, the color of a person is only mentioned in Scripture merely in a descriptive and not proscriptive manner: The deeply tanned Israelite women who married Solomon (Sg 1:6) and the skin tone of the Kushite (Sudanese) person (Jer 13:23). But language and other indicators of ethno-linguistic diversity are used multiple times throughout the warp and woof of Scripture again as I have demonstrated in a previous work.[44]

Example Three. In addition to this, the implication of several passages in C&S 1986 and 1990 seem to be that Scripture demands some sort of holistic, structural unity of all Christian churches in a single visible institution called "the Church." This provided the more radical DRC leaders a manifesto to engage in comprehensive ecumenicism whose eventual goal is to reunite

---

43 The NASB 2020 note correctly points out: "Two Gr[eek] words in the text, prob. both submissive and dominant male [homosexuals]."

44 See again, Kreitzer, *Ethnicity*, 115–22 [ch. 4].

58   WHEN A THEOLOGICAL SHIFT CHANGED A NATION

all Christian denominations in one visible organization. The following paragraphs state this ecclesial point clearly. The one body of Christ is indivisible, consequently any division at all in it is a sin that must be confessed and actively turned away from. Apartheid color-based churches are evil as well as any development of indigenous churches in former "mission fields." In the following paragraphs there is much to be commended such as the emphasis upon "mutual love" and the rejection of "unwillingness to accept each other, misunderstanding and misconceptions absolutising of the diversity." However, the total message is in practice a rejection of orthopraxis and become actually antithetical to Christ's Great Commission to literally "disciple all people-groups."[45] C&S 84–7 reads:

> **This means** ... that this unity becomes primarily visible in mutual love; ... that Christians may never be content with disunity among the churches, especially among those with the same confession, but must acknowledge and confess it as a sin; ... that the church bears the responsibility, in so far as it is practically possible, to experience and make visible its unity with all believers.[46]

C&S, 82 also clearly states this principle along with much good to commend:

> **2.9.3 The church has the responsibility to confess its profound, inviolable unity in Christ and to experience and make this unity visible in this broken and divided world.**
> **2.9.3.1 It is essential that this unity be experienced and made visible.**
> As a result of sin the unity of the church has been endangered from the beginning by various factors, such as carnal attitudes, lovelessness, unwillingness to accept each other, misunderstanding and misconceptions absolutising of the diversity, a superficial and spiritualised conception of unity as well as political and other interests. The result was that through the centuries the church fell into a state of division and disunity.[47]

The implication again here seems to be that God-created ethnic identity absolutizes that which is imperfect and less spiritually good than the perfect, eternal good of unity. The universal Church, as a sign of the new world to come, must become visibly a present sign-post pointing to the future in which no Jew or Greek, male or female, slave or free, black or white or any other social distinction will be overcome.

---

45   Kreitzer, *Ethnicity*, 432–42.
46   C&S, 84–7; see also 93 below.
47   C&S, 82; bold in original

THE TRINITARIAN PRINCIPLE AS KEY 59

Furthermore, "lovelessness," "sin," "carnal attitudes," "[theological] error" (*dwaling*), "refusal to accept one another," are all tied with "absolutising diversity." Lovelessness and all its kindred abominations are tied with absolutizing diversity. Interestingly enough, the English strengthens this connection by leaving out a crucial comma in the Afrikaans original, making it, perhaps, more palatable to the world ecumenical movement.[48] This diversity must certainly include absolutizing ethnic and gender diversity when the 1986 and 1990 General Synod decisions that both reject apartheid and mandate the ordination of women are taken into account.

In summary, these paragraphs illicitly connect negative sins and attitudes with the fact of ethnic and gender diversity as creational norms. This is a logical fault named colloquially "Poisoning the Waters." It is a false "guilt by association," an illicit *ad hominem* argument. Interestingly enough, the unconscious model behind these above C&S passages may be something like the medieval Roman Church with its pretensions of universality (catholicity), while excommunicating the Eastern Orthodox, the Church of the East, and other groups. Would the new Uniting Reformed Churches deliberately exclude Zulu, Xhosa, Venda, and dare I say Afrikaner indigenous denominations who still express desire to show visible unity in evangelical, confederal rather than unitary structures? In addition, the Uniting Church movement has shown its cards by supporting the new unitary South African state. It has done this for the last several decades while implicitly or often explicitly disdaining all ethnic secessionist political movements such as an independent KwaZulu-Natal or an independent and geographically contiguous KwaXhosa political unit. However, I must ask. Would it be really divisive and evil to biblical Christian ethics to peacefully "tear apart" the present, extremely unstable new South Africa through the negotiated and pacific secession of large portions of the present Eastern Cape Province which is overwhelmingly Xhosa speaking? After all, that is exactly what Lesotho, Kingdom of Eswatini (formerly Swaziland), and Botswana are. Could this not be a way forward for all the imperialist-defined borders within Africa?

Example Four. The consequence of C&S's holistic doctrine is also found in later paragraphs: "Christians may never be content with disunity among the churches, especially among those with the same confession, but must acknowledge and confess it as a sin."[49] In other words, first confess sin then take

---

48 The translation changes the intent of the original: *"misverstand en dwaling,* [note comma] *verabsolutering van die verkeidenheid."*

49 C&S, 85.

60 WHEN A THEOLOGICAL SHIFT CHANGED A NATION

action to destroy the root and rotten fruit of that sin as the following citations demonstrate. Again there is much to commend such as visible interrelations of churches in confederal structures. My personal problem with the way the process proceeded over the last three decades was that the formally orthodox Reformed theology of the DRC has been almost complete abandoned in the process of rejoining the world ecumenical or conciliar movements such as the WARC and the WCC. Biblically, this is akin to spiritual adultery and abhorrent to our good Father as the prophets everywhere affirmed (see e.g., Ez 16, 23).

2.9.3.3 Church liaison and ecumenical relationships are an essential expression of the church's unity

Whereas we are in a situation of division and disruption in the church of Christ, it is our calling to seek the unity of the church in the hope that the present division and disunity [literally "torn apartness"] can be done away with and the unity of the church be restored. Even though this ideal may appear to be unobtainable as a result of the deep seated disunity, we nevertheless should endeavour through ecumenical relationships to make visible the spiritual unity of the church as far as possible, amongst others, in a spirit of cooperation and united witness in the world.

This means ... that the church is called to seek ecumenical relationships with other churches; ... that varying degrees of ecumenical relationships are established, depending on confessional compatability [sic] between the churches.[50]

Certainly also it is necessary and true to seek some sort of visible structural unity among all churches of Christ, especially those of the same confession. However, these passages seem to imply something in addition to this noble effort. C&S here again seems to suggest that all present divisions based on ethnic and linguistic particularity are as evil as those caused by ethical breaches. Being evil, divisions based on ethnic diversity are to be "confess[ed] ... as a sin."

---

50 C&S, 93–5; bold in original.

· 4 ·

THE TRINITARIAN PRINCIPLE APPLIED: REFORMERS AND C&S DIFFER ON ETHNO-CHURCHES

The Reformers Welcomed Language-Based Ecclesial Groups

My point throughout the former chapter had been to emphasize that the type of unity C&S emphasizes is not that which the more scripturally-founded Reformers taught. The Reformers and their children allowed independent Reformed congregations in Geneva for the various ethno-linguistic groups such as the Dutch, English, and Scots who sought refuge there.[1] So did the original Church Order of the Synod of Dort make allowances for French-Walloon and Dutch-speaking congregations, classes, and synods if all would meet regularly in (con)federal Synods, as I have mentioned previously.

They did not see the separateness of these language-based groups as sinful so that they worked for unitarian structures such as the C&S was seeking to accomplish. In addition, I do not agree that the civil government should serve as the basis for visible unity as it seemed to do in Geneva. Geneva perhaps should have had one General Assembly comprised of various ethnic synods.[2] Nor did they agree with C&S' ideal of unity: One structurally unified church

---

1 Potgieter, *C&S Essence.*
2 See Potgieter, *C&S Essence.*

62   WHEN A THEOLOGICAL SHIFT CHANGED A NATION

with provisions in the structure for unity-in-diversity so long as the diversity serves that which is primary, good and eternal.

Note the following paragraphs making concession to linguistic and cultural diversity:

> **3.2.4 In the structuring of the church, provision may be made for linguistic and cultural differences related to the diversity of peoples, but then in such a way that the church's unity is not jeopardised but served.**[3]
>
> **Unity does not obliterate the diversity among God's people, but encompasses it.**
> The diversity in the church of the New Testament is always diversity within unity . . .
> **This means** . . . that the diversity . . . must not be used as a pretext for disunity in the church.[4]

The Reformers were content with confessional and disciplinary unity for each national church, whether in Geneva itself or in each country. They definitely did not want to return to a Romanized, monolithic, unitarian church structure. They saw that such a holistic emphasis upon unity would eventually lead—though it has not happened yet in Catholic social theory—to the total swallowing up of the individual and every other distinction, including private property and separate wives, in the absolute rebellion against Trinitarian Christianity. This is exactly what happened in the most consequent of the Radical Anabaptists, and this is why the Reformers so strongly fought against certain Radical Reformation presupposition and why the fathers included Article 36 in *The Belgic Confession*. It anathematizes the Radical Reformation's bias toward communal property as well as its rebellion against God's law-order in rejecting Christian civil rulers.[5]

C&S and Church Unity in John 17. One foundational passage that C&S uses to justify its definition of the relationship of unity to diversity is John 17. C&S teaches that our Lord prayed for an undivided unity in the church in John 17. For example, C&S, 82 and 83 discusses the division and disunity of the church through the ages. It then cites our Lord's prayer for church unity in John 17 as demanding "clearly visible" unity, implying "that the church bears

---

3   C&S 122, bold emphasis in original; see C&S, 78–81.
4   C&S, 79, 80; bold in original.
5   Willem Balke, *Calvin and the Anabaptist Radicals*, trans. William Heynen (Eugene, OR: Wipf and Stock, 1999).

THE TRINITARIAN PRINCIPLE APPLIED

the responsibility in so far as it is practically possible, to experience and make visible its unity [in structures] with all believers."[6]

A holistic presupposition would claim that Jesus asked the Father to destroy the evil of all church divisions. This indeed seems to be the intent of C&S, 83–6, and 93. The relevant paragraphs are as follows:

> Christ, however, prayed for the unity of the church (John 17:23). It is indeed true that the unity of believers was given in Christ, but the visible revelation thereof in the unity of his church is of the utmost importance for Christ, "so that the world may know that you sent me." The clearly visible unity of the church is a confirmation to the world of the authenticity of Jesus's [sic] mission and therefore the church should seek it for Christ's sake.
>
> **This means** . . . that Christians may never be content with disunity among the churches, especially among those with the same confession, but must acknowledge and confess it as a sin; that the church bears the responsibility, in so far as it is practically possible, to experience and make visible its unity with all believers.[7]
>
> Whereas we are in a situation of division and disruption [verskeurdheid] in the church of Christ, it is our calling to seek the unity of the church in the hope that the present division and disunity [verskeurdheid] can be done away with and the unity of the church be restored.[8]

C&S here once again implies, under the cover of rightly rejecting a color and race-based denomination, that any and all divisions in the church are sins that must be confessed. This would include those establishing ethno-linguistic diversity by planting language specific congregations, classes, and synods, it seems. Remember, the DRC is to this day (2023) almost 100% Afrikaans speaking. C&S by implication excludes, as we saw earlier, sex and gender diversity in leadership as well because both cause division and "torn-apartness." Consequently, the present, independent, self-governing DRC as an Afrikaner ethno-church is still sinning. However, its decision to ordain biological females to all ecclesial offices and its decision not to resist the court decision mandating the full inclusion of gay clergy as well would be implicitly supported by C&S. In addition, this must be the correct interpretation considering the later decisions tentatively to move toward structurally uniting with all the various ethno-racial daughter churches it has planted.[9]

6 C&S 86.
7 C&S, 83–6.
8 C&S, 93.
9 See Dionne Crafford and Gustav Gous, eds., *Een Liggaam—Baie Lede: Die Kerk se Ekumeniese Roeping Wêreldwyd en in Suid-Afrika* [One Body—Many Members: The Church's Ecumenical Calling Worldwide and in South Africa] (Pretoria: Verba Vitae, 1993).

64   WHEN A THEOLOGICAL SHIFT CHANGED A NATION

Now, I unequivocally agree that diversion from the biblical norm is sin. However, assuming as does C&S that unity is primary over any diversity in the New Testament, confessions are themselves also ultimately evil because of their divisive characteristic. Pushed to its logical end, C&S would disallow even the division of the Reformation. At that time, the Roman church was declared a non-church to justify the schism (see *Belgic Confession*, 27–9).

In conclusion, the implication of the above discussion as well as C&S' use of Christ's prayer (Jn 17), it seems, is that there should be only one church in each geographical location with only some practical concessions for linguistic diversity. Geographical separation, thus, is the only diversity seemingly allowed. However, C&S makes allowance for no other creational or providential distinctions such as linguistic, ethno-covenantal, gender, or cultural style. However, that in itself is not logically consequent. If one creational distinction (geographical location) is allowable, there is no compelling reason why others should not be allowed as well.

It must be emphasized again at this point that the Trinitarian principle agrees that visible structural unity is indeed demanded by John 17 so long as the unity structures allow for the fundamental expression of the equal ultimacy of true self-determining diversity *along with* structural unity.

There is a more logically and contextually correct understanding of John 17. In the context of John 17:21, Jesus does not ask the Father to create a monolithic, equalitarian church, the non-ethnic, nonsexist, non-ageist, and non-classist unified church (and state) ideal of the world ecumenical movement and the logical end result of C&S' ecclesiology. Christ prays:

> My prayer is not for them alone. I pray also for those who will believe in me through their message, that all of them may be one, Father, just as you are in me and I am in you. May they also be in us so that the world may believe that you have sent me. I have given them the glory that you gave me, that they may be *one as we are one*: I in them and you in me. May they be brought complete unity to let the world know that you sent me and have loved them even as you have loved me. (Jn 17:20–3 NIV; emphasis added)

Jesus is praying, first of all, for the whole church, on earth at that time, and all those who will believe in the future. In other words, the church across the generations. Second, he is praying for unity like that found in the Godhead, in other words, true unity and real self-determining diversity. After all, Jesus said "I have come down from heaven, not to do my own will but the will of him who sent me" that is the Father (Jn 6:38 ESV). The decisions of the Triune always are one but within the Triune Godhead, by implication, the

THE TRINITARIAN PRINCIPLE APPLIED 65

preincarnate Word had desires and determinations just as the Spirit in the present economy has desires and determined choices as we see in, for example, 1 Corinthians 12:11. The three always, however, work together to implement one action in the outworking of creation-redemptive history.

Wesley L. Duewel, in a paper read at Trinity Missions Consultation Number Two entitled "Christian Unity: The Biblical Basis and Practical Outgrowth," explains this further:

> The unity for which Christ prayed is a oneness like the oneness of the Godhead, a trinitarian oneness. Father and Son are one in the Spirit. Their unity is a unity of doctrine (John 17:16; 8:26, 28; 12:49), purpose (John 6:38, 40; 17:4), and love (John 10:17; 14:31; 15:9; 17:23,24,26). But it is far more. It is a oneness infinitely real yet preserving distinctiveness. The persons of the Trinity are not merged. They are distinct yet one. God's highest created unity, the unity of the ecclesia in the Spirit, is a spiritual unity like the unity of the Trinity. Despite all differences of language, . . . and background . . ., the all-pervading unity of all true believers is blessedly real in the Holy Spirit. In the Spirit there is no tension between unity and diversity; unity does not require the merging of diversity. It does require that all diversity must exist in spiritual unity.[10]

I would only add to Duewel's description that a visible confederal structural unity demonstrates the essence "spiritual unity." The Trinitarian principle corrects C&S' view that Jesus demands a structurally unified church of all ethnic groups with the same confession (C&S, 86) as the only answer to his prayer. On the contrary, biblical Trinitarian teaching leads to the development of true federal and confederal structures in both the ecclesiastical and civil government spheres, as Abraham Kuyper would describe them.

As I mentioned previously C&S conceded the necessity of some indigenization and contextualization of the Word into specific ethno-linguistic and cultural groups. The previous paragraphs that I have discussed above do not seem to contradict C&S 32, 38 which allows language and culture as legitimate ministry needs. The reason it gives is that such diversity is only relative, that is relative to the absolute, the priority of the unity of the church. Therefore, diversity must be *pragmatically* worked into the priority structural unity. However, to do this responsibly must ultimately lead to the Trinitarian Principle of the "equal ultimacy of the one and the many." C&S attempted to take diversity

---

10 Wesley L. Duewel, "Christian Unity: The Biblical Basis and Practical Outgrowth," in *New Horizons in World Mission: Evangelicals and the Christian Mission in the 1980's—Papers given at Trinity Consultation No. 2*, ed. David J. Hesselgrave (Grand Rapids: Baker, 1979), 268–9.

66   WHEN A THEOLOGICAL SHIFT CHANGED A NATION

into consideration using the miracle of Pentecost and Paul's admonition to contextualize.

> The New Testament is realistic in its handling of the practical problems arising from specific needs of various people. The language miracle of Pentecost . . . [means] that each listener heard of the great deeds of God in his own language. Therefore, what is of importance is the effective ministry of the Word. The same motive is also apparent when Paul states that for the Jews he became a Jew and all things to all men for the sake of the Gospel. Geographical factors, social conditions, etc., can also be a factor in meeting specific needs. The ministry must be structured in such a way as to enrich the unity of the church and to promote the fellowship of people.[11]

A bit later, C&S vaguely explained what this means: "With a view to the effective ministry of the Word and in order to minister to the needs of various linguistic and cultural groups, allowance may be made for the church to be indigenous."[12] However, I must ask what does an "allowance" mean in practice without real self-determining diversity being seriously considered? The Uniting Reformed Church of Southern Africa, whether the Afrikaner DRC ever actually joins or not, will have to deal with language and language-governance issues eventually, if history has anything to teach us.

Furthermore, those familiar with the theology of Karl Barth should observe the neo-orthodox, kerygma- or word-proclamation centeredness of the church in these paragraphs. With no background from the Old Testament and in sharp contrast, C&S here minimizes orthodox covenantal Dutch Reformed theology. Classic covenantal theology confesses that the new covenant is the foundation of the church but also that the new covenant is in direct continuity with the old covenant. Consequently, the new covenant, contrary to Barth, is in direct continuity with all the covenants of the previous dispensation, especially the Abrahamic covenant. Paul explicitly connects that covenant to ethno-linguistic diversity in both Romans 4 and Galatians 3. I have discussed this explicitly in "Ethnic Solidarity, Babel-Pentecost Relationship, and the New Covenant."[13] Word-, gospel-, and kerygma-centeredness reduces theology to the Second Article of the Apostle's Creed as I will discuss more in coming chapters. This makes the word alone and individualized faith alone the only

11   C&S, 38.
12   C&S, 38.
13   Mark R. Kreitzer, "Ethnic Solidarity, Babel-Pentecost Relationship, and the New Covenant," *Global Missiology English* (April 10, 2010), https://www.academia.edu/es/65046607/Ethnic_Solidarity_Babel_Pentecost_Relationship_and_the_New_Covenant.

determinant of church membership, reducing the church to a believer's church without any reference to the Abrahamic covenant's fulfillment in the new covenant and whole-family covenant baptism.[14]

Consequently, kerygmatic theology, similar to pietist and dispensationalist doctrines, ultimately cuts children of believers out of covenant promises and curses, from the baptismal font, and from the visible community of faith as Karl Barth was well-known for doing.

The comprehensive Word, founded in the creation-covenantal order, and not merely the new covenant word-proclamation is foundational to the covenant. Thus the church is founded upon both blood (i.e., genetic "seed," descent) *and* faith in the biblical kerygma-word as I discuss in the Covenant Principle in this volume. The holistic assumption that C&S seems to accept here is that the DRC "fell" from "primal" unity into the present unjust system of churches divided by ethno-racial background. However, redemption heals all such injustice and sinfulness, C&S affirms. Therefore, the Christ of C&S came to restore racial unity within a non-ethnic, nonsexist, now non-homophobic, and non-classist holistic church and eventually a similar social-political unity throughout the earth. By doing so, such an anti-biblical definition of redemption destroys all *created* ethno-linguistic and gender-sexual divisions, among others. In addition as well, it implicitly supports the non-classist, neo-Marxian philosophy of Liberation Theology, which was so evident in the anti-apartheid movement in the mainline denominations of South Africa from the 1970s to the early 1990s. That type of theology after going underground a couple of decades has raised its head up again in various postmodern "social justice" movements.

However, in these following paragraphs and as a concession to reality, C&S allows a certain form of diversity, though that diversity is never specifically defined as I have mentioned.[15] C&S states, however, that unity must be only participate in the enrichment of unity and must be encompassed by unity.[16] Therefore, it has no real and separate "ultimacy" equal in value, importance, and yes human dignity to human unity. C&S defines the relationship between unity and diversity similar to modern holistic-pantheistic philosophy. It does not deny the existence of diversity but downgrades true diversity, making it of lesser importance than unity itself. As a consequence in the text of C&S, diversity is always "diversity within unity."[17] It certainly is not real

14 See C&S, 42–4.
15 See again C&S, 32, 38.
16 See again C&S, 79–89.
17 C&S, 79.

68 WHEN A THEOLOGICAL SHIFT CHANGED A NATION

self-determining diversity that, C&S seems to be claiming, is "used as a pretext for disunity"[18] and "a threat to the church's unity."[19]

Pay attention again to C&S, 79–81:

> Although this unity is given in Christ, it can be denied and obscured through the sin of division and disunity. Because Christ is not divided, the church may also not be divided.
>
> **This unity does not obliterate the diversity** [1986 text added: "in God's creation and"] **among God's people, but encompasses it.**
>
> The diversity in the church of the New Testament is always a diversity within unity. This is clearly evident in the image of the church as the one body of Christ, consisting of many parts. It is precisely, and only, because they belong to the one body that the diversity of members can be of service and a blessing to each other.
>
> **This means** ... that the diversity which according to the Bible is clearly evident in the church, must not be used as a pretext for disunity in the church; ... that diversity must not be seen as a threat to the church's unity, but as enriching it and as an opportunity for mutual service.
>
> **2.9.3 The church has the responsibility to confess its profound, inviolable unity in Christ and to experience and make this unity visible in this broken and divided world.**
> **2.9.3.1 It is essential that this unity be experienced and made visible in this broken and divided world.**[20]

This citation makes it clear that recognition of ethno-cultural diversity is only a concession because unity must be confessed and lived out as a witness of unifying redemption against one major, if not the major, evil of this world, its divided state: "this broken and divided world."

The following section 82 states that "sin endangered from the beginning" the unity of the church. This is certainly true both biblically and confessionally. However, sin also endangers true diversity as collective man seeks to obliterate all human distinctives in the collective humanity. Ultimately humanity wants to remove the last true distinction, that between himself and his Creator. The former mentor of many of the previous generations of Dutch Reformed scholars in South Africa saw this clearly in his still very relevant speech he gave in

---

18 The original reads "*as grond vir kerklike verskeurdheid*," which a rather wooden literal translation reads "as the grounds for the tearing-apart of church unity" (C&S, 80).

19 C&S, 81.

20 C&S, 79–82, bold emphasis in original.

THE TRINITARIAN PRINCIPLE APPLIED 69

1869: "Uniformity, the Curse of Modern Life: Lecture held in the Odéon in Amsterdam."[21]

Does C&S really absolutize unity? This leads me to another question many readers may have at this point. Does C&S actually absolutize unity without considering diversity? No, as we have seen but could it not be then that C&S absolutizes unity and relativizes diversity, while accusing apartheid proponents of absolutizing diversity and relativizing unity? Clearly, that is what occurs when C&S prioritizes unity above diversity and something that encompasses diversity. However, the sword cuts both ways. To absolutize one or the other principle is idolatrous. Both the apartheid theologians ultimately made idols: On the one hand, the idolatry of the *volk*—Afrikaner people (small "v" in Afrikaans) and on the other hand, the universal collective. Neither correctly understood what the late F. J. M Potgieter correctly termed the "Trinitarian Key,"[22] possibly not even Potgieter himself as he never made a clean break with race as a defining factor of ethno-cultural identity. However, his key along with the four other principles I discuss in this volume are a biblical and much more confessionally sound way forward out of the idolatrous morass of both the extremes—apartheid theology and ecumenical-conciliar theology of the World Council of Churches.

On this basis, C&S' prophetic charge that "absolutising of the diversity" and "superficial and spiritualised conception of unity" is sinful and endangering true church unity, is hollow in this context. It is true, of course, that platonic concepts of spiritualized unity have been rampant in the church virtually since the beginning. It is also true that many have so overemphasized diversity that, for example, the boundaries of "race" have become totally rigid. However, a Scripture-taught emphasis upon true God-formed ethno-cultural, gender, age, even social class diversity is not absolutizing that created diversity to the sinful expense of unity. Both can and must co-exist in harmony the church within the scriptural guidelines it gives (see the chapter, the Whole Scripture Principle). In other words, C&S seems to again assume the ancient Neoplatonic and Medieval European viewpoint that "unifying grace" must redeem and destroy the "divisions of nature." The new sacramental grace-order in the Church destroys the old, divided and broken, natural creation order in a totally new unifying, creation order. That new order, the unitary church is the unique

---

21 Abraham Kuyper, "Uniformity, the Curse of Modern Life: Lecture held in the Odéon in Amsterdam [1869]," 19–44, in *Abraham Kuyper: A Centennial Reader* [Kuyper's Uniformity], ed. James D. Bratt (Grand Rapids: Eerdmans, 1998).

22 Potgieter, *C&S Essence*.

70   WHEN A THEOLOGICAL SHIFT CHANGED A NATION

creation of God, the new man. This assume that the new creation is not the old, natural creation renewed and freed from the enslaving and twisting effects of sin. Instead, C&S seems to presume a nature-grace dualism, which Herman Bavinck, Kuyper's colleague at the Free University of Amsterdam, clearly refuted. Christ's redemption, his salvific work, instead restores creation. If the authors of C&S had carefully studied Bavinck and Kuyper, they may have gone in another direction than that of following Karl Barth. Jan Veenhof analyzes this refutation succinctly in a now-translated Dutch monograph from Dordt College Press in the USA: *Nature and Grace in Herman Bavinck* (2006).[23] I will discuss this principle with much more depth in the Creation Restoration Principle.

Logical Conclusions

What can I conclude from this first scan through the Church and Society Synod document. First, philosophical theories positing a strong dialectical tension between unity and diversity with a priority given to unity tend like pietism and the Radical Reformation to define social division as evil or at least imperfect. As seen in the case of C&S, this results in ever-increasing social-ethical radicalism to tear down all social diversities to be replaced with unifying and collective totalities. Social-political ideologies that make this same presupposition lead inevitably to a centralized and coercive State structures that relativize all diversities, subsuming them under the collective. This occurs also in ecclesial institutions as well that begin to mandate full inclusion of females, LGBT+ people, and soon open advocates of pedophilia in every office and as full communing members. In other words, true role distinction between male and female oppresses women, trans-people, and same-sex couples of all types. True self-determining ethno-cultural distinction in church and state, therefore, by definition, are also evil like apartheid.

When these movements become politically engaged, they assume that all diversity in every human institution—family, civil governmental, and church—must be leveled, because they are unjust and oppressive. Historically this led to the massive bloodshed, and especially in the twentieth and now the twenty-first centuries including the abortion holocaust as we shall see. These kinds of philosophical theories assume that all borders and boundaries in society cause oppression and consequently, all such distinctions, borders, and

---

23 C&S, 24–6. See Jan Veenhof, ed., *Nature and Grace in Herman Bavinck* [Nature and Grace] (Orange City, IA: Dordt College Press, 2006).

THE TRINITARIAN PRINCIPLE APPLIED   71

boundaries are either less than perfect or outright evil. In the final analysis, all such boundaries non-loving and unfair. Pushing the logic of C&S' bias toward unity and oneness brings one to the following non-biblical conclusions.

First, breaking down ethno-linguistic, cultural, gender, age, socio-economic exclusiveness must become the long-term goal of the reconciling work of the church. Growing inclusiveness must occur now, making the church an antici-patory "window on the future."[24] Granted, many DRC theologians still believe that perfect, loving inclusiveness, of course, will happen only at the resurrection. However, as institutions continue to radicalize the not yet is absorbed into the already as we shall see occurred in the case of the most radical in the Radical Reformation.

Second, those factors which lead to unified, group inclusiveness must be "good," "reconciling," "just," and "loving" by definition. Creational diversities should be only tolerated now in the in-between-time until the end. All these groups, smaller than the whole, divide the unity of humanity in Christ. They must, therefore, be de-emphasized and abolished, slowly or radically and rapidly, depending on the emotional and spiritual state of the advocates.

Third, the ideal of much of futurist dialectical theology, as we shall see, and the most logically consequent of the descendants of the Radical Reformation, is that all individuals are to be stripped from a God-created group as discussed in Scripture. These racist, sexist, homo- and transphobic structures must be abol-ished by the coercive weaponry, ultimately of the centralized and idolatrous State exactly like the independent landowning class of *kulaks* was crushed by the Soviet commissars. These individuals can then be united in unitary, inclusive ecclesial and political institutions. There is little difference between this vision and that of beyond-postmodernist humanism: No discrimination on the basis of ethnic group, language, gender, sexual orientation, class, age, bodily condition or even species.

Throughout the almost two-decade revolutionary run-up to the 1994 inclusive election of Nelson Mandela and the inauguration of the new South Africa, the Barthian-influenced, Alliance of Black Reformed Christians in South Africa (ABRECSA), agreed with this sentiment. The signatories of their founding charter were several prominent theologians from the DRC fam-ily. The its theological basis reads: "The unity of the Church must be visibly manifest in the one people of God. The indivisibility of the body of Christ

24 C&S, 72.

demands that the barriers of race, culture, ethnicity, language and sex be transcended."[25]

The late, radical Mennonite-Anabaptist theologian, John Howard Yoder, in "The Social Shape of the Gospel," also explains:

> [Believing Jews and Gentiles] ... together form the new humankind (Eph. 2:15). What has happened is the creation of a new socio-history which is neither Jew nor Greek, or is both Jew and Greek .... The reality is so new that the words Paul uses for it are *new creation* ... and *new humanity*. In none of these usages ... is the new thing [that] Paul is talking about an individual. But neither is he talking about an existing ethnic group. He is talking about a new group which is so much like an ethnic group that it can be called a nation or a people, but whose constitutive definition is that it is made up of both kinds or many kinds of people.

Yoder concludes his comments by misusing 2 Corinthians 5:17: "'If one is in Christ,' there is a whole new world. Ethnic standards have ceased to count."[26]

Yoder's critique here was actually of Church Growth Missiology. This theology rejected apartheid theology's desire to found color and race-based denominations. Instead, it desired to plant self-governing ethno-linguistically based churches though unfortunately under the rubric of the Homogeneous Unit Principle (HUP), which was easily misunderstood and misused. Many at the time illicitly confounded that more or less theology-based missiology with Apartheid theology. Yoder's critique presupposed like C&S and others in the broader ecumenical movement that *any* social division in the church was imperfect or even evil.

Anglo-South African theologian John De Gruchy agreed. In commenting on Dietrich Bonhoeffer's definition of "community" in the new humanity in Christ, he described the "far-reaching social, political, and economic ramifications" of this holistic philosophy, which he advocated. To accomplish these ramifications, he wrote,

> the church must be liberated from being the mirror image of broken community "in Adam" in order to become a sign of the new humanity of Christ. The true unity of

---

25 M. John Lamola, "D9.2 Alliance of Reformed Christians in South Africa, 1981, ABRESCA Charter [Chapter 53]," in *Sowing in Tears: A Documentary History of the Church Struggle against Apartheid 1960–90* (Grant Park, RSA: African Perspectives, 2021), https://zoboko. com/text/156rd9g4/sowing-in-tears-a-documentary-history-of-the-church-struggle-against-apartheid-1960-1990/53.

26 John Howard Yoder, "The Social Shape of the Gospel [Social Shape]," in *Exploring Church Growth*, ed. Wilbert R. Shenk, 277–84 (Grand Rapids: Eerdmans, 1983), 182–3.

THE TRINITARIAN PRINCIPLE APPLIED

the church is thus the contradiction of apartheid or any division on the basis of race, culture, or class, just as these are antithetical to the reconciliation made possible through the cross of Jesus Christ.[27]

Fourth, because unity encompasses particularity, all diversity loses "equally ultimate" existence in itself. Consequently, logically, even the individual has lost any permanent particular identity and self-determination. He must be encompassed by unity to participate in the good. Hence, the individual must "lose all of himself," that is "deny himself" even his very particular diverse Zulu, Xhosa, Tswana, or Afrikaner culture to be united to the "good" of the new humanity coming.

Marx and other social holists, correctly saw how this understanding of the relationship of unity to diversity inevitably leads to control by an enlightened, elitist leadership who understand the priority of unity over diversity. This top-down control almost inevitably is exercised with propounded altruistic justifications, often in the form of Social Democracy with "free elections." The leaders often call themselves the "Benefactors" or "Friends of the People," as our Lord said concerning the global imperialists of his day (Lk 22:25 NIV, NLT). It can also operate in the name of a presbyterial-synodal ecclesiastical system such as the DRC and in the USA the Presbyterian Church (USA).

This type of social vision is fundamentally the same as that of the Neoplatonic influenced, Gnostic heresy as a multitude of scholars over the last half-century have conclusively demonstrated.[28] Historically, Gnostics and gnostic-like social philosophies, like other dualists and holists, drew inspiration from Plato's ideal top-down social order in *Republic*.[29] Ruler-philosophers and the military classes in this almost Hindu social caste system rule as Benefactors over the masses. Beyond postmodernity influenced theologians *radicalize* this vision further. The masses are to be totally individualized with no group identity other than the cosmopolis—the All City. Herbert Schlossberg's, *Idols for Destruction* as well as Theologian Peter Jones' volume *The Other Worldview: Exposing*

---

27 John W. De Gruchy, *Bonhoeffer and South Africa: Theology in Dialogue* (Grand Rapids: Eerdmans, 1984), 81.

28 (1) Cohn, *Pursuit*; (2) Philip J. Lee, *Against the Protestant Gnostics* (Oxford: Oxford University Press, 1993); (3) Voegelin, *Gnosticism*; (4) Peter Jones, *The Gnostic Empire Strikes Back* [Gnostic Empire] (Phillipsburg, NJ: P&R, 1992).

29 See Plato, *The Republic*, trans. Desmond Lee (New York: Penguin, 2007).

Christianity's Greatest Threat (and his other works on Gnosticism) serve as an excellent introduction this and other related philosophical theologies.[30]

The Scripture, on the other hand, teaches that everything that our good God created including the created social divisions are good and not to be rejected such as marriage between a biological male and female and even eating animals slaughtered for food (1 Tm 4:1–5). All created distinction that exists within the boundaries of the Decalogue are in-built into God's created design-order. Among these are the God-human and male-female and privatized, binary marriages distinctions (in contrast to communal cohabitation and communal children). In addition, the six-day work one day rest, private property divided up among citizens, indentured servants-freeman, parent-child, and truth-falsehood distinctions are essential to a Christian social order. Discriminating on the basis of those radical distinctions is not evil or oppressive in itself. It is only evil discrimination if the boundaries are overstepped by tyrants on either side of the divide. Two examples that come ready to mind are (1) false gods such as the State taking the place of the family, ecclesial, and voluntary societies in providing a security and (2) when male-husbands snatch the role of king, and law-maker, and judge over their wives and families such as occurred in ancient Roman culture. There are many more similar examples.

It is important also to realize that the Decalogue does support a citizen and alien distinction as well in the Rest Day command of Exodus and Deuteronomy: "On it you shall not do any work, neither you . . . nor any foreigner residing in your towns" (Ex 20:10 NIV). This distinction was part and parcel of the biblical worldview. It clearly does allot land and citizenship to ethno-covenantal groups while rejecting apartheid-discriminatory legislation. I demonstrate this systematically in *The Concept of Ethnicity in the Bible: A Theological Analysis* and will summarize in especially Chapter 8.[31]

Conclusion. Presupposing a type of church or social unity that rejects real gender role distinctions and true ethnic self-determination calls something a sin that God does not define as sin. Instead, it is a "commandment and doctrine of man," against which the Reformers mightily struggled. The resulting guilt is a false guilt. When submitted to, it logically leads to suicidal tendencies,

---

30 (1) Herbert Schlossberg, *Idols for Destruction: The Conflict of Christian Faith and American Culture* [Idols] (Wheaton: Crossway, 1993); (2) Peter Jones, *The Other Worldview: Exposing Christianity's Greatest Threat* [Other] (Bellingham, WA: Kirkdale, 2015). See, Peter Jones, *One or Two: Seeing a World of Difference* (Escondido, CA: Main Entry Editions, 2010) and Jones, *Gnostic Empire.*

31 Kreitzer, *The Concept of Ethnicity.*

THE TRINITARIAN PRINCIPLE APPLIED 75

personally and ethnically. "He who hates me [God's wisdom], loves death" (Prv 8:36). God does not make suicidal demands. God desires individuals and peoples, instead, to protect the good of created individual and group particularity. God created the internal instinct for individual and group self-protection. That instinct is good if God-designed priorities are followed: God, others, and yourself. If this were not true, no one would cloth, feed, or rest oneself (Phil 2:3–4). Neither would one care for one's wife (see Eph 5:24–6).

Many medieval, solitary monks, Hindu mystics, and Buddhist recluses, however, have taken this philosophy to its logical extremes. The resulting filthy appearance, begging for money, forced wakefulness, and other extreme measures are an attempt to escape from this old, divided world into the bliss of a unifying vision. The triune God does not make unity primary to real self-determining, ethno-covenantal diversity. This would deny his nature in which dwells unity and diversity as equally ultimate. Neither should his church prioritize one or the other. The evil in southern Africa and in the DRC family is not apartheid-based, racial-ethnic churches nor "this broken and divided world." Evil according to Scripture is disobedience to God's tôranic wisdom revealed in Scripture and especially the Pentateuch (see The Whole Scripture Principle).

Several Practical Questions

In the C&S document, the relation of the model for the ecclesial community and the civil communities are deeply interrelated because its roots are still reformed though not consistently so as we have seen and will see more in-depth as each chapter unfolds. After all the document is entitled *Church and Society*. So each of the following models for diversity in the communities of Christ have specific overflow ramifications for a social order.

Are One-Building, Several-Congregation Churches Sin?

First of all, C&S assumes pragmatic diversity for the sake of the diaconal ministry of the church and the fulfilling of the cultural and Great Commission mandates. Would this allow truly indigenous, biblically contextualized, local congregations? Would multiethnic congregations in one building with several church councils reflecting ethnicity be allowed? No, it seems not, if C&S' logic mandating the priority of unity over diversity is carried out to its greatest extent. When that occurs as it normally happens in human social

76 WHEN A THEOLOGICAL SHIFT CHANGED A NATION

institutions, then all local congregations should be ethnically mixed. (After all, every human groups becomes like the image of divinity its worships. If the true god that is worshiped is ultimately a simple One, then all of life will begin to reflect that holistic unity [see, e.g., Ps 115:1–8]).

Consequently, age, sexual orientation, social class, gender, and ethnic mix should reflect the geographic area surrounding the church building. We can see the basic outworking of this holistic presupposition in many of the inclusivist movements within the USA. For example, the Supreme Court and business management teams must reflect the diversity of the surrounding social order. To create this, affirmative action must be exercised often enforced by civil legislation and the weaponry of the State. Logically, then, each ethnically mixed area, for example, should have one council and one culturally diverse body. One local church building would not be allowed to contain several cooperating yet ethnically diverse church councils and congregations.

This then raises questions of geographic (congregation, classis, synod) versus gathered church polity. Which of these is biblically justifiable? After all, according to traditional DRC polity, no one from outside the local congregation's geographic borders were allowed to attend, vote, or serve in the church council of that church. This was officially changed in the same period of time I am examining. The DRC opened all parish boundaries (to use an Episcopalian term), thus abolishing the parish church model. Was it discriminatory and exclusive? It seemed when the logic of the inclusivity argument began to be pushed to its extreme—consciously or unconsciously, each pillar of the old "apartheid-discriminatory" social order began to be knocked down one by one.

Are Ethnic-Based Gatherings Wrong?

Second, for the same reasons, would an ethno-linguistically indigenous, self-governing circuit (classis) be allowed as did the Synod of Dort's original Church Order, as we have seen? What about an ethnically indigenous regional synod or ethnically distinct General Synod within a National Synod of confessionally similar "denominations"? Again, the answer seems to be negative. According to C&S 32–8, 67, and 85, which I have previously examined, the local church must include all within the boundaries of its parish. At the same time, these sections state that the DRC must make some accommodations to meet the pastoral needs of those having differing language and so forth, as we have seen. However, this affirmation and retraction of concessions in the same

THE TRINITARIAN PRINCIPLE APPLIED 77

document shows first a subtle underlying nature-grace distinction and further a rejection of the invisible/visible church distinction in Reformed literature.

First, showing the medieval nature-grace distinction, C&S states that the church in the New Testament is universal and the unity principle has priority. As a result, the church cannot be made exclusive or particular to any ethnocultural group because the diversity principle is secondary. Grace is above and prior to natural-created distinctions and will erase these distinctions ultimately. In addition, the C&S also subtly rejects the invisible/visible distinction. This means that the church as the universal, invisible body of Christ and the church as local, indigenous body should be mixed and not distinguished. What is true of the universal body, the holy, universal, apostolic Church must be made visible in each local congregation as a sign of the coming new order of the Resurrection: "**This means** ... that the church, as the one universal people of God, may not be restricted exclusively to one nation or group, nor may it exclude anyone on the basis of origin, national allegiance, language or culture."[32] Certainly this is true and correct for the universal body of Christ but cannot always be manifested in any local congregation, which must be founded upon language and culture, at least. Grace does not erase created distinctions, and language is one of these. Instead, grace restores all that was ruined and perverted by the rebellion of sin against the Creation. The equal ultimacy principle, furthermore, will recognize both the real unity in the Spirit of all brothers and sisters but also the real necessity to found congregations of people who can understand the Gospel in their own language and culture *without* excluding any person from the attendance or any true believer from the Lord's Table or baptism.

The result of this confusion of the relationship of nature to grace and the visible-invisible church distinction results in "conglomerate congregations." Church of Christ missiologist, Donald McGavran, developed this descriptive term as a result of his decades-long tenure in and reflection upon the ecclesial context of the Indian subcontinent. He noted that theologies imported from the West developed in India a similar anti-ethnic, anti-caste and anti-jati ideology as did the anti-racist theology did in South Africa. India is the archetypical apartheid culture so Western missionaries imported such a pro-inclusive

---

32 C&S, 67. Compare C&S, 66 and 67 to see this Barthian-type dialectical distinction. For an original Afrikaner-Kuyperian critic, see P. G. W. Snyman, "Die Barthiaanse Teologie (Dialektiese Teologie) [The Barthian Theology (Dialektical Theology)]," in *Koers in die Krisis II* [Course in the Crisis II], ed. H. G. Stoker, J. D. Vorster (Stellenbosch: Pro Ecclesia, 1940), 106ff.

78 WHEN A THEOLOGICAL SHIFT CHANGED A NATION

diversity argument to destroy the caste system. They based their argument on the fact, they believed, that the church must be as non-ethnic as they believed Paul was in Galatians 3:28 and other similar passages taken out of context.

However, McGavran and his disciples demonstrated that these types of churches do not grow. An ethnic group whose distinct identity as a religious, intermarried, and linguistically related social system reacts to any proselytism as a body reacts to and rejects a virus. His seminal three volumes, all written before C&S: *The Bridges of God, Ethnic Realities and the Church: Lessons from India* and *Social Structure and Church Growth* generated many volumes of research that supported his pro-ethnic ecclesial theology in multiple other countries around the world. These works agreed that when people are extracted from ethno-linguistic solidarities and joined to a foreign-appearing religious body, those groups react—sometimes violently—against the foreign "attacker." Consequently, conglomerate congregations made up of extracted individuals taken out of a multiethnic social order tend to be almost universally shadow banned or actively canceled.

The exceptions are in highly assimilated urban centers where churches founded mainly on individuals do not become non-ethnic, but eventually form a new, intermarrying and distinctive ethnic group in themselves. Likewise, he observed in India that only a few scattered individuals will come into the conglomerate churches in areas with high ethnic solidarity and that these individuals together became an almost caste-like social order in itself. These sociological observations have implications both for the ecclesial but also for the social-political order as well. However, more on this issue below.[33]

When Does Ethno-Linguistic Diversity Endanger Unity?

A third important question this perspective generates is this. At what point will the unity of the church be "obscure[d] or endanger[ed]" by true ethno-linguistic diversity within the Uniting Reformed Church of Southern Africa (which the DRC has not yet joined)?[34] As seen, C&S does allow some sort of accommodation to linguist diversity, and rightly so, but only pragmatically,

---

33 See, e.g.: (1) Donald A. McGavran, *The Bridges of God: A Study in the Strategy of Missions* (Eugene, OR: Wipf and Stock, 1955/2005); (2) Donald McGavran, *Ethnic Realities and the Church: Lessons from India* [Ethnic Realities] (Pasadena, CA: Wm. Carey, 1979); (3) Donald McGavran, *Understanding Church Growth* [Understanding], 2nd ed. (Grand Rapids: Eerdmans, 1980).

34 See, e.g., C&S 1986, 53; see parallel in C&S 1990, 32.

never confessionally. However, it never specifies what amount of indigeneity is good and justifiable and what is evil.

Within this practical accommodation, then, would groups of Afrikaners in English dominated Rondebosch, a suburb of Cape Town, Zulu hostel dwellers in Johannesburg, or Xhosa-speaking domestic workers in Afrikaner majority suburbs of Pretoria, be encouraged to meet separately to hear the word of God in their own language within the same local congregationally owned building? Should then the ethnic Other be encouraged and/or required to meet in the same sanctuary with headphones for translation of the sermon, for example? Would this obscure unity as C&S implies?[35] Would this enrich the unity of the church and further mutual fellowship? Or would these practical accommodations be accused of separatism and divisiveness when the logic is pushed—when it inevitably will be? In the long term, would not the ethnic Other, whether Afrikaner, Anglo-South African or Zulu and Tswana, feel completely ill at ease in the foreign ecclesial language, culture, theological emphases, leadership styles, and music of the majority?

As a result of these questions most likely being answered in the negative, I can come to only one conclusion. Clearly, the building of one new people of God that is neither Jew nor Greek is the ecclesiastical parallel to the one new rainbow South African nation. What language would prevail in this one new people of God? Will English prevail as it seemingly is in the new South African and Namibian states over the last three decades? Does that not imply that imperialism has prevailed, ironically?

These questions have yet to be definitively answered. However, Zulus, Afrikaners, or Xhosas who love their own language, culture and people, will probably dread that they will be required to give up their own God-created language and culture with the accusation that clinging to these is divisive. English unites, tribal languages divide, seems to be a logical sloganized outcome of this direction.

Of course this is a common issue throughout the world in ethnically diverse, imperialistically founded nation-states. These include, for example, to show how pervasive the issue is throughout the globe, The Peoples' Republic of China with its annexation of Tibet and the far western Uyghur province, the United States expansion from the east to the west coasts while annexing all of the native American ethnic-territories, Ethiopia with its shrinking Amharic

---

35 C&S 1986, 53.

80 WHEN A THEOLOGICAL SHIFT CHANGED A NATION

ruling ethnic group, Arab Algeria with its Berber minority, and Arab Iraq, Turkey and Iran with their large Kurdish-speaking regions.

Could Ethnically Distinct Congregations Be Planted?

C&S, it seems clear then, would forbid the planting of ethno-culturally separate congregations. In other words, ordained DRC evangelists can no longer justly seek to plant ethno-linguistically distinct, internally financing, propagating and determining, *local* congregations in order to help the growth and/ or consolidation of Christ-following communities in each ethno-linguistic people of Southern Africa. However, even in 2023 most Afrikaner members of congregations and many leaders instinctively reject, for whatever motives, the logic of C&S being pushed to such extremes because the DRC has not yet officially joined the Uniting Reformed Church of Southern Africa.

The late, world-respected New Testament scholar and anti-apartheid theologian, David Bosch spoke for many leaders in the DRC just before the time the Synod approved the first edition of C&S in 1986.

> An unbiased reading of Paul cannot but lead one to the conclusion that his entire theology militates against even the possibility of establishing separate Churches for different cultural groups. He pleads unceasingly for the *unity* of the Church made up of *both* Jews and Gentiles. God has made the two one, 'a single new humanity', 'a single body' (Eph. 2:14–16) (NEB). . . . The Church is one, indivisible, and it transcends all differences. The sociological impossibility (Hoekendijk) is theological possible . . .. The One body of Christ [is] the 'one new man.' The early Christians called themselves a '*triton genos*', a 'third race', next to and transcending the two existing races of Jews and Gentiles, whose enmity was proverbial.[36]

In the same volume, Bosch gives a good commentary on the thought milieu in which C&S was written. "[What I am saying is that t]his most certainly does not mean that culture is not to play any role in the Church and that cultural differences should not be accommodated." The reason, he continues, is that "almost everybody now accepts that the Church should be indigenized or . . . 'contextualized' into the very fabric of a local community, culturally, sociologically and otherwise." He then gave another notable and it seems clear, contradictory concession: "This is the legitimate element" in both Donald McGavran's (1897–1990) "Church Growth missiology" and in the views of

---

36 David J. Bosch, *The Church as Alternative Community* (Potchefstroom, RSA: Instituut vir Reformatoriese Studie, 1982), 29, emphasis in original.

THE TRINITARIAN PRINCIPLE APPLIED 81

earlier German missiological-theologian Gustav Warneck (1834–1910) and his school of missiology. However, what he gives with one hand, he immediately takes back with the other:

> However, cultural diversity should in no way militate against the unity of the Church. Such diversity in fact should serve the unity. It thus belongs to the *well-being* of the Church, whereas unity is part of its *being*. To play the one off against the other is to miss the entire point. Unity and socio-cultural diversity belong to different *orders*. Unity can be *confessed*. Not so diversity. To elevate cultural diversity to the level of an article of faith is to give culture a positive theological light which easily makes it into a 'revelation' [similar to Kuyperianism].[37]

Note Professor Bosch's conscious or subconscious rejection of the "equal ultimacy" of "unity and diversity" that I have been building upon. If the single Ultimate Reality, who is both immanent in and transcendent above the creation, that is the Triune Creator, possesses two different types of "order" within the divine ontology, then either diversity is ultimate (tritheistic polytheism) or unity is ultimate (monist pantheism).

Therefore, would C&S' logic allow for ethnically distinct congregations to separate from a mother church to help the discipling of a specific *ethnos*? The answer again is most likely negative. C&S would logically reject ethnically distinct congregations, classes, and linguistic synods being planted. These self-determining, linguistically exclusive congregations, classes or synods would divide the church. In order to have an ethnically exclusive, indigenous church on classis and regional synod level, one lingual-cultural group must be preferred. In doing so others must be excluded on the basis of family, language, culture and historical grounds. This exclusion may be totally unintentional and may even occur with the best intention of drawing people from other groups into the fellowship.

Years of missiological experience show that when a church is truly indigenous (or contextual) people from other ethno-linguistic groups both do not understand and do not feel at home in these congregations. I personally experienced this in the post-Vietnam War years. My family's congregation in Southern California sponsored Vietnamese refugees with great joy and welcoming hospitality. Yet when a Vietnamese-speaking evangelical pastor planted a nearby congregation, "our immigrants" (as we saw them) immediately left to join this new fellowship of their "kind of people" (yet still with great appreciation for how we helped them resettle). "We" were hurt nevertheless. "How

---

37 Bosch, *Alternative*, 30.

could 'they' do that?" all of us as the "we" thought. (Notice the "us/we" over against "they/them" language). We were likely thinking, "Why can't 'they' be like 'us' and like 'our' kind of people and 'our' way of doing things?"

Diversity of language and religious vocabulary used, different liturgy, music, preaching style, organization, and emphases in theology are part and parcel of the beautiful diversity and unity and of unity and diversity within the global Community of Christ. Consequently, an ethnic Other attending a truly con-textualized congregation strongly tends to leave that congregation to join one made up of "our kind of people" because "their kind of people" is so different. This is not necessarily "racist" or "hateful" but based on creational realities. The late sociologist and Church Growth School theologian C. Peter Wagner (1930–2016) wrote *Our Kind of People* (1979) and *Church Growth and the Whole Gospel* (1981) before C&S was conceived. His goal was to demonstrate that biblical ethics and creation-based sociological realities give a positive warrant for an ethnic minority in a majority or dominant culture hiving off. However, he would add, the hiving off should have the goal of better serving and evan-gelizing their own people.[38] Later, when the "they/them" assimilate into the dominant language and culture group (the "us") can a full rejoining occur in the same congregations. That happens often only in the third generation and beyond when the two distinct cultures assimilate into one language and culture.

I cut my teeth on those volumes before I went to live and serve in South Africa (1983–92) with, ironically, the heart intention to help free the oppressed African population. As a result, I began not only to champion each South African ethnies' liberation but also that of the liberation of the Afrikaner. That is if that were at all possible because of the Afrikaners generally dispersed population throughout southern Africa. Interestingly enough, Dr. Andrew Ong, a third-generation ABC (American-Born Chinese), has also substanti-ated these same ethical principles from Kuyperian and Reformational perspec-tive, sometimes citing my work. Ong wrote an article "Neo-Calvinism and Ethnic Churches in Multiethnic Contexts" that summarizes his PhD thesis.[39] In it he repudiates, as I also do, "the evils of apartheid." Yet at the same time he

---

38 See C. Peter Wagner, *Our Kind of People: The Ethical Dimension of Church Growth in Amer-ica* [Our People] (Louisville, KY: Knox, 1979), 179–81; C. Peter Wagner, *Church Growth and the Whole Gospel: A Biblical Mandate* [Whole Gospel] (San Francisco: Harper and Row, 1981).

39 Andrew Ong, "Toward a Chinese American Evangelical Theology: The Promise of Neo-Calvinism" (PhD thesis, New College, The University of Edinburgh, 2019).

THE TRINITARIAN PRINCIPLE APPLIED

seeks, as I also do, "to defend the legitimacy of ethnic churches within multi-ethnic communities by retrieving theological concepts and emphases from the neo-Calvinist tradition" of Abraham Kuyper.

I agree with him that a definite historical link existed "between [the] neo-Calvinism" of Kuyper, "and apartheid." He wrote further that this link stemmed "from an inconsistent and imbalanced appropriation of neo-Calvinism for the sake of evil ends." I agree both with that previous statement and the following statement, "A more consistent and balanced appropriation of neo-Calvinism ... can and should be retrieved for contemporary evangelical discussions concerning ethnic churches."[40] Ong summarizes:

> Utilizing the same Second Adam Christology of Bavinck, Kreitzer argues that while there is a new creational unity in the Second Adam, it does not erase creational particularities. Just as Jesus rose from the grave as a physical, Galilean Jewish male, so also will New Covenant believers retain their gender and ethnolinguistic particularities. Following Cornelius Van Til, Kreitzer maintains the equal ultimacy of unity and diversity. He asserts that any false unity that would destroy ethnic identity in Christ has succumbed to social Unitarianism. For the God-ordained diversity of ethnicities among a united humanity reflects God's triunity.[41]

Ong also wrote approvingly of how I described the view of the late John Howard Yoder. Both of us strongly disagree with Yoder's summary: "'If one is in Christ,' there is a whole new world. Ethnic standards have ceased to count."[42] "Mark Kreitzer, a Vantillian missiologist," Ong writes, "rightly rejects this way of thinking about ethnicity." He continues:

> Contrary to those who view the multiformity [diversity] of peoples at the Tower of Babel as a mere curse, Kreitzer follows Kuyper's interpretation. While the sinners at Shinar pursued an empire of uniformity, God scattered them into peoples according to his original pre-fall plan for human multiformity. The existence of distinct nations and peoples was divinely ordained, and this rich diversity of tribes, tongues, and nations was always an eschatological goal.[43]

In summary, during the decade before the DRC approved C&S (1986), I was reading the Trinitarian literature of Dutch-American Apologist and Theologian, C. A. Van Til and his followers, the VanTillians. In addition,

---

40 Andrew Ong, "Neo-Calvinism and Ethnic Church in Multiethnic Contexts [Ethnic Church]," *Journal of Reformed Theology* 12 (2018): 297.

41 Ong, *Ethnic Church*, 316.

42 Yoder, *Social Shape*, 283.

43 Ong, *Ethnic Church*, 316.

I meditated deeply on the thought world of the Dutch, Amsterdam school founded by Abraham Kuyper and Herman Bavinck. I discovered in these scholars' exegesis of Scripture keys to a biblical third way distinct from both Apartheid Theology and the paradigm shift that the C&S introduced. These keys did not include an implicit or explicit divorce between sociology (nature) and theology (grace). That divorce is explicit in Yoder, David Bosch following Yoder, and more or less in C&S.

Furthermore, Christ's third way does not reject the Trinitarian Principle of the VanTillians. The third way accepts that both unity and diversity within God and his creation are equally valuable and equally ultimate. Both unity and diversity in balance are inescapable in God-ordained reality, as Ong also noted: "Following Cornelius Van Til, Kreitzer maintains the equal ultimacy of unity and diversity."[44] God designed the creation to reflect the glory of the triune divine nature. I summarized this teaching elsewhere: "Biblical Christianity is therefore not platonic-gnostic" in other words, biblical Christianity does not "de-particularize" humanity in order to form "a non-ethnic, androgynous person as the ideal." The reason is, I wrote further: "Redemptive history does not move away from so-called divisive social identities of the first creation, but rather establishes them in mature and restored form."[45] Any kind of unity that destroys "ethnic identity in Christ," Ong quoted me, "has succumbed to social Unitarianism."[46] Consequently, true unity and real diversity, contra David Bosch, must *both* equally be confessed as of ultimate value. Only then ecclesial and dare I say, socio-political, structures can be designed to express *both* visible unity and self-governing diversity *within biblical parameters*.

C&S, 32 and C&S, 63–7, on the other hand, seem clearly to reject the paradigmatic principle of true self-governing ethnic diversity as we have seen. No form of exclusivity seems to be allowed in the church which is universal. This confuses the invisible church through the ages with the visible, local manifestation of that church. Ultimately, the principle of no exclusivity allowed is a logical deduction from the priority of unity over diversity. Furthermore, the theologians who developed Apartheid theology neglected other further biblical parameters such as "neighbor love," as I will continue to unfold in coming

---

44 Ong, *Ethnic Church*, 316.

45 (1) Kreitzer, *Ethnicity*, 394–5; (2) Mark R. Kreitzer, "Ethnic Solidarity, Babel-Pentecost Relationship, and the New Covenant," *Global Missiology English* (April 10, 2010): n.p., https://www.academia.edu/es/65046607/Ethnic_Solidarity_Babel_Pentecost_Relationship_and_the_New_Covenant.

46 Ong, *Ethnic Church*, 316.

chapters. C&S had an opportunity to truly reform the previous theological paradigm but instead introduced a complete paradigm change. Their paradigm shift did transform the Republic of South Africa, but that transformation has not been positive for the flourishing of all the ethnic solidarities of the Republic. There was and is a much more biblical alternative in the path forward, as we shall see.

Suggested Alternative Structures for Federal/Covenantal Unity

In summary, C&S motivated a progressive paradigm shift that sought to move the DRC into what is now the rainbow, inclusive new South Africa that occurred after the election of Nelson Mandela in 1994. This new South Africa is still building upon the unity of individuals in a unified and centralized State and it still rejects any real self-determining ethno-cultural or ethno-linguistic diversity in the ecclesial and civil spheres. Likewise, it also rejects any natural role distinction between the only two sexes God created.

C&S hints at minimal parameters for determining the relationship of unity to diversity. (C&S 122 is cited above). However, how this would look in the culture of the church and in society can be inferred from what occurred in the New South Africa post 1994. What happened since then is a direct result of the paradigm shift C&S helped introduce to the country's old apartheid regime and its leadership. These leaders directly participated in developing the present South African constitution with its strong bias to a centralized, unitary state. C&S's model of a more centralized institutional Church provided an important model that spilled over into the social and political model of a strong centralized state. A tight description of the influence of C&S upon the present social constitution is not possible to ascertain apart from careful research in primary sources and is something beyond the scope of this volume. However, historically, the Reformers have seen a decentralized, presbyterial-synodal system as adequate to express true unity in real diversity within various ethno-national churches. This model did spill over into the Reformed Constitutions of such countries as the USA, the Netherlands, and even the UK.[47]

---

47 See, e.g.: (1) Abraham Kuyper, "Calvinism: Source and Stronghold of Our Constitutional Liberties," in *Abraham Kuyper: A Centennial Reader*, ed. James D. Bratt (Grand Rapids: Eerdmans, 1998), 279–322; (2) Douglas F. Kelly, *The Emergence of Liberty in the Modern World: The Influence of Calvin on Five Governments from the 16th Through 18th Centuries* (Phillipsburg, NJ: P&R, 1992); (3) Glenn S. Sonshine, *Slaying Leviathan: Limited Government and Resistance in the Christian Tradition* (Moscow, ID: Canon, 2020).

86 WHEN A THEOLOGICAL SHIFT CHANGED A NATION

The Scripture provides several basic parameters for holding true unity and real ethno-linguistic diversity in biblical balance: Mandatory community stipulations for (con)federal, ethno-churches; Concentric-circle shaped (con) federal gatherings; Compact geographical areas; Appellate jurisdiction only; Ethnic diversity at all levels if existing; and Multi-congregations in one geographical parish.

Three Mandatory Stipulations for (Con)federated, Ethno-Churches. C&S rejected a decentralized model in the church and helped lay the foundation of the modern South African democratic socialist, centralized regime. On the other hand, I propose the following (con)federal principles as an alternative to the centralized unitary structures of the new South Africa to express visible, structural unity *and* real multiethnic diversity. Each of the following biblical stipulations is *mandatory* for fellowship within and between ethno-linguistic-based churches in what I propose to be a (con)federation of churches and by implication for a future, proposed, post New South Africa. These principles imply constant fraternal communication within the various branches of the new Reformed Church of Southern Africa that I would envision. They also imply formal gatherings of at least elders in local areas. Meeting together of parishioners of various linguistic and cultural groups is also highly commendable.

The three mandatory community stipulations are:

1. **Open Community.** Community is only developed through three further stipulations: (a) Fellowship and partnership between individuals, families, and congregations, (b) Proclamation of the word, and (c) Open Lord's Table (communion) and open baptismal fonts for all true believers of whatever class, language group, or sex (Jas 2:1–10; Gal 2:11–14, 28–9). Here, C&S is correct.[48] Such neighbor love, as we shall see in a coming chapter, demands that all believers can and should be allowed into church buildings to hear the proclaimed word to express true unity (Jas 2:8–10).

On the other hand, does it biblically follow that this visitor can demand *in* his or her *own language* equal voting and leadership rights for himself and his linguistically alien friends in, to that visitor, an *alien* ethno-linguistically based congregation? I think not. That would destroy true diversity. Voting and governing rights are not rights coming from our shared humanity, but covenantal

48 C&S 36–7, 40, 90–2.

THE TRINITARIAN PRINCIPLE APPLIED 87

rights *and* responsibilities coming from an ethno-linguistic group that covenants together in their *own* language to serve the Lord. After all, trust and faith coming from being able to hear the Word. No one can hear the Word with power except in one's own mother language. Also, for example, every country intuitively sees that these two rights flow from covenant citizenship. A third basic biblical principle is that leadership ought always to come out of a people-group, an ethno-linguistic group, as Moses mandated (Dt 17: 1:9–18). These leaders are chosen by that specific people, which is a group of ethno-historically related, intermarried families sharing a common covenantal faith and language, again as we shall see.

Both equal human rights and ethno-covenantal rights are, consequently, equally ultimate. Therefore, also, it is just and right to have congregations, classes, and synods of one kind of linguistically based people-group.

Logically, this principle certainly also applies to true ethno-linguistic-based social-political orders as well. In what may be an apocryphal account, Paul Kruger (1825–1904) President of the old Transvaal Republic, told the tale that once an old man was driving his oxcart to Johannesburg, founded by Afrikaans-speaking settlers. Along the way, he picked up several English-speaking guest workers employed in that Boer Republic's gold mines. However, they voted that since they were now in the majority, the oxcart belonged to them. So the old owner could ride along if he wished but they were going to take *their* cart where they wanted. In Kruger's mind, this was an injustice and a matter of natural law built into human consciences by their common creator (see Rom 2:14–16). Neighbor love does not steal (Rom 13:8–10), he could have reasoned, but it also provides abundant hospitality to show them that he loved them like himself, something our Lord also emphasized in the Parable of the Good Samaritan (see, e.g., Lv 19:34; Lk 10:25–37).

This was Kruger's legendary justification for resisting the British Empire's annexation of the Transvaal Republic over the lack of voting rights for English guest workers. I agree. In addition, there was no moral justification whatsoever for the Empire to annex the independent Zulu Kingdom. Nor was it ever justified for the British Empire to annex the independent Xhosa territories and join them into their imperial Union of South Africa as well. Could not this intuitively correct (and biblically correct) principle also provide a negotiated way forward in the post New South Africa and for that matter the whole of postcolonial African continent? Yes. Sadly, the Afrikaner apartheid regime used the first part of Paul Kruger's parable in their justification of apartheid's top-down, indeed it was also imperial, partitioning of the country, but not the

88 WHEN A THEOLOGICAL SHIFT CHANGED A NATION

second vital aspect as well, again as we shall see. Peaceful and negotiated partitioning is not evil but good.

2. **Single Confession** renegotiated among all (con)federal branches of a truly uniting reformed denomination. It is time for a new South African confession, still biblically orthodox and teaching biblical orthopraxy (biblical practice), to be negotiated and written. All must accept this one common Confession, that is the one common gospel that establishes the one law of God. This common confession can be used to develop a new consensus without losing any of Scripture's essential core teachings.

3. **Mutual Recognition of Church Discipline.** All members and branches of this new ecclesial confederation should negotiate mutually acceptable wording so that all units could to be under the same doctrinal *and* ethical principles for church discipline. Therefore, the jurisdiction of each unit's church disciplinary gatherings must be respected by all the other gatherings at all levels and linguistic units. This implies a rejection of both absolute congregational autonomy and top-down prelacy. The first presupposes a bias to absolute diversity, whereas the second, prelacy with its authoritarian bishops, presupposes a bias toward uniformity and for unity, as the most foundational principle that merely embracing diversity without denying unity's logical priority. Eventually these three principles should result in a common polity that is built upon the minimum of rule of elected congregational elders and concentric-circle shaped, connectional government.

Concentric-Circle Shaped (Con)federal Gatherings. All of this presupposes in the best of Dutch Reformed teaching, that the unity of such multiethnic church gatherings should be expressed in a series of (con)federalized gatherings structured as concentric circles. The continental Reformed teaching rejected a top-down pyramid such as in the Roman Catholic Church.[49] These gatherings exist in a common socio-politically defined, geographical areas. These are (1) local parish boundaries with, eventually, multiple gathering points, (2) larger classis/presbytery boundaries, (3) even larger regional synod, (4) national synod (e.g., Lesotho), (5) regional multi-national synod (e.g., Southern Africa), and the largest, (6) world general synod boundaries.[50] This means that each language

---

49 See, e.g., E. P. J. Kleynhans, *Gereformeerde Kerkreg* [Reformed Church Law], vol. I, *Inleiding* [Introduction] (Pretoria: N.G. Kerkboekhandel Transvaal, 1982), I:82–3.

50 See a discussion in C&S, 93–5.

group in multi-lingual South Africa should develop their own non-color-based, but language and dialect-based congregations, classes, and regional synods. In urban areas *especially*, but not exclusively, multiple "colors" could very well agree to meet *together* as a newly developed, English-speaking urban South African ethnic group that intermarries and has the other characteristics of an ethnic group.

Compact Geographical areas. Each presbytery or classis (and on up to the world-encompassing International General Synod) would exist in a compact geographic area with many congregations. All of the elders in each area ought, then, to consider themselves one local ecclesial unit that is traditionally translated as "church" in English. In Scripture, however, this seemed to be the structure of the primary governing unit, for example, the church of Rome, Corinth, Ephesus. Each classis/presbytery, for example, will consist of multiple gathering places. Most will be home or store-front based as in the early church, but certainly not all.

As the number of members grew, especially the urban areas should be divided into smaller but still geographically determined units such as, in South Africa of the time of the C&S document, the DRC classes of North, West, East and Central Pretoria. The regional synods, then should be seen, in this best of Reformed biblical exegesis, not to be a "church" (singular) but a (con) federation of *churches*—a that is of classes or in the Scots polity, of presbyteries. This can be seen in Scripture as the "churches" of the Roman province of Judea, Asia, Macedonia, and so forth (e.g., 1 Thes 2:14; 1 Cor 16:19; 2 Cor 8:1). The same principle could hold true for the other larger gatherings as well.[51]

Appellate Jurisdiction Only. The progressively larger gathering only has appellate jurisdiction over any discipline-oriented gathering immediately next to it and smaller than it in this postulated concentric-circle-shaped superstructure. The larger gatherings do not have direct authority over all the other smaller disciplinary actions nor over all individuals. No policy statements nor confessional changes should be originated in any other than a compact, geographically-based classis/presbytery. The geographically larger gatherings of elders are for discussion and opinion only. They must never be top-down in enforcement. For the smallest level, policy statements such as, for example, a C&S replacement, would then be passed along to the broader circles for comment, discussion, and evaluation. Consequently, all broader circles of synods

---

51 See, e.g., Thomas Witherow, "The Apostolic Church: Which Is It?" in *I Will Build My Church: Selected Writings on Church Polity, Baptism, and the Sabbath*, ed. Jonathan Gibson, foreword (Philadelphia: Westminster Seminary Press, 2022).

would serve as appeal forums alone, not as a top-down enforced policymakers, which amount to tyranny. Scripture is replete with warning on such pyramidal structures (e.g., Gn 11 and Rv 13).[52]

Ethnic Diversity at All Levels. Local, regional, and/or national synods could consist of self-governing, self-theologizing ethno-churches. Even those assemblies (congregations) that claim not to be "race," or ethnic-based *but* are speaking together a lingua franca such as English can and should be included in any level of government.

In South African practice, these synods will include Zulu, Xhosa, Sotho, Afrikaner, Anglo-South African and multi-color English-speaking churches in an ever-larger circles. A provincial region can be where the churches choose to meet (e.g., Western Cape Province) or an ethno-linguistic based, but post-color church such as a transformed *Afrikaans Protestante Kerk* may choose to meet with other broader synodical assemblies only on a national, or subcontinental (Southern African) level.

Multi-Congregations in One Geographical Parish. Last, this (con)federal or covenantal model could allow flexibility for several ethno-linguistic based congregations to meet in one local geographical "parish" building, to use a more episcopal term. It could also allow for several ethno-linguistic based congregations meeting in one local ecclesial building with different variations on ruling bodies for these congregations.

Conclusion

The Trinitarian principle rejects the to-down, centralized Roman Catholic, theoretical (though not actually practiced) model of one congregation for each geographic area no matter what varying types of ethno-linguistic groups live in it. The Trinitarian model does not exclude churches who choose not to be ethno-linguistically exclusive. Nor does it exclude fellowship between congregations, classes, and regional synods of various language and culture groups with the above stipulations put into practice.

---

52 For similar Presbytian warnings, see, e.g.: (1) Robert J. Breckinridge, *Presbyterian Government: Not a Hierarchy, but a Commonwealth*, ed. Kevin Reed (Dallas: Presbyterian Heritage Publications, 1843/1988); (2) Thomas Smyth, *Complete Works of Rev. Thomas Smyth, D.D.*, 2nd ed., ed. J. W. Flinn, vol. III, *Ecclesiastical Republicanism or the Republicanism, Liberality and Catholicity of Presbytery in Contrast with Prelacy and Popery* (Columbia, SC: R. L. Bryan, 1908).

This model of (con)federalism is the Reformed, Protestant presbyterial-synodal structure followed through logically to include peoples and to include the reality of true unity and real diversity. If "peopleness" is not evil in itself "in Christ," then it is an ethical "good" both in the church invisible and visible and in distinct ethno-states, some totally independent, others cantonally confederated like Switzerland or federated like Germany.

· 5 ·

THE SCRIPTURE ALONE PRINCIPLE AND THE DRC

Introduction to Classic *Sola Scriptura* Doctrine

The second most foundational question I wish to address in this volume is what view of biblical authority does the DRC adopt in its paradigm-shifting document, *Church and Society*? If C&S denied the historic Dutch Reformed understanding of Scripture, it denied a foundational principle of the Reformation itself. If this is truly accurate, as I will contend, it will bring an even deeper oppression as the history of the last three decades has demonstrated it has. I assert, further, that instead of paving the way forward into a progressive, new and more just society, the nation-changing paradigm shift that C&S brought actually turned its back on the comprehensive freedom Reformation-based, biblical Christianity brought and still brings. It instead pointed the Afrikaner and other southern African ethnic and cultural groups back to another deeper and more powerful "Egypt" of human bondage.

Ironically, the ecclesial and social-political liberation movements which strongly pressured the DRC and motivated C&S 1986 and 1990 led to deeper enslavement to human idolatry. Instead of cutting off the chains of all of the oppressed Southern African people-groups including those in Namibia,

94 WHEN A THEOLOGICAL SHIFT CHANGED A NATION

Zimbabwe, and South Africa, it tightly bound them in much stronger and darker spiritual chains. The post New South Africa needs a return to a chastened but more biblically enlightened Reformational movement of both grace and truth. So does almost every nation-state in the continent of Africa, and throughout the earth. Both the ecclesial and socio-political arenas of life should be so reformed. *Semper Reformanda*—always Reforming—but only according to sound exegesis of the infallible and inerrant Scripture.

Infallibility: Foundational Presupposition

Scripture is both infallible, incapable of teaching any untruth or lie and without error, it never errs. Consequently as the Creator's only verbal revelation, it serves as the foundational framework and sometimes even as a broad blueprint for Christ-followers to transform culture according to the standards of Christ's kingdom in the power of the resurrected and indwelling Christ. In addition, the doctrine of Scripture upon which the DRC was founded is based on a single two-sided presupposition. On one side, God-trusting humans have the necessary and sufficient Word of God and should be submitting their whole being to its perspicuous and infallible authority in every area of life because it is the veritable word of their Lord and King. As Paul wrote: "We also thank God continually because, when you received the word of God, which you heard from us, you accepted it not as a human word, but as it actually is, the word of God, which is indeed at work in you who believe" (1 Thes 2:13 NIV). Or, alternatively, rebellious humanity will inevitably grasp to himself another "word" and then put this self-made law, truth, and reality above God's fully reliable Word.[1] This provides what Paul—and the Kuyperians—call an antithesis between the wisdom of God and the folly of humans "devoid of the Spirit" (1 Cor 1:21, 3:18–21; Jude 19 ESV).

Our Lord insisted that man has only two foundations upon which he can build his whole life. Either he builds upon the Rock, Christ's Word revealed in the whole Bible, or he builds on the sand, his own word of wisdom (Mt 7:23–39). Implicitly, Christ teaches that every human must not ask "whether" he or she has an authority upon which to build his life. Instead, each person needs to ask, upon "whose" authoritative word each will build. Lutheran

---

1 See, e.g.: (1) R. J. Rushdoony, *Infallibility: An Inescapable Concept* (Vallecito, CA: Ross House, 1978a); (2) Joseph Boot, "In Understanding be Men: The Crisis of our Age and the Recovery of the Gospel," in *The Mission of God: A Manifesto of Hope for Society* [Mission of God], 2nd ed. (London: Wilberforce Publications, 2016).

THE SCRIPTURE ALONE PRINCIPLE AND THE DRC 95

scholar, Robert Preus asks: If *sola Scriptura* is not the sole "source and norm of Christian doctrine," and I might add, of ethics, "then it is not the source and norm at all; any violation of the sola scriptura principle is a violation of biblical authority *per se*."[2]

Summing up classic Reformed confessions, Anthony Lane concurs: "[The] essence of the *sola Scriptura* principle . . . is that Scripture is the final authority or norm for Christian belief."[3] Those who reject this, claim that the "interpreter is the final norm." A bit later in the same work, he stated that the historic doctrine of "*sola Scriptura* asserts the supremacy of the text over its interpreter," whether it be an individual or an institution.[4] This truth strategically is utterly crucial to understand the paradigm shift that the DRC has undergone to change the South African nation.

Now certainly it is true that the doctrine of "infallibility" must be deduced from relevant scriptural passages. Infallibility was once a term that the Dutch Reformed Church of South Africa fully supported out of its own confession of faith, the *Belgic Confession*, Art. 7. The deductive pattern is true for the later term "inerrancy" and the meaning of the biblical words for "truth."[5] However, this does not detract from the fact that this doctrine of comprehensive biblical authority is inescapable. After all, the Dutch Reformed Three Forms of Unity and all Reformed movements stated that all teaching must be either directly supported by Scripture or from express Scripture by good and necessary consequences. This position was that which Herman Bavinck and Abraham Kuyper took concerning the Scripture as Richard Gaffin demonstrates in *God's Word in Servant-Form: Abraham Kuyper and Herman Bavinck and the Doctrine of Scripture* (2008).[6]

2   Earl Radmacher and Robert D. Preus, eds., *Hermeneutics, Inerrancy, and the Bible: Papers from ICBI Summit II* (Grand Rapids: Zondervan, Academie Books, 1984), 125. See also, Robert Preus, "The View of the Bible Held by the Church: The Early Church through Luther," in *Inerrancy*, ed. Norman L. Geisler (Grand Rapids: Zondervan, 1980).
3   Anthony N. S. Lane, "Sola Scriptura? Making Sense of a Post-Reformation Slogan [Sola Scriptura]," in *A Pathway into the Holy Scripture*, ed. Philip E. Satterthwaite and David F. Wright (Grand Rapids: Eerdmans, 1994), 297–327, 323.
4   Lane, *Sola Scriptura*, 326.
5   See, Paul Feinberg, "The Meaning of Inerrancy," in *Inerrancy*, ed. Norman L. Geisler (Grand Rapids: Zondervan, 1980), 263–304; (2) Paul Feinberg, "Truth: Relationship of Theories of Truth to Hermeneutics," in *Hermeneutics, Inerrancy, and the Bible: Papers from ICBI summit II*, ed. Earl Radmacher and Robert Preus (Grand Rapids: Zondervan, Academie Books. 1984), 3–50.
6   Richard Gaffin, *God's Word in Servant-Form: Abraham Kuyper and Herman Bavinck and the Doctrine of Scripture*, foreword by Peter Lillback (Jackson, MS: Reformed Academic, 2008).

Consequently, when this foundational doctrine, like that of the Trinity, is ever denied in practice (orthopraxis) and/or teaching (orthodoxy) it inevitably leads to the destruction of a denomination's actual claim to a biblical form of Christianity. The contemporary DRC in 2023 is well along this path, a direction taken by multiple ancient and Reformation denominations over the last two millennia.

The broader evangelical movement, which the DRC once was a part of, has made much progress in developing the doctrine of sola Scriptura and its implications over the last century. For example, the missionary based, Lausanne Covenant (1974), shows the inseparable connection between the two terms "infallibility" and "inerrancy": "We affirm the divine inspiration, truthfulness and authority of both Old and New Testament Scriptures in their entirety as the only written Word of God, without error in all that it affirms, and the only infallible rule of faith and practice."[7] This document was later expanded and nuanced by the consensual *Chicago Statement on Biblical Inerrancy and Hermeneutics*.[8]

The classic Reformed perspective has consistently taught that out of the sola Scriptura principle came the term "infallibility." When that lost its original meaning of "without error or fallibility," biblically sound brothers introduced the technical term "inerrancy." I will use both terms as interchangeable synonyms.[9] This was the essence of the theological battle with Rome and now with, for example, the Neo-Marxian Liberation Theology and the Social Justice movements in Christ's universal Community. *Sola Scripture* and its concomitants, infallibility and inerrancy, taught that the church, its synods, popes, and doctors have erred and will continue to err as the *Belgic Confession*, Articles 5, 7 state. Scripture will not and cannot be fallible, that is able to error, nor is it ever erroneous, that is Scripture is inerrant, in any area in which it speaks.

---

7 ICWE, *Let the Earth Hear His Voice: Official Reference Volume, Papers, and Responses. International Congress of World Evangelization, Lausanne, Switzerland*, ed. J. D. Douglas (Minneapolis: World Wide Publications, 1974).

8 ICBI, "The Chicago Statement on Biblical Inerrancy," *Evangelical Review of Theology* 4, no. 1 (April 1980): 8ff.

9 See (1) R. C. Sproul, "Sola Scriptura: Crucial to Evangelicalism," in *The Foundation of Biblical Authority*, ed. James M. Boice (Grand Rapids: Zondervan, 1978), 103–19; (2) John Hannah, ed., *Inerrancy and the Church* (Chicago: Moody Press, 1984); (3) Don Kistler, ed., *Sola Scriptura: The Protestant Position on the Bible*, 2nd ed. (Orlando, FL: Ligonier Ministries, 2009); (4) R. C. Sproul, *Scripture Alone: The Evangelical Doctrine* [Scripture Alone] (Phillipsburg, NJ: P&R, 2013).

A Pluralistic View of Scripture

Development of the DRC's View of Scripture

The DRC and its predecessor churches have gone through several periods of transition away from and back to, and then again away from an infallibilist (inerrantist) view of Scripture. The DRC at the time of the General Synod's approval of C&S, officially denies its former doctrine of the infallibility/inerrancy of Scripture. The following citations are designed *not* to prove a consensus on any specific theory of Scripture but to demonstrate the pluralistic standpoint on Scripture in the DRC.

These citations are also designed to give examples of the almost universal rejection of the classic definition of sola Scriptura and infallibility within synods and theological leadership of the DRC. Many of these leaders participated in the agitation for, as well as the writing and revision of, C&S.

A major work edited by the late DRC theologian, Professor Ferdinand Deist, who was quite progressive in his time documented this paradigm shift: *Experience, Reason, and Method in Scripture Interpretation* [*Ervaring, Rede en Metode in Skrifuitleg*]. The well-respected DRC authors of the articles within the volume candidly approved and documented the DRC's internal dispute and resulting change in the many decades leading up to the election of Nelson Mandela in 1994. Once again, this pivotal paradigm shift in Scripture did indeed help change a whole nation.[10]

The first almost imperceptible change in the doctrine Scripture both occurred and was then repudiated within the British-dominated Cape Colony during the first third of the nineteenth century. Only by 1880 and largely as the result of the founding of Stellenbosch Seminary was this anti-infallibility movement overcome.[11] Ironically, the seminary that was founded to overthrow the higher critical movement in the Cape Colony is now on the forefront of the radically progressive element in the DRC.

The next major stand for the Reformed sola Scriptura doctrine of inerrancy was the church, and later civil, court case involving Johannes du Plessis, Professor of Missions, nonetheless, also at Stellenbosch University.[12] Johannes

---

10 Deist, *Experience*.

11 Deist, *Experience*. See also DRC Church historian, P. B. Van der Watt, P. B., *Die Nederduitse Gereformeerde Kerk: 1825–1905* [The DRC: 1825–1905] (Pretoria: N.G. Kerkboekhandel, 1980).

12 P. B. Van der Watt, P. B., *Die Nederduitse Gereformeerde Kerk: 1905–75* [The DRC: 1905–75] (Pretoria: N.G. Kerkboekhandel., 1987).

Du Plessis claimed that the *Belgic Confession* allowed for several interpretations on inspiration and infallibility. He used this defense to deny the inerrancy/infallibility of Scripture, the divinity of Christ, and the Mosaic authorship of the Pentateuch. Denying these core doctrines and supporting among other dogmas such as evolution left him and his students without any Good News for the many ethno-cultural groups of the Southern African subcontinent in an academic post dedicated to reaching these very groups beginning with South Africa.

The charge against Du Plessis was that he taught "that the holy Scripture was not infallibly inspired in all its parts."[13] After quoting Articles 3, 4, 5, 6 and 7 of the *Belgic Confession*, the charge of the then biblically orthodox DRC stated: "Not only do our Confessions know no distinction between errant/fallible and inerrant/infallible parts of God's Word, but the Holy Scriptures themselves struggle against such a distinction. 1 Thes. 2:13 . . .." It then referenced Articles 3–7 of the *Belgic Confession* and added: "Based upon these articles, the history [of creation and redemption] as it is *prima facie* taught by the Scripture must be accepted. . . . This history is accepted as the truth by the Lord Jesus Himself." In the teaching ministry of our Lord, the charge adds, "He establishes the historicity of Adam and Eve (Mt. 19:4); Abel and his murder by Cain (Lk. 11:51); Noah and the Flood (Mt. 24:37–9); Abraham, Isaac and Jacob . . . " along with the Mosaic authorship of the Pentateuch, citing Mt 19:8; Mk 10:3; Jn. 3:14; Jn 5:45, 46, 7:19. In 1930, the DRC's highest court expelled Du Plessis from his professorship at Stellenbosch Seminary. The DRC reinstated him reluctantly after he won a subsequent civil court case in the Cape Town Supreme Court but was immediately put on administrative leave so he could not further his non-orthodox teaching.

At that time, the DRC courageously refused to bow the knee to the civil authority on principle. However, it ignored this brave precedent in 2019 when it refused to resist the Pretoria High Court's decision to mandate the full inclusion of LGBTQ+ persons into membership and clergy in 2019, which I mentioned in the first chapters.

In another volume, Ferdinand Deist discussed this incident in a volume whose title echoed, it seems, the Serpent's claim in the Garden, *Sê God So?* [Does God Say This?] (Gn 3:1). He claimed that this 1930 Synod decision showed the negative influence of Kuyperian "fundamentalism" and strengthened the hand of the "orthodox and fundamentalist majority" for years to come.[14] I stand in

---

13 F. S. Malan, *Ons Kerk en Prof. Du Plessis* [Our Church and Prof. Du Plessis] [Our Church] (Cape Town: Nasionale Pers, 1933), 298.

14 Ferdinand Deist, *Sê God So?* [Does God Say This?] (Cape Town: Tafelberg, 1982), 37–9.

THE SCRIPTURE ALONE PRINCIPLE AND THE DRC   99

complete agreement with this Synod's decision in expelling Prof. Du Plessis and will build my argument for an alternative to C&S's doctrine of the church and its social theology upon this foundation. Last, the charges state that Professor Du Plessis is in accordance with the German-developed "higher-critical school" of theology, a school of thought that I also thoroughly reject because it is based on an *a priori* presupposition of anti-supernaturalism and equating inspiration with the dictation method of revelation.[15] Grievously, Du Plessis has been totally rehabilitated and celebrated by the DRC of the twenty-first century.

Influence of G. C. Berkouwer's Paradigm Shift

This good Kuyperian consensus on Scripture held on tenaciously until the late 1960s. At that time a paradigm shift began to occur especially under the influence of Dutch theologians influenced by Karl Barth such as the later G. C. Berkouwer and H. Ridderbos. In the 1950s under this Barthian influence, Berkouwer and Ridderbos reversed their former orthodox views that were virtually the same as what we now call "inerrancy." They introduced Barth's neo-orthodox position on Scripture to Dutch Reformed circles worldwide, South Africa included. Seventy years later, Berkouwer's denomination that began as a movement back to complete infallibility of Scripture is no longer in existence. It lost its biblical saltiness and merged with other theologically progressive denominations in the Netherlands that have adopted the agenda and theology of the West's present beyond-postmodern culture. Once the door was cracked to the unbelief of the higher critical, Scripture critical approach, Pandora's box opened to a menagerie of spirits flowing into the once orthodox churches of the Dutch tradition in the USA, South Africa, and elsewhere where there is a Dutch diaspora.

Berkouwer's views are the most important for our purpose because of his immense authority. Briefly, he accused Kuyper's inerrantist theory of inspiration of being a "mechanical," "dictation theory." At the same time, however, he acknowledges that "no one deliberately takes" this fundamentalist mechanical view. In his paradigm-shifting volume, *Holy Scripture*, Berkouwer inaccurately correlates faith in the absolute trustworthiness of Scripture with the mechanical theory. He again followed Karl Barth, who attacked inerrancy as the idolatry of the Bible (bibliolatry). Berkouwer's antidote to his previous belief in

---

15 Malan, *Our Church*, 300–1.

inerrancy is not to link faith with Scripture but to link faith with God. He thus emphasizes the leading of the Spirit through the *church* to find God's voice in the Scripture. In other words, the Spirit is *not* directly tied to the careful, exegetically derived meaning of every word of Scripture as in the earlier Reformed, and especially Kuyperian teaching. Instead, the Spirit can work outside of and alongside of the Bible for a new leading and a new direction.[16]

He further makes the accusation that those who ignorantly hold to this "dictation" theory reject the full humanity of the Bible, because he believes that humanity must always be at times fallible.[17] However, logically, this would imply that our fully human Lord himself must be fallible. Grievously, Berkouwer does not interact with Kuyper and Bavinck's thorough refutation of this mechanical theory in their teaching on Scripture as organically inspired.

By organic inspiration they mean that God's Spirit works through the full humanity of the writers of Scripture while protecting the infallible authority of what they speak. After all, Paul has no problem in writing that the message of the Gospel is the "word of God" delivered by the apostles and prophets of the New Testament. Believers, who received it did not receive it "as the word of men, but as it actually is, the word of God, which is at work in you" (1 Thes 2:13). In other words, the word spoken and written by those with the prophetic gifting also infallibly speak the very words "breathed out" of the mouth of God (2 Ti 3:16 NIV). Consequently, our Lord is certainly able as God to work by his Spirit through the human organs of mind, mouth, and hand. God himself guarantees that the non-erring truth of both the written and spoken words of Scripture have the imprimatur of the Spirit of truth himself. The writer of Hebrews even claims that the ancient words of Psalm 95:7–11 is the Spirit still speaking through, what some would say "that antique Psalm" even now with the voice of "the living God": "So, as the Holy Spirit says"—present tense—"'Today, if you hear his voice' do not harden your hearts" (Heb 3:7, 12, 18).

Secondly, and again he follows Barth, he made a sharp subjective distinction between two elements. The first more objective element is the "essential content," scopus, or intention of Scripture. This is infallible. The second element, however, because it is the "time-related form" or periphery, cannot be inerrant. Consequently, it is open to scientific analysis using higher critical processes.[18] He shifted to embrace the form-content (*vorm en inhoud*) distinction

---

16   G. C. Berkouwer, *The Holy Scripture*, trans. and ed. Jack B. Rogers (Grand Rapids: Eerdmans, 1975), 15, 47–8.

17   Berkouwer, *Holy Scripture*, 18–20, 153.

18   Berkouwer, *Holy Scripture*, 175.

THE SCRIPTURE ALONE PRINCIPLE AND THE DRC   101

between "kernel and husk," "fact and clothing of the fact," that he previously rejected in his early, pre-Barthian work on Scripture.[19]

Significantly, both Berkouwer's earlier and later perspectives has parallels in DRC synods' doctrine of Scripture and DRC professor's scriptural critique. A major example to be dealt with later is the late DRC Professor Johan Heyns, who had a major influence upon C&S and the General Synod's doctrine of Scripture during the decades leading up to the publication of C&S. He followed the lead of Berkouwer, his esteemed Th.D. promoter, in several works on Scripture, for example, *Bridge between God and Mankind* [*Brug tussen God en Mens*].[20]

DRC's Synodical Views of Scripture

1986 General Synod on Biblical Authority. Professor J. Heyn's views are also paralleled in a somewhat moderated form in the DRC's official policy document on Scripture (S&S). It is extremely important to note that the same General Synod that approved the first edition of C&S (1986) also passed a crucial paradigm-shifting document on the authority of Scripture. It is entitled, "The Authority and Use of Scripture: Policy document of the DRC, Approved by the General Synod, 1986"[21] (henceforth S&S). Like Berkouwer, S&S caricatures and in effect ridicules the Scripture informed, Reformed and Kuyperian doctrine of organic-verbal inspiration as a mechanical-dictation theory of biblical authority. It replaces this view with what it calls "dialogical inspiration," a term used by Professor Johan Heyns, who was then General Synod Moderator, to describe his theory of inspiration.[22]

19 G. P. Berkouwer, *Het Probleem der Skriftkritiek* [The Problem of Higher Criticism] (Kampen: Kok, 1938), 129. See refutation by Dutch-American theologian, Henry Krabbendam, "The Functional Theology of G. C. Berkouwer," in *Challenges to Inerrancy: A Theological Response*, ed. Gordon R. Lewis and Bruce Demarest (Chicago: Moody, 1984), 285–316. See also Henry Krabbendam, "B. B. Warfield versus G. C. Berkouwer on Scripture," in *Inerrancy*, ed. Norman L. Geisler (Zondervan: Academie Books, 1980), 413–46.

20 Johan Heyns, *Brug tussen God en Mens: Oor die Bybel* [Bridge between God and Mankind: Concerning the Bible] [Bridge] (Pretoria: N.G. Kerkboekhandel, 1976); chapter 4: "Die sentrum en die periferie in die Bybel" [The center and periphery in the Bible].

21 Algemene Sinode [General Synod], "*Skrifgesag en Skrifgebruik: Beleidstuk van die Nederduitse Gereformeerde Kerk, soos Goedgekeur deur die Algemene Sinode, 1986*" [The authority and use of Scripture: Policy document of the *Nederduitse Gereformeerde Kerk* [DRC], as approved by the General Synod], in *Skrif, Dogma en Verkondiging*, ed. Pieter Potgieter (Kaapstad: Lux Verbi, 1990), 59–67.

22 See S&S, 1.2; Heyns, *Bridge*.

Furthermore, S&S, somewhat like Berkouwer, has a strong tendency to limit the authority of Scripture to merely *religious* and *spiritual salvation* matters. In this regard, the General Synod seems to contradict itself. It wants to hold, in an orthodox manner, to the "reliability and truthfulness of everything that is proclaimed in the Holy Scripture" as the *Belgic Confession* affirms in Article 5, correctly claiming that "the whole message of the Bible is truly dependent on the reliability of the history of God's salvation-deeds that are proclaimed in it" (S&S, 2.3). On the other hand, the Synod also claims that a "modern-Western" theory of truth is "abstract, rational and positivistic." In other words, it is Enlightenment, that is Modernity based. The Synod further claimed that this theory does not "reckon with the unique character of the Scripture."[23]

This false theory, S&S claims, should be rejected because it does not consider the central, *limiting* scopus (or focus) of the Scripture, which is wisdom unto salvation. The implication is that inerrancy doctrines are based on an autonomous, humanistic concept divorced from the reality of the errors of the Scripture phenomena. The reason given is that Scripture does not "strive after scientific precision" and is "not a textbook of science or history."[24] Consequently, S&S claims that the redemptive history proclaimed in Scripture occurred in general, but certainly not every detail is accurate: "The Bible does not handle history in the modern-Western manner. It does not strive for scientific precision and comprehensiveness." What that means, I am not certain, but it could include details such as how God created the heavens and earth, who wrote the Pentateuch, and whether the story of Jonah and the great fish actually happened. This attempt appears to be moderate and hermeneutically accurate but does open the door to grievous error, such as eventually denying the bodily resurrection of Christ. Or, not as far down the road to apostasy, it could result in denying that the creation account of a binary couple, Adam and Eve, actually has anything to do with how the modern family should be defined and lived out. This is contrary, of course, to what our Lord did in defining when divorce is just and what constitutes marriage. Certainly, by logical deduction, this applies to the gay marriage dilemma in the contemporary church worldwide (e.g., Mt 19:1–12). Or again, as the same General Synod also decided, that the account of the creation of languages at Babel had anything to do with developing a contemporary theory of the relationship of church and

---

23 S&S, 2.3.
24 See S&S, 2.2 and 2.3.

THE SCRIPTURE ALONE PRINCIPLE AND THE DRC 103

society. Essentially, these shifts have been occurring in the last almost four decades since the 1986 General Synod.[25]

In summary, the 1986 Synod's moderate Barthianism at this point was seemingly still better than adopting the radical and consequent higher critical theory, which presupposes that no supernatural sphere exists at all. However, the door was cracked opened to accommodate not merely alleged unimportant scientific errors but also even theological error. Historically when the door is cracked open against the full infallibility of Scripture, all the other errors flood in and force the door wide open to all errors including a purely anti-supernatural bias. The crack in the dam of biblical infallibility published in 1986 when S&S appeared, represented a major paradigm shift that began to be lived out in C&S 1986 and 1990. S&S seemed to anticipate this danger: "The historical-critical method ... puts the confession concerning the infallibility of the Scripture under severe pressure." In addition S&S's section on "Dangers" and the last section on "Interpretation" attempt to warn against some of these errors using principles that seem on the surface to be using sound hermeneutical principles of interpretation.[26] But perhaps this was only a concession to the remnant of the Kuyperians left in the DRC because the denomination ignored its own Synod's warnings in its rush to rejoin the World Council of Churches with its modernity-bound higher critical and often now postmodern bias.

The Western Cape Regional Synod. The Commission on Doctrine and Contemporary Affairs of the Western Cape regional synod (Kommissie van Leer-en Aktuele Sake) (KLAS-WK) published *The Reformational Sola Scriptura and the Appeal to Scripture in Ethical Questions [Die Reformatoriese Sola Scriptura en die Skrifberoep in Etiese Vrae]*, written by Professor Willem Daniël Jonker ("Willie") Jonker from Stellenbosch University.[27]

The document, though still relatively moderate at the time it first appeared (1979), shows a strong tendency toward reducing sola Scriptura to "narrower" personal sanctification issues. The reason was that social ethics must deal with the intimidating verities of the physical and social sciences. It specifically addresses and then questions whether the application of Scripture to the social spheres, as Kuyperians would apply them, is appropriate at all.

---

25 S&S 2.3, "Scopus of the Scripture."

26 S&S, 2.1, 2.7, 2.6.

27 KLAS-WK [Western Cape Regional Synod], *Die Reformatoriese Sola Scriptura en die Skrifberoep in Etiese Vrae* [The Reformational Sola Scriptura and the Appeal to Scripture in Ethical Questions] [Reformational] (Wellington, South Africa: NG Kerk-Uitgewers, 1980), https://williejonker.co.za/20110901-2/.

104   WHEN A THEOLOGICAL SHIFT CHANGED A NATION

It asked "whether the Scripture is also perspicuous and sufficient and necessary whenever we seek light in all the various areas of our lives, such as science, politics, economics, culture, and ethics" and whether "we can and must allow ourselves to be led in all these areas through the Scripture alone [sola Scriptura]? Is that the purpose of Scripture?" Certainly classic Calvinism, of which the DRC is an heir, answered these questions with a hearty yes! And certainly this includes the Neo-Calvinism of the maligned Kuyperians, which seems to be the interlocuter in the background. To the contrary, however, "the commission is convinced that the Scripture offers the final . . . answer for all religious questions (in the narrower meaning of the word)." Nevertheless, taking back what is just stated, Scripture does speak to modern "ethical questions" but in a "markedly more complicated" manner than "specific religious questions." In addition to reversing classic and Neo-Calvinist insights, it retreats to a typical dualism distinguishing between core and periphery or form and content dualities. "As soon as it deals with the social ethic, in which the sanctification of the society in its various contexts is dealt with, it becomes more difficult because such things as science, culture, politics and economics are introduced."[28]

In effect, this actually denies the infallibility of Scripture and the Reformational teaching on the sufficiency of Scripture in every area that it speaks. And it does speak clearly without question to social and cultural areas as the Lord, Paul, and the other NT writers often stress (e.g., Mt 5:17–20; Rom 3:31, 7:12, 13:8–10, 15:4; 1 Cor 5:3, 10:6, 11; 1 Ti 1:8–11; Tm 3:16–17). It seems to be a variant form of social antinomianism.

---

28   KLAS-WK, *Reformational*, conclusions, 5.2, 5.3, 5.8.

· 6 ·

APPLYING THE SCRIPTURE ALONE PRINCIPLE TO C&S

Sola Scriptura Denied by Key C&S Theologians

As was discussed in the first chapter, several internationally respected scholars have noted a shift by important DRC theologians in the doctrine of Scripture.

DRC Theologians Document Paradigm Shift. A good example was, Professor Ferdinand Deist, although not a member of a DRC seminary, was a professor in the Department of Ancient Near Eastern Studies at the prestigious University of Stellenbosch. He was a DRC member and a major leader of those within the DRC propagating the anti-reformed paradigm shift in Scripture that has occurred.[1] In 1986, the year the first edition of C&S appeared, he approvingly stated that

> the fact that younger ministers and lecturers now stand up publicly and claim that contradictions and even errors occur in the Bible, that Moses did not write the first

---

1 Deist himself denies that sola Scriptura includes inerrancy: Ferdinand Deist, *Kan ons die Bybel dan nog Glo: Onderweg na 'n Gereformeerde Skrifbeskouing* [Can We Still Believe the Bible? Underway to a Reformed View of Scripture] [Can We Still Believe] (Pretoria: J. L. van Schaik, 1986).

106   WHEN A THEOLOGICAL SHIFT CHANGED A NATION

five books of the Bible, that Isaiah wrote only a part of the book of Isaiah and another part of the book came into being only after the Babylonian Captivity, that the book of Daniel came into being only in the 2nd century B.C. and that such a book as Jonah probably is not based on historical material (to only use Old Testament illustrations)—such things are experienced by the younger generation as a necessary contribution to the understanding of the Bible. The older generation, on the other hand, felt that all these teachings were an attack on the authority of the Scripture and upon the faithfulness, infallibility and inspiration of the Bible. In short, it was seen as an attack on everything that was believed and proclaimed about the Bible up to this point.[2]

Deist wrote other volumes on the doctrine of Scripture and the relationship of Scripture to society, claiming that Scripture gives no certain, unambiguous answers for the basic questions of contemporary social theology, inter alia inter-ethnic relations, economics, and political difficulties.

J. J. F. Durand, then a member of the Dutch Reformed Mission Church's theological faculty in Cape Town, also recognized that there had indeed been a paradigm shift in the understanding of Scripture among DRC theologians before publication of C&S. He approvingly believed that the source was Barthian theology and that Marxian social analysis was kept at bay until the late 1960s. The chief antagonist holding both back was a strongly inerrantist Kuyperian theology and its "sphere sovereignty" social analysis. In "Church and State in South Africa: Karl Barth vs. Abraham Kuyper," Durand claims that a major paradigm shift occurred in hermeneutical principles as the younger DRC theologians had adopted the New Hermeneutic as advocated in the Barthian-influenced circle of theologians.

Durand wrote first concerning the Kuyperian resistance: "From the beginning of the 1930s to the end of the 1950s, Barthian theology had such a formidable opponent in Kuyperianism that it was never able to obtain a firm foothold in the field of Afrikaner theological thinking." The DRC consensus rejected Barth's neo-orthodox views about Scripture only containing the word of God but not being God's very word in written form. Only in the 1960s and early 1970s, he continued, did this paradigm begin to shift with a growing Barthian backlash that "began to take hold among young Afrikaner theologians and new thoughts with a definite Barthian flavour made significant inroads into the debate on church and society." This flowed together with a paradigm shift in how to interpret Scripture that only contained God's word: "[Can] theologians drawing on the Bible . . . make meaningful pronouncements about

2 Deist, *Can We Still Believe*, 1.

APPLYING THE SCRIPTURE ALONE PRINCIPLE TO C&S   107

any subject, given the historical gap between biblical times and the present." This issue, Durand believed, must consider "the respective influences of Barthian and Kuyperian theology on the issue of the relationship between state and church in South Africa."[3]

In another work coauthored with Professor D. J. Smit, Durand developed this theme further concerning the time period from disciplining process against Professor Johannes Du Plessis process to the 1960s. He claimed that "it was always the more Kuyperian oriented theologians and . . . students who took up the case" against those in the DRC that wanted to follow "Du Plessis's apparently liberal and non-orthodox standpoint." The reason for this was, he suggested wrongly I believe, that "it was actually impossible for a South African Kuyperian suddenly to appear as an opponent of the theological and political developments of the day," that is the development of Apartheid as a legally enforced comprehensive social ideal. The reason, he stated, "is the idea that the Word of God contained eternal and unchangeable norms or principles for the totality of life together with a very biblicistic approach to the Bible in which little respect is shown for the context and historical situation," code words for higher critical influenced exegesis. All inerrantist, Reformed-Evangelicals hold that contextual and historical factors must be taken into account. But these factors do not imply accepting the consensually assured results of higher critical scholars with their evolutionary and methodologically atheist presuppositions.

However, for those who held to the New Hermeneutic and the Barthian view of Scripture, Kuyperianism was abhorrent. Higher Critical theory, which Barth and his followers blithely accepted seemingly without sound reflection upon the other side of the issue, read into Scripture modernity-bound philosophical presuppositions. These included such biblically alien concepts as "the modern skeptical scholar knows better than the scientifically naïve, pre-modern Hebrews knew and wrote down about." However, these original authors witnessed events first-hand and wrote down at that time what happened under the guidance of the Holy Spirit. These processes the Higher Critical Movement vehemently rejected then and still today. They alone knew, so they thought, who actually penned the Pentateuch, for example, and that it was passed after many generations. On the other hand, Scripture writers, including those who

---

3   J. J. F. Durand, "Church and State in South Africa: Karl Barth vs. Abraham Kuyper," in *On Reading Karl Barth in South Africa*, ed. Charles Villa-Vicencio (Grand Rapids: Eerdmans, 1988), 122.

108 WHEN A THEOLOGICAL SHIFT CHANGED A NATION

faithfully recorded our Lord's words and opinions, uniformly held to Mosaic authorship as even a cursory reading of both Testaments demonstrates.

When a denomination rejects the Reformational sola Scriptura principle that the Kuyperians thoughtfully followed, then any modern or postmodern ideology can be read into Scripture. This has been occurring with quickening tempo in the DRC of the late twentieth and twenty-first centuries with its adoption of such anti-Scriptural concepts as LGBTQ+ ideology. Certainly, Durand and Smit correctly warned about accepting every principle claimed to be biblical: "When certain principles are first accepted as being Biblical, the rejection of these principles can easily be seen as a rejection of the Bible itself."[4] However, the way forward was not to reject the principles of creation designnorms and biblical authority in every sphere of life in the first place. Instead, DRC theologians should have built a critique of apartheid theology, mission theory, and social application using the very principles of Scripture alone, such as what I am advocating is this volume and in *The Concept of Ethnicity in the Bible: A Theological Analysis*.[5]

For example, the elite *Stellenbosch Theological Journal* includes recent articles stating that excluding the Queer community from full participation in every aspect of ecclesial life robs them of full humanity. Theologians in the twenty-first century RSA as in the USA now argue that just as white racism and apartheid robbed brown and black Americans and South Africans of their full human dignity so cisgender heterosexual identity does the same. Internal critiques from within the DRC clergy now include active attempts to include the Queer community with an explicit movement away from the "white male"—exactly the same as is occurring in the European Union and North America. Louis R. Van der Riet, and Cobus G. J. Van Wyngaard wrote in 2021:

> It is increasingly evident that modern conceptions of the human—including those explicitly named as Christian—have centred around the white male, and that something different from a mere expansion of the human to include female, queer or black bodies would be required. [6]

4 J. J. F. Durand and D. J. Smit, eds., *Teks Binne Konteks 1: Versamelde Opstelle oor Kerk en Politiek* [Texts within Contexts 1: Collected Essays on Church and Politics] (Cape Town: University of the Western Cape, n.d.), 166–7.

5 Kreitzer, *The Concept of Ethnicity*.

6 Louis R. Van der Riet and Cobus G. J. Van Wyngaard, "The Other Side of Whiteness: The Dutch Reformed Church and the Search for a Theology of Racial Reconciliation in the Afterlife of Apartheid," *Stellenbosch Theological Journal* 7, no. 1 (2021): 1–25, http://dx.doi.org/10.17570/stj.2021.v7n1.t2.

APPLYING THE SCRIPTURE ALONE PRINCIPLE TO C&S 109

Clearly, at present, the standards of modernity ("modern conceptions")—actually active postmodernity—have replaced sola Scriptura as the final standard of life and practice. This is the penultimate outworking of Paul's prophetic proclamation concerning the idolatrous nations (Rom 1:18–32) and of the DRC course begun in the paradigm shift that C&S represented. A culture in total collapse with values totally opposite of those found in Scripture is the last stage. The last step is "the crack of doom," as Cornelius Van Til stated and Paul affirms in the second chapter of Romans. There is no partiality with our Creator (Rom 2:5–11).

Further Examples of DRC Professors' Paradigm Shifts

Professor Pieter Potgieter, UOVS theologian and 1990 General Synod moderator. Pieter Potgieter followed his father, F. J. M. Potgieter, as a professor of Theology in the DRC. However, unlike his father, Potgieter equates inerrancy with the Barthian misunderstanding that infallibility mandated a merely mechanical theory of inspiration. This he caricaturizes as the doctrine of absolute fault-lessness (*foutloosheid*) in the original manuscripts. Instead, a more accurate term that is less pejorative is errorlessness, without error, or inerrancy (*feiloosheid*). Now certainly, there are grammatical "errors" or "faults" most likely deliberately brought into the text by those who wrote them so as to accurately describe circumstances and relationships. A ready example that comes to mind is when John records Jesus as stating that the Spirit, neuter in the Greek, was a personal, masculine "he" and not an impersonal "it." That is a grammatical error but an actual theological fact. Such a caricature of "faultlessness" is not what the important orthodox Reformed fathers meant by "infallibility" (the Scripture is not able to err), and more recently "inerrancy" (the Scripture does not ever err). As R. C. Sproul wrote: "The Bible provides information about every area of life, such as mathematics or physics." I would add also cosmology, geographic and geological history, and redemptive history as well. Infallibility, he concludes, "affirms that what the Bible teaches, it teaches infallibly."[7]

Potgieter's account, consequently, of how errors are explained demonstrates that he has not taken to heart nor understood much of the extensive

---

7 Sproul, *Scripture Alone*, 21; See, e.g.: (1) Norman L. Geisler, William C. Roach, with a Foreword by J. I. Packer, *Defending Inerrancy: Affirming the Accuracy of Scripture for a New Generation* (Grand Rapids: Baker, 2012); (2) Gregory K. Beale, *The Erosion of Inerrancy in Evangelicalism: Responding to New Challenges to Biblical Authority* (Wheaton, IL: Crossway, 2008); (3) Norman Geisler, ed., *Inerrancy* (Grand Rapids: Zondervan, 1980).

evangelical and Reformed, literature on the subject, not even that from the pen of his own father, F. J. M. Potgieter. Pieter Potgieter describes the carefully developed doctrine or verbal organic inspiration as a "mechanical doctrine": "The advocates ... do not want to recognize that the human writers of the Bible have any independent role in the inscripturation of the Word." Instead of being truly human organisms with unique vocabulary, style, and circumstance, "they were merely instruments in the hand of the Holy Spirit, through whom He literally caused to be written word for word that which He spoke to them." He claims that this implies further that "In the Bible, there can be no single fault of whatever type due to the human factor. As the Word of God, the Bible is, in the original autographs ..., not only infallible but without fault." In other words, even such clearly "apparent errors such as different accounts of the same event by different Biblical authors," they must be explained away virtually mindlessly "as a transmission error in the later copies of the original manuscripts." Here again, he fails to interact with the huge literature of biblical faithful scholars. Potgieter concludes: "Such 'faults/errors' in the autographs would mean that the Holy Spirit made an error and that, naturally, cannot occur."[8] The biblically orthodox scholars of the previous era where certainly quite aware of all of this and, though not yet being able to solve every conundrum, certainly made much progress in this. It would have been wiser to build upon these scholars instead of blindly pursuing a heady new direction toward what now happening in the New South Africa.

Last, Potgieter falsely equates infallibility as inerrancy with a sectarian "fundamentalism," again a movement he does not understand nor interact with. However along with some of his colleagues at the time, he uses the moniker as a pejorative cudgel to discredit those holding to classic DRC infallibility doctrine such as his own distinguished father held to. He was a very distinguished Dogmatics Professor, F. J. M. Potgieter, whom I had the privilege to interact with in his retirement in Stellenbosch, South Africa. I also personally experienced his son's strong disapproval when I served as the Head of Research and Communication in an official commission of all three DRC sisters Churches, CERCOS. The Centre for Reformed and Contemporary Studies, based in Pretoria in the late 1980s and early 1990s was a Broederbond[9] connected, but also remaining a Kuyperian research center. CERCOS, led by

---

8 Pieter C. Potgieter, *Skrif, Dogma en Verkondiging* [Scripture, Dogma, and Proclamation] [Scripture and Dogma] (Cape Town: Lux Verbi, 1990), 19.

9 "Afrikaner-Broederbond," Britannica, accessed August 3, 2023, https://www.britannica.com/topic/Afrikaner-Broederbond.

APPLYING THE SCRIPTURE ALONE PRINCIPLE TO C&S 111

the late Dr. Christiaan L. Jordaan, rejected classic apartheid discrimination while also holding to a strong view of biblical infallibility and application of Scripture to all areas of life. We were attempting to educate the Afrikaner members in the three largest Dutch Reformed "sisters" denominations about the ideological attack upon both the churches and the country.[10]

However, the son, Professor Pieter Potgieter, disapprovingly writes against this classic Kuyperian viewpoint: "A fatal fundamentalistic approach is to make the infallibility of the Scripture equivalent to a Bible without factual error in the sense of scientific exactness."[11] Certainly, this paradigm shift opens the door to destroy a Scripture-based culture and ecclesial life—Church and Society, as has been occurring over the last forty-plus years in South Africa. He gives no parameters as to what "scientific exactness" means at all and no check on "scientism," the doctrine that positivist-empiricist human science trumps every clear description of geological, biological, cosmological description in any Scripture whatsoever. Open even a crack in the door to this idolatry and eventually, it happens everywhere in every denomination, culture degenerates to the last stage of Romans 1. That last stage is a "disapproved" or as older translations state, a "depraved mind" that pushes the Creator totally out of an individual's and culture's thinking processes and community life. He becomes totally unnecessary in every area of life with the resulting moral chaos bringing God wrath (Rom 1:21–3, 28–32, 2:1–16). A better way forward is the "Chicago Statement on Biblical Inerrancy."[12]

Johan Heyns, University of Pretoria Dogmatics Professor. Another clear example of the influence of Karl Barth through G. C. Berkouwer is that of the very influential DRC Professor Johan Heyns. He was Professor of Theology at Pretoria, moderator of the DRC's watershed 1986 General Synod, and member of the commission which wrote C&S. Though he rejects Barth's terminology, Barth's influence can be seen in several of Heyns' works such as his volume on

---

10 See, for example, the bilingual basic edition of the following work, C. L. Jordaan and M. R. Kreitzer, *'n Manifes vir Christene in Suiderlike Afrika* [A Manifesto for Christian in Southern Africa] (Pretoria: Christian Action Africa, 1991).

11 Potgieter, *Scripture and Dogma*, 31.

12 R. C. Sproul and Norman Geisler, *Explaining Biblical Inerrancy: The Chicago Statement on Biblical Inerrancy, Hermeneutics and Application with Official ICBI Commentary* (Arlington, TX: The International Council on Biblical Inerrancy/Bastion, 2013).

For a Kuyperian DRC viewpoint before Karl Barth's influence, C. J. H. De Wet, "Bybelgeloof—Bybelkritiek—Bybelfoute" [Biblical Faith—Biblical [Higher] Criticism—Biblical Errors], in *Koers in die Krisis* [Course in the Crisis], ed. H. G. Stoker and F. J. M. Potgieter (Stellenbosch: Pro Ecclesia, 1935), 1:89ff.

112   WHEN A THEOLOGICAL SHIFT CHANGED A NATION

the doctrine of Scripture, entitled *Brug tussen God en Mens* [Bridge between God and Man] (1976) or his later *Dogmatiek* [Dogmatics] (1978). A concise example of this neo-orthodox view of Scripture is found in "Bible, Church and Proclamation," originally presented at the Reformed Ecumenical Synod's 1972 conference on "Scripture and Its Authority" held in Sydney, Australia.[13] Because Heyns was such a powerful leader of the change movement in the DRC, this last-named article, along with references to his other works, serves as a commentary on relevant sections of C&S, for example on sections 13–23.

First, Heyns rejects verbal inspiration and the Reformed organic doctrines of Scripture because they show "mechanical traits," again that Barthian calumny.[14] In contrast to these and other theories, he propounds a "dialogical inspiration theory": Scripture is a dialogue between God and man,[15] a theory profoundly influenced ultimately by Barth.

According to this theory, the first dialogue was between the seers and the Divine Spirit. They reacted with obedience to that revelation as *best they could*. In the process of obedience, the prophets have irrevocably changed and sifted the word in their act of receiving and writing it. Thus we do not receive a pure inerrant word in the Bible but a human interpretation of the original revelation: "God's first pure and naked Word which he gave these writers and which they alone heard, we do not possess, for the simple reason that we are not the writers of the Bible." The Bible, then, is merely the writers' response ". . . to God's Word and their answer has become God's word to us." The result of this dialogical view of inspiration is that the Bible merely contains words of God mixed with the fallible interpretations and culturally bound fallacies of men, a Barthian conceptualization: "The words of the Bible remain the words of men, sought by men, and found by men. However, in and among these words which remain words of men, the Word of God is present."[16]

The Holy Spirit never "violently overwhelmed" the prophets so as to eliminate "all typically human characteristics and activities." Hence, Scripture authors wrote in thought patterns and limited pre-scientific images of their day. They were not "changed from pre-scientific observers of the world around

---

13   Johan A. Heyns, "Bible, Church and Proclamation," in *Scripture and Its Authority: Conference papers, RES Conference on Scripture, Sydney 1972* [Bible Church]. *International Reformed Bulletin* 54 (1973).

14   See, e.g., Heyns, *Bridge*, 1976, 48, 55.

15   Johan A. Heyns, *Dogmatiek* [Dogmatics] (Pretoria: N.G. Kerkboekhandel Transvaal, 1978), 21.

16   Heyns, *Dogmatics*, 38.

APPLYING THE SCRIPTURE ALONE PRINCIPLE TO C&S   113

them to the [*sic*] scientific researchers." Instead of being scientific researchers, the Scripture writers made fallible "use of certain naive, contemporary and thus limited conceptions about the world, . . . [with which] they gave . . . testimony to God." This testimony is "unmistakably characteristic of the time of its origin and inevitably influenced by the cultural and spiritual life of the East."[17]

Because of this "dialogic structure of the origin of the Bible," the issues of infallibility and truthfulness are beside the point: "It is clear that the Bible is a book of purpose and destiny; . . . the matter of non-authenticity or untrustworthiness is irrelevant." He further states that the central message (scopus) of the Bible is the kingdom of God. The scopus of the Kingdom is God's revelation in Jesus Christ. The consequence is that the peripheral data, that is "the historical and cosmic information in the Bible is not in itself . . . of any importance."[18]

Peripheral information, he believes, can be erroneous, but that does not affect the truth of the message, he claims. "The Bible, then, has authority, yet it is not directly normative to us in all matters."[19] In other words, Heyns claims that only the central "spiritual" message is truly normative. The peripheral subjects, therefore, cannot provide clear and unchanging models or standards with respect to science, sociology, psychology, history, political science, nor inter-ethnic relationships *except* for spiritual principles related to the central scopus, the kingdom: "Generally speaking, one can say that the writers were not primarily interested in the nature of things but chiefly in their relation towards God and His relation towards them."[20]

F. Klopper, an Old Testament scholar at the University of South Africa (UNISA) gives the logical consequence of this dialogical view. She writes, for example, that "In modern society it is not possible to rest findings for or against capital punishment solely upon Scriptural testimony," for example. Instead, she rests her view of the social application of Scripture on "a relational view of Scripture" that "takes into account [that] the text is historically determined" as defined by Higher Critical scholars, and "was meant to fulfil a particular function in an ancient society and was therefore written from a perspectivist view on reality." In other words, this viewpoint that is very similar to Heyns,

17   Heyns, *Dogmatics*, 39.
18   Heyns *Dogmatics*, 40, 42.
19   Heyns, *Bible Church*, 44.
20   Heyns *Dogmatics*, 40.

114   WHEN A THEOLOGICAL SHIFT CHANGED A NATION

"denies that Scriptural norms are directly applicable to all times and in every situation."[21]

This is similar, though not exactly the same sort of conclusion to which C&S comes with respect to socio-political models. Certainly, however, continental and DRC Kuyperian and North American inerrantist scholars consider "ancient society" and the context but still see in every word of God a word that speaks "Today," just as the author of Hebrews saw the ancient Psalm speaking directly to his contemporary context (see Heb 3:7, 4:7; Ps 95:7). In other words, to acquiesce or worse to totally capitulate to biblical errancy and its corollaries, biblical non-objectivity and lack of perspicuity even when the text is clear, is to devastate any attempt at forming a truly biblical world and life view. This perspective, then, rejects a biblical missiology, a biblical social theology, and a truly biblical social ethic exactly as the C&S document does, which Johan Heyns fostered. Without such a biblical world and life view, the "course of this age" as it is controlled by dark spiritual powers (Eph 2:1–2) forces its way onto the agenda of any denomination, as has been exceedingly evident since at least 1980 in the DRC.

A. B. Du Toit: UP New Testament professor. The last example is Andrie B. Du Toit, DRC New Testament professor also at the University of Pretoria. He published a highly inaccurate article in the Afrikaans press entitled "Fundamentalism." In the beginning of this article, he claims that his way is a via media between both nineteenth-century Higher Critical-dominated theological liberalism and the twentieth-century reaction, fundamentalism. That "middle" way, generally, has been the Neo-orthodoxy led by Karl Barth. Both movements, he claims, are problematic and are causing confusion among Christians. Fundamentalism, he reports accurately, was a reaction against liberal theology and that the leaders "defended a number" of "fundamental convictions." Among these "were the inspiration of Scripture, the divine nature of Christ, the virgin birth, redemption from sin, creation not evolution, etc."[22]

However, he further inaccurately claimed that fundamentalists force a historical novelty upon the theological scene that "doesn't do justice to what the Bible is ... namely a religious book in which God speaks his perfect Gospel

---

21 F. Kloppers, "Skrifgebruik in die Beoordeling van Uitsprake oor die Doodstraf [The use of Scripture and the judgment of sayings concerning the death penalty]," *Skrif en Kerk* 11, no. 2 (1990): 174.

22 Andrie B. Du Toit, "Fundamentalisme: Konsep van Onfeilbaarheid op Bybel Afgedruk" [Fundamentalism: Concept of Infallibility Forced upon the Bible]" [Fundamentalism], *Beeld* (Johannesburg, RSA), November 26, 1991, 12.

word through fallible people in their specific historical situation and in a truly human manner." In other words, for the "fundamentalists," again notice that pejorative, "infallibility means that the Bible contains no errors at all and that the Bible books are timeless documents that place everyone on the same level." Again, inaccurately, he writes that these sectarians find biblical "dictums [that] can be immediately applied to our [then contemporary] situation." The reason, again, is the same calumny: "The historical situation as well as the unique character, and the special defined kind of literature of Biblical books are never earnestly taken into consideration."[23]

Clenching his case, Du Toit uses another logical fallacy, Guilt by Association. He connects inerrantist fundamentalists with those who must enforce ceremonial-dietary laws as well as believe in "seven day creationism" [*sic*] and premillennialism. They, in turn, must also force women to wear hats and be totally silent in church. No European, Oceanic, or African inerrantist-evangelical scholar would see themselves in this classic "straw man" type argument, which does not consider the voluminous literature to the contrary.[24] No connection even existed between inerrancy and chiliastic premillennial doctrines. Dutch Reformed developers of inerrancy, for example Kuyper and Bavinck, were amillennialists and the American Presbyterian developers Charles Hodge and B. B. Warfield were postmillennialists. Du Toit's comments summarized the inaccurate lack of scholarship, or worse, defamatory hostility that helped produce the paradigm shift in viewpoint on Scripture among DRC leaders. That change remains to this day (2023).

Specific Application to C&S

As we shall see below, Potgieter, Heyns, and Du Toit's views cracked the door to be pushed wide open by world ecumenical forces antithetical to whole Bible application of tôranic wisdom to all areas of life such as Abraham Kuyper, albeit imperfectly, advocated. This paradigm shift was not the way forward into a realm of peace and justice in the Kingdom of God as some might have thought. It pushed in the opposite direction from which our Lord causes his true people to escape when he rescues them from the "domain of darkness" and transfers them into "the kingdom of his beloved Son" (Col 1:13).

23 Du Toit, *Fundamentalism*, 12.
24 Du Toit, *Fundamentalism*, 12.

C&S' Noble Attempt to Maintain Biblical Authority

C&S' did make a noble attempt to see the Bible as relevant for all of life and as "the church's sole yardstick," a Kuyperian theme.

> **1.2 The Bible is the church's sole yardstick.** We believe and confess that Holy Scripture is the complete revelation of God, authoritative revelation for all time. Thus for us it is the sole yardstick by which all standpoints, attitudes and actions in the South African situation must be tested.
>
> **This means** . . . that . . . we need to study Scripture carefully and correctly, in order to determine what message and mandate comes to us out of the Word and how we must apply it in our own situation.
>
> We must constantly be on our guard that no other voice, however appealing or beguiling—be it that of a particular ideology, school of thought, political trend, tradition, personal bias, national sentiment, or whatever—speaks decisively to us above or alongside the truth of the Bible.
>
> . . . .
>
> The new covenant proclaims that through Jesus Christ, God has reconciled the world to himself. Furthermore, that he has brought together in his church all those who believe in him and have accepted the message, giving them the vocation to serve him as king in all spheres of life, and to be a blessing to the world until that day when he brings all things to consummation.[25]

Now, read in the light of classic sola Scriptura doctrine, these paragraphs appear accurate and sound. However, these words sound like an empty shell of the once robust DRC affirmations of biblical authority when several factors are considered.

First of all, the emphasis on the "humanity" of the Bible and the New Hermeneutic within the DRC should be recognized as the underlying premise behind the following words: "specific nature, context, style, purpose and historical situation."[26] This passage could then presuppose the neo-orthodox and classic liberal emphasis upon the errors and fallibility of the packaging around the central scopus of the Word as we have seen. The door is opened by ambiguity to a deceiving double interpretation as some critics correctly saw. For example, DRC theologian and apartheid-defending politician A. P. Treurnicht, a former Broederbond Chairman and a Kuyperian, cited several clear cases of

---

25 C&S, 13–15, 20; emphasis in original.
26 C&S, 17.

APPLYING THE SCRIPTURE ALONE PRINCIPLE TO C&S   117

C&S paragraphs in crucial sections that "leave room for a double interpretation."[27]

For example, it claimed that because the Bible is a fallible human witness of God's word, "one may not read into the Bible our own circumstances and problems, thus reducing the Word of God to a contemporary recipe book with instant solutions for all human problems."[28] Certainly, on the one hand, C&S was correct here. An interpreter must be very careful to not read into Scripture a contemporary context. On the other hand, one could understand in this C&S passage that the text of Scripture is relative. In other words, it is only a witness of the dialogue between God and man, as Heyns asserted, and has no supra-cultural and pan-temporal relevance anywhere in its pages. In other words, no certain word that can be applied to contemporary culture can be taken from it. The reason is simple. Fallible humans wrote Scripture in a pre-scientific context with the erroneous worldview of a long-lost era. Hence there remains a major gap between the cultures of that day and today which strongly undermines any contemporary application.

A further implication could be derived from C&S that human interpreters cannot take *any* of the truths of the Bible at face value. For example, the creation of male and female with Adam as the leader and Eve as the Helper cannot be used to justify binary marriages and deny gay and lesbian or for that matter polygamist rights (as has been asserted in RSA at present). Presupposing error in the packaging of Scripture truth must also cast grave doubt on *any* doctrinal truth surrounded by the packaging. How do we know what is the Lord's word and man's interpretative and fallible words? The Lord's words cut to the core of the issue: He who can be trusted in very little can also be trusted in much and he who is unfaithful and dishonest in small things cannot be trusted with larger things (Lk 16:10). Certainly for infallibilist scholars all of this does pose difficulty but they are not insurmountable ones because over the centuries many such problems have been solved.

27 Treurnicht summarizes this in a letter to official DRC newsletter, *Kerbode*: A. P. Treurnich, "Apartheidsbesluit Gee Probleme [The Decision on Apartheid Is Problematic]," *Die Kerkbode*, November 29, 1991.

28 C&S, 18.

Attack on Certainty Applied

Secondly, Barthian-influenced dialectical theology leads to confessional ambiguity. Barth was notorious for asserting and denying the same proposition.[29] This ambiguity is also true of C&S. This is one of the biggest complaints of both inclusivist theologians such as Charles Villa-Vicencio and Johann Kinghorn, and traditional "apartheid" theologians such as A. P. Treurnicht.[30] All agree that C&S is ambiguous and even contradictory in several key paragraphs.[31]

Neo-orthodox or dialectical theology, consequently, inevitably leads directly to a dualistic dilemma: The Bible is both authoritative in all areas but yet is an exclusively "spiritual message of spiritual redemption." Therefore, it is "not a political manual from which specific political models can be deduced."[32] This teaching makes the Bible merely a vague book with nonspecific "principles and norms" into which theologians can read a man-created ecumenical agenda. C&S purposefully disallows specific models, blueprints and unchanging practical standards derived from the Word. These are necessary to help struggling modern men out of the morass into which humanist-influenced theology has caused them to sink.

C&S therefore denies that the Christian exegete can ever find a solid socio-political or even ecclesiastical model valid for all times and all places. "Scripture is not a political manual from which specific political models can be deduced."[33] In other words, grounds for unity come out of negotiations that have no necessary foundation in Scripture-derived principles, such as Kuyper would have described it: "The structures in which this unity ['one church bond' between DRC family of churches] are to be expressed, is at this stage not clear." That will be determined through discussions with the parties concerned.[34]

In other words, the synodal-presbyterial form of government for church and civil orders, deduced from Scripture by an earlier generation of Reformed exegetes, is no longer transculturally valid. All that remains are generalized thoughts about love, justice, and dignity that are not necessarily derived from Scripture Alone. C&S continues the thought: "Scripture proclaims norms

---

29 See Klaas Runia, *Karl Barth's Doctrine of Holy Scripture* (Eugene, OR: Wipf and Stock, 2018).

30 See, e.g., inclusivists: Villa-Vicencio, *Safe Synod*; Kinghorn, *Home for Everyone*. Note also, A. P. Treurnicht, "Insertion," *OMSENDBRIEF* (November 28, 1991).

31 E.g., C&S, 274–88, on apartheid; 13–15 with 19–23, etc.

32 See C&S, 19, 274.

33 C&S, 274.

34 C&S, 236.

APPLYING THE SCRIPTURE ALONE PRINCIPLE TO C&S 119

and principles such as love, justice, human dignity and peace which must be embodied in society." However, this is virtually vacuous because it immediately states: "Therefore the church may not prescribe political models to the government, but by virtue of its prophetic function the church will continue to test every existing and proposed political model against the Biblical principles and norms."[35] In other words, the prophetic voice cannot tell the "king" that his confiscation of private property held by generations of forefathers is evil and worthy of God's just judgment as did Elijah (1 Kgs 21). Nor can a prophetic voice ever say with certain authority that a centralized imperialist state is evil as did the Prophets of Israel (Is 10:1–14, 25; Jer 4:7–8, 5:14–17, 6:22–3; Hb 1:7, 2:4–5, 9–10, 12, 17; Na 1:15).

C&S, then, seems to be truly self-contradictory. Abstract principles and norms can be deduced from Scripture, but not specific models. A vivid contrast to this approach to Scripture is Reformed, biblical orthodoxy's firm and unwavering "Thus says the Lord God of hosts." Reformed orthodoxy's humble, yet clear trumpet call to trusting and obedient action is based on the presupposition of a clear Word (perspicuity) that hears the commands of God in the inerrant words of Scripture and the logical deductions that can and must spring from these words.

The above statements from C&S, thus, seem to assume a drastically limited scopus of Scripture. Second, C&S seems to reject the logical-deductive method of classic Reformed theology. One major consequence of this dialectical reduction of biblical authority is that C&S seems to indicate truth cannot be directly expressed in propositions and deductions from propositions. One can only experience biblical truth as a sense of awe and reverence, such as Barth seemed to be saying. That awesome feeling, however, can never arrive at any real objective comprehension of truth, in any exact form, nor real actions springing from repentant trust.

C&S must be read in the light of this neo-Orthodox theological background. In the following passage, at least superficially, C&S seems to be teaching a truly biblical humility. However, considering the dialogical and dialectical war on certainty through the New Hermeneutic and other neo-orthodox directions, these paragraphs give a justification for a complete paradigm shift away from the older logical-deductive method of finding truth. This shift, again, changed the nation of South Africa drastically. No theological

35 C&S, 275.

deduction, hence is final: "In this seeking after God's will we cannot afford the luxury of regarding our reflections as final at any particular stage."

The document supports this with the following reasoning some are true and some not: "Believers have to keep on growing in a better understanding of God's will." The reason is that "we live in a dynamic situation which is continually changing; . . . the validity of previous pronouncements has to be continually tested," again true. It then concludes: "The insights . . . of other churches . . . induces us to think again and so to come to a richer and deeper understanding of God's will."[36]

However, this document provides no means to discover a cross-culturally valid standard based upon sound exegesis. However, God's character does determine his will, and he is above all cultures and never changes. Consequently, his will is valid in every culture. Certainly, it is good to listen to other true believer's and church's insights. I advocate strongly for this. But to kowtow to them to curry favor so as to be accepted into arrogant anti-biblical world ecumenical circles is evil. These circles were championing then and still are at present perversions that are directly against God's creation design-norms.

For example, could the DRC using the principles of C&S speak unwavering Scripture truth against the perversion of Robert Mugabe's Marxist movement taking over Zimbabwe? Or would it acquiesce to the world consensus and term his movement good and advancing the Kingdom of God as some WCC notables notoriously did at that time? Would it speak with a clarion call to pray God's imprecation upon the State that permitted the perversion of same-sex marriage as the present RSA constitution does with the connivance of the then present DRC? Could it speak against the apartheid law allowing Zulu males to work in Johannesburg without their wives for months at a time as did the former regime?

Sadly, the Kuyperianism guiding the regime's prophets did not make a peep when that atrocity of a law passed Parliament. It could and should have. After all, intact families are a divine design norm! The result of no prophetic voice from the Lord as found in Scripture upon social evils in both the former and the present regime has led to drastic social and economic decline in RSA. No economy, for example, can thrive when corrupt State officials siphon off hundreds of millions of Rands allocated to build and maintain the power grid. Twelve hours of load shedding is common in 2022–3 in RSA. In Zimbabwe's case, no word from the Lord from the evangelical Churches has led to an

---

36 C&S, 8–12.

APPLYING THE SCRIPTURE ALONE PRINCIPLE TO C&S 121

almost total economic collapse. A paradigm shift did change the South African nation, but not for the good.

Sola Scriptura Implies Models Can Be Deduced from Scripture. Contrary to C&S, Reformed theologians, synods, and confessions have classically claimed that the doctrine of sola Scriptura results in a Bible of certain truths that can be applied to all areas of culture. Scripture, they historically taught, can be carefully searched and analyzed with the purpose of reaching certainty on many areas that it addresses. These certain areas have indeed included such social and physical science subjects as origin biology, economics, political science, social ethics, and inter-ethnic relations. The catechisms and confessions are full of socio-economic, political and cultural applications of biblical laws. For example, the Anglo-American Puritans, correctly deduced from Scripture the ideal of a Christocratic, republican form of government with no monarchy except Jesus, the Anointed King from heaven (Christ) (using, e.g., Dt 4:5–8; Jgs 9; 1 Sm 8–12; Hos 10:3–7, 13–15, 13:4, 9–11).

This is explicitly denied by C&S (1986), which states that the Bible is a virtual spiritual-platonic form with no direct and specific relevance to the details of modern culture:

> As the Book of God and His kingdom, the Bible is exclusively a "religious" book . . ..
> **This means** . . . that the Bible, because of the decisive spiritual character of its message, may not be used as a manual for solving social, economic or political problems. Consequently all present and previous attempts to read into the Bible a particular social or political policy . . . must be emphatically rejected.[37]

This paragraph in C&S (1986) so limited the scopus (focus) of Scripture that C&S (1990) removes the offending words. However, a similar de-particularizing of a very earthly and relevant biblical Christianity seems also to be described in the following corrective words of the 1990 C&S:

> **The Bible focuses on God and his Kingdom.** . . . The Bible as proclamation of God's Kingdom is not a textbook [*handboek*] on, inter alia, sociology, economics or politics. The Bible is the Good News that God in his grace seeks out human beings, alienated from him through their sin. He then redeems them, makes them his own, and entrusts them as his chosen people with a supreme calling.[38]

This is true if C&S means by the words "manual" or "textbook" "a systematized textbook of information on political or socio-economic models." Of

---

37 C&S 1986, 42–3; bold in original.
38 C&S 1990, 19, emphasis in original.

122   WHEN A THEOLOGICAL SHIFT CHANGED A NATION

course, the Bible is not that. Much systematization and exegesis must be done to discover biblical models and blueprints. However, as the words "manual" or "textbook/handbook" are so often used to mean "having no specific and practical relevance to a subject apart from general, spiritual principles," it is possible this is the meaning here. For example, some have said that biblical chronologies cannot be trusted because Scripture is not a "handbook of history." Or it is not a "handbook of origins science" because Genesis 1–2 "was never intended to provide lessons in biology, or tell us exactly what we must think about anthropogenesis." Such higher critical influenced biblical scholars "cannot even decide for us whether man came from a single or from several lines of origin" based on Scripture.[39]

However, assuming the rejection of sola Scriptura, as discussed above, C&S seems to imply a "blueprint-less," "model-less" Christianity for social and political transformation, contrary to the Neo-Calvinism of the Kuyperians and earlier streams that flowed out of the Genevan Reformation. Paradoxically, C&S correctly denied that the Bible is irrelevant. However, it again contradicted itself by rejecting, without any attempt at exegesis, some of the most relevant passages needed for developing a transforming social theological ethic for southern Africa. The reason, evidently, was that former Synods used these passages to justify the apartheid system of color-based discrimination *and* of partitioning the imperially designed State into ethnic units. The first, I vehemently reject on biblical grounds; the other I have a measured sympathy for on biblical grounds as we shall see.

In other words, C&S rejected those passages that would provide biblical support for the defense of the right to self-determination and independent ethno-cultural identities. What remained is the artificial British imperial ideal of a singular South African "national identity" to which the DRC capitulated. C&S canceled any other socio-political or economic system without discussion of other standpoints except that imperial ideal. In C&S's putative attempt to decolonize, ironically the colonialists were victorious. C&S gave up on at least one hundred years of the Boer's somewhat Christianized resistance to English imperialism in the following passage. Instead of becoming a light of the comprehensive Gospel to the surrounding nations (e.g., Is 42:6, 49:6, 51:4; Acts 13:47–8), for example, the Tswana, the Zulu, and the Xhosa, the Afrikaner theologians abandoned them to the Anglo-American, English dominated world hegemony.[40]

---

39 Verkuyl, *Break Down*, 23.

40 See prestigious Georgetown University Professor's books about UK/USA joint foreign policy, (1) Carroll Quigley, *The Anglo-American Establishment* (San Pedro, CA: GSG,

APPLYING THE SCRIPTURE ALONE PRINCIPLE TO C&S   123

This means . . . that the Bible, because of it's [*sic*] own nature and character may not be used as a manual for solving social, economic or political problems. Consequently all present and previous attempts to deduce a particular social or political policy from the Bible, whether it be apartheid or separate development or a policy of integration must be emphatically rejected; . . . that portions of the Bible such as Gen 2:18, 10–20, 11:1, 7–9, Deut 32:8, Pr 22:28; Matt 24:7, John 17:20–23, Acts 2:8, 17:26, 1 Cor 12, Gal 3:28–29 and Rev 21:3, 24 may therefore not be used as a Scriptural basis for political models.[41]

A basic question remains. How can Jesus exercise dominion and kingship over every sphere of life as C&S also claimed, if he does not have specific, just and wise words through which to rule therein? If we excise many relevant passages of the Bible, as paragraph 22 does, how can we say that a "policy document" is in any way based on a Reformed principle, which the sola Scriptura doctrine is? The DRC, in effect, proclaimed itself non-Reformed in this document, surreptitiously but truly. This was a monumental paradigm shift.

Final Summary

C&S seemed to desire to maintain the sola Scriptura principle that accepts Scripture is relevant to all of life. However, C&S is not consistent due to anti-biblical presuppositions coming from the actual rejection of its own classic sola Scriptura principle. These presuppositions reject the concept, rightly included in C&S, that "no other voice, however appealing or beguiling . . . [must] speak decisively to us above or alongside the truth of the Bible."[42]

To be fair, C&S genuinely desired to escape from the non-biblical rationalizations for coerced racial separateness that helped justify the Apartheid system. However, even granting this, its dialectical view of Scripture still did its corrupting work of gradually destroying consistency, specificity, and certainty. It is for this reason that C&S did not listen to the historical consensus of theologians, creeds, and synods concerning what the Scripture says about itself. Instead, in interacting with the contemporary and ever-changing critique of modern theologies, C&S syncretized many of their presuppositions into itself

---

1981) and (2) Carroll Quigley, *Tragedy and Hope: The History of the World of our Time* (New York: MacMillan/Dauphin, 1966/2014). See also, Abraham Kuyper, "The South African Crisis," in *Abraham Kuyper: A Centennial Reader*, ed. James D. Bratt (Grand Rapids: Eerdmans, 1998), 323–60.

41 C&S, 21–2.

42 C&S, 15.

WHEN A THEOLOGICAL SHIFT CHANGED A NATION

creating an at times covert and in other paragraphs an overt paradigm shift. I suggest that C&S is an example of an opposite form of syncretism from the syncretism of the older Kuyperian-influenced apartheid social theological paradigm.

Thus the beguiling voice of humanism's "particular ideology, school of thought, political trend, tradition, personal bias, national sentiment," with its then politically correct agenda, was the grave danger implicit within C&S. This will be progressively clearer as each chapter unfolds.

Therefore, in rejecting sola Scriptura, the DRC has not followed the voice of the Spirit of Christ, who only speaks Scripture truth in Synod decision. In this rejection, is not the DRC running the danger of returning to an institutional infallibility, to a synodocracy, against which some then clearly warned? Is a new priestly class, an enlightened elite, that are the ones who now mediate Scripture to the laity. Is Scripture no longer clear and hence should not be read, because a "naïve reading" would lead to abominations that the world conciliar movement condemned then and now. The following four decades have demonstrated that C&S's paradigm shift continually provided fuel to the fire that has been overthrowing so many verities of the past. I am not speaking about atrocities such as apartheid social discrimination but those never accepted by the consensus of the church throughout its many eras of existence that were based on sound biblical exegesis and not mere tradition. The overthrow of the biblical doctrine of creation and created design-norms were then and remain examples very relevant to this study. Overturning the prohibition of females and practicing homosexuals in church offices are merely results of this overthrow. This segues directly into the next chapter.

· 7 ·

THE CREATION RESTORATION PRINCIPLE AND C&S

Recapitulation and Restoration of Creation

Introduction

Redemptive history is not static but moves toward the unveiling of a restored and mature renewed creation order. God's creation began with a "very good" *creatio ex nihilo* (Gn 1:1). Next, God worked both directly and through human agents to develop this creation, resulting in growing differentiation (Gn 1:2–11:32). In the process of this growth came the Fall (Gn 3). Next, to prepare for the coming comprehensive restoration of the fallen creation, he chose Abraham's family (Gn 12). He then sent the law and the prophets and promised a final Davidic monarch. When the Davidic Anointed One came, the final stage arrived. Up to the present, God's holy people have been involved in the progressive application of Christ's finished work until the end.[1]

---

1   See Herman Dooyeweerd, *Roots of Western Culture: Pagan, Secular, and Christian Options* [Roots] (Jordan Station, ON: Paideia Press/Reformational Publishing Project, 2012); Wolters, *Regained*; Spykman, *Reformational*, 1992.

126   WHEN A THEOLOGICAL SHIFT CHANGED A NATION

A classic, reformed eschatology can be both long-term culturally optimistic and victorious in its outlook though it definitely does not have to be classic Postmillennial with its over-optimism and historicist view of the book of Revelation.[2] A Reformational scholar can also be amillennial and optimistic. On the other hand, paradoxically, it accepts a backward-looking, creationist perspective yet remains both forward-looking and socially progressive in a positive biblical sense. By this I emphatically do not mean that God is moving the earth forward to a socialist-globalist order of a boundary-less one-world system. Instead, God is moving progressively forward to the recapitulation of the creation in a matured form, a matured protology. In other words, Scripture expects a return to the first things, that is the creation design, in developed and maturing form.

Scripture further expects that all the ethno-linguistic people-groups of the earth will be discipled by believers in King Jesus our Lord. All then will mature step-by-step as they learn about and apply all the instructions of their covenanted Lord to all areas of life. The last enemy to be destroyed is death. Before that time of the Resurrection, the Lord Christ will conquer all his other enemies (1 Cor 15:20–8). After all, in the Reformational perspective, the commands disciples will learn begin with the Cultural Mandate of Genesis 1 and continue to the last command in Revelation 22:18–19. Consequently, the classic Reformed faith is a dynamic, whole Bible, and restorative faith. In other words, all that God created in the beginning will grow and be repeated and restored in the end in the completed work of Christ and his ongoing work of transforming the whole earth. As the only restorative, recapitulative faith, it looks to creation for its norms (e.g., Gn 2:2; Ex 20:8; Mt 19:4; 1 Cor 11:7–9; Col 1:15–16; 1 Tm 2:12–15). Christians fulfill the first Adam's mandate by means of the second Adam's Great Commission accomplished in the resurrection power of the Holy Spirit (Mt 28:17–20; Acts 1:8–9).

---

2 See classic, postmillennial: (1) Iain Murray, *The Puritan Hope: Revival and the Interpretation of Prophecy* [Puritan] (Edinburgh: Banner of Truth, 2014); (2) J. A. De Jong, *As the Waters Cover the Sea: Millennial Expectations in the Rise of Anglo-American Missions 1640–1810* (Laurel, MS: Audubon, 2006). For modern optimistic eschatology, see: (1) Kenneth Gentry, *He Shall Have Dominion: A Postmillennial Eschatology*, 3rd ed. (Chesnee, SC: Victorious Hope, 2021) [Neo-postmillennialism]; (2) Cornelis P. Venema, *The Promise of the Future* (Edinburgh: Banner of Truth, 2000) [Optimistic Amillennialism].

Background

The antidote to anti-creational worldviews is the "comprehensive and balanced trinitarian approach" pioneered by the Apostolic Confession.[3] This is constructed around the work of the Father (creation, world), the Son (his humanity, historical redemption, kingdom), and the Spirit (the formation of the church and its bodily resurrection). Calvin follows this "order of right teaching" (Institutes 1.2.1; 1.61; 2.1.1; 2.6.1). It is the basic redemptive-historical order the *Institutes* follow: creation, fall, redemption, and consummation.

Trinitarian Approach Protects Against Imbalance. Reduction of the work of any one of the three Persons "inevitably results in a one-sided gospel and a sectarian church."[4] As Lutheran theologian Carl Braaten in *Eschatology and Ethics: Essays on the Theology and Ethics of the Kingdom of God* convincingly demonstrates, throughout church history the consequences of such doctrinal reduction is quite evident. Thus, ironically, movements over-emphasizing the Second Article of the Apostles' Creed, "[We/I believe] in Jesus Christ," for example, the Roman Church, neo-orthodoxy led by Karl Barth, and pietism that reduces Scripture to merely personal salvation, all tend to reduce Christianity to the church as an institution. This is the direction that C&S seems to have taken. That institution, consequently, is always sectarian and culture-bound even when attempting to model the kingdom, which is above culture and sect.

Furthermore, nineteenth-century theological liberalism and its descendants have almost always overemphasized the First Article: "I/we believe in God the Father Almighty." It tended to reduce the church to a vanguard group espousing the secular and humanist agenda popular in each generation. That always divides the church. The Holiness Movement, "Enthusiasm" or as the German's termed it, *Schwärmerei*, and many similar forms of revivalism overemphasized the Third Article, "We/I believe in the Holy Spirit." The result is the tendency of such groups to withdraw into an inner-worldly utopia, as found in radical communalist groups such as the Shakers, and withdrawal Mennonite groups such as the Amish, and Hutterites. Or, they withdraw into congregations of believers with an other-worldly future vision of a rapture-escape from this old, unredeemable and inevitably declining world.

---

3 Spykman, *Reformational*, 142.
4 Carl E. Braaten, *Eschatology and Ethics: Essays on the Theology and Ethics of the Kingdom of God* [Eschatology] (Eugene, OR: Wipf and Stock, 2017), 79.

128 WHEN A THEOLOGICAL SHIFT CHANGED A NATION

The twentieth-century church, including the DRC that we are studying, had its share in all three of these types of imbalance. First, according to American Dutch Reformed Theologian, Gordon Spykman, modernism as the heir of nineteenth-century liberalism had an unbalanced emphasis on the fatherhood of God. In other words, this movement overemphasized that we are all children of God as humans. God, then, is solely a grandfather-like God of love. This is a first-article theology. Barthian, neo-orthodoxy and evangelical pietism overreacted with something like Jesus- or Christo-monism, a second-article theology. Pentecostalism and modern Theologies of Hope "drift . . . toward third-article theology," according to Spykman.[5]

Interestingly enough, among modernity- and postmodernity-bound ecumenical theology, at present, the "gravitational center" of doctrine is indeed shifting steadily toward futurist, Third Article emphases. These are especially influenced by Moltmann and his disciples. In this imbalance, "creation gets absorbed into the process of salvation history" with evident ramifications in "social theology."[6]

Brunner and Moltmann Absorb the First Article into the Third. The German theologians, the late Emil Brunner and the still living Jürgen Moltmann had views on creation, eschaton, and ethics that reveal this absorption process. These future-oriented theologians are typical of much modern theology. Both cut culture and truth off from *any* normative design framework from the past activity of God the Father, who created the heavens and the earth. They postulate a radical discontinuity between the *protos* (the beginning of earth and human history, which did not occur as the Scripture describes) and the *eschatos*, the end of history.

Dutch-American Reformed theologian Douglas Schuurman has done a masterful study of these two scholars: *Creation, Eschaton, and Ethics: The Ethical Significance of the Creation-Eschaton Relation in the Thought of Emil Brunner and Jürgen Moltmann.* In this important work, he summarizes Brunner's and Moltmann's rejection of a creation-based ethic. These are what I have termed, "creation design-norms." Future orientations, they claim, lead to "an open future and a revolutionary social ethic." Schuurman continues somewhat later, "[Brunner], like Moltmann, believes that an emphasis upon creation coheres with conservative acceptance of the [creation] orders," something Abraham Kuyper, for example, emphasized. On the other hand, "an emphasis upon eschatology coheres with revolutionary rejection" of these creation orders. In

5 Spykman, *Reformational*, 146.
6 Spykman, *Reformational*, 60.

THE CREATION RESTORATION PRINCIPLE AND C&S   129

other words, they reject backward-looking norms as "the conservative ethics of creation," such as those norms that limit pastoral and familial leadership to males alone and restrict the recognition of gender roles to the tradition binary male-female roles.[7] This leaves these types of reactionary ethics "closed to the future," and, I add, closed to any totally new work of the Spirit.[8]

Consequently, future-oriented social norms and social-political structures, seen "primarily in light of eschatology" of hope, will leap over the social forms of this old broken age. These antiquated norms are built on the *protos*, the "created" beginning. Furthermore, they assume that this protological creation actually was *not* good, contrary to the Mosaic and Pauline description (e.g., Gn 1; 1 Tm 4:1–4). Therefore, futurist theologians teach that protological-creational social forms are inherently evil. Moltmann names these the inevitably declining "forces of history [that] bear the names of law, sin and death."[9] Because of a key presupposition he shares with non-orthodox modern theology, Moltmann postulates the in-breaking (irruption) of a totally good, future creation into the present. This assumption is informed by the "post-Darwinian insight" concerning an originally defective present creation. According to this insight, as Swedish Lutheran Theologian Gustaf Wingren said, "biotic processes have a built-in cruelty," a history of billions of years of death and an ever-threatening divisive chaos.[10]

It is against that threat of the encroaching of socially divisive chaos that collective man-in-the-State must ever be diligently battling with legislation mandating the equalizing and unifying coercion of social justice. Therefore, implicitly, the norms of the Mosaic law are outdated as part of a divisive and outdated social order based on creation. In place of Mosaic and creational norms, only the good, "desirable and hoped for future" is normative. This new thing cannot "be extrapolated from the entrails of present [evil] history," Moltmann claims. The future social forms are totally different from the oppressive present orders of creation, the *Schöpfungsordungen* [creation orders] of the Nazi-affirming German Christians in the 1930s. Extrapolation from the present orders and social structures onto the future "kills the very future character of the future."[11]

7   Schuurman, *Creation-Eschaton*, 139, n. 1, 150.
8   Jürgen Moltmann, *The Future of Creation: Collected Essays* [Future] (Philadelphia: Fortress, 1979), 55.
9   Moltmann, *Future*, 53.
10   Gustaf Wingren, *Creation and Gospel: The New Situation in European Theology* [Creation and Gospel] (New York: Edwin Mellon, 1979), 136, 141–2.
11   Moltmann, *Future*, 55, 43.

Therefore, "the only people who have any interest in prolonging this rule of the present over the future are those who possess and dominate the present." These are the oppressors suppressing the right and freedom of those victimized by the present structures. These are "the have-nots, the suffering and the guilty," who are asking "for a different future; they ask for change and liberation."[12]

Only in "the Christ who was condemned according to the law and crucified by the state," do we find the desirable "anticipation of God's future," breaking into this evil age. The gathering place, thus, in the "social order" where future hope and love "ought to be found" is where the people with whom Christ identified are. This is *the church*. The church, then, should be a radical church not allied to the "progressive leaders of society, the spearheads of economic development," those on top of the social order. Christ identified himself with the "victims" of the powerful spearheads of development.[13] He identified with the marginalized and outcast, the lowest rank of society. The motivation for *at least* Moltmann's radically futurist perspective, thus, seems to be a socio-political option to side with the struggle of poor and oppressed to cast off the backward-looking structures of now present society. In South Africa's case in the 1970s and 1980s, and to a great extent still today, these are the oppressed black and brown children of God subjugated by apartheid and the remains of a capitalistic economy with its "systemic oppression," as it is termed. For these reasons and more, Jürgen Moltmann has been a great inspiration for ecclesial revolutionary movements in the last five decades or more.

Relationship of Protology to Eschatology: Options

This, then, leads us to even further background study as unearthed by Douglas Schuurman's excellent research. Throughout church history there have been three chief options for the relationship of protology (creation) to eschatology (creation consummated): (1) Annihilation of the present world-system (*annihiliatio mundi*) with a completely new creation ex nihilo in the eschaton (*nova creatio*). (2) A simple return to the first creation, a *restitutio ad integrum* or repristination, restoring the original golden era before the fall. And last, (3) a transformation of creation (*transformatio mundi*) by restoring, in a matured form, that which was lost through sin in a recapitulation (*recapitulatio*) process.[14]

---

12 Moltmann, *Future*, 43.
13 Moltmann, *Future*, 53–4.
14 Schuurman, *Creation-Eschaton*, 147–52.

THE CREATION RESTORATION PRINCIPLE AND C&S   131

The last is the viewpoint that I will take in this volume. It provides a real biblical hope for the future with the in-breaking (irruption) of the long-promised eschatological Kingdom in Christ's first coming, which is now growing, but will not be consummated until Christ's second coming.

Recapitulatio: Not a Nova Creatio. Futurist theologians who base their doctrine on the Third Article of the creed tend to opt for the first of the above. They tend to believe in a radical discontinuity between the proton and the eschaton, the first creation and the new creation. The new creation is a virtual absolutely new, *nova creatio.* Moltmann, for example, moderated this emphasis in later writings, yet his stress is still upon a radically discontinuous new creation even with some continuity.[15] Futurist-oriented dialectical theologies thus conceal a utopian agenda. Utopia, in this meaning, retains the original sense of the word utopia, that is, "no-place." For them, the history of redemption is moving to a future form never before seen or imagined by man in this creation.

Moltmann realistically modified the revolutionary implications of this theory by accepting the already-but-not-yet tension of contemporary eschatology. However, even in doing this, the utopian future principle that his theory introduced into the present still acted as a radical signpost of a hoped-for future. The institutional church, as the sphere of the nova creatio, must be the present model of the future.[16]

The moderating aspect of Moltmann's theory that he brought in later comes from the patience and realism that the already-but-not-yet schema introduced to his radical rejection of protological design-norms and creational structures. This allowed him to reject most structure-overturning, revolutionary violence, the methodology of classic Marxism-Leninism and many forms of Liberation Theology.

Moltmann and most other nova creationists seem to prefer the slow but steady incremental overturning of "backward-looking" social structures through the ballot box or as we are increasingly seeing in the second decade of the twenty-first century, the fixing of the ballot box results. This is the methodology of European and American social democracy movements. It is as coercive as revolutionary violence. Both use the weapons of state police and armies. It, however, substitutes gradual coercion for revolutionary violence so that the reactionary majorities can become gradually acclimated to the in-breaking of the revolutionary, totally new future.

---

15 Schuurman, *Creation-Eschaton.*
16 Moltmann, *Future.*

In conclusion, such theologies of hope, as well as other related theologies, all reject "reactionary" creational theologies. The result is that they are sympathetic with structure-overturning ideologies seeking social forms never before realized in human history. Therefore, these theologies tend to favor the ordination of women and practicing homosexuals and reject any form of church built upon ethno-cultural solidarity. The future, according to these theologies is built upon a group-pless, self-identified individual united in a global state, as envisioned by utopians for millennia.

Nova creatio futurist theologies, hence, strongly tend to social radicalism even when structure-overturning rhetoric is moderated and an incremental approach to change is advocated. This may explain the difference between the radical doctrinal and moderate application sections of C&S (see Chapter 2).

Theologian term this position of a future, totally new creation (nova creatio) which begins to be worked out now in anticipation of that new future, a "proleptive" in-breaking (irruption) of the future into the present. This view is actually similar to that of several of the adherents of the Radical Reformation. Apartheid theologian F. J. M. Potgieter correctly cites Herman Bavinck to warn that the doctrine of nova creatio is "not Reformed but *Anabaptistic*."[17] In contrast to this, the biblically orthodox position has always been, as exemplified by Abraham Kuyper's colleague, Herman Bavinck, that "grace does not destroy but perfects nature"; thus the "goal of grace" is not a completely new "*creatio ex nihilo*" but a renovated, renewed world in Christ by his Spirit.[18] The Gospel is not revolutionary. Instead, it is a step-by-step transformative as Paul affirmed in 1 Corinthians 15:20–8, that leads to the progressive healing of the wounds of Adam and his offspring's treason against their King and Lord. Paul states that Christ must reign until he makes all his enemies a footstool under his feet. The last enemy to be subjected is death.

Recapitulation: Not a Return to a Pristine Eden. The second alternative in the attempt to relate protology to eschatology is that of repristination, the return to a pristine Edenic existence in the end. This view has often had a small minority following throughout church history and is based on a cyclical view of history that inevitably returns to a mythical golden age. It normally manifests itself in libertine, communalist sects that imagine the first creation as a totally egalitarian paradise without law, social class, marriage and work as especially as Norman Cohn described in *The Pursuit of the Millennium: Revolutionary*

---

17 Potgieter, *C&S Essence*, 45; see also Balke, *Anabaptist Radicals*.

18 See Veenhof, *Nature and Grace*, 157.

THE CREATION RESTORATION PRINCIPLE AND C&S   133

Millenarians and Mystical Anarchists of the Middle Ages.[19] In the end, these movements advocate a society similar to that envisioned by nova creationists.

Ironically, Moltmann accuses the orthodox recapitulatio or renovatio (repairing) view of being based on this cyclical return myth. Orthodox time orientation, however, has never been cyclical, but always linear. Creation moves inexorably on from a literal creation a few thousand years ago until the Final Day, the Consummation. This is the true basis for a biblical doctrine of progressive, social dynamism.[20] In other words, to be socially dynamic and transformative, the biblical Christ-following movement does not need to look forward to a future utopia coming from the past. Instead, Christ-followers look forward to the progress in wholistically discipling all the nations as Scripture teaches (Gn 12:3; Pss 2, 110; Mt 12:17–21, 28:18–20) as we shall see in a coming chapter.

Recapitulatio, the word Irenaeus used in the Latin translation of his works against the Gnostics, does not, therefore, imply a simple repristination of the creation in Christ, because Eden is gone forever. Recapitulation "is rather the present and future restoration of the fallen creation to all it was meant to be."[21]

Recapitulatio: Transformation of the World. The last and most biblical alternative, therefore, in discovering the relationship of protology to eschatology is that of transformation of the human systems of the whole world (*transformatio mundi*). It has historically been the orthodox position both in the Genevan Reformation and its precursors. It found its culmination in Calvin and his followers, though not now, in the twenty-first century exclusively only there. In brief, the renewed, transformed creation has arrived in union with its Messiah, its Anointed King Jesus Christ. Although it has been growing from the size of a mustard seed, and rapidly the last many decades, it has not nor will be totally perfected until our Lord comes to destroy his last enemy, death. There are several characteristics differentiating the classic Reformational position from other worldviews.

First of all, recapitulation does not add something to an always imperfect nature as in dualist worldviews. In Roman Catholic dualism, for example, grace adds something to nature, so that "salvation is something basically

---

19 Cohn, *Pursuit,* chapter 10: "The Equalitarian State of Nature;" Micea Eliade, *The Myth of the Eternal Return: Cosmos and History,* trans. Willard R. Trask, 2nd ed. (Princeton, NJ: Princeton University Press, 2018).

20 See, e.g., Eliade, *Myth;* Robert Nisbet, *The History of the Idea of Progress,* 2nd ed. (New York: Routledge, 2017).

21 Spykman, *Reformational,* 143.

'non-creational,' supercreational, or even anticreational." These dualists believe that what Christ adds to creation is a holy, ecclesiastical realm, the holy Roman Church, while the creation itself belongs to a worldly or secular realm.[22] A similar sort of dualism is shared by many pietistic evangelicals and by dialectical theology.[23]

Secondly, recapitulation does not leave creation orders and structures (*Ordnungen*) virtually intact under natural law as in Luther's view and the early twentieth-century viewpoint of the Nazi-oriented German Christians, who twisted and misused Luther. Sin has corrupted and polluted "every structure of humanity and the world." However, "God's abundant grace in Christ triumph[s] . . . even more" than sin. The Gospel is "a joyful tiding" of the transforming renewal of "not only the individual person but also for humanity, for the family, for society, for the state, for art and science, for the whole groaning creation," groaning under the curse, as Dutch Theologian, Herman Bavinck, wrote.[24]

Thirdly, the future in a Reformational worldview follows historic, creedal orthodoxy. Both see continuity with the past healed from its rebellion in the concept of renewal of creation design-norms, and both extrapolate the originally good creation into a future that is progressively partaking of the cosmic redemption work of Messiah Jesus. Orthodoxy organizes history "around the central insight that 'grace restores nature.'" Salvation thus is "to salvage a sin-disrupted creation," according to Albert Wolters.[25] Douglas Schuurman adds: "History is paradise lost; redemption is paradise regained. Sin perverts, and grace restores, the good creation. The eschaton, accordingly, is the full restoration of the good original creation,"[26] contrary to Moltmann and his Eschatology of Hope.

---

22 Wolters, *Regained*, 12.

23 See Dooyeweerd, *Roots*.

24 Herman Bavinck, "The Catholicity of Christianity and the Church," trans. John Bolt, *Calvin Theological Journal* 27 (1992): 224.

25 Wolters, *Regained*, 12.

26 Douglas Schuurman, *Creation, Eschaton, and Ethics: The Ethical Significance of the Creation-Eschaton Relation in the Thought of Emil Brunner and Jürgen Moltmann* [Creation-Eschaton] (New York: Peter Lang, 1991), 104.

Creation-Eschaton Relation: The Last Correlated with the First

The end also, then, is a maturation of the beginning. The late DRC theologian, Adrio König, wrote correctly: "The Bible begins and ends with creation terms!"[27] Norwegian theologian N. H. Dahl's classic article entitled *The Background of the New Testament and its Eschatology* ascribes this "positive correlation of 'eschatology' and 'protology'" as holding "a very firm position within the ancient Church." Not only the anti-Gnostic fathers, but the New Testament writers and the "common tradition of the Church [agreed] . . .. The idea that God will make "the last things like the first things" (Barn. vi.13) is used as a [common] hermeneutical principle for the interpretation of Genesis." Dahl surveys similar concepts in the New Testament (e.g., Rom 5:12ff; 1 Cor 15:22ff; 2 Cor 4:4; Eph 1:22ff, 2:15, 4:24, 5:21–33; Col 1:15–20, 2:10, 19, 3:10).[28]

The Meaning of Recapitulation. Church Father Irenaeus used recapitulation to describe this process of correlating the end with the beginning. The word has several implications. First, all things, including all men, are to be summed up under Christ's headship (see Eph 1:10, Irenaeus' key text). The protological sin never affected our Lord so only in him, all of mankind returns to his proper head as the only source of life. From this flows "the renewal of life in men's public and private lives," according to Gustaf Wingren.[29] Irenaeus clearly saw redemptive history as the growth of the church in every people and tongue.

Second according to Irenaeus, the word recapitulation implies restoration to a matured form of the original creation. Paul in Romans (8:18–39) clearly states that the first creation will not be destroyed but fully saved from all the effects of Adam's rebellion and treason against his rightful King. The future thus brings the maturity of the original creation. Just as a flower is the outworking of the created potential of the bud, or just as a child grows up into adulthood, so the City of New Jerusalem is the outworking of Edenic potentials. The garden becomes a city! Recapitulation implies, therefore, a backward and forward look. Grace in Christ restores and reforms the original creation, bringing with it a growing maturity which wars against and overcomes sin.

---

27 Adrio König, *New and Greater things: Re-evaluating the Biblical Message on Creation* (Pretoria: University of South Africa, 1988), 108.

28 N. A. Dahl, "Christ, Creation and the Church," in *The Background of the New Testament and its Eschatology: In Honour of Charles Harold Dodd* [Christ Creation], reprint ed., ed. W. D. Davies and D. Daube (Cambridge: At the University Press, 1964), 423–4.

29 Gustaf Wingren, *Man and the Incarnation: A Study in the Biblical Theology of Irenaeus* [Man and Incarnation] (Edinburgh: Oliver & Boyd, 1959), 174.

136 WHEN A THEOLOGICAL SHIFT CHANGED A NATION

Third, recapitulation implies repetition. The second Adam repeats the first Adam's history with opposite results. However, man in Christ has been growing and differentiating. Hence the word, in Irenaeus, does not imply mere reversion to mankind's original pristine immaturity. Recapitulation "contains the idea of perfection or consummation" because "man's growth is resumed and renewed" in Christ, as Wingren describes it.[30] Christ, then, is the Recapitulator, the "pattern of the new humanity," in orthodox, anti-Gnostic theology.[31] Our Lord repeated Adamic history in his sinless birth as the second Adam. In his life, resurrection, ascension he repeats, restores and consummates all things lost by Adam until his Second coming when he sums up all things in Himself in actuality. "There is an unbroken unity in the whole of Christ's work right up to the events of the last time—everything is *recapitulatio*" (Acts 3:21ff). Irenaeus saw this clearly: "From beginning to end *recapitualtio* involves a continuum which stage by stage is realised in time."[32] Here, it seems, Irenaeus was expositing the Apostle Paul in his powerful resurrection chapter of 1 Corinthians 15:20–6 (NIV):

> But Christ has indeed been raised from the dead, the first fruits of those who have fallen asleep. For since death came through a man, the resurrection of the dead comes also through a man. For as in Adam all die, so in Christ all will be made alive. But each in turn: Christ, the first fruits; then, when he comes, those who belong to him. Then the end will come, when he hands over the kingdom to God the Father after he has destroyed all dominion, authority and power. For he must reign until he has put all his enemies under his feet. The last enemy to be destroyed is death.

As a manifestation of Christ's recapitulation, the Body of Christ, as the people of God militant in culture, act as leaven, salt, and light in all institutions of society. They must do so, but if not "they will be trampled under foot" literally, as occurred with the Jews, that our Lord was addressing, only about 40 years later in the Roman conquest of Jerusalem (Mt 5:12–13). Christ as the Recapitulator is now working in and through his body until the last day, the day of the Resurrection as the passage in 1 Corinthian cited above states in turn quoting selected sections of the most quoted Psalm in the New Testament (Ps 110). Gustaf Wingren again concisely summarizes Irenaeus' thought: "Christ's

---

30 Wingren, *Man and Incarnation*, 174.

31 H. Wayne House, "Creation and Redemption: A Study of Kingdom Interplay," *Journal of the Evangelical Theological Society* 35 (March 1992): 13.

32 Wingren, *Man and Incarnation*, 194, 193.

THE CREATION RESTORATION PRINCIPLE AND C&S 137

work in itself is finished and complete, but it has not yet extended to every part of human life."[33] Christ thus is the proton and the eschaton, the first and last.

Conclusion. In conclusion, I follow classic biblical orthodoxy in eschatology. Thus, the last things are "squarely based upon biblical protology, [in which] the ending of history could only be comprehensible within categories by which the beginning of history is described," as biblical theologian Warren Gage stated.[34] Mankind-in-Christ is restored in Christ already, but also looks forward to being restored both as individuals and communities. A recapitulated Christian person and a restored Christian society is fully and healthily human, as they were designed to be. Hence Christian society and Christian individuals are not eccentric or out-of-step with the development of history. The effect is that the church as God's steward "is turned outwards towards the world. Its function is to protect whatever has been created from the forces that destroy life."[35] Only in this sense is biblical Christianity conservative, contrary to its many critics. The DRC of South Africa attempted culture transformation but did so on faulty biblical grounds with some correct insights from Kuyper and others yet twisted or ignored other of those insights. The forward way into true reformation of South African culture remains open.

Recapitulation Does Not End the Creation Covenant's Law-Order. The recapitulation principle of realistic, *long-term* victorious eschatology of Scripture does not accept the perspective followed by Luther. This view "puts an end to the law by announcing its fulfillment," as important Lutheran theologian Carl Braaten wrote.[36] Man was created in covenant with the Creator as Sovereign King and Lord of the Universe: "in creation God covenanted his kingdom into existence."[37] Part of his kingdom's rule was an implicit covenant with an ethical standard, a norm. God revealed his instruction as King and Father, and after all that is the root meaning of the original Hebrew, both in the heart of man and in the explicit words of that he spoke (see, e.g., Gn 1:26, 29; 2:16–17, 24). That pattern continues. That law-order, since it is based on the character of the Creator who is unchanging and upon his wise creation design, provides norms that are also absolute and unchanging (Pss 19, 119). Though the

---

33 Wingren, *Man and Incarnation*, 171.

34 Warren Austin Gage, *The Gospel of Genesis: Studies in Protology and Eschatology* (Winona Lake, IN: Carpenter, 1984), 8.

35 Gustaf Wingren, *The Flight from Creation* [Flight] (Minneapolis: Augsburg, 1971), 8.

36 Braaten, *Eschatology*, 119.

37 Spykman, *Reformational*, 11.

138   WHEN A THEOLOGICAL SHIFT CHANGED A NATION

external form of a command does change yet its internal meaning never does, as the *Belgic Confession* states (BC, art. 25).

Mankind-in-Adam broke this royal law, and God sent a covenantal curse upon Adam, his seed through history, and the creation (see Gn 3; Rom 8:19ff). However, the Suzerain graciously consented to restore man and cursed creation through the redemptive renewal of the original covenant of creation through the solidarity of redeemed humanity in Christ, the Last Adam.

Recapitulation assumes the continuity of the historical covenants with his people starting with Adam and his wife in Genesis 3:15 and 3:21 and continuing through Noah, Abraham, Moses, David until the Greater David comes. Those covenants began in the Garden and are progressively renewed until Christ completes their intention in his renewed covenant "in Christ." Christ the King restored the broken covenantal law by obeying it completely as it was originally designed to be (Gn 3:15; Rom 5:12ff, 16:20; Rv 12:7–9). Each renewal of the covenant of the King reaffirmed the originally revealed design-norms of Eden in a progressively more specific manner though clothed in a culturally specific form.

Grace that our King promised in the coming Victor, the Messiah, therefore, does not abolish the created covenantal design-norms such as the binary family and the one day in seven rest day. Neither does it abolish the King's wisdom and character, which is the norm behind the design. Instead, Christ, the King's Anointed Son (Ps 2; Ac 2), affirms and restores the correct use of the creation as he restores the King's covenant law (Mt 5:19ff). The King commands dominion-oriented, covenant-keeping families to transform their various cultures on the basis of the comprehensive rule of the covenantal law-ethic first given in the Garden. "Covenant and kingdom are like two sides of a single coin," American Dutch Reformed theologian Gordon Spykman correctly wrote. The message of the gracious covenant, promising redemption is kingdom-oriented from the beginning. The "original covenant stands forever as the abiding foundation and norm for life in God's world."[38]

Implications of Recapitulation for Social Theology

Christ Recapitulates Moses. The recapitulation principle rejects the dialectical view of the law, followed by Luther, Anabaptists, most pietists, and neo-orthodoxy. These teachers and movements do not understand that the

---

38 Spykman, *Reformational*, 11, 12.

THE CREATION RESTORATION PRINCIPLE AND C&S   139

covenant law of Moses was essentially the original covenant law of creation applied and exposited to all areas of life. That, in turn, finds true restoration in the new covenant in Christ, who will write his law on the hearts of believers.

On the other hand, dialectical and neo-orthodox worldviews tend to teach instead that Jesus introduces a neo-nomos, a new law, that "presuppos[es] [radically new] eschatological provisions of the [future] kingdom." Futurist-oriented, dialectical theologians, such as Jürgen Moltmann, often teach that the rule of justice through the law is an inherent part of the *fallen* order of this age. The old law is not part of the "perfections of Christ" in the new order. This is similar to what the early Anabaptists taught. In Christ, a "new law of love is at work in the same contexts of life" dealt with by the old law.[39] Again similar to the views of the Radical Reformation, this ultimately results in two differing norms for the secular and spiritual kingdoms, a two-kingdom perspective instead of a one Kingdom, biblical law-norm perspective of classical continental Reformed theology.[40]

The recapitulation principle teaches the opposite because of its continuity principle. Instead of two norms, it teaches that there is only one normative order for all spheres of life and for all cultures. The Mosaic-Prophetic law is a model for all peoples as the Torah and the Prophets abundantly made plain (see, e.g., Lv 18:1–23, esp. 24–30; Dt 4:5–8; Ps 9:5–12; Jer 50:14–15, 29; Ez 5:5–6, 14:12–23). The Psalms and Proverbs universalize the Torah for all nations and peoples. Jesus, the Davidic King, is thus a "second Moses," delivering from the Mount the correct interpretation of the law. He is the Great Prophet foreseen by Moses (Dt 18:18; Acts 3:22–3, 7:37). Moses was, in turn, in continuity with Abraham, Noah and the covenant norms of the Garden. Herman Ridderbos, though influenced by Karl Barth, discussed this in 1982 about the time that the DRC scholars of South Africa were working on C&S. His excellent volume, *When the Time Had Fully Come: Studies in New Testament Theology*, was one of several works in the Dutch-Kuyperian tradition that could have helped move the DRC into a more biblical and transformative stream.[41]

---

39 Braaten, *Eschatology*, 119.

40 For classic one-kingdom Kuyperian perspectives, see (1) Ryan C. McIlhenny, ed., *Kingdoms Apart: Engaging the Two Kingdoms Perspective* (Phillipsburg, NJ: P&R Publishing, 2012); (2) Willem J. Ouweneel, *The World is Christ's: A Critique of Two Kingdoms Theology* (Toronto: Ezra Press, 2018).

41 Herman N. Ridderbos, *When the Time had Fully Come: Studies in New Testament Theology* (Jordan Station, ON: Paideia Press, 1982).

140 WHEN A THEOLOGICAL SHIFT CHANGED A NATION

Christ's kingdom and his law, as understood in orthodoxy, is therefore not merely future-looking. In a real sense, it is also backward-looking. The principle of recapitulation is both conservative, if that which is to be conserved is indeed built on created design-norms, and dynamically transformative. There is continuity between creation and eschaton, not conflictual, dialectical dualism. As a result, there is no theological necessity to give "hermeneutical priority" to either the beginning or the end as Douglas Schuurman summarizes the topic. It is a both-and situation and not an either-or.[42]

The Second Moses Restores All of Culture. Furthermore, recapitulation in union with Christ, the Second Moses, does not imply that the institutional church is the *only part* of the creation that partakes of restoration as do the more recent Reformed Two Kingdoms advocates emphasize. The reason is clear. All things have come under our Lord's sovereignty over heaven and earth as an inheritance from his Father (Ps 2; Dn 7:13–14; Mt 28:18). All things are *presently* being brought under his headship, his grace, and his commands as he himself mandates his people to participate in. This includes all kings, families and peoples of earth (Pss 2, 47 [NIV], 96, 110; Mt 12:18–21; Acts 2; Eph 1:20; Heb 2). The last thing to be totally conquered by him is death itself. That occurs at the resurrection (1 Cor 15:20–8). In the meantime, he is progressively putting all his enemies under his feet (Ps 110).

Classic Puritan Hope Versus the Modern Eschatological Hope

I support an addition to the orthodox recapitulation theme, which is a modified form of the classic "Puritan Hope" that drove both mission to the ends of the earth[43] and a vision for transformation of culture based on the "general equity" of the Mosaic polity (WCF 19.4) as empowered by the Spirit of the indwelling Christ (Rom 8:2–4). That term comes from the *Westminster Confession* mandated by the British Puritan Parliament after the decapitation of Charles I. Since the Puritan era, this type of optimistic eschatology has fallen on very hard times. It has been much refined from that previous time up to about 1900 with this over-optimistic postmillennialism was the consensus of most denominations at one time or another. The vast majority of contemporary Bible-believing scholarship has abandoned that historicist interpretation

42 Schuurman, *Creation-Eschaton*, 151–3.
43 See Murray, *Puritan.*

THE CREATION RESTORATION PRINCIPLE AND C&S 141

of the Apocalypse of John. Most have adopted either a futurist premillennial or an idealist-platonic (dehistoricized) view of the future. However, a growing minority have adopted a creedally faithful preterist view, which is actually an optimistic amillennial vision for that book and its precursor, the Olivet Discourse (Mt 23:33–25:46; Mk 13; Lk 21).

I adopt this third viewpoint as an "eschatology of victory," a term I borrow from Dutch-American theologian J. Marcellus Kik (though he calls his view Postmillennialism). Alternatively, it can be termed optimillennialism to describe this position of realistic but still long-term optimism that our King's mandate will be fulfilled before the Second Coming.[44] After all, he promised he would be with us always even to the end of the age, when the work of disciplining all the ethno-peoples of the earth will be finished.

My use of "optimillennialism" combines the "already-but-not-yet" consensus of progressive dispensationalism and amillennialism with the realistic anticipation that the peoples and cultures of the world will be substantially discipled before the second coming. In addition, it welcomes the exegesis of the Apocalypse that takes its genre seriously as a book of symbols drawn from previous prophetic literature of the old covenant. One of these often-used symbols is that of the number 1000, which is a metaphor throughout the Old Testament meaning an uncountably long period or number (e.g., Dt 32:30; Jo 23:10; Pss 50:10, 90:4; Eccl 6:6, 7:28; Is 60:22). In summary, what this means is that Christ's reign has earthly effects as it is progressively actualized upon earth by the collective, faith-filled works of God's people, who pray: "Your Name be set apart as holy, Your Kingdom come, Your will be done on earth as it is in heaven" (Mt 6:9–13, my translation; see WLC, 191; HC, 48).

Certainly, I do not imply that mankind brings in the kingdom. Christ has already brought it in (Mt 12:28) and it working from his throne in heaven to destroy all his enemies. However, as the King works now through his people, his kingdom acts as leaven in and like a mustard seed upon all the peoples and cultures of earth (Mt 13:31–3). The Spirit of the King works *now already*, through obedient men and women, to bring comprehensive kingdom growth. That work, on the other hand, is *not yet* perfect, *nor will it be* until the resurrection. This allows for a realistic faith that the Great Commission can and must be fulfilled before Christ comes yet realism remains because "in this world you will have tribulations" (Jn 16:33). However, that must mean we should always look forward to ever-greater works he will give to us to do and an ever-greater

44 Gary North, Gary North, *Millennialism and Social Theory* [Millennialism and Social Theory] (Tyler, TX: Institute for Christian Economics, 1991).

142 WHEN A THEOLOGICAL SHIFT CHANGED A NATION

spread of his kingdom before the end. Paul asks for prayer that "the message of the Lord may spread rapidly and be honored, just as it was with you" (2 Thes 3:1) and that ever more glory will come to our Lord as all the peoples praise him (see Ps 67:3–5; 2 Cor 4:15; Rom 15:8–12).

Optimillennialism gives a biblical futurist orientation to God's people's dominion work under the Cultural Mandate that is long-term, realizing that the Kingdom has great periods of growth, as is occurring in the Majority, Global South, as well as periods of deep declension as is happening in the West in contemporary times but historically in the Byzantine world under the onslaught of Islam. This is in direct contrast to much of the futurist orientation of contemporary theology, which is ultimately quite culturally pessimistic. The modern evangelical theological consensus in North America, on the other hand, accepts the church as an exclusively eschatological interim event, one not in continuity with the creation and its future restoration nor with the covenants of the past variously joined together as the old dispensation of the single, overarching covenant of grace.

Church as Eschatological "Sign" of Future Kingdom

Viewing the church as an eschatological event means that the church is *not* founded upon the past Edenic Dominion Covenant (Gn 1:26–8), its renewal in the "First Gospel"—the protoevangelium and to Noah, and the renewal in the covenant promises of the patriarchs Abraham, Isaac, and Jacob, and of the prophets Moses and David, the king. It is thus not modeled upon the design of Abraham's created extended family, a national unity in sub-ethnic diversity. In other words, Israel is a nation consisting of twelve tribal, sub-ethnic parts (thirteen if Levi is included). This classic Reformational principle of covenantal continuity focuses upon a foundation consisting of both the individual *and* the family group(s) in covenant with the Creator-Redeemer.

In direct contrast, the modern consensus at least among the Neo-orthodox seems instead to teach that the church is founded upon the work of Christ's *kerygma* (proclamation) heard now in the Word that is exclusively applied to the individual hearer or responder alone. The groups of the Old Testament past are an anachronism, overcome by the always-present that is in the word presently proclaimed (*kerygma*). Emphasis upon group solidarity, because it comes from the past, is thus relativized or denied. The church, therefore, is the preliminary and anticipatory form in today's world of an exclusively future kingdom that Christ brought to humanity. This view seems more similar to the various forms of dispensationalism found in the Radical Reformation and revivalism than to Reformed covenantally.

Proleptic Eschatology is Exclusively Future-Oriented. Much of contemporary theology sees this exclusively future kingdom as proleptively present now. "Prolepsis" means "anticipation." Therefore, the kingdom is present "in the person of Christ first, and then in those incorporated into his love, into his freedom, his peace and the fullness of his life," that is, his church.[45] In other words, the present church anticipates *now* what *will be* in the future.

Proleptic Eschatology has specific ethical implications. According to many proleptic theologians, the opposite of proleptic eschatology is anachronistic theology and anachronistic eschatology. Proleptic eschatology perceives the church to be a microcosm and anticipation of what the future world will look like. The church must therefore reject in every one of its structures all backward looking to the creation such as is found in anachronistic eschatology. Furthermore, it must reject every aspect of the anachronistic structures and social order built upon the past. "Just as anachronism limps after time, so prolepsis hurries ahead of it, already realizing today what is to be tomorrow." Modern theology thus completely rejects Kuyperian theology and related eschatologies that desire to recapitulate in the future the past creation structures. The doctrine of prolepsis has a third ethical implication. "Just as the coming God already antedates his future, giving it in advance in history," Moltmann states, "men and women can and should anticipate this future in knowledge and in deed." The church and its ministry of word and sacrament are therefore the "spearhead of the kingdom of God, which moves through both the church and the world."[46]

The result of this spearhead or to put it is Marxist terms, vanguard effect is that the in-breaking Kingdom sets up "signs of the kingdom not only in the church's sacraments but also in the world's struggles for brotherhood, equality and freedom."[47] Such proleptic anticipation creates hope for those who have identified with the poor, and "who with the poor hope for the new, liberating future of God." Proleptic eschatology then "is not content with the present, but does not take the place of consummation either. It is the 'now already' in the midst of the 'not yet,'" Moltmann writes, citing the contemporary consensus on the already-but-not-yet of the kingdom.[48]

---

45 Braaten, *Eschatology*, 82.
46 Moltmann, *Future*, 47.
47 Braaten, *Eschatology*, 83.
48 Moltmann, *Future*, 47.

144   WHEN A THEOLOGICAL SHIFT CHANGED A NATION

In other words, the signs of God's kingdom for which people must now unite to work are the three slogans of the French Revolution: fraternity, equality, and liberty. This alone anticipates the final eschaton. Proleptic eschatology must therefore work backward from a postulated equalitarian future to the oppressive non-equalitarian present. Prolepsis teaches that there "cannot be an extrapolation of the future from history." The opposite is the case. The present must begin to anticipate the never-before-seen future. The in-breaking future brings liberation into present oppression.[49]

The WCC and Proleptic Eschatology. Around the same time as the publication of C&S, the WCC has published a comprehensive survey of the growing consensus in the world church (Roman Catholic, WCC, and Orthodox) concerning this proleptic eschatology entitled, *Church Kingdom World: The Church as Mystery and Prophetic Sign,* published by the Faith and Order Commission.[50] Günther Gassmann, who was then Director of the WCC's Faith and Order Commission, surveys the adoption of the "newly adopted ecclesiological terminology," which describes the unity of the church using the "terms sacrament, sign and instrument."[51]

In this growing ecumenical consensus, the unity of the church was never seen as an end it itself. It is a sign, that is a "pointer, symbol, example and model," and a sacrament, in the sense of "anticipation" in itself of the coming unity of humanity in the kingdom. It is also an "effective means or tool" in itself to help bring that coming unity into effect. "The church is sign, sacrament and instrument of God's love, of his rule, his universal plan of salvation for all humankind in Jesus Christ." Consequently, the church in itself is the "sign of the coming union of all human beings in God's kingdom, the redemption of creation and the fulfilment of all things." Gassmann further explains that the unity of humankind that is to come was initially understood in realized eschatological terms (Cullman and Dodd) but has been shifting to an "eschatological perspective" (likely under influence of various futurist eschatologies spawned by J. Moltmann and W. Pannenberg). The totally new future is now proleptically present in the church. The church, thus, is the vanguard

---

49 Moltmann, *Future,* 48.
50 Gennadios Limouris, ed., *Church Kingdom World: The Church as Mystery and Prophetic Sign* (Geneva: World Council of Churches, 1986).
51 Günther Gassmann, "The Church as Sacrament, Sign and Instrument [Church as Sacrament]," in *Church Kingdom World: The Church as Mystery and Prophetic Sign,* ed. Gennadios Limouris (Geneva: World Council of Churches, 1986), 13. See also, Avery Cardinal Dulles, "The Church as Sacrament," in *Models of the Church* (New York: Image, 2002).

THE CREATION RESTORATION PRINCIPLE AND C&S   145

of the coming unified and just world. It is an "anticipatory sign" of a future perfected reconciliation and hope for the world and for humanity.[52]

Therefore, logically I might add, the church in its institutional structures must model the future kingdom's unity, liberty, justice and brotherhood to the world. The church gives to the world an encouraging model of how it should dismantle and replace unjust, divisive relationships and oppressive social structures. The application to the oppressive order of apartheid South Africa was crystal clear. This new paradigm provided a well-defined path to the New South Africa. However, was it felicitous? Did it lead to true human flourishing?

Evaluation of Proleptic Eschatology

There is some truth in the concept that the present must anticipate the future. In orthodox theology, the church must indeed model or be a sign now of perfected kingdom relationships. "The Church is summoned to be the militant vanguard of God's Kingdom in an ecclesiastical way," Johan Heyns Moderator of the Synod that produced C&S and one of the leading Theologians of the DRC wrote in 1980.[53] However, since WCC theology did not accept the classic recapitulative eschatological perspective outlined above, it departed significantly from classic continental Reformed orthodoxy. First of all, it must be socially antinomian (the subject of a later chapter) and second, it must be at least moderately utopian. In other words, the defining norm for justice, liberty, unity, and brotherhood is a never-before-seen future vision of the kingdom. That kingdom is cut off from any creational norms as summarized in the Decalogue.

For example, using Moltmann's theology as a base, J. M. Lochman wrote the following for a WCC colloquium in 1986. He claimed that the Spirit combats all "obstacles and rifts between human beings which are barriers to the achievement of unity." He listed "cultural, social and religious" barriers as examples. Consequently the Spirit, he said, is "determined to overcome obstacles and to tear down barriers which keep human beings apart ... so as to renew human community." He concluded, "Every form of 'apartheid' is sin—indeed, in this concrete sense, the sin against the Holy Spirit."[54] Clearly for

---

52 Gassmann, *Church as Sacrament*, 14.

53 Johan Adam Heyns, *The Church*, trans. D. Roy Briggs (Pretoria: N.G. Kerkboekhandel Transvaal, 1980), 28.

54 Jan Milic Lochman, "Church and World in the Light of the Kingdom of God," in *Church Kingdom World: The Church as Mystery and Prophetic Sign*, ed. Gennadios Limouris (Geneva: World Council of Churches, 1986), 71.

146   WHEN A THEOLOGICAL SHIFT CHANGED A NATION

Lochman, since the defining social norms are not derived from a careful exegetical understanding of the law-order of revelation, they must be derived from the surrounding humanist culture. Biblical norms are then redefined by the standards of humanist culture. What is rejected is the explicit biblical content of social norms as classically defined within the context of the one continuously present covenant of grace. This, as shall be demonstrated in this and the following chapters, is also what the DRC's C&S document does.

Socio-Cultural Implications of Proleptic Eschatology

Gassmann, as mentioned earlier, spelled out some of the implications of this new understanding of the relationship of the church, the future kingdom, and its norms to the world's society. "The sign-character of the church is not purely "spiritual" but, according to an incarnational understanding of the church, needs to be set in relationship to the conflicts, needs and hopes of our world."[55] For the WCC, the unity of the church is closely connected to the unity of humankind as an official WCC publication spelled out in 1978 within the pages of *Unity in Today's World*. The Faith and Order Studies on "Unity of the Church—Unity of Humankind."[56]

Putting its teaching into practice, the WCC spent many millions of its parishioners' money to help build, what they termed, a unified, just, and more equal world in the 1960s, 1970s, and 1980s. The Program to Combat Racism (PCR) in southern Africa, with the millions given to southern African revolutionary liberation movements, is an example.[57] This type of social activism is a logical outworking of the futurist, equalitarian eschatology adopted by the WCC. The results were the rise to power of one-party rule: The late Robert Mugabe's Marxist-oriented ZANU-PF party in Zimbabwe and the African National Congress/South African Communist Party Alliance in South Africa (though the latter maintains the mirage of a multi-party system). Both economies have suffered greatly by the change that actually resulted in replacing one hegemonic people-group with another, in Zimbabwe Mugabe's Shonas and in RSA, the Xhosa-Zulu alliance replaced the English and in South Africa, the Afrikaner-English alliance.

---

55 Gassmann, *Church as Sacrament*, 14.
56 Geiko Müller-Fahrenholz, *Unity in Today's World*. The Faith and Order Studies on "Unity of the Church—Unity of Humankind" (Geneva: World Council of Churches, 1978).
57 See, e.g., Rachel Tingle, *Revolution or Reconciliation: The Struggle in the Church in South Africa* (London: Christian Studies Centre, 1992).

THE CREATION RESTORATION PRINCIPLE AND C&S   147

The working for the unity of the church as a model pointing to the future of the world globalizes not just international politics but also national and local politics. For example, the official documents of the WCC's World Conference on Church and Society in 1966 have a definite bias for centralization of power. Was this an ecumenical precedent for the title of the Afrikaner DRC's document C&S? I am not certain. However, the conference clearly stated that the implication of the fact that God "created and redeemed the whole world" was that national sovereignty must be diminished in the search for a global "just distribution not only of wealth but also of health, education, security, housing and opportunity." The WCC was urged to study global taxation and certain "regional and world-wide institutions" to coordinate redistributionary social justice.[58]

Consequently, the WCC interprets "protection or advancement of sectional interests" as morally repugnant and inconsistent with the love of God for the "whole of his creation." The WCC defines "sectional interests" as *particular* nations, classes, industries, or individuals. To emphasize these is always "at the expense of the good of [the whole of] humanity." Accordingly, centralized structures are best because decentralized units of even a federal or confederal state can "preserve local injustices that the federal government seeks to remove."[59]

Furthermore, the WCC's church and society documents gratefully acknowledged the Universal Declaration of Human Rights, not Scripture, as a standard for social justice. The WCC praises that declaration as already having achieved a "significant impact" in social justice though not yet a sufficient impact. Furthermore, the documents claim that national unity with these universal human rights should be the goal in all multiethnic countries such as South Africa. This is because this ideal best serves the "effective mobilization of the economic resources of the state in order to achieve social justice."

Instead of having one inerrant authority for these norms, the WCC conference postulated a series of multiple authorities: "Holy Scripture, Christian history, contemporary Christian experience, and the insights of the social sciences and other secular disciplines do inform the situation."[60] The WCC here clearly opted for an ideal socio-political order a unified, powerful, centralized

---

58 World Council of Churches [WCC], *World Conference on Church and Society: Christians in the Technical and Social Revolutions of our Time* [Conference] (Geneva: World Council of Churches, 1967), 89, 92.

59 WCC, *Conference*, 89, 99.

60 WCC, *Conference*, 111; compare C&S, 13–23, with 274–88.

148   WHEN A THEOLOGICAL SHIFT CHANGED A NATION

state checked only by UN guaranteed human rights. This description would apply equally to most Social Democratic states including the United States. This ideal has been realized in the present South African constitution and anticipated the ideal state of that the *Church and Society* (1990) document of the DRC postulated and advocated.[61]

The Church and Society Synod document of the DRC also denied the existence of a "clear set of universally valid rules" or a set of "abstract principles" to apply to "concrete situations." These classically have been derived from careful, context-sensitive exegesis and not eisegesis, reading into the text human ideologies. C&S, as I see it, inaccurately characterized the classical perspective that Scripture alone *inerrantly* and *perspicuously* reveals creation-based design-norms that can be applied to world cultures. This leaves room for human autonomy that rushes to fill authority vacuum with the sole fallible authority of a human document from which universal, transculturally valid principles could be derived. In other words, as we shall see, C&S like the WCC, replaces divine with human authority in its paradigm shift that changed the nation.

Several Logical Deductions from Recapitulative Eschatology

In summary, I would like to suggest eight logical deductions from a classic biblical recapitulative eschatology.

1. A good creation implies that the universe is not in danger of falling into chaotic division destroying primal unity. Unity is therefore not in danger of being compromised by renewed structures that include both unity and diversity in balance that reflect the glory of the Triune God.
2. Redemptive history is, therefore, not a movement away from an always impinging human division. Redemptive history is not a movement toward social-equalitarian unity in centralized-unified institutions. True redemptive history restores covenant fidelity to the Creator's original design, in matured form for all spheres.
3. The structures of created reality are revelatory of divine design-norms and are not merely descriptive givens, even when polluted by death and sin. Certainly, reading nature must be done through the clarifying "glasses" of sound, context-sensitive biblical exegesis that considers genre, human authorship preserved from error by the Holy Spirit, and the era of progressive revelation that the text was written without

---

61 WCC, *Conference*, 103, 107; see C&S, 184–205, 267.

THE CREATION RESTORATION PRINCIPLE AND C&S   149

higher critical biases such as anti-supernaturalism and so forth. In other words, for example, the image of God is broken in humans but not destroyed and can be restored in Christ (e.g., Eph 4:24; Col 3:10; Jas 3:9–12). The image of God includes only a binary of sexes and just gender roles as Scripture abundantly witnesses.

4. Gender, class, or lingual-culture group divisions are not evil in themselves but come out of the creation and can be restored and renewed in the new humanity in Christ.

5. Creation orders (*Schöpfungsordungen*) that are static and non-developing orders, designed to protect against an ever-impinging human social chaos-division, are not biblical.

6. God gave man stewardship for cultivating, protecting, and advancing God's providential design. This includes God-created languages and culture groups.

7. Both indigenous church planting in each language group of earth and the transformation of ethno-culture are top priorities in the Great Commission of Christ.

8. To develop and preserve, for example, a Zulu, Tswana, Xhosa or Afrikaner Christianized culture and language is just, *if* truly directed by biblical norms in the power of the resurrection.

· 8 ·

THE CREATION RESTORATION PRINCIPLE APPLIED TO C&S

C&S Reduces Gospel to Second or Third Article

As seen in previous chapters and sections, C&S rejects, among other key passages, those found in the proto-history (Gn 1–11). The reason is that the Bible's "own nature and character"[1] (C&S, 21) is an exclusively kerygmatic, kingdom-oriented document: "The Bible as proclamation of God's kingdom is not a textbook . . .." Instead, it is the book of the "Good News [i.e. Gospel] that God in his grace seeks out human beings, . . . redeems them, . . . and entrusts them . . . with a supreme calling."[2]

"The DRC and Scripture" (chap. 3 of C&S) discusses this issue extensively. Of particular note are the comments concerning the use of Scripture as a textbook or manual (*handboek*) for the social sciences. In sum, the General Synod explicitly denies that the excluded passages can be used "as a Scriptural basis for political models" and thus certainly cannot be used as a "textbook on, *inter alia*, sociology, economics or politics." All the excluded passages listed in

---

1 C&S, 21.
2 C&S, 19.

152   WHEN A THEOLOGICAL SHIFT CHANGED A NATION

C&S, 22 have been used by various groups to give norms for the judging of or "deduc[ing]' a particular social or political policy."[3]

Evaluation. First of all, the excised passages theoretically should exclude any Christian group from developing and applying biblical models for socio-political renewal and rebuilding. This does not seem to be the case. In actual fact, it seems those passages that would aid confessional conservatives in (re)building a Christian society are more likely to be excluded than those aiding social and theological radicals with their vision.

For example, confessional conservatives in South Africa have used the following passages that C&S excludes. First, Genesis 2:18 deals with the making of Eve as Adam's helper and aids in building a just binary social structure of only two sexes and two gender roles. Second, Genesis 10–11; Deuteronomy 32:8; Proverbs 22:28; Acts 2:8, 17:26; Galatians 3:28–9; and Revelation 21:3, 24 give factual, background information necessary to construct a biblical doctrine of (a) the creation of the ethnic groups, (b) their continuation into the eschaton, and (c) the necessity of all peoples coming into the one church of Christ. All of these, except Galatians 3:28–9, are used by the exclusivists and Afrikaner proponents of apartheid but that does not make them prima facie evil. Any Scripture can be twisted and misused. Misuse does not vitiate true use if exegeted carefully and wisely.

It seems clear that C&S is contradictory at this point. Whereas C&S, 22 rejects the use of certain passages by exclusivists, it also allows several of the same and similar type of passages to be used to construct a doctrine of human unity, a favorite theme of inclusivists. Actually both uses are correct and so it is befitting to use the whole Bible in developing a balanced doctrine of humanity (Anthropology). Mankind in Adam and in the Second Adam is a real Unity and true Diversity, reflecting the equal ultimacy of the One and the Many within the Godhead. Notice how C&S, 96 prioritizes unity without mentioning diversity.

3.1.1 Scripture views the human race as a unity

The creation narrative, which traces the entire human race back to one pair of progenitors, views mankind as an essential unity. This point of view is confirmed by the genealogical registers in Genesis 10, 1 Chronicles 1–9, and Luke 3:23–38, where world history is seen as an extended family history. In Acts 17:26 it is stated that God made every nation 'from one man'. In the same spirit Christ is described as the 'second Adam' who involves the whole human race as an organic unity in his ministry of redemption.[4]

---

3 C&S 22, 19, 21.
4 C&S, 96; bold in original.

THE CREATION RESTORATION PRINCIPLE APPLIED TO C&S   153

In addition, social radicals invalidate the use of the following passages. For example, several of the passages C&S excluded dealt with *both* the unity and diversity of the church (e.g., Jn 17:20–3, 1 Cor 12). Their excision from the corpus of relevant Scriptures implicitly *denies* that the structure of the church, as a unified Body, is actually a proleptic sign of how the future of the world will look in *both* its real diversity together with true unity (the Trinitarian Principle). Consequently, C&S implicitly said that the excised passages teach nothing about, first, what ideals socio-political and economic institutions should follow with respect to unity and diversity together. In addition, C&S implicitly, second, that the diverse-unified structure of the church is not a metaphor in any way or form concerning God's future plan for the rest of the institutions of creation.

If this is a correct implication, then C&S rejected the use of these passages by social radicals and creation design norm advocates (e.g., Kuyperians). If true also, it seems that the document is internally contradictory because C&S definitely did say the church is a paradigmatic sign of the future, as we will note below.

Two Possible Theories for Excision of Passages. In summary, the reason for these exclusions could thus possibly be explained by two theories. Either one or both of the theories seem to be the only viable possibilities for the arbitrary excision of the passages listed. In the case that both possible theories have some validity, then the document is internally contradictory at this point.

First of all, C&S could possibly have moved to a focus upon the kingdom as an exclusively spiritual phenomenon not dealing with specific mundane affairs. As seen above, this is common in pietistic circles and among dialectical theologians. C&S (1986), 42–3 explicitly claimed that the Bible is reduced to a spiritual gospel. However, the 1990 version removes this passage from the revised edition. Even though the Synod of 1990 removed this specific passage and context, this could still remain an implicit theme within the document as a whole. The second theory is that the DRC adopted some form of Third Article futurism as I discussed above.

I will examine both in order, but first, I would like to address a possible motive for the paradigm shift.

Ecumenically Correct Expediency as Possible Motive. Could expediency possibly be a crucial motive for the reason why such excised passages listed above are singled out as not applicable to the development of a viable Reformed social theology and ethic for southern Africa? As I have demonstrated, there are very strong voices and directions in the church moving it toward rapprochement

154   WHEN A THEOLOGICAL SHIFT CHANGED A NATION

with the SACC and the WCC. Thus, there seemed to be a strong pragmatic need at the time to reject the relevance of most of these embarrassing passages because they were and are used by proponents of an ethnically exclusive church and state.

This the WCC emphatically rejects. For one representative example, note that the WCC's conference on church and society urged its member churches everywhere make careful organized attempts "to eradicate from the Church and Christian community" every kind "of discrimination based on race, colour or ethnic origin in the selection of persons for church leadership, admission to the membership of congregations." Furthermore, member churches must adapt "social and cultural values and traditions to the present."[5] Certainly in the first third of the twenty-first century, adapting to the present means adapting to the LGB and now transsexual (T) plus (+) movements as well (LGBTQ+). The evidence seems to point to such a pragmatic need.

Higher Critical Rejection of First Article Absolutes. However, a theological paradigm shift is most likely the deepest underlying motive. Therefore, a first hypothesis as to why C&S excises the relevant passages is that it adopts Second Article reductionism. Only a comprehensive biblical faith that uses such First Article concepts as design-norms, covenantal law, and so forth can develop socio-political models. A reduced social policy, emphasizing a relationship with Jesus and his loving welcome for all, is the result. Without First Article emphases, this Second Article reduction can and has led to huge biblical distortions in social and political ethics.

Furthermore, C&S taught that Scripture must not be read directly into "our own circumstances and problems," reducing it to a "recipe book with instant solutions for all human problems." Instead, the distinctive "character, composition and style," and each book's "particular situation" must be considered. Thus "any superficial interpretation or application of biblical statements" must be "completely rejected" because they ignore "the specific nature, context, style, purpose and historical situation" of each pericope, book, and genre.[6]

Certainly, this type of statement could very well be harmonized with classic Reformed hermeneutics. However, as seen above, many in the DRC accept the higher critical assumption that Scripture is made up of more than one theology. These are sometimes complementary, sometimes parallel, and

---

5 WCC, *Conference*, 175–6; see (1) Neville Richardson, *The World Council of Churches and Race Relations, 1960 to 1969* (Frankfurt am Main: Lang, 1977); (2) Webb, *Long Struggle*, for comprehensive documentation.

6 C&S, 18.

THE CREATION RESTORATION PRINCIPLE APPLIED TO C&S   155

sometimes contradictory to one another. Therefore, the Bible does not speak with one unified voice throughout. Consequently, using higher critical presuppositions, a doctrine is thus not discovered by the compilation of all relevant data. This compiled data cannot be correlated, harmonized, systematized, and applied to culture as in classic Scripture-based hermeneutics. This new hermeneutic denies perspicuity and the concept that fallen human nature and hence Scriptural norms and remedies are the same for all humans in all times and cultures. As a consequence of adopting the higher critical paradigm shift, Scripture has no direct application to contemporary culture if it ever did at all.

Secondly, most major theologians in the DRC at the time of C&S and especially today reject the creation account and the rest of the proto-history as factual history. A great many would reject the fifteenth-century BC date of the composition of the Pentateuch, adopting some form of the Documentary Hypothesis (DH). This means that no statement in these books can ever be taken at face value but must be reinterpreted through the lenses of the DH or its then present permutation. This is termed historical exegesis or something similar like taking the historical context into account.

Taking the point to its logical conclusion, the creation account or the Decalogue, for example, cannot be used as a "recipe book with instant solutions," as C&S, 18 boldly stated, to the issues directly addressed in these accounts (e.g., Gn 1:28 and Ps 8; Gn 2:2 and Ex 20:11, 31:17; Heb 4:4; Gn 2:24 and Mt 19:5 and 1 Cor 6:16; Eph 5:31; Gn 1–2 and Rom 5:12ff).

On the other hand, following Christ and the Apostles, classic Reformed theology has always taught, for example, that both the First History (Gn 1–11) (the accounts of the creation to just before Abraham) and the Decalogue are immediately applicable to every group and time in human history. The creation to Abraham account is the necessary prologue to both the law and the gospel. This both our Lord and the Apostle's claimed in such passages that deal, for example, with marriage and sexuality, the fall into sin, the universal flood of Noah all the way to the call and covenant with Abraham. Even the story of Abraham Christ and especially Paul saw as paradigmatic for believers everywhere.

Therefore, taking these higher critical assumptions as a given, C&S' main authors seem to have meant that the excised passages have been subjected to complex higher critical syllogisms and have come out being rejected as relevant truth for contemporary culture. The substratum of relevant truth left to the church is merely the gospel truths proclaimed in the Second Article about Christ's redemption. However, stripping Christ from his historical context

156   WHEN A THEOLOGICAL SHIFT CHANGED A NATION

calls into question even his own history leaving humanity with no certain joyful news.

The implication thus is that only ecclesiastical experts trained in the various Redaction and Form Critical theories or the various theories of the origin of the Pentateuch, the historical books, the pre- and post-exilic prophets, the pseudonymous books (e.g., Daniel), the Synoptics, Acts, the Epistles, and so forth can understand these and other passages. Scripture becomes a dark book to the man in the pew. By taking the Bible out of the hands of the people, the General Synod has made itself into a collective, Medieval papacy—a virtual synodocracy.

Old Testament professor P. A. Verhoef, writing in a commentary on the C&S commissioned by the General Synod, tried to refute this conclusion. "Now does this mean, some want to know, that the Bible can only be exposited by experts?" Verhoef writes. "In this perspective, are we not in the process of becoming Roman Catholic? Is not the Bible meant for the normal believer?"[7]

Verhoef's answer was two-fold. First, he claims that the synod was mistaken on several things in the past and, in like manner, has now "come to other, deeper insights." Verhoef, however, does not explain why the new insights of the present, higher critically trained experts and theologians contradict certain foundational truths validated by previous synods. This includes even the synods that adopted and promoted the *Belgic Confession*. For example, to deny the use of significant Scripture passages, using such new insight as "the scopus of Scripture is largely kingdom, kerygma and gospel oriented," is certainly a fundamental paradigm shift. The classic Reformed position as exhibited by the Heidelberg Catechism uses the First History and even the Mosaic case laws to apply to contemporary societies.

Verhoef next claims that "the Bible speak[s] in clear language," but only concerning the gospel. Hence, it is only the gospel that people can understand "without necessary intermediaries to exposit the Bible for us."[8] The rest of Scripture not dealing specifically with the gospel, Verhoef concludes, cannot be understand apart from experts. For the rest, "theologians are necessary."[9]

This is not only overconfident but ecclesiocentric, that is centered on the churchly academic bureaucracy, exactly as was the Medieval Roman Church's

---

7 Pieter A. Verhoef, *Bybellig op Verhoudings. "Kerk en Samelewing" vir die Gewone Lidmaat.* ... [Biblical Light upon Relationships. "Church and Society" For the Normal Member. ...] [Bible Light] (Wellington, RSA: Bybelkor, 1987), 6.

8 Verhoef, *Bible Light*, 10, 11.

9 Verhoef, *Bible Light*, 11.

THE CREATION RESTORATION PRINCIPLE APPLIED TO C&S 157

magisterium. Further, his assertion seemed to deny the redemptive-historical movement from the old to the new covenant. Before, God the Spirit was with the people of God, speaking through prophets and priests (Jn 14:17; Neh 9:20, 30). Now he is in each one as the prophetic Spirit (Jl 2:28–32; Acts 2:17–18). Now God has spoken (aorist) in the Son once and for all (Heb 1:1–2; Jude 2). All have the anointing Holy Spirit to discern truth and to teach believers through Scripture (1 Jn 2:20–1, 26–7). This is the key Reformational doctrine of the priesthood of believers (1 Pt 2:9). All of these fit within the hypothesis that the General Synod adopted a form of Second Article reductionism sketched in preceding pages and has thus, in effect, rejected the Reformation.

Third Article Reductionism: The Church as Nova Creatio. A second theory is that C&S has adopted a form of Third Article futurism. As discussed earlier, this ecumenical theology views the kingdom as a future reality that introduces into the church totally new creation (*nova creatio*) role relationships. In this nova creatio, the kingdom is always in the process of becoming, and hence it has always been cut off from any normative root in a literal creation. According to this interpretation, the passages excised from the proto-history are by and large based upon mythological accounts that do not teach fact but only a moral ideal. That ideal is the unity of mankind that has been "lost" and needs to be "restored" in the kingdom of God by the redemption in Christ. Therefore, the world is in itself "broken and divided." The church, as the proclaimer of the unique, new creation-kingdom, must "make this unity visible."[10]

> **2.8 The church is a window to God's imminent new world**
> As God's new creation, and as the sphere of the Holy Spirit's operation, the church must in all its activities provide a glimpse of the future. The divisions within the church must not be accepted as normal. In the church, love must triumph over enmity and hate, the truth over falsehood, unity over division, reconciliation and peace over violence and confrontation. Only in this way will the church be a true church, and prove to be a credible window to the future of our Lord Jesus Christ.

This gives us a first indication of the futurist, Third Article influence in C&S. The church thus has come as the model for the world. This means, the next section 23 states, "that the new relationships in which the citizens of the Kingdom were placed ... causes them to have a solemn calling which must be practised in all walks of life." The implication seems to be that Christians must first center on the church as institution as the agent of change: "For this reason attention is given firstly to the nature and calling of the church and

10 C&S, 72, bold in original. See C&S, 81, pt. 2.9.3.

158   WHEN A THEOLOGICAL SHIFT CHANGED A NATION

the relationships which result therefrom, and secondly to **personal** and **group relationships** as viewed from the perspective of the [future] kingdom."[11]

Professor Johann Kinghorn understands the radical implications of this change in the definition of the church in his *Commentary on Church and Society*. This paradigm-shifting change, he perceives, had already begun even by 1989 to permeate the rest of the DRC's social theology as well. C&S' "church-centered" ecclesiology was experiencing a "de-ideologization" from apartheid's "non-ecclesial ideas." The individualist, believer's church concept was non-ideological, he indicated but the idea of an indigenous-people's church, he seems to have claimed, shows syncretism with "ideology," by which he means, most likely, with apartheid.[12]

On the other hand from the perspective I am emphasizing, quite possibly the opposite contention has more truth. C&S now saw that individual faith alone, irrespective of ethnic or racial background, was the only prerequisite for full voting membership in a local congregation irrespective of language or culture. This was a rediscovery, via Barth, of the concept of the "church as the community of the believers." As I will demonstrate later, this implicitly accepts the Radical Reformation's ideal of a believer's church. That in turn is a denial of the covenant continuity doctrine of the Genevan Reformers from which the DRC derives its lineage.

In other words, each local congregation must both reflect and make full accommodation to the language and culture differences for all those living in the vicinity and incorporate them into the kingdom community. Often this would imply in practice that a worship service or business meeting of the congregation would be in a local trade language or in the case of South Africa, in English, the imperial language. This paradigm shift in ecclesiology was of "greatest importance," Johann Kinghorn continued, because he anticipated, it can "overflow in the end with a fundamental shift in the [DRC's] standpoint on apartheid [in society]."[13] Ultimately, apartheid and all its roots and shoots must be utterly dismantled. The Medieval Latin Mass would be an analogy.

However, would it not more loving to plant distinct congregations for each language-cultural group living in a circumscribed geographical area if, at least, every service was open for attendance by whomever would come? This is what

11 C&S, 72, 22, 23, emphasis in the original.
12 Johann Kinghorn, "'n Rondte Meer [A Round Sea]," in *Kommentaar op Kerk en Samelewing* [Commentary on Church and Society] (Potchefstroom, RSA: Instituut vir Reformatoriese Studie, 1989), 38, 37.
13 Kinghorn, *Commentary on Church and Society*, 38.

THE CREATION RESTORATION PRINCIPLE APPLIED TO C&S   159

the Reformers emphasized, I would assert. Even post-Vatican 2 Catholics would agree. Therefore, this Third Article emphasizes upon the future kingdom makes the church the unique sphere of an absolutely new creation without any of the polluting marks of what some Third Article theologians may still call the old divisive creational structures. The church as institution thus becomes a "model" for all of society. In other words, the church as an equalitarian society must *preview* what all the rest of society should strive now to become.

This leads to a second indication of possible influence for a Third Article futurist orientation. This springs from C&S' direct use of terminology claiming that the church is a window upon the coming future kingdom. For example is the passage I cited above: "**The church is a window to God's imminent new world.**" Therefore, "as God's new creation, and as the sphere of the Holy Spirit's operation, the church must ... provide a glimpse of the future." Another example is C&S' point 3.4.3, which states: "The church must summon its members, equip them, and send them out to serve the coming of the kingdom in society."[14]

Now, taken by itself, many orthodox theologians could have written this. However, the following paragraphs clarify the meaning. "3.4.4 The church must furnish society with a living example of what God's work of re-creation accomplishes in people's lives." To accomplish this, and to "lend credibility to its [kingdom] proclamation," "the church must in its very existence establish a visible symbol and concrete expression of the Kingdom of God." This means, as described in a later practical application section, that the "church must be a living display window of what God in his grace accomplishes." The following C&S paragraph shows the social structural implications of this social ethic: "In contrast to the social structures emanating from creation, the church is the only social structure which is the fruit of God's re-creation. It is the first-fruit of his new creation."[15] This paragraph served then as a commentary on the phrase used several times in C&S concerning the church as a "unique" fellowship: "As the unique new creation of God, the church is a fellowship of people"—without qualification.[16]

It seems certain that here C&S is not in continuity with covenantal thought on the nature of the church. Classic Reformed theology defines the church as the people of God through the ages beginning with the first family in the Garden and continuing into the family of Abraham, then fulfilled in

14   C&S, 227.
15   C&S, 229, 230.
16   C&S, 68, see also 24–5, 232.

160   WHEN A THEOLOGICAL SHIFT CHANGED A NATION

the family of Abraham's seed, who is the Second Adam (BC, 27). Reformed Theology teaches that the New Testament universal assembly (the *ekklesia* as the body of Christ) is truly a multi-national and multi-lingual people of God, the assembly of YHWH (*qahal Yahweh*) in the new covenant and the legal assembly of the Creator. However, now it is not merely for one people-group (the Hebrews) but for every people-group of earth. At the same time, it is not merely an institution which is a "unique wonder of regeneration by God in a sinful and broken world."[17] The church of Christ is the community of faithful, covenant-and-language-bound families, who live out their trusting obedience as salt and light in the socio-political order, the family, the school, private organizations, and in the worship cultus.[18]

In the best of Reformed and especially those in the broad Kuyperian, Neo-Calvinist school, the church as institute is not the center of Kingdom life but only one of several institutions partaking of new covenant life. The goal is to have the world and its kingdoms become indeed what they are in title, the kingdom of God, which his Christ (the Anointed King) has inherited and given to Abraham's Seed (e.g., Ps 2; Dn 7; Jn 1:2–3; Gal 3; Col 1:13–20; Heb 1:2–3, 2:5–18; Rv 11:15).

C&S sees the church as the exact opposite. As a "unique creation," the "unique nature of the church" must be respected. We must "not assess it in terms of the notions of this sinful, passing world, or confuse it with the institutions of the present sinful reality." In other words, Christ did *not* come ultimately to teach all the peoples and nations everything he commanded from Genesis to Revelation. He came only to build a separate, totally new people that does *not* redeem, restore, and in that way transform every culture group of earth. He came *merely* to distinguish the divisive old from the totally new with the hope that the totally new will eventually triumph over the oppressive and divisive old. This is a Third Article overemphasis.[19] This then must model to the social order what the Kingdom should look like in its socio-political ramifications.

Again the above could perhaps be read in the light of orthodox theology. However, two theological errors need to be considered first to correctly understand what C&S seems to mean here. First of all, most DRC theologians do

---

17 C&S, 24.

18 See a Kuyperian-Dooyeweerd perspective, James H. Olthuis, and others, *Will All the King's Men. ... Out of Concern for the Church Phase II* (Toronto: Wedge Publishing Foundation, 1972).

19 C&S, 26.

not believe the creation account of the proto-history is literal history. This would then imply that death and evil must be inherent in the world itself because there never was any fallen creation that needed to be healed as a result of the redeeming work of the promised Messiah-King Jesus. The church, then, must become the only institution that has ever partaken of creation newness. The new creation is thus not a recapitulation of the first creation. If the creation were not *inherently* broken and deficient, then there would no need for a "unique" new creation. "In this sinful, broken, passing world, God made a new beginning, bringing into being a unique creation: his church." Without an originally defective creation, the new creation would merely be the restoration of the first creation in matured form as both Bavinck and Kuyper affirmed.[20]

It is in this sense, that C&S claimed the church is unique. In itself as structure, it should ideally anticipate the "total newness" of the future kingdom. The old apartheid DRC, however, rejected this total newness and desired to restore the creational diversity and hence failed as a "window" on the new creation, future kingdom. At this time sin and divisive evil will no longer be a constituent part of the essence of the old creation called in C&S "the passing world." (In its former project, I would add, the DRC failed miserably because it equated color and race to ethno-linguistic identity).

If this perspective on C&S is accurate, then Kinghorn's deductions concerning the meaning of this "uniqueness" of the church were again correct. "Logically," he wrote, "the church is not bound to the structures or biases of the society in which the church operates. In (the body of) Christ the normal distinctions between man and woman, slave and free man, and there also between race and nation, are not normative." In conclusion, he wrote, "obviously, this has far-reaching implications for the question as to how the unity of the church should take visible shape."[21]

Again, Professor Verhoef's commentary on C&S supported this understanding of an implicit nova creatio principle in C&S. He claimed that the church is not "rooted in the nation, but in the incarnation." It is not built upon creation order, or what I term, creational design-norms, but upon the recreation.[22] Similarly, the DRC's General Synod Commission (GSC) criticized a group of their own apartheid theologians and their document protesting C&S called *Faith and Protest* (F&P). The chief critique against F&P was that it determined the nature of the church by means of the fallen creation,

20 C&S, 25.
21 Kinghorn, *Home for Everyone*, 30.
22 Verhoef, *Bible Light*, 19.

162 WHEN A THEOLOGICAL SHIFT CHANGED A NATION

not the new creation: "Thus the origin of the church is situated not in nature but in grace."[23]

Evaluation. Neither faction, I might add, was biblically nor reformationally correct. The new community of the King is built upon a healed and renewed creation design and not merely upon a "grace" that has absolutely nothing to do with the fallen first creation. Apartheid did not consequently and comprehensively seek to heal the broken first creation. Instead, it merely considered race. However, race is never mentioned in Scripture but only ethno-linguistic groups. Color is only mentioned twice, the darkly tanned Shulamite woman and the Kushite, who could not change his color just like a leopard could not change his spots. The apartheid legal system, to which the DRC acquiesced, then merged together color as a very hurtful and crude ethnic demarcation indicator and ethno-linguistic diversity. Apartheid theology also rejected building its recommended legal system upon the Old and New Testaments' impartiality principle, which I will discuss later in this volume. So it was doomed to fail just as the new South Africa, built as it also is upon deviant theology, is failing and will ultimately collapse. When that will occur I do not predict nor know, but it certainly will, based on the revealed principles of justice belonging to the God of justice revealed in Scripture.

To accept this radical dichotomy between the creation and new creation means the theologians must accept two faulty doctrines, if they were logically consistent. First, it should teach a semi-Docetic Christology that claims that Christ possesses humanity not derived from the inherently imperfect first creation. Second, it should also teach a form of the Radical Reformation's dictum that Christ's body was a heavenly body not derived from Adam through Mary.[24] Both destroy Christ's right to recapitulate Adamic history in reverse, because to do so, Christ has to partake in the same created humanity that Adam possessed before the fall.

The implicit assumption here is that the original creation was not "very good," as the Scripture states. Contrary to Verhoef and the GSC, the church is built on both the creation and the new creation, both Adam's creation and the Second Adam's incarnation. New creation and incarnation are both in recapitulative continuity with the good original creation. Thus, it is not evil to build the church upon creational design-norms and creational forms (e.g., the

23 *Algemene Sinodale Kommissie* [General Synod Commission], *Antwoord van Ned. Geref. Kerk op Geloof en Protes* [Answer of the DRC to *Faith and Protest*] (N.p.: Algemene Sinodale Kommissie, 1988), 10, 11, 18.

24 See, e.g., Balke, *Anabaptist Radicals*; Potgieter, *C&S Essence*, 199.

THE CREATION RESTORATION PRINCIPLE APPLIED TO C&S   163

family and the extended family). As shall be seen, this is fundamental to the Reformation's covenantal doctrine of the church.

The DRC's Implicit Radical Model for Social Transformation

While denying that Christians may use Scripture-based models for social transformation, C&S actually turns around and uses one. This model's world-view assumptions are actually similar to those of the Radical Reformation and of dialectical theology influenced by Karl Barth. As Professor André Dumas of the Protestant Theological Faculty of Paris said at the WCC conference on church and society, "Revolutionary leaders find it hard to resist the messi-anic drawing power of a myth of absolute newness." However, as Dumas goes on to point out, once in power these leaders always "re-establish links with their ancestral and national past." Creational design-norms are inescapable for those who wish, even pragmatically, to build a lasting social order. This is true for all secular and religious prophets of newness. This pragmatic reality is what Dumas and other ecumenical leaders often point out when they note that Christ does not promise a "pure other-worldly utopia."[25]

According to many of these leaders, however, Christ did introduce the other-worldly future principle into the present fallen, passing, and divided world. This future principle as something not founded upon the institutions of creation creates tension between the old and new. This tension, they believed, was what drives history forward.[26] For example, already in 1966, the Harvard theologian Krister Stendahl could write prescient, now classic article, about how the radically new future breaks into the present, using Galatians (3:28). This is a passage, which he as so many other radicals do, tears out of its context. The old creation orders oppressed women (and powerless ethnic minorities), he implies, but the new gives them equality. Thus, the church does not need to be reminding people of the oppressive present oppressive reality. "We need badly the reminder of that which is new [the *not-yet*] . . . the forces toward renewal and re-creation."[27] When the church *now* gradually sets up equalitarian sign-posts of the expected not-yet kingdom, the new future order will gradually

---

25 WCC, *Conference*, 21.

26 For background, see Igor Shafarevich, *The Socialist Phenomenon: A Historical Survey of Socialist Policies and Ideals* [Socialist Phenomenon]. Translated by William Tjalsma. Foreword by Alexander Solzhenitsyn (Shawnee, KS: Gideon House, 2019); Cohn, *Pursuit*.

27 Krister Stendahl, *The Bible and the Role of Women: A Case Study in Hermeneutics*, trans. Emilie T. Sander (Philadelphia: Fortress, 1966), 37.

transcend the old. The church models for the social order what the totally new future kingdom looks like in practice, serving as a leavening force therein.

To accomplish this transformation of the present by means of the future, the Radical Reformation proposed two models: The gradualist "withdrawal model" (e.g., Amish, Mennonites, and Hutterites) and the "revolutionary model" led by inner light, holy spirit-led prophet, Thomas Müntzer and self-proclaimed prophet-king, Jan van Leyden. Against both these movements, Martin Luther strove mightily, sometimes with quite intemperate rhetoric. Recently retired, Calvin Theological Seminary Professor John Bolt, surveyed these Christianized ideologies in an excellent article titled, "Eschatological Hermeneutics, Women's Ordination, and the Reformed tradition." In it he carefully sketched the ideological roots of contemporary eschatological and gnostic-utopian movements and their eschatological ethics. I would dissent on only one issue. Contrary to Bolt's attempt to sharply distinguish the gradualist movements from those that are revolutionary, I am of the opinion that both share the same non-recapitulative presuppositions and are two species of the same genus. Consequently, both seek to introduce a utopian-revolutionary futurist ethic into society. One is perhaps more covert and gradual, for example, the Anabaptists of the Mennonite Central Committee, while the other is more overt and blatant such as the present homosexual and transsexual revolutionary propaganda within mainline denominations in the West.[28]

To its credit, C&S denied both models. Concerning the withdrawal model, C&S was forthright: "The church is not intended to be an alternative society replacing existing social structures." However, this was actually not as straight forward as it at first seems. The paragraph continued by explaining that "within society it must be an exemplary fellowship." In other words, the church "ought to be a fellowship that serves as an example to all, and in its very existence . . . provide an inspiring example of the power of the Holy Spirit who can also completely renew human relationships." Immediately, however, the "already," the futurist vision was again softened by the "not-yet": "Yet the church may never imply that it has attained everything or that it has reached its goal."[29]

28 John Bolt, "Eschatological Hermeneutics, Women's Ordination, and the Reformed Tradition [Eschatological Hermeneutics]," *Calvin Theological Journal* 26 (1991). See a moderate more biblical version of the Anabaptist vision, Perry B. Yoder, *Shalom: The Bible's Word for Salvation, Justice, & Peace* (Eugene, OR: Wipf and Stock, 2017).

29 C&S, 230.

THE CREATION RESTORATION PRINCIPLE APPLIED TO C&S   165

Radical Gradualism Described. In introducing a tension between the future and present, C&S seems to have adopted a perspective similar to Stendahl and the many ecumenical theologians who have used similar argumentation since his day in the 1960s. This can be termed radical gradualism or Fabianism, named after a British gradualist socialist movement begun in the 1880s. David Bosch, the late DRC minister and UNISA theologian, explained what will happen when the church, without withdrawing from society, gradually sets up signposts of the kingdom in the world. At the time of his writing, many leaders of the DRC would have recoiled, perhaps, from the logical extent to which Bosch pushes C&S' non-recapitulative, already-but-not-yet eschatology.

However, worldview presuppositions over time have profound consequences in culture. It is wise to plot out what those consequences could be. Bosch was not arguing in an intellectual vacuum. The vision he expounded has never-before been held by the orthodox Christian movement. However, it has been the staple of gnosticized-equalitarian sectarians that have fed utopian renewal movements for centuries.[30]

Professor Bosch explains: "Once Paul became aware of the reality of the new community he suddenly discovered that he was now living in another age and time." He continued, citing radical liberation theologian Juan Mattheos with approval. This gradually radicalizing community, provides "no privileges [for any individual], either racial, national, social, . . . class or sex (1 Cor 12:13; Gal 3:28; Col 3:11)." This new fellowship results in "a group where all barriers have fallen (Eph 2:13–16)." In other words, "There is no one on top or beneath," that is no hierarchy at all. Furthermore, "Here there is no mine or thine (Acts 4:32)." Everything will be held communally including wives in Jan Van Leyden's visionary practice. Bosch's vision accords with the sects' radical equalitarian, utopian vision in which all hierarchical relationships are removed, even those between magistrate and citizen. The property distinctions between the rich and poor are erased. All capitalistic and economic competition is replaced with harmonious distribution of the whole community's goods for which everyone works to the best of their ability. Bosch continued with another citation of Mattheos: "It is a group . . . where no rivalry or partasionship [*sic*] exists, but all are united in love . . . and authority means greater service not superiority."[31]

Conclusion. Needless to say, this was and remains a semi-Christianized, almost-Marxian version of the utopian vision that Friedrich Engles saw in

---

30 See, e.g., (1) Cohn, *Pursuit*; Shafarevich, *Socialist Phenomenon*; (2) bibliography of Bolt, *Eschatological Hermeneutics*.

31 Bosch, *Alternative*, 28–9.

166   WHEN A THEOLOGICAL SHIFT CHANGED A NATION

Thomas Müntzer and Jan Van Leyden's totally new creation ideology. In his 1850 work, *The Peasant War in Germany* he terms both "prophets" as pre-Marxist but also as religious precursors of the atheist revolution that he and Karl Marx foresaw inevitably would come upon the earth.[32] Interestingly enough, these kinds of Fabian, gradualist movements can rapidly switch into full on revolutionary mode and then back again. In North America, this same Fabian ideology has now morphed into the revolutionary neo-Marxian, official Black Lives Matter movement (though not shared by all co-demonstrators), the Antifa (a Marxist, Anti-Fascist) movement and the ideologically radical LGBTQ+ movement.

Therefore, if this second gradualist theory about the ideological roots of C&S is accurate, as it seems to be, then the DRC church had adopted in a moderated form the "unique," nova creatio perspective, a Third Article viewpoint. Whether gradualist or revolutionary both seek a realization of something totally new and never before seen. Several of the exclusivist theologians I surveyed in an earlier chapter gave evidence for the validity of this insight.

C&S and the Creation of the Peoples

Furthermore, it seems clear that C&S rejects HRLS' use of the First Article of the creed and thereby reduces it to the Second and/or Third Article. In so doing, C&S rejects the earlier DRC Synod document that sought to justify apartheid, *Human Relations in the Light of Scripture*.[33] That Synod policy statement grounded apartheid ideology on a First Article-like doctrine of the creation of the peoples. C&S explicitly states that the "existence and the diversity of peoples **per se** . . . is accepted as part of the given reality." Furthermore, as such it is "neither positively commended nor negatively viewed."[34] The peoples and their territories on the earth are merely described in relatively neutral terms as "a historic reality which occurred by God's providential ordering."[35] Ethno-linguistic diversity in Scripture, in other words, is merely descriptive and as such has no prescriptive and normative value at all. I have extensively

---

32 Friedrich Engles, *The Peasant War in Germany*. Routledge Revivals, trans. Moissaye J. Olgin (New York: Rouledge, 2017).

33 HRLS, 9.3.

34 C&S, 103; bold in original.

35 C&S, 16.

THE CREATION RESTORATION PRINCIPLE APPLIED TO C&S   167

refuted this allegation in *The Concept of Ethnicity in the Bible: A Theological Analysis* (2009).[36]

Reasons for C&S' Shift in the Assessment of Ethnicity

As shall be discussed more completely in the following chapter, this seems quite clearly parallel to how Barthians see peopleness. Merely a "historic reality" or part of "given reality," such passages as those concerning (1) the confusion of languages (Ge 11; C&S, 106), (2) Abraham's call (Ge 12; C&S, 107), and (3) the creation of the peoples (Dt 32:8 and Acts 17:26) speak of nothing more than "God is in control of everything."[37] In addition, according to C&S, the cause of this doctrinal reductionism is that ostensibly the "Bible does not concern itself with the discussion of such issues as national policy or the maintenance or abrogation of national identity."[38]

Evaluation and Chapter Conclusion

First, a paradigm shift from creation-oriented, Kuyperian theology to a pluralistic theology deeply influenced by higher criticism, Barthianism, and Third Article eschatology seems to be the cause of this reductionism. Since Barthian theology rejects "peopleness" (*volk* in Afrikaans) as a creation-founded social sphere, there seems to be more than a circumstantial connection here between the theological paradigm shift and the change in the understanding of ethnicity.

Second, Scripture explicitly states that God created the peoples to worship him (Ps 86:9; Acts 17:26). C&S denied the relevance of this type of passage for any sort of social or political model, as I have shown. This can again only be explained by the theological paradigm shift that has occurred. Both the Second Article Christological and gospel focus of C&S and neo-Orthodox views of revelation relegated created social, historical, and material entities into irrelevance. They were mere non-essential packaging around the real spiritual message of the Bible. With the denial of a literal creation and the protohistory, Barthians (and C&S) made the existence of the cultural mandate and the Babel account (Gn 10–11) irrelevant for social theology and social ethics. C&S saw both accounts as not historically factual, but again only teaching

36 Kreitzer, *Ethnicity in the Bible.*
37 C&S, 16.
38 C&S, 109.

168   WHEN A THEOLOGICAL SHIFT CHANGED A NATION

rather vague spiritual truth and nothing more. On the other hand, the previous decade's document, HRLS, was correct in founding the cultural mandate (Gn 1:17–18), along with both Kuyper and Bavinck, in the creation design and the covenantal connection between that mandate and the Babel pericope (compare Gn 1:28; 9:1, 7 with 11:4).[39] Its application, however, was extremely skewed by race-bound ideological "glasses."[40]

Third, all social phenomena, including the existence and continuation or extinction of ethno-cultural groups, occur at the specific command of the Creator God who guides providence. C&S got this right to a certain extent. On the other hand, this is the doctrine of the correlation of creation and providence, and all socio-cultural phenomena are revelational of God's will and foreordained plan. Especially with the guidance of the Word, therefore, such phenomena can be evaluated positively if honored and protected according to biblical design standards, or they can be negatively viewed when deified or denigrated. Clearly, then, ethnicity, nationhood, and related concepts are more than just mere observational givens in present reality.

Last, if the Barthian background for the paradigm shift from HRLS to C&S on ethnicity is rejected, then the only other explanation for reducing the creed to Christology, which this passage does, is escapist pietism as Wingren shows. However, C&S rejects such pietistic reductionism. Several paragraphs espouse the classic Reformed perspective of the relevance of the Scriptures for all of life.[41] Here, as I previously discussed, C&S is self-contradictory. It wants to limit the relevance of many applicable passages and still, at the same time, maintain somewhat of the comprehensive, classically Reformed vision for the transformation of all of society.

Notice examples of this self-contradiction in the following. C&S claimed, "by virtue of its particular nature God's Word contains no direct prescription regarding the regulation of relationships among peoples." This is because of its unique kingdom focus, as discussed earlier. Yet as the same time, C&S immediately stated that "this does not mean the Bible has no message concerning group relationships." These are found in the ethics of inter-individual relationships: "we have to look for [that message] . . . in the biblical guidelines for interpersonal behavior."[42] In making these claims, C&S forgets to mention the

39 See, e.g., Abraham Kuyper, "The Tower of Babel [Babel]," in *Common Grace*, vol. 1, ed. Jordan Ballor and Stephen Grabill (Bellingham, Washington: Lexham, 2016), 357–64.

40 See, as an example, HRLS 9.3.

41 See esp. C&S, 222–4, 227–8.

42 C&S, 123.

THE CREATION RESTORATION PRINCIPLE APPLIED TO C&S 169

extensive stranger laws of the Pentateuch, the background of the Parable of the Good Samaritan. The principle of love between peoples is more than mere inter-individual ethics.

Final Conclusion. C&S denied a wholistic Three Article creed. It reduced Christianity to the Second Article when useful to deny odious aspects of apartheid theology based on creation ordinances. It further introduced reductionistic Third Article themes to help paint a more or less covert picture of what a new South Africa could look like. These appeared to the authors of C&S to be useful in the attempt to re-enter the worldwide ecumenical discussion and ecclesial communities. On the other hand, however, when it appeared convenient to emphasize the all-comprehensive nature of Trinitarian kingdom themes and norms, then C&S returned in a contradictory manner to a more classic Reformed perspective. Perhaps this was to mollify the more conservative Kuyperian academic and membership base.

I suggest that a swing away from a Reformed recapitulation doctrine explains the DRC's covertly radical paradigm shift quite adequately. This doctrine teaches that Christ brings healing and then maturing into a still good yet actually twisted, literal creation. He has brought in the eschaton into the present evil age so that the two ages overlaps. The new eschatological age which the promised Davidic King brought gradually overwhelms the dark domain of the prince of rebellion and conquers it step-by-step.

The DRC's swing away from the biblical recapitulation theme also brought with it a reduced creed that focuses on either Christology or Third Article spiritualized futurism (or both). Both kinds of swings are common in dialectical and neo-orthodox circles. Consequently, while denying that Scripture can support socio-political models, C&S does indeed have such an embedded covert model. The future kingdom of God in the church breaks into the world with a totally new creation, a totally new, never before seen rainbow vision of a soon-to-come Rainbow Nation, the New South Africa led by the more or less ideologically egalitarian ANC-SACP (African National Congress, South African Communist Party) alliance (though not in actual practice). The DRC church, then according to the C&S, must model to all the whole world what the future will look like.[43] The New South Africa was the first nation in the world to guarantee LGBTQ+ rights, I believe. That Rainbow revolution, first officially constituted in the RSA, has now hit the West directly.

---

43 See, e.g., C&S, 303.

Alternative Critique of Apartheid Needed. To adequately critique apartheid social theology, however, this shift was never necessary. Scripture itself, the war cry of the Reformation, was then and remains sufficient to both critique Apartheid and to give a just alternative. Contrary to many, the creation design-norms elaborated by Moses and the prophets and interpreted by Christ and his Apostles did not create the genuinely oppressive aspects of apartheid social theology. If the C&S theologians, many of them disciples of Karl Barth, had followed the lead of Gustaf Wingren and many others, they could have used many varied sorts of creational-legal and Old Testament prophetic materials to refute their own biblicized Afrikaner nationalistic idolatries. These the Afrikaner National Party used to justify inter-ethnic oppression in the name of love of their nation and even in the name of love for their neighboring nations all within the imperialist designated borders of the Republic of South Africa.

· 9 ·

THE COVENANT PRINCIPLE AND
PEOPLENESS IN SCRIPTURE

Two Protestant Social Theologies

This chapter on the Covenant Principle will demonstrate that *Church and Society* reads alien presuppositions about covenant into Scripture. Biblical covenantal models bind together distinct yet foundational family, church and civil governments under the Lordship of King Jesus. C&S, I assert, make presupposition that are more akin to those of the individualistic, radical Reformers than the covenantal, family-oriented Reformers. Secondly, I argue that C&S (1990) applies these presuppositions primarily to the question of church unity and secondarily to the critique of Apartheid as a socio-political system.

The two most prominent forms of Protestant social theology are (1) covenantal and (2) non-covenantal or individualistic social theology. These two forms result in two streams of thought with much intermixture of the types.[1] British, North American, and Continental Calvinism are essentially covenantal

---

1 Some at that time resisted contrasting the two: (1) John Howard Yoder, "Reformed Versus Anabaptist Social Strategies: An Inadequate Typology," *Theological Students Fellowship* 8 (May–June 1985): 2–7; (2) Richard J. Mouw, "Abandoning the Typology: A Reformed Assist," *Theological Students Fellowship Bulletin* 8 (May–June 1985); (3) Richard J. Mouw and John H. Yoder, "Evangelical Ethics and the Anabaptist-Reformed Dialogue," *Journal of Religious Ethics* 17 (Fall 1989); (4) Hans Georg Vom Berg, Henk Kossen, Larry Miller, and

172 WHEN A THEOLOGICAL SHIFT CHANGED A NATION

built on the covenant family group, while still considering the necessity of an individual's own surrender of trust to the Lordship of King Jesus. On the other hand, the Radical Reformation or Anabaptist Movement is self-consciously non-covenantal and built on the individual believer. The Radicals consisted of the revolutionary and pacifist wings.[2] The cultural vision of the Radicals and that of the covenantal Reformers are antithetical (see chart below).[3] One group saw the church as made up of believing individuals; the other saw the church and civil order as founded upon believing covenanted families. The Radical Reformation's non-covenantal thought is a logical consequence of a rejection or re-interpretation of three classic Reformed doctrines: Scripture's infallible authority, its Trinitarian key, its optimistic yet restorative eschatology.

Non-Covenantal Individualism

Does C&S Overemphasize Individual Believer's Church Dogma?

An individualizing process is at work in C&S. The following quote from C&S, 40 possesses a distinctive baptistic emphasis: "In the New Testament the church is in all respects a fellowship of faith, confession and worship. Whoever believes the Gospel, confesses that Jesus is Lord, and truly worships God in spirit, is accepted into His church." It does not mention covenant baptism,

---

Lukas Vischer, *Mennonites and Reformed in Dialogue* (Geneva: World Alliance of Reformed Churches, 1986).

    The dialogue between progressive, Reformed Protestants and the descendants of the Radical Reformation is still ongoing. See, e.g.: (1) "Mennonite and Reformed Reconciliation in a Global Perspective," Mennonite World Conference, accessed August 17, 2023, https://mwc-cmm.org/en/stories/mennonite-and-reformed-reconciliation-global-perspective; (2) Leonard Verduin, *The Reformers and Their Stepchildren* [Stepchildren] (Grand Rapids: The Baptist Standard Bearer, 2001).

2 See George H. Williams, *The Radical Reformation* [Radical], 3rd ed. (Kirksville, MO: Truman State University, 1995).

3 Sources, see, e.g.: (1) Williams, *Radical*; (2) Guy F. Hershberger, ed., *The Recovery of the Anabaptist Vision: A Sixtieth Anniversary Tribute to Harold S. Bender* (Scottdale, PA: Herald, 1957); (3) Balke, *Anabaptist Radicals*; (4) C. Arnold Snyder, *Anabaptist History and Theology: An Introduction* (Kitchener, ON: Pandora, 2022); (5) Verduin, *Stepchildren*; (6) John E. Colwell, "A Radical Church? A Reappraisal of Anabaptist ecclesiology," *Tyndale Bulletin* 38 (1987), https://docslib.org/doc/9555934/a-radical-church-a-reappraisal-of-anabaptist-ecclesiology.

THE COVENANT PRINCIPLE AND PEOPLENESS IN SCRIPTURE 173

Table 1. Presuppositions of Covenantal vs. Radical Reformations

Covenantal Reformation	Radical Reformation
Augustinian, creedal	Semi-Pelagian, non-creedal
Sola Scriptura: Scripture alone plus logical deductions from it. Analogy of Scripture is the foundational principle of interpretation.	*Sola Scriptura*: only New Testament norms remain and no logical deduction about sacraments can be made from Old Testament covenant structure.
Unity of one covenant of grace.	Clear dispensational distinction between testaments.
One people of God: Israel enlarged by adoption of the ethnies/nations.	Two peoples of God (many make a Church/Israel distinction fundamental).
Trinitarian, covenantal culture; family, church and state under Christ as King. Every institution transformable.	Church separate, alternative society under Christ as Lord. Outside Church is irredeemable "world."
Decalogue as fundamental law. Christ *interprets* intent of the OT law in Sermon.	Sermon on the Mount as *neo-nomos*. Christ *contrasts* the old law with his new teaching.
Church and state distinct yet responsible to enforce *both* tablets of the law. Judicial law determines crimes and to certain extent punishments for criminals.	Church and state separate. Nonbelievers to rule state, which enforces only second tablet of law. State not bound to judicial law *in any way*.
State has sword authority within the authorization of the law of King Jesus. Christian may be a magistrate and soldier.	State has sword authority "outside the perfection of Christ." Christian may not be magistrate or soldier.
Church based on covenant family groups.	Church is regenerate individuals.
Social order built on the covenant family.	Church and society built on individuals.
World as the earth is good and to be affirmed. World-system of evil values to be avoided.	World is everything outside of church. It is evil, not redeemable, and to be avoided.
New creation is restoration and healing of first creation.	New creation is *nova creatio*: A totally new order.

covenant children, and covenant family bonds as it logically should in this context if within the covenant heritage of the DRC.

The meaning of this "faith fellowship" is spelled out in C&S, 42. Significantly, again, the covenant children of believers are not mentioned as members of the church. This is a large gap that needed to be addressed: "This means ... that faith in the Triune God and his revelation in Scripture is the *only*

174   WHEN A THEOLOGICAL SHIFT CHANGED A NATION

prerequisite for membership of the church of Jesus Christ."[4] C&S, 64 clarifies this further. Individual people are taken out of, that is extracted from, the "peoples" (ethno-covenantal solidarities) and united into one totally new people of God. This is what students of missions (missiologists) term an extractionist mission strategy. It has definite down-sides because advocates tend to teach, though not always, that because the universal community of Christ is, so to speak, pan-ethnic, the local congregation should also reflect as much of the universality as is possible. These as I explained in Chapter 1 result in conglomerate churches. They rarely grow.[5]

2.6 The church is a universal fellowship

Under the Old Testament dispensation the emphasis was strongly on the separateness of God's people, though not in the sense that Israel existed in and for herself. Her existence had far-reaching significance for the nations. Abraham was called and destined to be a blessing to all peoples of the earth. As a kingdom, Israel had a priestly function to serve God among the nations. Even then it was prophetically envisaged that a dispensation of universal salvation would come about.

In the New Testament dispensation the church is even less restricted to one nation or location. It includes people of all nations from the whole world, who through faith in Jesus Christ have become members of the true people of God. All believers from among all peoples become members of the one people of God.[6]

The Gospel Does Not Reject Group Solidarity. The above discussion was excellent, and I agree with it as far as it goes. However, this crucial section does not mention that a local congregation is not made up of mere individuals "out of" all people. This seems to be the implication of what C&S is saying. It does not make a distinction between the invisible and universal Community and the local, parochial community of the King. It thus relativizes and individualizes the covenant family and the covenanted, extended family group in a non-covenantal manner. To C&S' credit, however, it does not yet reject these and the biblical doctrine of covenant baptism as the seal and sign of that covenant.

In summary, then, the classic continental Reformed, biblical viewpoint has always been that a child is a member of the visible community of Christ because he or she is a member of the covenant. The child remains part of the

4 C&S, 42; emphasis added; see also C&S, 249.
5 For a discussion and rejection of extractionist missiology, see two classic works of McGavran, *Understanding*, and McGavran, *Ethnic Realities*.
6 C&S, 64–5.

THE COVENANT PRINCIPLE AND PEOPLENESS IN SCRIPTURE 175

covenant body until he or she does not or refuses to publicly confess regenerating faith and/or shows in action and non-Christian faith-confession that he or she deserves to be put under church discipline. This leads to eventual excommunication or at least removal from the rolls (Mt 18:17). Unfortunately, this is rarely consequently practiced in the DRC or most other denominations.

A clear conclusion is that if the family solidarity is incorporated into the church as a group, then the gospel is not anti-group, and it is not built of groupless individuals.

C&S Tends to Break Down Group Solidarity to the Individual. This theme of extraction out of the peoples is inevitably individualistic if logically thought through. It normally is a concomitant of radical Anabaptist and other utopian groups. This will be unmistakably seen with a careful reading of C&S, 115 and 116 (below).

The section of C&S claims that the church is taken *out of* the peoples and thus shows cultural peculiarities of the *various* peoples. This is right and true. However, the church can never be identified with, C&S teaches, such people-group nor serve the function of giving religious sanction for a people's values, ideals and ambitions. This is stated in absolute terms.

The following passage thus seems to imply that the unifying function of faith in Christ is more important than, and indeed something different from any of its specific and particular groups that add up to the unity. C&S, 115–17 reads as follows:

3.2 The relationship between church, nation and nations
3.2.1 By virtue of its universality or catholic nature the church is a church for the nations
The activity of the church has a close relationship with real human life. Through the proclamation of the Gospel to the nations, the church of Christ is formed from believers of different nations. Thereby the church in different countries and within different national and cultural communities will display characteristics which are typical of those communities. This indigenizing of the church is a positive sign that the Gospel has taken root at local level and within a specific community, that is to say, that it has become "contextualized."
3.2.2 Church and nation may not be identified as one
Through the ages the contextualisation of the Gospel owing to many factors, amongst others, those of a geographical and political nature, resulted in the establishment of people's churches or state churches in various countries. Side by side with the positive fruits that the christianisation of culture and public life brought about, there were also negative fruits in so far as church and nation were identified with each other, these people's churches to a great extent forfeited their true nature as a faith fellowship. Therefore it must be maintained that the indigenization of the

176   WHEN A THEOLOGICAL SHIFT CHANGED A NATION

> Gospel must never mean that church and nation become so interrelated that the church loses its character as a confessional church and becomes an exclusive church of a particular nation, which serves that nation and chiefly has the function to grant religious sanction to that nation's values, ideals and ambitions.[7]

This principle of unity in the church functions *in the long run* to destroy all the group parts that make up the whole. The male-female binary must be broken down into androgynous humanity that can self-identify as whatever "they" wish. Ethno-linguistic diversities must break down into homogenized mono-lingual humankind. The rich and poor must be leveled into amorphous equal persons, and so forth. Logically this means that out of the gradual destruction of the group parts, something absolutely new is created. That something is a "third race," a new humanity not made up of any group parts of the old fallen humanity as Professor David Bosch affirmed in the last chapter.

Therefore, no real, eternal, and substantial self-determining group diversity exists that comes from the old creation humanity healed in Christ. The binary sexuality of the creation account and its specific gender roles affirmed in, for example, the curse section of Genesis 3, is not necessarily normative according to many, though certainly not all, who hold this view. No family, extended family, or federation of extended families is eternal. They come from the old creation. Logically, then, every such old creation group must eventually be broken down to the individual. The implication is that every group is something smaller than, and thus less good than, the whole. These smaller group parts are considered *divisive* of the unity of the whole.

If the unity is more important than any group, then the smallest unit of that unity is the individual. All individuals must be united into unity in Christ. If the logic is pushed, even the individual as a part will be consumed in the inexorably growing unity, the oneness in Christ of all things. As discussed in the first chapter, this concept differs little from the monistic concept of "Holism" in *Holism and Evolution* taught by Afrikaner, British Imperial Field Marshall, Jan Smuts. He was one of the greatly important contributors of the League of Nations and inspirers of the United Nations' Universal Declaration of Human Rights.[8] American Education Professor John Dewey, signer of the original egalitarian *Humanist Manifesto* I, Karl Marx, and Adolf Hitler all used Smut's concept of holism to justify their rejection of the individual and his good as less important than the good of the whole.

---

7   C&S, 115–17.
8   Smuts, *Holism.*

THE COVENANT PRINCIPLE AND PEOPLENESS IN SCRIPTURE 177

Though many have defined the whole variously as Collective Humanity by Dewey, *das Volk* by Hitler, or the international proletariat by Marx and Engles, the results of these ideologies are similar. The individual is subsumed under the good of the collective whole and eventually millions of individuals must be sacrificed to the gods of Humanity in the abortion holocaust, the god of the *Volk* in the purging of Jews, Gypsies, disabled, and many other inferior groups in National Socialism, and the god of the Proletariat that led to the purging the *kulaks* in the Ukrainian Holodomor (death by famine) and other brutal Marxist purges in International Socialism.[9]

Questions and Discussion about the Breaking-Down Process. Several questions need to be asked about this section in C&S.

First, is this not using "believer's church" terminology in a manner virtually identical to the Radical's dogma of an exclusive church made up of believing individuals (see also C&S, 34: "the church is a faith, confession, and worshipping community")?

Second, what if those cultural ambitions, ideals and values are biblical values and the Zulu people, Afrikanervolk or any other people being discipled is becoming consistently more Christianized? Certainly this is good. Yet certainly, C&S' assertions are true concerning those values that are non-biblical. However, if they are biblical where else can a people get specific norms for all of life besides Scripture?

Third, to say that God does not make His covenant with people in their "peopleness" (*volkgewys*, ways of a people) rejects the covenant continuity of the Reformed confessions. In other words, this implies that God "cuts" His covenant in this age only with individuals out of the various ethno-cultures. He then melts them into a new humanity in which all the old creation groups are relativized, waiting to disappear. This is in direct opposition to the Prophets and Writings (e.g., Is 19:23ff; Pss 47:7ff; 86:4; see also Rv 15:4). Myriads of Old Testament passages predict the conversion of the peoples with their own leadership again as I demonstrate carefully in *The Concept of Ethnicity in the Bible: A Theological Analysis.*[10]

Therefore, C&S implies that because the church is made up of individuals out of the peoples, no local or geographical church can be exclusively limited to people from one people-group (ethno-covenantal solidarity). As I see it, this

9 See, e.g., Rushdoony, *One and Many.* Note also the Libertarian, nominalist study of Nazism and Fascism, Leonard Peikoff, *The Ominous Parallels: The End of Freedom in America* (New York: Meridian/Penguin, 1983).

10 See Kreitzer, *The Concept of Ethnicity.*

178 WHEN A THEOLOGICAL SHIFT CHANGED A NATION

concept includes two distinct errors. First, C&S's terminology confuses two differing types of churches and definitions of church unity. Visible unity, that is the local gathering of believers of one specific geographical and lingual-cultural area at one time and in one historical era as in C&S, 249, is confused with invisible unity, that is the unity of all the true saints in heaven and on earth. Invisible unity cuts across history and exists in every geographical area of the world. This is the universal and true church, those who find their hope and home in the New Jerusalem above.[11] Many Radicals reject this distinction due to their emphasis upon a believer's church of baptized persons.

Second, it confuses the local congregation, as well as the circuit and regional synod, with the whole universal, catholic church on earth and heaven (Eph 3:15 NIV 1984). It is logically incorrect to think that the "universal" of the universal church must be made visible in the local group to fulfill Christ's prayer (Jn 17). A part of the whole is merely that, a part. It does not contain the whole. To make such unity visible would mean that all would have to meet at one time, in one place, in one language, perhaps all dressed in uniform white. This concept is more akin to unitarian Islam with its radical leveling and uniformizing during the *hajj* in Mecca. Such a gathering will occur in heaven and then likely in language and ethnic affiliation, as John saw people from every tribe, language and nation (Rv 7:9; 21:24, 22:2). Knowing that God loves diversity, it would not at all be wrong to visualize each group wearing a cultural variation of the white clothing!

The New Covenant Does Not Destroy but Renews the Creation Design

Scripture clearly states that God made, designed and formed the peoples (Ge 10–11; Dt 32:8; Ps 86:8; Acts 17:26). It uses the same terminology as that used to describe the "forming" or creation of mankind (Gn 5:1–2). "All the peoples [*gôyim*] you have made will . . . worship . . . you, O Lord; they will bring glory to your name" (Ps 86:9). Jeremiah claims that YHWH is the King over all nations: "Who should not fear you, O King of the nations? This is your due" (Jer 10:7; see Rv 15:3).

Any attempt to theologically describe the Church as an absolutely new entity, one that is not made up of the renewed and regenerated "divided parts" of the first creation design, is not orthodox.

---

11 C&S 42, 65, BC, 27.

THE COVENANT PRINCIPLE AND PEOPLENESS IN SCRIPTURE   179

Louis Berkhof and Creation Design. American Dutch Reformed theologian, Louis Berkhof agrees that any attempt to see imperfection and evil in a "divided" creation design is clearly Radical Reformational and Barthian. For example, C&S, 24 claims that the church in its Old and New Testament forms is a "unique divine miracle of recreation in a sinful and broken world." Is this an attempt to support the Reformed position or to assert the Anabaptist error with respect to the Old Testament church? It is vague.[12] Berkhof continues by stating that the Radical Reformation as a whole, though not every individual reject "the doctrine of common grace" because this Reformational doctrine recognizes that "good elements" still exist in the created order, "the natural order of things" as Berkhof wrote. That recognition goes against their "fundamental position" that everything in the created order is violent and irredeemable, hence no Mennonite, for example, will serve in civil government nor any of its coercive arms such as police and military. In other words, as Berkhof put it, "they regard the natural creation with contempt, stress the fact that Adam was of the earth earthy, and see only impurity in the natural order as such." In contradistinction to the natural order,

> Christ established a new supernatural order of things, and to that order the regenerate man, who is not merely a renewed, but an entirely new man, also belongs. He has nothing in common with the world round about him and should therefore take no part in its life: never swear an oath, take no part in war, recognize no civil authority [see BC, 36], avoid worldly clothing, and so on.

In other words, all good Christ-followers, ideally, should avoid private property and opt for the poor and oppressed (BC, 36; WCF, 26.3). On Radical's position there is no other grace than saving grace.[13]

Berkhof connects this rejection with various movements such as "Pietism, the Moravian brethren, and several other sects." To this he adds Karl Barth's "denial of common grace," which, he believes, "seems to be following along these same lines." The reason is that for Barth also, "creaturliness and sinfulness are practically identical." In other words, there is no originally good creation design and design norm for anything other than the individual's relationship with the creator through the direct speaking of the Holy Spirit through the Scripture. Berkhof concludes with Emil Brunner's "summary of

---

12 See [F. J. M.] Potgieter, *C&S Essence*, 45ff, section 3: "Re-Creation" (*Herskepping*), for a summary of the debate in the *Kerkbode*, the official DRC layman's newspaper between David Bosch and himself on this and related topics.

13 Berkhof, *Theology*, 446.

Barth's view" which claims that there is no common grace, which maintains the world from the beginning. There is only, as Barth wrote "the singleness of the [saving] grace of Christ."

> Similarly, the new creation is in no wise a fulfillment but exclusively a replacement accomplished by a complete annihilation of what went before, a substitution of the new man for the old. The proposition, *gratia non tollit naturam sed perficit* [grace does not destroy nature, but perfects it], is not true [according to Barth] but is altogether an arch-heresy. Brunner rejects this view and is more in line with the Reformed thought on this point.[14]

In summary, then, C&S seems definitely to be under the influence of the Radical Reformation's presuppositions via Karl Barth. These indicate that every group division in Christ is imperfect or, in a sense, "evil." The implication is that all group-dividing barriers must be broken down. C&S either implied or blatantly stated that each person comes to Christ as an individual *alone*. It seems to define the church as made up of the whole lot of those individuals who believe and experience Jesus Christ. These individuals have been extracted out of the peoples and groups as C&S, 42 cited above implied. They then form a new unity or a new humanity of individuals in which language and culture bonds are relativized.

Furthermore, it appears that C&S gives excessive, perhaps exclusive emphasis to the personal faith of the groupless individual in the formation of the church. According to this individualistic, "extractionist" type of theology, the church is a totally new society. In other words, it is a totally new humanity: non-ethnic, non-gender, non-classist and non-ageist oriented. At present, the DRC would likely add, non-homophobic and non-transphobic as well. The totally new humanity is made up of individuals taken out of their previous identity as given something absolutely new. Therefore, they are stripped or extracted from real and substantial age, gender, linguistic, etc. group identity. Again, this standpoint is very similar, if not identical to, a consequent form of the Radical Reformation's groupless individualism.

Descent and Faith of Equal and Non-Contradictory Validity. Contrary to C&S, the Bible would teach as read through covenantal eyes that both physical descent and unifying faith possess equal validity. In other words, they cannot contradict one another as long as they remain within the Scripture's norms. On the other hand, the Synod in C&S, 39, 40, and 100 attempted to show that even the old covenant church made covenantal faith (i.e., unity)

---

14 Berkhof, *Theology*, 446.

THE COVENANT PRINCIPLE AND PEOPLENESS IN SCRIPTURE   181

primary and the family blood relationship (creation diversity) of only second-ary importance. C&S implies that this creation-oriented, blood relationship is further radically relativized in the New Testament so that faith remains totally primary.

2.3 The church is a fellowship of faith, confession and worship

Being one of "the people of Israel" was an important factor in the religious life of the old dispensation. Yet that was not the decisive factor. What was crucial was the fact that God had chosen this people and established a covenant with them. More important than the blood tie was the relationship to God and the confession that he is the only God. Whoever confessed Him as his God, could, once certain provisos have been met, become a member of the assembly of the Lord, even if he was not of the people of Israel.

In the New Testament the church is in all respects a fellowship of faith, con-fession and worship. Whoever believes the Gospel, confesses that Jesus is Lord, and truly worships God in spirit, is accepted into His church.

The true maintenance of the confession is of vital importance to the New Tes-tament church . . ..

This means . . . that faith in the Triune God and his revelation in Scripture is the only prerequisite for membership of the church of Jesus Christ.[15]

However, this understanding is definitely not based on a covenantal exegesis. Both covenant faith, that is unity with all believers, *and* blood or descent, that is the covenant family as a part of true created diversity, are of equal validity and equal importance. Neither is to be rejected, nor prioritized, nor relativized. Paul claims this as well, "What advantage, then, is there in being a Jew, or what value is there in circumcision," he asks (Rom 3:1). Later he speaks of his "great sorrow and unceasing anguish in my heart," wishing that he could be "cursed and cut off from Christ for the sake of my brother, those of my own" genetic kind, the Israelites (Rom 9:1–4). He never denied being "of the people of Israel . . . and the tribe of Benjamin, a Hebrew of Hebrews" (Php 3:5). He believed even that "all ethnic-Israel" will one day be saved as the context abun-dantly attests when the full number of the gentilic peoples "come in," that is into the Kingdom through Christ (Rom 11:26).[16]

Faith in Christ is indeed the basis for membership in the universal and invisible Body of Christ, the New Jerusalem above. Confessional faith is one of the several expressions of real unity (see Eph 4:3ff; 1 Cor 8:6). However, faith-unity does not of necessity mean that true creational diversity is destroyed.

---

15 C&S, 39–40, see 100.
16 See Kreitzer, *Theology of Ethnicity*, chapter 7, "Ethnicity and Paul's Covenant Theology."

182   WHEN A THEOLOGICAL SHIFT CHANGED A NATION

In other words, it could be that a right to vote and hold office of elder in a local congregation, classis/circuit, or synod may be an expression of real created diversity dwelling in harmony with the unity of the church. Against this both C&S and the World Alliance of Reformed Churches mightily strive. For example, the WARC document, *Farewell to apartheid? Church relations in South Africa. The WARC consultation in South Africa March 1–5, 1993* shows the sometimes-contradictory nature of C&S.[17] Both the WARC and the DRC documents accepted the concept of "faith" was the only prerequisite for church membership. However, the WARC document rejects the notion that the church council may make the determination "to structure itself in terms of a common language and culture" as C&S, 253 then did.[18] It continues: "The inner logic of this makes provision for a rejection in the vestry because the only proof required is that you couldn't be matched with the pastoral character of the local congregation." The WARC document next pointed out the obvious:

> Where cultural positivism takes on regulating features, the question may be asked: How open is open? In a church which is home to so many right-wingers, and especially since Afrikaners claim to have their own separate culture, this option to structure the congregation along cultural lines effectively closes a significant number of doors on black people. Instead, it opens the door for white Christians to make a mockery of the Reformed notion that faith is the only requirement for membership.[19]

This was painfully obvious then and still is because there was a good measure of truth to Botman's assertion. Certainly, I affirm with my whole heart that it is necessary to keep all building doors open for worshipers, who are human and help them understand the Good News. Clearly, many brown Afrikaans speakers will identify as Afrikaners in, for example, the Cape Province. Others will not and seek for a distinct unifying identity that all Christ-followers should respect and help them develop. Some, on the other hand, will speak an Afrikaans dialect but will identify as Griqua or in Namibia as Rehoboth Basters. However, this principle also applies to Zulu citizens and Shona illegal aliens in KwaZulu-Natal Province as well. It applies to Navaho and Cherokee in the USA as well. It is a necessary balance to be found and one that must be maintained within gracious love of God the Father through Christ by the

17   Réamonn, *Farewell to Apartheid.*
18   H. Russel Botman, "The Decisions of the Dutch Reformed Church [Decisions]," in *Farewell to Apartheid? ...,* ed. Páraic Réamonn (Geneva: World Alliance of Reformed Churches, 1994), 45.
19   Botman, *Decisions,* 45–6.

THE COVENANT PRINCIPLE AND PEOPLENESS IN SCRIPTURE 183

Spirit. Both creational identity and faith need to be given *equal* ultimacy in balance. In other words, as essential aspect of identity is a distinct ethno-linguistic group and biological sex, male or female, all of which are creational. The new aspect of my identity is that a person, male or female, are "in Christ" the last Adam and the New Man. Both identities will be carried with us beyond the resurrection, after all, Y'shua remained a Jewish male, seed of the woman Mary, and descendant of David and Abraham, after the resurrection.

Furthermore, I assert that C&S is clearly inadequate in its understanding of the old covenant church, as covenant theology terms it. The paragraphs cited above state that the "assembly of the Lord" was open to any person after he had performed "certain provisos" (perhaps meaning circumcision?). It attempts to make the confession of faith the first and most important fact above and beyond covenantal descent as a determining factor in allowing an ethnic alien into the assembly of Yahweh. However, this is not exactly accurate.

Biblical law did not allow the believing and circumcised alien male into full membership of the legal assembly of the LORD (*qahal Yahweh*) until at least the third generation. Some people were not allowed in until the "tenth generation," whatever that may exactly mean. Certainly, he was to be treated with kindness and dignity under the same legal standard as the "native-born." However, he is not given absolutely the same rights as the covenant-born and faithful member until his time of full adoption into the people had arrived. Thus, it is illicit to read back into the Old Testament individualistic assumptions about the church of Yahweh as an exclusively faith fellowship. When the third generation arrived, the male proselyte was officially adopted into the covenant family of God as full members (see Dt 23:3–7).

What this implies, then, is that covenantal relationship involves more than merely individualistic "faith" alone. Covenantal "faith" is a trusting oath of covenant loyalty in the King as the example of Ruth demonstrates (1:16). Covenantal faith also submits to the other necessary structural elements of covenant such as the covenant responsibility of following ethics and necessary sanctions for obedience or disobedience. Passing all of this on to the covenant partner's seed is extremely important in any covenantal formulation.

Long-Term Implications of the Confessing-Believers Church Theology. Lastly, as stated, it is not dogmatically accurate to claim that a confession of faith is the only condition for membership in the body of Christ unless one claims that there is no covenantal continuity between the old and new covenants. The church, thus, is not just a Radical "faith, confessing, and worship fellowship" (C&S, 40) ruled by Jesus "through the proclamation of his Word and the

184   WHEN A THEOLOGICAL SHIFT CHANGED A NATION

operation of his Spirit" (C&S, 27). Instead, it is a holy body that baptizes both covenant children and new adult believers and their children.

Furthermore, those baptized covenant members, child, teenage, and adult, are to be in submission to elders ruling by means of the Word and Spirit. When a child comes to mature understanding and can publicly give a credible and convincing confession of biblical trust in Christ alone, the elders and congregation admit them to the Lord's Table. Later, when they come of the age of adulthood, probably should be 20 on analogy of Israel, a baptized and confessing child can be admitted to the ruling/voting functions of the assembly. Furthermore, Christ charged elders to practice discipline and teach the covenant standards of God (BC, 29; HC, ques. 3, 83–5). Both the commonwealth of ancient Israel and that of the New Israel, therefore, have excommunicating sanctions. When the person or group violate the norm of God they must be cut off or expelled from the covenant of the People of God (see Mt 18:15ff; 1 Cor 5:13: Paul cites a case law found in Dt 17:7, 19:19, 22:21, 24, 24:7). Why are these covenantal qualifiers so uniformly left out of the C&S? Consequently, there are guidelines for a biblical church and membership in it that include more than merely a profession of the true faith.

With the DRC's new individualistic, Radical hermeneutic, the following scenario could easily happen. An ethnically different, materially poorer denomination or churches could demand unconditional admission to a materially better-off church that is predominantly made up of one ethno-linguistic group (as is the case with the DRC). The new members, all of whom are ethno-linguistically different, could demand the following because they are the majority: (1) English or Xhosa or any other language should be the language of the congregations, classes, and Synods. (2) Every pastor should be paid exactly the same as every other. (3) The leading bureaucratic positions of the uniting church be put into their hands as the majority.

This leads to exactly the same type of bureaucratic, top-down redistributionist church government as what the WCC envisions for a world Church. After a few more decades of hermeneutical juggling and doctrinal defection, the next step could be to rejoin with Rome and throwing out the remnants of the Reformation. After all, the *doleantie* (grievance) church of Kuyper and Bavinck, the *Gereformeerde Kerken van die Nederlanden* (The Reformed Church of the Netherlands), no longer exists. It has taken exactly that kind of step to rejoin the State-dominated Hervormde Church along with an equally liberal Lutheran denomination to form the Protestant Church in the Netherlands (PKN).

THE COVENANT PRINCIPLE AND PEOPLENESS IN SCRIPTURE 185

In principle, this is also basically what has been occurring since 1994 in the Uniting Reformed Church of South Africa. Talks between URCSA and the Afrikaner DRC have been held in earnest since 2006 to discuss the denominations reuniting. Will this mean that Afrikaans, Tswana, and Zulu, for example, will become secondary in circuit and synod meetings with the only common language, English the imperialist language, dominating? Will all pastors of Xhosa or Zulu linguistic background be paid the same as those from the economically better-off Cape-Afrikaans-speaking congregations? Will this make the church a ward of international, ecumenical welfare? This is what happens in socialist-unitarian, political systems as well as what is occurring in the South African state at present. It is definitely not evil in light of the Lord's High Priestly Prayer in John 17 and other similar passages to desire visible unity of Christ's followers. However, the C&S way is not the biblical way forward.

Both Covenants Teach Blood/Descent and Covenant Faith. That the New Testament continues the Old Testament's emphasis on blood/descent and covenant faith is clear. First, Paul strongly rebuked those who rejected honoring and providing for their blood family in God-given love. This included at least the extended family of parents and grandparents. Those who do neglect them, he says, have denied the faith and are worse than unbelievers (1 Tm 5:3–16). This apparently includes even unbelieving parents and grandparents (see Prv 1:8ff; 13:1, 15:5; Eph 6:1ff citing the 5th commandment). As L. Berkhof pointed out above, it is a mark of almost all sectarians to preach *total* separation from family and culture. This meant turning away from all that is of "this old, divided, and passing-away world," including war, parents, inheritance, money, and school. When separated in this manner, then sectarians teach that the new proselyte must be united into a new Super Church of individual believers which swallows up all natural-created divisions. Clearly this involves anti-Christian Platonic assumptions.[20]

Furthermore, Christ criticizes the Pharisees for not caring for their aged parents because that would somehow invalidate a faith-oath they made to the temple (Mt 15:1ff). This, Jesus said, violated the 5th Commandment.

On the other hand, however, true to their form, the Pharisees overemphasized blood descent and drastically de-emphasized faith. The modern parallel is the British-Israelite and Afrikaner *Israelvisie* (Israel Vision) movements. Both claim their European ethnic groups is part of ethnic Israel. To combat this sort of imbalance, John the Baptist said that God could create sons of Abraham

---

20 Berkhof, *Theology*, 141.

186 WHEN A THEOLOGICAL SHIFT CHANGED A NATION

out of the stones of the earth. And indeed God has created sons of Abraham from the formerly "rock hard" formerly idolatrous ethnies, who are now, fully-trusting Jesus as the King of the Nations. The Pharisees' pride in their "blood" and "circumcision" without the fruit of faith-and-repentance, was worthless (Lk 3:7–9; see also Gal 2:15–16; Rom 2:25–9). The consequence was that for unbelieving Jews, for example, the Pharisees who depended on the flesh (Php 3:2ff), were that God excommunicated them out of his covenant. They were to be covenantally divorced, awaiting future repentance (Rom 11:7ff; Jer 3:1ff; Is 50:1). Furthermore, their city was to be burned with fire (Mt 22:7) and the kingdom given to a new people led by the twelve Apostles (Mt 21:43).

Second, Paul said that circumcision with faith was of great benefit for the Jews. "Circumcision" is a symbol of, at least, descent and birth but also remains a sign and seal of true justifying faith (Rom 4:11). That symbol, however, without regeneration resulting in faith-obedience (i.e., love) was worth less than nothing (Rom 2:25–3:2; see Phil 3:2ff; Col 2:20ff; 1 Cor 7:19; Gal 5:6, 6:15). Consequently, not all born from Abraham were children of Abraham nor all born of Israel were true children of Israel. Both descent and faith were and are necessary to become an Israelite. To become a child of Abraham is by trust in the Israelite King, Y'shua (Jesus, Yesu, Isa) because he was to become father of the whole world of people-groups (Rom 4:13), all circumcised and uncircumcised believers (Rom 4:11–12), the mass of the nations (Rom 4:17–18), which is equivalent to all the clans and ethnic solidarities of the earth as all versions of the Abrahamic covenant in Genesis assert (Ge 12:3, 17:5, 18:18, 22:18, 26:4, 28:14–15, 49:10).

Third, Christ said that his true brothers and sisters were those who do the will of his Father. That is, those who exercise true faith in every people-group are part of the family of Abraham without become ethnic Judeans nor religious Jews (Mt 12:50; Lk 8:21, Ac 10:34; 1 Jn 2:17; see Gal 3). James of Jerusalem, citing Amos of the old covenant's prediction, summarized the first Ecumenical Synod. He said in effect: "Do not trouble the former idolatrous peoples (Gentiles)" with the implication from the context that it is no longer necessary to be accounted a "child of Abraham" through being circumcised. All that they must do is to be sensitive to Jews inhibitions (Ac 15:14–20).

Certainly, this was a contextualizing concession to help win Jews in every town in the Empire as Paul himself taught in his first letter to the Corinthians: "To the Jews I become like a Jew to win the Jews" (9:19–23). James and Paul agreed even in the context of Acts 15: "For the law of Moses has been preached in every city from the earliest times and is read in the synagogues on

THE COVENANT PRINCIPLE AND PEOPLENESS IN SCRIPTURE 187

every Sabbath." In other words, Christ predicted that his flock would include other sheep of other pastures. He would gather them also into the covenantal faith (see Rom 11; Eph 2; Mt 28:18ff; Jn 11:52). They would become one even as he and his Father are one, a true unity and real diversity at the same time (Jn 17:21). Both true unity and real diversity are equally important and equally ultimate in the Godhead and in the Church universal.

The meaning of all these sayings and passages cited is clear. The renewed Israel of the new covenant was to be a multiethnic people of God. This nation is eventually to be made up of all believing peoples in their ethno-covenantal solidarity—a kingdom-nation of peoples as I have shown extensively in *The Concept of Ethnicity in the Bible.*[21] The Abrahamic covenant promises predicted this new multiethnic solidarity as it is expounded by the Psalmists and Prophets (e.g., Pss 22:27ff; 72:12, 96:1–10; Is 19:23–5). The Day of Pentecost fulfilled the Abrahamic covenant as a foreshadowing of a greater harvest to come. Interestingly enough, C&S 32 gives the correct interpretation of the Pentecost miracle.

All these themes can also be traced in the Old Testament. Jesus did not come to change the law, but to fulfill it, that is to be in continuity with it, to correctly interpret it, and perform it for us (Mt 5:17ff). Therefore, there is *normally* no need to choose between blood (i.e., descent) and faith. Peter says clearly that the new covenant promise of the Spirit of the resurrected Christ was "for you and your children" (Ac 2:39, echoing Is 59:21). (Certainly, if we must choose the Lord Jesus over a family that rejects him, we are to choose him as the pearl of great price and the hidden treasure in the field above all else). Paul speaks about such a covenantal unity in First Corinthians (10:1ff): All of the believers (including, per implication, their children) were baptized into Christ just as the Hebrews were all baptized into Moses in the rain (Ps 77:16-19) and the cloud when they passed through the Red Sea. This is specifically analogous to circumcision except that all bloody signs cease with Christ, who fulfilled them all. Covenant family baptism replaces covenant circumcision as the "sign and seal" of the covenant of Abraham (Rom 4).

In conclusion, therefore, the community of the King, the invisible and universal church of Christ in the biblical, Reformed view is a covenantal unity of families in their intergenerational solidarity. The gentilic peoples do not have to become Hebrews to enter their King's Kingdom. They can remain in their ethno-covenantal solidarity with their families intact, while at the same

---

21 Kreitzer, *The Concept of Ethnicity.*

time rejecting their rebellious customs and idols to serve the living and true God. This means both faith and descent. In other words, the everlasting covenant includes an oath of faith-loyalty and promises for the blood-seed of those believers from the idolatrous peoples as well as the Jews, who trust in Y'shua as King.

C&S Claims That Emphasizing Family and Extended Family Group Is Divisive. However, according to several passages in C&S, this concept that ethno-covenantal group solidarity remains in the new covenant is divisive. In other words, it divides the new holistic unity of believing individuals within the one true church, which Christ came to bring. Hence, such family solidarity in trusting our Lord is somehow not as holy as mere individual faith. This view contradicts biblical, covenantal exegesis. Note the following: "In the New Testament the church is in all respects a fellowship of faith, confession and worship. Whoever believes the Gospel, confesses that Jesus is Lord, and truly worships God in spirit, is accepted into His church." This means in practice that "the true maintenance of the confession is of vital importance to the New Testament church" and "that faith in the Triune God and his revelation in Scripture is the only prerequisite for membership of the church of Jesus Christ."[22] Again without question this remains true for the universal and invisible Community, the body of Christ but cannot be true for the local congregation, as we have seen.

In addition, C&S states unequivocally, "All believers from among all peoples become members of the one people of God." Therefore, it confesses: "We acknowledge this great truth when in the words of the Apostles' Creed, we confess that we believe in a universal church." Again, no one denies this. C&S continues: "This universality of the church denotes, first and foremost, the world as a whole and its entire past: the church encompasses **all** believers from **all** peoples of **all** places, who have ever lived or still live."[23] This contention is not based on covenantal exegesis if applied to a local church or even a classis. The visible, local church is a covenantal union of believing, that is, confessionally and ethically sound, Christian families and extended families. It does not consist merely of believing individuals as the Radical theologians claim. God does not reject blood bonds, that is, extended family. By extension, it seems logical that he does not reject ethno-covenantal solidarity in the new covenant, as C&S, 42–3 clearly by implication seems to do.

---

22 C&S, 40–2.
23 C&S, 65c–66; bold in original.

New Covenant, Ethno-Covenantal Solidarity, and Baptism

It seems quite clear that if the DRC continues on this Radical-like individualizing paradigm shift as it has for almost four decades, it must also begin questioning the biblical basis for covenant baptism. If it rejects "group" in the universal church as "exclusive" and "discriminatory," logically it then must reject the ultimate of exclusive and discriminatory groups: the family group. Karl Barth actually also followed this logical line of thought and began to question, if not outright reject, covenant baptism.

Covenant theology teaches that God did not move from divisive "group" to unifying "individual"—an irony if there ever was one—when he instituted the new covenant. Furthermore, it is also clear that God's law is not "nondiscriminatory." It teaches just discrimination between God and idols, God and man, one man's wife from another man's wife, truth from falsehood, and work from rest, among several other discriminations. The Bible teaches the ethical and covenantal continuity between the Testaments, the abiding validity of the Abrahamic covenant, and true just discernment (just discrimination) but only as he defines these concepts in his infallible Word.

If the DRC holds to these three crucial biblical doctrines, it cannot reject considering, in a real manner, extended family solidarity. Such an extended family is a group of covenanted and intermarried families with a common language, religious confession, history and geographic provenance. I proposed this to be the definition of a "people-group" or ethno-covenantal solidarity[24] in biblical theology in *The Concept of Ethnicity in the Bible: A Theological Analysis*.

In that volume, I demonstrated that God holds people-groups responsible for obeying his creation-founded norms as ethno-covenantal solidarities. He does exactly the same in the new covenant era as he did in the old covenant times. Time and time again, the prophets pronounced judgments on specific people-groups for their evil ways. They also prophesied that when Messiah comes, the peoples as ethnic solidarities along with their leadership corps intact will turn to the Lord God of Israel. In fact, J. Alex Motyer wrote in his Isaiah commentary:

> Universalism was implicit in Israel's cult. Pss. 46–48 thematically show the defeat of world-wide foes (46), the nations' princes becoming 'the people of the God of Abraham' (47:9) and the centrality of Zion (48). Ps. 87 universalizes the idea of a register of Zion's citizens to include Egypt, Babylon, Philistia etc. The sequence

---

24 Kreitzer, *The Concept of Ethnicity*.

190   WHEN A THEOLOGICAL SHIFT CHANGED A NATION

Pss. 95–100 begins with 'us' as the Lord's flock (95:7) and ends with a world-wide flock (100:3).[25]

Now, if God still sees a people-group (volk) as a responsible, religious and socio-political entity in the new covenant, then there is no logical problem in concluding that he sees it as a living and self-governing religious reality within the true unity and real diversity of the body of Christ. C&S seems to read an individualistic version of holistic philosophy into "ethnic passages," the so-called Apartheid verses. With these philosophical glasses, the clear teaching of true ethnic diversity is missed. With Trinitarian lenses, using the presupposition of the equal ultimacy of the one and the many, the message cannot be missed. The issue, then, is basically presuppositional. As I shared in the first chapter, Reformed Protestants have two basic philosophical major premises: (1) *Sola Scriptura* and (2) its revelation of a Triune reality which God reflects into every area of the creation as an inescapable witness to his existence and glory (Rom 1:18–21).

Covenant Theologians and People-Groups. Reformed theologians just prior to the publication of C&S, who did not have to respond to Apartheid, emotionally or otherwise, saw this concept of ethno-covenantal solidarities or people-groups distinctly. The DRC scholars needed to have been reading much more widely. Or did they reject well-respected British Philologist and Historical Theologian Geoffrey Bromiley, and American scholars Professor Daniel Fuller (PhD from the University of Basel) and Harvard-educated double PhD in Theology and Psychology James Hurley (University of Cambridge and Florida State University) for being fundamentalist? I do not know. But I could have cited other excellent examples from that time period and the ensuing four decades to the present.

G. W. Bromiley writes concerning "the two New Testament types of baptism, the ark and the Red Sea passage," found in 1 Peter 3:20–1 and 1 Corinthians 10:1–10, "children are included with their parents in the separation as a covenant people and therefore in the covenant sign. God does not deal with the individual in isolation, but with the individual in a family or people." The reason for this oikos or household principle in Scripture he states later concerning God's covenant relationship with humanity "is not with the individual in isolation but with the individual in a family or people." A page later he explains further, that God's desire for a covenant relationship with Adam's

---

25 J. Alec Motyer, *The Prophecy of Isaiah: An Introduction and Commentary* (Downers Grove, IL: InterVarsity, 1993), 131, n. 1; see Ps(s) 22, 47, 67, 96.

THE COVENANT PRINCIPLE AND PEOPLENESS IN SCRIPTURE   191

children is not canceled out in the new covenant. In classic Reformed exegesis, covenant remains into the era that our Lord inaugurated. After all it is a new covenant, not an absolutely new covenant but a renewal and extension of the former covenant relationship.

Therefore, Bromiley adds that God gave the covenant originally to Abraham and his "seed" but it never neglected the other peoples and clans (e.g., Gn 12:3). The relationship promised to Abraham "remains—filled out, extended" that is it is now applicable to "all the peoples" (Gal 3:6–9, 14, 29), to "the whole world" of "clans and peoples" (Rom 4:12–17) "as promised in the Abrahamic covenant." Yet at the same time, he continues, it is "unaltered in essential character and certainly not discarded. The promise is still 'unto you, and to your children'" and I might add to "all those far off." Here Peter is almost certainly quoting from the important new covenant prophecy in Isaiah (59:21; Ac 2:39) concerning the outpouring of the Spirit upon nearby Jewish and "far off" gentilic families, clans and ethno-nations. "There is no reason whatever to suppose that when these believers from the nations are added God changes course and begins to deal only with individuals in isolation" that is as group-less individuals, Bromiley asserts correctly. Speaking clearly of the sacraments, Bromiley adds a page later: "In the events which prefigure baptism and in the sign which it replaces, the purpose and work of God are not with solitary individuals but with families and groups and the individuals within them." God is interested in creational solidarities not merely with the mere individual so he concludes: "From the very beginning the covenant carried with it the creation of a redeemed and renewed people, at first restricted in the main to a single nation" in other words it was mono-ethnic, "but then broadened to embrace all nations." In other words, the covenant became multi, not non-ethnic.[26]

Another example is that of the late Professor Daniel P. Fuller. Even though he had an idiosyncratic view of covenant theology, still his comments in this area remain accurate. Fuller shows that the Pauline statement concerning "no distinction" between Jew and Gentile does not destroy the ethno-linguistic distinction between groups. Rather, the background of this statement is found ultimately in the Abrahamic covenant and the equality of all families, clans, and ethnic solidarities under the Lordship of the one God and his long-awaited Anointed One, King Jesus.

Fuller argues from the Shema (Dt 6:4) as Paul expounds it in Romans 3:29. From this allusion, "Paul draws two corollary conclusions." First, "God is just

26 Geoffrey Bromiley, *Children of Promise: The Case for Baptizing Infants* (Grand Rapids: Eerdmans, 1979), 19, 23–5.

as much the God of the Gentiles as he is of the Jews" against potential Jewish objection, which many "early rabbis" would have agreed. God was not exclusionary in his covenant relationship with Abraham. Fuller writes that "the Shema and the Abrahamic covenant were intertwined, being part of the same covenant from the beginning." Though here Fuller conflates the primal covenant relationship, most term the Legal Covenant or the Covenant of Works with the Covenant of Grace made immediately after the Fall, he argument still remains valid even from a bicovenantal perspective. Arguing from Paul's use of Genesis 12:3, "in you shall all the families of the peoples be blessed" (NASV) in Galatians 3:8, Fuller correctly claims that "all the ethnic entities of earth were to enjoy the blessings that Abraham and his posterity enjoyed because God was equally the God of all men." Fuller adds that Paul could have used Isaiah 54:5, "The God of the whole earth he is called," or even Isaiah 45:22, "Turn to me and be saved, all the ends of the earth! For I am God, and there is no other." In other words, Fuller concludes, reading the Shema, in correlation "with Genesis 12:3 and other Old Testament passages, would prove the conclusion that the one God was the God of both the Jews and the Gentiles who desired to bless each equally."[27]

Fuller then draws out a second close interconnection in Pauline thought in Romans 3:29–30 between the Hebrew confession, the Abrahamic covenant, and ethno-covenantal solidarity. It was exactly the same conclusion Paul made in Galatians 3:8 when he cited Genesis 12:3, the Abrahamic promise of blessing to all peoples. Both passage support Paul's commission from the Lord Jesus to reach all ethnic groups with the Good News. God desires that "all the ethnic entities of earth to have equal access to his blessings." This is because God alone is the one God of all the earth. Therefore, "the great diversity in cultural distinctives and behavioral characteristics between various peoples due to heredity and past history" does not create in God an antipathy to one people or a love for another. In other words, only one condition that any and all individuals from the ethno-nations must do is "believe in" that is to wholly trust in Christ alone, as C&S correctly states. "All peoples, despite their great diversities" must cease "to place any value on some particular distinctive they possess, in contrast to that of some other ethnic entity." Instead, they must trust "in the God who holds before all men the merciful promise to be their God." In other words, "if God favored one nation because of some distinctive like circumcision, then it would not be true that he was equally the God

---

27 Daniel P. Fuller, *Gospel and Law: Contrast or Continuum? The Hermeneutics of Dispensationalism and Covenant Theology* [Gospel and Law] (Grand Rapids: Eerdmans, 1980), 101.

THE COVENANT PRINCIPLE AND PEOPLENESS IN SCRIPTURE 193

of other nations who did not practice circumcision."[28] Our God loves people within their own ethno-cultural solidarity without forcing them to become culturally and linguistically part of a "chosen" people.

The Jews, Fuller contended, were twisting the Shema to their own ethnocentric ends so that they could remain exclusively unique from all the other ethno-nations. They boasted in cultural externals as a sign of their special relationship with God. Certainly, the Second Temple Jews of Paul's day did not reject proselytes that joined their unique religious-cultural fellowship as the Book of Acts demonstrates. But to be accepted without a second-class citizenship status, the former idolaters must go all the way from merely fearing the Jewish God to practicing the Judeans' religion with the same externals as they did. This is why God removed "the middle wall of separation," the ceremonial law's prohibitions for any unclean ethnies except "clean" Jews to "come near" to his presence. However, there is no hint at all that God removed ethnic identity as a condition for former idolaters from the multitude of ethno-nations to come to him (see Eph 2:1, 15 and parallel Col 2:11–17).[29] He removed the "middle wall" so that the Jews and the heathen peoples could be justified by faith alone and not on the basis of ceremonial (or any other law-keeping). At present, ethnic Jews and ethnic Greeks, barbarians and Scythians have equal access to God (Eph 2:17–18). They are no longer "foreigners and aliens" to the Abrahamic covenant of promise. All are equally covenantal citizens of the heavenly Jerusalem, the commonwealth of Israel above, *without* sacrifice of their ethno-cultural and linguistic identity (Eph 2:19–22, 3:6).

C&S added no such biblical nuance to its doctrine that "faith" was the only prerequisite for entry into the new covenant community. Yes, Paul agrees that trust alone in the Jew's Anointed King alone was necessary. But he refused to homogenize that faith nor to acquiesce to the Judaizers perversion of his trinitarian gospel that welcomes real cultural diversity with their unifying trust in the one God of all the earth, as Fuller correctly stated as well.

Another excellent example of a Reformed theologian who substantiated this thesis at the time of the writing of C&S was Professor James Hurley in his study of Galatians 3:28 (1981). This text was misused in the same Synod that approved C&S. That text was also used as out of context to pave the way forward to female ordination into all offices as the egalitarians used it in that Synod to demand the removal of all ethno-linguistic distinctives in the

---

28 Fuller, *Gospel and Law*, 101–2.
29 Fuller, *Gospel and Law*, 102–3. See Kreitzer, *Theology of Ethnicity* for comprehensive documentation.

194   WHEN A THEOLOGICAL SHIFT CHANGED A NATION

denomination, except for small concession to "pastoral" concerns. Harvard-educated James Hurley set the tone for his justification for only male leadership in the assemblies of Christ the King.

First, he states that the most crucial issue in Galatians 3 and 4 was the "role of the law in relation to faith." The second theme was the equal approach to God on the basis of true faith, trust in the promises of that same God through Christ. "It is within this frame that our text must be read," he adds. The immediate prior context is Galatians 3:22, which states that the Law of Moses was "not a special avenue of approach to God, open only to Jews, but a statement from which God condemns both Jews and Gentiles." Since all are not made right through Jewish cultural-religious nor even moral uprightness all humans "come before God on the equal footing" irrespective of "race"—a better term is ethnic solidarity—their "state of bondage, and sex (Jew/Greek, slave/free, male/female) having no effect whatsoever on their right to stand before God." In other words, Paul says, "You are all sons of God through faith in Christ Jesus .... There is neither Jew nor Greek, slave nor free, male nor female, for you are all one in Christ Jesus. If you belong to Christ, then you are Abraham's seed."[30]

Hurley concludes, then, that within its context, the contended passage answers the question of "'Who may become a son of God, and on what basis?' It answers that any person, regardless of race [ethnicity], sex or civil status, may do so by faith in Christ." In other words, this is the Apostle's "equivalent of Jesus' welcoming of the outcasts and the Samaritans and Canaanite women. The gospel is for all persons." So far, the authors of C&S would possibly agree. But then Hurley writes something, if they had read it while preparing for the final version of their Synod pronouncement, would have rejected. The context, Hurley states, "was not reflecting upon *relations* within the body of Christ when he had the text penned. He was thinking about the *basis of membership* in the body of Christ." In other words, it is erroneous to apply this passage about "'all one' in Christ means that there are no distinctions within the body."[31]

To illustrate this contention, Hurley using an analogy about joining the army or a soccer team. All without distinction can join but not all have the same role, rank or job description in the military or the same position as "goalies or full-backs." Using these analogies should not be pushed too far when applied to Christ's community, still it remains an inescapable conclusion "that Paul himself did not seem to feel any tension between his proclamation that

---

30 James B. Hurley, *Man and Woman in Biblical Perspective: A Study in Roles* [Man and Woman] (Eugene OR: Wipf and Stock, 2002), 126.

31 Hurley, *Man and Woman*, 126–7.

THE COVENANT PRINCIPLE AND PEOPLENESS IN SCRIPTURE   195

all are one in Christ and his teaching that the one body of Christ has many different members or that his own authority was distinctive and all who would not acknowledge it should not be acknowledged."[32] In other words, true unity in Christ, our oneness, is absolutely compatible with real diversity of cultural and linguistic diversity. This again flows out of the Trinity Principle.

Summary and Conclusion. In 1990, Mission scholars Edward Dayton and David Fraser in *Planning Strategies for World Evangelization* summarize this biblical, covenantal theme of created diversity by contrasting New and Old Testament terms for ethnic groups. They summarize conclusions that DRC scholars should have followed and considered in C&S. The discussion of ethnicity, Babel, and Pentecost were ongoing in evangelical missiological circles from at least the epochal Lausanne Conference in 1974. South African apartheid was also a definite topic in these discussions about planting an indigenous Christ-following community in every people-group on earth.

First, Dayton and Fraser acknowledge that the New Testament terms are "set within a different phase of God's redemptive action" that those of the Old Testament. Second, they discern a difference of "accent" between the Testaments. The Old Testament sought "cultural uniformity in a single, holy people set apart to serve Yahweh," that is mono-ethnicity. However, the "stress in the New Testament is upon a unity that incorporates great cultural diversity" within the new people of God, the children of Abraham. The New Testament, then, does not destroy real ethnic diversity, it does not reverse Babel as I extensively documented in *The Concept of Ethnicity in the Bible: A Theological Analysis.* Instead, it celebrates and establishes multi-ethnicity in the single Kingdom of the Lord of heaven and earth.

Dayton and Fraser's conclusions on the Babel and Pentecost relationship in 1990 did not change in their second edition (2003). They concluded both times that Pentecost was not a reversal of the ethno-linguistic diversity that God created at Babel but was "a signal that the new people of God will incorporate the vast array of tribes, clans, castes, languages, and subcultures" of the earth into its unity. Again, notice that they believe that the move from Old Testament to the New Testament was not from one nation to the individual but from mono-ethnicity to multi-ethnicity, and not from one nation to a non-ethnic state that unites the whole earth. (Again, I must ask the very pragmatic question: "In what language will the non-ethnics understand each

---

32 Hurley, *Man and Woman,* 127.

other?"). "The miracle of tongues," the authors continue, "signals that each language group is to hear the mighty acts of God in its own tongue."[33]

In other words, the Christian movement "does not reduce the people of God to one culture," which I add is the heresy of the Judaizers. Nor does it reduce it to just "one people in the same sense that Israel was single people sharing a single culture." On the other hand, they write, "the people of God is a community sharing a common loyalty to the same Lord, confessing the same faith, and yet retaining distinctive ethnic and cultural ways of life." Then comes a solid conclusion that I agree with in part: "The unity of the church is a unity of the Spirit, not of cultural or linguistic uniformity."[34] I say "in part" because I believe it is ideal to express unity visibly in decentralized, confederal structures as I discussed in the first chapters.

Consequently, when C&S states that no biblical conclusion can be made about the "diversity of peoples" (C&S, 22; see 101), it ignored much data and much real-life experience of oppression cause by imperialism. This includes the horrible oppression the Afrikaners by the British empire in the Anglo-Boer War (1899–1902) in which a large percentage of the Afrikaner women and children population died in "concentration camps," a term pioneered by the Empire. That oppression also, grievously, included Afrikaner oppression of the several African ethnies in South Africa as well with the apartheid-discriminatory legislation. C&S's attempt to address that real oppression led the church and the country in an epoch paradigm shift in exactly the opposite direction than the earlier DRC social theology had taken. This opposite direction was in every area of life as well.

C&S ignored much of the contrary discussion in the literature of that day and, I might add, the DRC still does up to the present as well. For example, I would highly recommend Dewi A. Hughes outstanding volume, *Ethnic Identity from the Margins: A Christian Perspective* (2012). This is the second edition of a book first published in 2001. It takes a similar position on many, but not all, respects that this present volume and my volume on ethnicity take.[35] In his Introduction to the present edition of his book originally entitled, *Castrating Culture: A Christian Perspective on Ethnic Identity from the Margins*, the late Dr. Dewi Hughes wrote the following as a proud Welshman from an ethno-

---

33   Edward Dayton and David A. Fraser, *Planning Strategies for World Evangelization* [Strategies] (Grand Rapids: Eerdmans, 1980), 118–19. See also the newest edition,

34   Dayton and Fraser, *Strategies*, 118–19.

35   Dewi A. Hughes, *Ethnic Identity from the Margins: A Christian Perspective* [Ethnic Identity] (Pasadena, CA: William Carey Library, 2012).

THE COVENANT PRINCIPLE AND PEOPLENESS IN SCRIPTURE   197

nation long oppressed by Anglo-Saxon imperialism. This Introduction provided the author's warrant both for the original title and for the new one. I quote at length because of its utmost importance.

> I took [the original title] from a statement by a Peruvian Quechua Indian [pastor], Artidoro Tuanama. . . . Artidoro's statement takes us to the heart of the concern of this whole book.
>
>> We simply want to take our place as indigenous and native Quechua people, understanding and living out the gospel. We assume our identity without shame, retaliation or indignation against those who have caused harm to our past and castrated our culture.
>
> Artidoro has understood something of the genius of the gospel. . . . He has understood that, having welcomed the gospel, his little people by the world's standards have a responsibility to live out the gospel in the context of their history and culture. Sadly that history and culture has been harmed and castrated.
>
>> From the perspective of this book, which is Artidoro's perspective, history is the story of the terrible harm and violence that has been done to less powerful ethnic identities by the more powerful ones. I hesitated for a long time before deciding to use the "castrating" in the original title because it is certainly not a nice word and I was afraid of offending Christian sensibilities—and as it transpired my worst fears were realized. However, it expresses well the sort of violence that has been done to less powerful ethnic identities. . . .
>>
>> It is impossible for a castrated creature to be fruitful and to multiply and to pass on its genes or genius to another generation. This is precisely what powerful ethnic identities do to less powerful ones. It is not surprising that many ethnic identities that have suffered such humiliation have answered violence with violence. . . .
>>
>> One of the most devastating effects of ethnic oppression is to make people ashamed of who they are to the point that they try not to be who they are and adopt the identity of the oppressors.[36]

The much-maligned Theology Professor and Dutch Prime Minister Abraham Kuyper would have understood Artidoro intimately. The former generations of Afrikaner theologians took to heart what their mentor was writing. In a defense of small nations, especially his beloved Netherlands, Kuyper wrote, for example, the following in his famous speech at a Christian young men's club in 1869, well before his tenure as prime minister of the Netherlands (1901–5). His speech, "Uniformity: The Curse of Modern Life" is even more applicable now than it was then. To get the full effect of his speech, I quote extensively:

---

36 Hughes, *Ethnic Identity*, Introduction.

198 WHEN A THEOLOGICAL SHIFT CHANGED A NATION

The bare *political* unity of the past was metamorphosed by the catastrophe of 1789 [in the French Revolution] into a *social* unity. Just read what history tells you [of Nebuchadnezzar, Alexander, Cyrus, Caesar, of Charlemagne, or Charles V] . . . and you will find in each the immediate goal of founding an empire [political unity]. That unity was effected by the sword. Violence shackled together peoples whose mutual aversion was virtually inborn. Only when that imperial unity had been achieved by a mighty military arm did the vain attempt begin to melt that diversity into a single unity. But what does experience teach? That the unity shattered and the peoples broke apart over and over because the necessary unity and homogeneity of social life was missing. It was precisely national differences, the peoples' diversity of character, the ineradicable uniqueness of their ethnicity, that time and again broke up imperial unity. . . .

Since the direct pursuit of this goal had brought nothing but disappointment, with the French Revolution people opted for another strategy. They prepared to take a longer road, one that would lead them all the more surely, even infallibly, to the great goal. If imperial unity kept foundering on the national diversity of ethnic groups, eliminating that diversity was the goal inherent in the French Revolution. "Liberty, equality, fraternity" is therefore the basic principle it seeks to inscribe in the constitutions of the peoples. For once the peoples have been robbed of their characteristic genius and rendered homogeneous, the triumph of imperial unity is assured. . . .

. . . The cries for brotherhood and love of fellow-man are but a slogan. Not fraternity but a false uniformity is the goal toward which its glittering images drive us.[37]

Perhaps the Afrikaner authors of C&S should have assumed their creational Afrikaner identity without "shame, retaliation or indignation" against those who have caused harm in their past and castrated their culture, to slightly paraphrase Artidoro. The Boer Republics were brutally crushed by the British Empire. Its descendant, the Anglo-American led "rules based international system" crushed the Afrikaner attempt to mold the country into its separation plan. Yes, the Apartheid Regime did grant some land and language rights to the scattered pieces of the "African" homelands, or what their opponents termed, Bantustans. Yet the plan failed miserably greatly because the Afrikaner kept about 87% of the land for their own people and did not grant full autonomy and financial independence to each "homeland"?

Under the Apartheid policy's attempt to break up South Africa, the Xhosa and Zulu, for example, were treated as only quasi-independent ethno-nations

---

37 Kuyper, *Kuyper's Uniformity*, 25. See also survey of Kuyper's discussion of the Boer Cause in the context of three Dutch crises in his time, Robert J. Joustra, "Abraham Kuyper among the Nations," *Politics and Religion* 11, no. 1 (March 2018): 146–68, https://doi.org/10.1017/S1755048317000554.

still heavily dependent up RSA for budget shortfalls. In contrast, South Africa was melded together by the oppressive British empire, which brutally crushed especially both Zulu and the independent Boer-Afrikaner Republics. To their credit, the Xhosa and Zulu elites now ruling over the whole of South Africa are still very proud of their language and culture to this day. Many still, however, seem to want English as the official language of theological education in their ethnic territorial heartland. This my wife and I experienced first-hand in a theological teaching time of a few weeks in 2022 in King Williams Town in the Eastern Cape province of South Africa. Is this option for English also a result of the shaming effect of colonialism upon Zulu and Xhosa that Artidoro mentioned? Or is it a desire to be educated in the world language alone? Or both. I would suspect it is both.

Therefore, unfortunately, in the Xhosa-Zulu attempt to decolonize the whole of present South Africa these two ruling ethnies need to decolonize the decolonizers who often, it seems, still cling to English, their original conquerors' language. It is a truism that mother-tongue education is the best way for individuals to learn and that includes theology. Ironically, in rejecting the Afrikaners' attempt to break up the British Empire's original unifying and homogenizing intention, the leading two ethnies in present South Africa have swallowed whole the British Empire's intent. The same is now happening too often even among Afrikaners, something their Kuyperian forefathers foresaw and worked mightily against. And yes, I might add, it worked so often quite oppressively against the indigenous and imported people-groups (though certainly not in every aspect of the National Party rule over "their" RSA).

Now since the paradigm shifting 1994 election the large, the large South African urban centers are becoming once again massive English assimilation machines. In the century before the Afrikaner-dominated National Party took over the reins of the State in 1948, Anglicization was often the overt and covert strategy of the Empire. Would not mother-language education all their way through graduate school, working together with robust teaching the world language English, be a wiser way forward? Would this not be a policy more in line with God's creational design-norms? But this was the oppressive Afrikaner regime's strategy and so must be rejected out of hand. But I am anticipating.

Consequently, C&S summarizes the theological core of the paradigm shift capsulized in the constitution and election of 1994. It seems to me, however, that the C&S theologians very possibly absorbed the shame and indignation against their own people that the Anglo-American and the World Ecumenical Movement heaped upon them. Shame is a well-known manipulation technique

200   WHEN A THEOLOGICAL SHIFT CHANGED A NATION

to create people, who see themselves both as constitutionally "defective" and "as irremediably and unequivocally different from an ideal image" of themselves than what was the previous image of themselves. They "do not feel ashamed because of the actions [they] have done, but because of who [they] are."[38] Again I have sadly witnessed the identity manipulation that has occurred among both Nguni-African during Apartheid and among Euro-African people-groups in the New South Africa.

Yes, absolutely this unique Euro-African people could and should have treated their neighboring Nguni-African ethnies with biblical neighbor love as both Testaments command. Yet remember that both African Afrikaner ethnies are those who felt the oppressive Anglicization machine for well over a century and a half before 1948. The Afrikaner elite tried unsuccessfully, yes and many times oppressively, to develop a separate land, language, existence for themselves and also for the other largest ethnic groups during those official Apartheid years. That regime, gratefully, ended officially in 1994. But the homogenizing machine continues now under the slogan of freedom, unity, and a centralized rainbow State, not too dissimilar from the French Revolution's slogan of liberty, equality, and fraternity just as Abraham Kuyper predicted.

In summary, instead of using the many good Reformed and Kuyperian insights and reforming their policy according to Scripture alone, C&S read into Scripture the philosophical presuppositions of their enemies and absorbed their shame and contempt. Instead of returning to Scripture, the C&S swallowed whole the Radical Reformation's holistic individualism, the radical individualist holism of the French—and Marxist—Revolutions, and the higher critical led, World Council of Churches' one-world holism. All three of these movements were and are hostile to the Afrikaner's desire for independence and liberty under God. (And yes, I will say it again, in their apartheid project they in turn genuinely oppressed their neighbors). On the other hand, they were and are also hostile to, for example, an independent, Zulu civil order (KwaZulu-Natal) and a similar Xhosa order in a large consolidated part of the present South African Eastern Cape province like that of totally independent Lesotho, Swaziland now Eswatini, and Botswana, all released by the Empire before Apartheid. The present Anglo-American dominated "rules based international system" is also hostile to the same process in every other colonially

---

38   Simone Redaelli, "The Psychology of Shame: What Happens When We Feel Ashamed of Ourselves in Public," *Psychology Today*, September 27, 2020, https://www.psychologytoday.com/us/blog/sonnet-freud/202009/the-psychology-shame.

THE COVENANT PRINCIPLE AND PEOPLENESS IN SCRIPTURE   201

defined nation as well, supposedly because it "has produced unprecedented levels of peace, prosperity" since World War II.[39]

The Creation of the Peoples, Babel, and Pentecost

This conclusion to the discussion of Pentecost and Babel leads directly to the next point. As stated, Scripture explicitly claims that God formed or created the peoples (Gn 10–11; Ps 86:9; Acts 17:26). Deuteronomy 32:8 agrees though it is a bit more controversial but still in agreement with my point. Contrary to some, the meaning of the passage is changed little whether the variant reading "sons of God," found in the LXX and Dead Sea Scrolls replaces "sons of Israel" in the Masoretic text. Clearly, the "Most High" both created each ethnolinguistic solidarity when he divided mankind; and gave each a land-inheritance with boundaries.

Secondly, Scripture explicitly regulates inter-ethnic relations even in the summary of the tôranic instruction in the Decalogue of Moses. This is especially true of the Fourth Commandment in which the ethnic alien servant must be allowed to rest one day in seven showing the legislation's divinely inspired impartiality. The other stranger (*ger*) laws throughout the Pentateuch also clearly teach the same.

It is certainly true that people are destroyed and new peoples come into existence (like the Afrikaner, the Palestinian, and the American). The Bible witnesses to this fact itself (Gn 18–19; Is 40:22ff, 41:2, 44:26; Jer 1:10; 18:5–10, 31:28; Ez 32:18; Dn 2:36–45, 4:34–5; Am 3:6). However, God, not man, is the first cause of the creation and destruction of peoples based on their obedience or disobedience to his normative instruction. For example, Leviticus 18:26–30 applied the sexual morality norms given to Israel also to the surrounding Canaanite peoples' egregious violations of those same norms as well.

God expressly condemns imperialism in the Prophets as I mentioned in the first chapters. The king of heathen Assyria comes under the Prophet Isaiah's strong censure for arrogantly claiming, "[I] . . . removed the boundaries of the peoples and plundered their treasures; like a mighty one I subdued their kings" (Is 10:13; see Hb 2:8–10, 17 of Babylon). Speaking of Cyrus, Yahweh claims that he alone creates such calamity and disaster (Is 45:1–12; Lam 3:37–8). God says that he moved the Israelites, the Philistines, and the Arameans

---

39 Jeffrey Cimmino and Matthew Kroenig, "Strategic Context: The Rules-Based International System," *Atlantic Council*, Atlantic Council Strategy Paper Series, December 16, 2020.

202   WHEN A THEOLOGICAL SHIFT CHANGED A NATION

(Am 9:7). Surely, he has placed the Afrikaner and all the various Sotho and Nguni peoples, as well as the new emerging English-speaking, urban ethnies in southern Africa for his sovereign purpose. However, woe to the state that moves the peoples—not modern nation-states—unjustly that is not in a just war, and their "boundary stones" (Hos 5:10; Dt 19:14, 27:17) because God has set the boundaries of their habitation (Acts 17:26; see Is 10:13 LXX showing a verbal connection between the two). This applies equally as well to the former "apartheid" state as to the present "democratic" homogenizing state.

Is this not explicit ethical information on the diversity of peoples, denied by the authors of C&S, who wrote it off perhaps based on higher critical presuppositions. God created that real ethnic diversity and does not want it to be destroyed by arrogant man. Therefore C&S' conclusion (C&S, 108) is clearly wrong. It states that questions such as civil government policy concerning the maintenance or removal of ethnic identity are not discussed in the Bible.

Furthermore, the following seems to be another case of reading the Radical Reformation's individualism that C&S read into Scriptures: "The Bible does not concern itself with the discussion of such issues as national policy or the maintenance or abrogation of national identity," contrary to what we have just seen. "When a nation maintains it's [sic] national identity and cultural values, the **manner** in which it is done, must always conform to the demands of God's Word," something I agree with the surface meaning but not in the depth perspective as I have discussed.[40]

---

40   C&S, 109, bold in original.

· 1 0 ·

COVENANT AND PEOPLENESS APPLIED TO C&S

C&S Reverses HRLS' Interpretation of the Babel Pericope

C&S, it seems, directly contradicts the early much more biblically faithful but horrible misused interpretation of Babel in the earlier Synod document, HRLS. In its total message, HRLS certainly supported the doctrine of separate development (apartheid). Discussing Babel, C&S definitely implied that the confusion of languages at Babel was a negative judgment of God. Now, certainly, it was a "judgment" in the sense that there was a negative divine judicial decree in the context against the city and tower building project. However, C&S implied more than this. It implied that the judgment was something that caused humanity to move away from the ideal good, that is the unity of humanity. In that sense it was negative. Therefore, division into ethno-linguistic groups was not God's ideal even though he included both grace and blessing in the decree to ensure the future survival of man. The implication seems to be that God's ideal was the former state of "one language and a common speech" (Ge 11:1).

Read carefully what is states about the "confusion of languages" in Genesis 11. The text described it "as God's judgement on sinful human pride. Yet this

204 WHEN A THEOLOGICAL SHIFT CHANGED A NATION

judgement also includes mercy and blessing inasmuch as it ensures humanity's continued existence, and God in this way achieves his creative purposes with mankind."[1] But this is equivocal and confusing. Was the confusion of languages a negative judgment of God? In other words, were it not for sin, humankind would not be divided? Or was it within the planned, creation design of Yahweh? C&S seems to choose the first, following Radical and ecumenical opinion, especially if one compares C&S with the crystal-clear exposition of HRLS.

After affirming, like C&S, the essential unity of mankind, HRLS, however, states the following: "The Scriptures also teach and uphold the ethnic diversity of the human race." Under this heading, HRLS proceeds to explain in rather technical language. "Ethnic diversity does not have a polyphylogenetic origin." In other words, human ethnic diversity did not evolve from different hominid genetic descent groups but from Adam, "progenitor" and his wife Eve. HRLS continues:

> Whether or not the differentiation process first started with Babel, or whether it was already implicit in the fact of Creation and the cultural injunction (Genesis 1:28), makes no essential difference to the conclusion that ethnic diversity is in its very origin in accordance with the will of God for this dispensation. The choice between these alternative explanations of origins depends on an examination of the important chapters 10 and 11 of the book of Genesis. The universal message of the "genealogical table of peoples" (Gen. 10) is that God created all peoples from one progenitor.

Clearly, according to the Barthian-influenced younger generation of non-Kuyperian theologians, HRLS was truly "fundamentalist" or better, without the pejorative connotation, "inerrantist" or "infallibilist." It continued immediately, by denying that racism of any kind is biblical, though it does so using social science terms. The biblical narrative, avoids "the danger of ethnocentricism" on the one hand, it said, and also it rejects the globalism of no borders and nations under the term "cosmopolitanism." This was a remarkably balanced biblically grounded teaching, founded in missiology, that was sadly quickly reversed by virtually equating "races" with ethnicity, or "peoples."

> [A]nd that this view of the human race not only avoids the danger of ethnocentrism, but also that of cosmopolitanism. Gen. 10 and 11, which should be read in conjunction, each individually recounts the fact and process of the division and distribution of peoples. According to Gen. 10, the diversity of peoples is the result of a progressive

---

1 C&S, 106.

COVENANT AND PEOPLENESS APPLIED TO C&S   205

split in the genealogical line, while Gen. 11:1–9 presents it as being the result of dispersal. The two processes are not unrelated. In Gen. 11 the spontaneous development of generations is given its momentum and specific character. In the process of progressive differentiation the human race into peoples and races there is not only a curse, but also a blessing, not only a judgment on the sinful arrogance of the builders of Babel, but also an active mercy preserving mankind from destruction so "That they should seek the Lord" (Acts. 17:27) and so that God's purpose for the fulfilment of the earth should be achieved.[2]

In summary, I could have agreed with this long paragraph almost completely if it were torn out of the context of the whole HRLS document, though with two caveats. First, it almost arbitrarily throws in the word "race" to help lead the whole document to the conclusion of a separate development based on color *and* ethnicity. As I unequivocally stated earlier, the concept of color-based race group is never mentioned in Scripture. Second, it does not show specifically what was a judgment and what was a blessing springing from God.

Correctly, I would add, HRLS gave the following conclusion about the connection between the Creation Mandate and the division of languages. This shows the intimate historical connection between the two, demonstrating that the division of languages was not a "non-ideal," that is an afterthought of God:

Verse [11:]6 states: "Behold the people ('am) is one and they have all one language." These people clearly valued the unity of language and community because, apart from the motive of making a name for themselves, their city and tower had to serve specifically to prevent their being "scattered abroad upon the face of the whole earth" [as God had commanded in the Creation Mandate] (v. 4). From the sequel to this history it is clear that the undertaking and the intentions of these people where [sic] in conflict with the will of God. Apart from the reckless arrogance that is evident in their desire to make a name for themselves, the deliberate concentration on one spot was in conflict with God's command to replenish the earth. (Gen. 1:28; 9:1, 7)[3]

Concluding the theme of the Babel story, HRLS *implicitly* stated—while again deviously equating ethnic and racial-color diversity—that the account supported the Afrikaner-dominated State's apartheid strategy. It claimed that the meaning of the Babel account was "overrated in a certain sense by those who think there would have been no question of a diversity of races and peoples if there had been no confusion of tongues." In other words, some claimed that diversity of "races and peoples" came only and merely because God created

2 HRLS, 14.
3 HRLS, 16.

206   WHEN A THEOLOGICAL SHIFT CHANGED A NATION

new languages. After the flood of Noah yet before the Babel incident, then, humanity was "not yet differentiated biologically," notice again the biological emphasis, "politically or culturally into separate community units." However, the document continued, "the confusion of tongues gave a specific character and momentum to the process of differentiation," as it should because no cooperation was possible. It seems then that the HRLS theologians believed that all three factors, biology (i.e., color and hair differences, for example) as well as politics and culture were the primary factors in causing humanity to grow "apart" from each other into distinct racial-ethnic groups. The biblical Babel account (Gn 10–11), on the other hand, only considered language as the single most important factor in that growing distinctiveness. Scripture only later considers the political and cultural differences. I have extensively documented this process in *The Concept of Ethnicity in the Bible: A Theological Analysis*.[4]

To its syncretistic observation, HRLS adds five considerations. First, "that diversity was implicit in the fact of Creation (Acts 17:26) and the cultural injunction (Gen. 1:28; 9:1, 7)."[5] Second, "the confusion of tongues occurred at a time when the process of differentiation into separate 'families' or community units had already, according to Gen. 10:25, been in progress for quite some time," a Kuyperian insight. Furthermore, third, collective humanity resisted "the process of progressive differentiation . . . as is evident from the fact that up to that stage they had also lived together in one geographic region (Gen. 11:2)." In other words, the authors state "the 'unity' had been artificial and clearly" violated God's twice spoken "intention that mankind should be spread across the face of the earth." Fourth, HRLS continues, "sin as a dividing factor was not restricted to events at Babel (cf. Gen. 6)," the account of utter human violence and rebellion against their Creator. "It therefore does not go without saying that the family relationship would have remained characteristic of mutual relationships if the confusion of tongues had not taken place." Last, fifth, "it specifically strikes us that the judgement of the confusion of tongues was not 'arbitrary', but resolved itself in the course of generations: the dispersal at Babel took place within the family division of the sons of Noah (cf. Gen. 10:25)."[6]

With the caveat concerning my deep concern about equating ethnolinguistic diversity with race, these conclusions cannot be overlooked or ignored. The insight that the dispersal of the peoples along clan and extended family lines was also an insight noticed by Abraham Kuyper in the first volume

4   Kreitzer, *Theology of Ethnicity*, 123–70 ["Dominion Covenant, Babel and Ethnic Solidarity"].
5   HRLS, 16.
6   HRLS, 16.

COVENANT AND PEOPLENESS APPLIED TO C&S   207

of *Common Grace*, that is sociologically accurate and predicted from the text itself.[7]

Independent Parallels to HRLS' Exegesis of the Babel Pericope.

The assumption that true, self-determining, ethnic diversity was *not* part of God's original intention for righteous mankind is common. Much of ancient and contemporary scholarship, both in evangelical and ecumenical circles accept this presupposition. For example, ecumenical theologian, Gerhard von Rad, claims the outcome of Babel was "disorder in the international world … [that] was not willed by God but is punishment for the sinful rebellion against God."[8]

However, the view making cultural diversity rooted in human rebellion rather than in the creation design itself is definitely not the only approach to the question of human ethno-linguistic diversity. There has been a growing movement outside of South Africa for several decades now in another direction, though from perhaps 2000 to the present there has been a backlash not among Ecumenical scholars but inerrantist Evangelicals. In summary, other key theologians agreed, at this point alone, with the HRLS document in the same time frame that C&S was being written and that important movement is still ongoing. For a contemporary review of the development of this teaching, see James Eglinton's article and the recent literature cited: "From Babel to Pentecost Via Paris and Amsterdam: Multi-Lingualism in Neo-Calvinist and [French] Revolutionary Thought."[9]

Three Independent Schools of Thought Also Connect Creation and Babel

Three North American schools of thought independently agreed with the HRLS' ethno-covenantal exegesis connecting the Creation Mandate and the

7 Abraham Kuyper, *Babel*, 357–64.
8 Gerhard Von Rad, *Genesis: A Commentary*, 2nd ed. (Philadelphia: The Westminster, 2016), 152.
9 James Eglinton, "From Babel to Pentecost Via Paris and Amsterdam: Multi-Lingualism in Neo-Calvinist and [French] Revolutionary Thought," in *Neo-Calvinism and the French Revolution*, eds., James Eglington and George Harinck, 31–60 (London: Bloombury T&T Clark, 2014).

208   WHEN A THEOLOGICAL SHIFT CHANGED A NATION

Babel pericope. First was the Church Growth School of Missiology (Pasadena, CA) led by late Professors Donald McGavran, C. Peter Wagner, and Ralph Winter and supported by the Missions Advanced Research Corporation and the US Center for World Missions. A second school of thought was a Roman Catholic and Ecumenical group of scholars led by Andrew Greenley and Bernhard Anderson, and a third were the Reconstructionists. The Reconstructionists, who also apply a similar Babel exegesis, advocated for decentralized civil governments in a future Christianized world of covenantal Christian states, each acknowledging Christ as King and his tôranic wisdom (Pentateuch) and Prophets as the basis for constitution and common law. Anything else is the "society of Satan."[10]

Andrew Greenley. "Theology of Pluralism" scholar Andrew Greeley, a non-infallibilist, claimed that the often-negative interpretation of the Tower of Babel comes from reading holistic assumptions into Scripture, not true exegesis of the Babel pericope itself. These were led by the "great Scholastic theologians of the Middle Ages," who concluded "largely from the tower-of-Babel myth—that if it were not for sin there would be no diversity in the human condition. In other words, the fantastic pluralism of cultures in the world is at best an evil caused by human sinfulness."[11]

---

10   1. The Church Growth School of Missiology (Pasadena, CA): (a) The Fuller School of World Mission (see works by Donald McGavran and C.P. Wagner, especially Wagner, *Our People*); (b) World Vision and MARC (see, e.g., Dayton and Fraser, *Strategies* [2003]), and (c) the US Center for World Missions (see, e.g., Ralph D. Winter and Steven C. Hawthorne, ed., *Perspective on the World Christian Movement: A Reader*, 4th ed. [Pasadena, CA: Wm. Carey Library, 2009]). This school attempts to apply a similar form of Babel exegesis to the question of ethnic diversity.

   2. See (1) R. J. Rushdoony, *This Independent Republic: Studies in the Nature and Meaning of American History* (Vallecito, CA, 2002a), 1, 10, 132–3, 142, 146–8; (2) R. J. Rushdoony, "The Society of Satan," *Christian Economics* (August). Quoted in *Genesis: The Dominion Covenant*, 2nd ed. (Tyler, TX: Institute for Christian Economics, 1964), 151; (3) Gary North, *Sovereignty and Dominion: An Economic Commentary on Genesis*, vol. 1 (Dallas, GA: Point Five Press, 2020d), 197–202, https://www.garynorth.com/SovereigntyAndDo minion1.pdf.

   3. The Ecumenical-Roman Catholic school's Theology of Pluralism: Andrew Greeley, Bernhard Anderson, Gregory Baum, Michael Novak, and others. See the collection of essays, Andrew M. Greenley and Gregory Baum, eds., *Ethnicity* (New York: The Seabury, 1977).

11   Andrew M. Greenley, "Notes on a Theology of Pluralism," *Christian Century* (3–10 July 1974): 697, quoted in C. Peter Wagner, *Our Kind of People: The Ethical Dimensions of Church Growth in America* (Atlanta: John Knox, 1979), 111.

COVENANT AND PEOPLENESS APPLIED TO C&S 209

C. Peter Wagner. Church growth missiologist C. Peter Wagner agreed:

> Another reasonable interpretation of the Babel incident sees the people of the earth making an attempt to counteract what they correctly understood to be God's purpose in diversifying the human race. God had been in the process of separating people from one another in order to implement his desire that humankind should "be fruitful and multiply, and fill the earth . . .." (Gen. 1:28) However, the early human race, which still all spoke one language (Gen. 11:1), rebelled against this plan. They therefore undertook to build a city and "make a name for ourselves" for one explicit purpose: "lest we be scattered abroad upon the face of the whole earth" (Gen. 11:4).[12]

The reason for this rebellion was clear. Post-flood mankind had perceived that God's intention of pluralizing the human race was inexorably working itself out as they grew in number and began to wander from one another. They intuitively recognized the sociological axiom that social separation causes cultural differentiation, and they rebelled against it, determined to maintain their human uniformity whether or not it was God's will.[13]

This parallel with HRLS' understanding of a key socio-historical process is quite noteworthy: separation over time causes ethno-cultural diversity. Wagner showed no evidence at that time of having read that DRC document. Wagner claimed to have discovered this teaching himself. He confessed in a footnote, however, that he later came across Bernhard Anderson's article written two years previously (mentioned below). Only later did Wagner and Ralph Winter react to DRC misuse of this principle as supporting apartheid. Wagner, for example, felt then that possibly South Africa could be a case where white, Afrikaner churches should deliberately take in black members to "visibly display the acceptance of all races in Jesus Christ, knowing ahead of time that such action would in all probability reduce their evangelistic effectiveness."[14] Wagner then interpreted Yahweh's subsequent action as making it quite clear that ethno-linguistic uniformity was his original design-plan:

> The city they were building around the Tower of Babel was never completed. God intervened and decided to accelerate his program for the decentralization of humankind, so he "confused the language of all the earth" and "scattered them abroad over the face of all the earth" (Gen. 11:9). This, of course, was a punitive act, but it was also preventative. It was designed to prove to men and women that they could not frustrate God's plan for human pluralism. H. C. Leupold sees the tower as a "symbol

---

12 Wagner, *Our People*, 111–12.
13 Wagner, *Our People*, 112.
14 Wagner, *Whole Gospel*, 169, n. 12; 112.

of defiance of God" because the people "preferred to remain a closely welded unit and to refuse to obey God's injunction" . . . "to replenish the earth." Apparently, then, God punished this early resistance to pluralism.[15]

Bernhard Anderson. Another parallel is from Princeton Professor Bernard Anderson's article: "The Babel Story: Paradigm of Human Unity and Diversity."

> The story of the building of Babel/Babylon . . . portrays a clash of human and divine wills, a conflict of centripetal and centrifugal forces. Surprisingly, it is human beings who strive to maintain a primeval unity, based on one language, a central living-space, and a single aim. It is God who counteracts the movement toward a center with a centrifugal force that disperses them into linguistic, spatial, and ethnic diversity . . ..
>
> Often the narrative has been regarded as a story of tragic failure, of the loss of the unity that God intended for his creation. The assignment to write this essay was accompanied by the editors' reminder that in the Middle Ages scholastic theologians understood the story to mean that ethnic pluralism was largely the unfortunate result of human sinfulness. In one way or another this negative view has survived in Christian circles to the present day.[16]

However, this was not God's original perspective, he claimed:

> In the larger perspective of the *Urgeschichte* [proto-history] the diffusion and diversification of humankind clearly is God's positive intention. In the beginning, God lavished diversity upon his creation; and his creative blessing, renewed after the Flood, resulted in ethnic pluralism (Gen. 10). Furthermore, eschatological portrayals of the consummation of God's historical purpose do not envision a homogenized humanity but human unity in diversity. According to the Isaianic vision (Isa. 2:1–4), when the peoples in the last days stream to Zion, the City par excellence, they will come as nations with their respective ethnic identities. And when the Spirit was given at Pentecost, . . . human beings "from every nation under heaven" heard the gospel, each "in his own native language," in the city of Jerusalem.[17]

In support of this contention, Anderson added a conclusion that Wagner later independently discovered:

---

15 Wagner, *Our People*, 111–12.

16 Bernhard Anderson, "The Babel Story: Paradigm of Human Unity and Diversity [Babel Story]," in *Ethnicity*, ed. Andrew M. Greenley and Gregory Baum (New York: The Seabury, 1977), 63.

17 Anderson, *Babel Story*, 63–4.

COVENANT AND PEOPLENESS APPLIED TO C&S   211

It is noteworthy that, when dealing with the post-diluvian [post-Noahic flood] period, [the redactor] displayed a special interest in the "scattering" motif, thrice repeated in the Old Epic Babel story [Gn 9:9–18; 10:18; 10:32]. In these instances, ethnic diversity is understood to be the fruit of the divine blessing given at the creation and renewed in the new creation after the Flood . . .. From the "one" [Noah] God brought into being "the many" through the ordinary course of human increase and population expansion.

In conclusion, Anderson contends:

One thing is clear: when the Babel story is read in its literary context there is no basis for the negative view that pluralism is God's judgment upon human sinfulness. Diversity is not a condemnation. Long ago Calvin perceived this truth. . . . [See Calvin's comments on Gn 11:8].

Viewed in this light, the Babel story has profound significance for a biblical theology of pluralism. First of all, God's will for his creation is diversity rather than homogeneity. Ethnic pluralism is to be welcomed as a divine blessing . . .. But something more must be added. . . . Human beings strive for unity and fear diversity. Perhaps they do not pit themselves against God in Promethean defiance, at least consciously; but even in their secularity they are driven, like the builders of Babel, by a corresponding fear of becoming restless, rootless wanderers.[18]

Lastly, Anderson correctly provided the internal thematic connection between the proto-history and the call of Abraham. "On the other hand, their 'will to greatness,' which also reflects anxiety, prompts an assertion of power which stands under the judgment of God." The judgment in the narrative was because of human sin not because of human linguistic diversity. Anderson then acknowledged that "human beings are . . . a broken, fragmented society in which God's will for unity in diversity is transformed into conflicting division." To this Anderson pointed out the literary connections that lead directly to the story of Abram/Abraham: "The *Urgeschichte*, however, leads beyond the Babel story toward the call of Abraham . . .. [H]e is a paradigm of a new people through whom all the families of humankind are to experience blessing, not by surrendering their ethnic identities, but by being embraced within the saving purpose of the God who rejoices in the diversity of his creation" (cf. Rv 7:9–12).[19]

Christopher J. H. Wright. Well-respected British missionary theologian, C. J. H. Wright, among the other writers at the time C&S was being composed, was also not reticent to draw lessons about the existence and relationships of

18 Anderson, *Babel Story*, 68.
19 Anderson *Babel Story*, 68–9.

212   WHEN A THEOLOGICAL SHIFT CHANGED A NATION

ethno-covenantal groups from (1) the Babel pericope and (2) the true unity and real diversity within the Trinity. For example, Christopher J. H. Wright wrote in 1983 just before C&S:

> The rich diversity of the economic resources of the earth ... have their counter-part in the wide ethnic diversity of mankind and its ever-changing kaleidoscope of national, cultural, and political variations. The Bible enables us to see the one as just as much part of God's creative purpose as the other. Speaking as a Jew to Gentiles in an evangelistic context, Paul takes for granted the diversity of nations within the unity of humanity, and attributes it to the Creator. [Acts 17:26]. Although ... [Paul] goes on to quote from Greek writers, his language in this verse is drawn from the Old Testament, from the ancient song of Moses in Deuteronomy 32[:8].

Wright then summarizes: "So the equality and ordering of relationships between the different groupings of mankind forms part of man's accountability to his Creator God." A bit later Wright also invoked what I have termed "the Trinitarian Principle":

> God himself, therefore, in the mystery of the Trinity, subsists in the harmonious rela-tionship of equal Persons, each of whom possesses his proper function and authority. Man, in his image, was created to live in the harmony of personal equality but with social organization that required functional structures of authority. The ordering of social relationships and structures, locally, nationally and globally, is of direct con-cern to our Creator God, then.[20]

Preliminary conclusion. A significant minority of the Christian scholarly world then was beginning to see the biblical justice of true, self-determining ethnic diversity within the confessional unity of the church. This is parallel to that of HRLS perspective. Unfortunately, again, HRLS tainted its excellent biblical perception on ethno-linguistic diversity with a race-based worldview grid that caused it to justify many racial separation laws and methods abomi-nable to Scripture.

C&S Rejected Both Racism *and* Real Ethno-Covenantal Diversity

In contrast to this, it is significant that C&S seemed to be rejecting the bibli-cally correct missiological insights of the previous HRLS Afrikaner theologians

---

20   Christoper J. H. Wright, *An Eye for an Eye: The Place of Old Testament Ethics Today* [Eye for Eye] (Downers Grove: IVP, 1983), 103–5.

COVENANT AND PEOPLENESS APPLIED TO C&S 213

except for the caveats I mentioned above. C&S so overemphasized, almost absolutized, the *biblical* doctrine of human unity, that it neglected or tried to relativize the true ethno-covenantal as well as the binary, duo-gender diversity.

First, it misrepresents Bavinck and Kuyper's Second Adam teaching. The following citation made two crucial theological errors.

3.1.1 Scripture views the human race as a unity

The creation narrative, which traces the entire human race back to one pair of progenitors, views mankind as an essential unity. This point of view is confirmed by the genealogical registers in Genesis 10, 1 Chronicles 1–9, and Luke 3:23–38, where world history is seen as an extended family history. In Acts 17:26 it is stated that God made every nation 'from one man'. In the same spirit Christ is described as the 'second Adam' who involves the whole human race as an organic unity in his ministry of redemption.

This concept of the fundamental unity of the human race is of immense importance to the biblical perspective regarding the dignity, the duties and the responsibility of every person. In the Bible this unity is always referred to in its religious context, namely man's God-given status, calling, destiny, and the universal presentation of the Gospel message.[21]

The Second Adam and the Division of Humankind

The first error is crucial. The doctrine of the second Adam teaches the fundamental division of humanity, not its organic unity. Without this division, there is no redemption. It teaches that there are two federal or covenantal heads of mankind: Adam and Christ. All in Adam, individual and multiple peoples, are dead on account of sin (Rom 5:12–22). All in Christ, including individuals and multiple peoples, are alive because of his righteousness (Rom 5:17–21). Christ, the second Adam (1 Cor 15:45ff; Rom 5:12ff), does not teach the holistic-individualistic unity of humanity. Christ states that he did not come to bring the unity of mankind but to create its fundamental, trust-based, creedal division: Covenant Keepers and Covenant Breakers. Out of that division, the new unity of the new mankind-in-Messiah will come.

Furthermore, our Lord said that he came to bring a sword of division into mankind (Lk 12:49ff; Mt 10:34ff), not peace, and certainly not non-confrontation and holistic reconciliation with anti-Christian Adamites (men in the fallen First Adam). This division will last until the end of the age as the

---

21 C&S, 96–7.

Parable of the Weeds in the Field teaches (Mt. 13:24ff). Mankind-in-Christ is different from mankind-in-Adam. Therefore, mankind is forever divided.

If C&S theologians continue with anti-covenantal assumptions as they have in the following four- and one-half decades, then to be consequent, they must eventually reject eternal punishment for the lost and rejected. (This is again something that Karl Barth struggled with as well). They must work, as they have, for a holistic "peace and reconciliation" between those peoples who have had no conscious, *covenantal* relationship to Jesus Christ and those who have had such as the Afrikaner as a whole.

As John Calvin wrote concerning this: "If we are minded to affirm Christ's Kingdom as we ought, we must wage irreconcilable war with him who is plotting its ruin. Again, if we care about our salvation at all, we ought to have neither peace nor truce with him who continually lays traps to destroy it" (*Institutes* 1.14.15).

The Second Adam is not a Unitary, Renewed Humanity. The second egregious doctrinal error involves the second Adam. This biblical teaching does not promote a unitary, renewed mankind. It teaches the recapitulative renewal of the original creation design but "in Christ," the Messiah of God (Eph 1:10; Ps 2). All mankind, in all its beautiful diversity—ethnic, gender, and age—is now to be redeemed and transformed in the New Creation brought by Christ according to the promise of the Abrahamic covenant (see Eph 1:10ff; Col 1:15ff; Rom 3:29–4:18, 11:11f, 15:9–12; Gal 3:6ff). Pentecost is a substantiation of this true unity and real diversity "in Christ" even as C&S, 32 stated.

Now, in the age of the Spirit of the new covenant, the promise to Abraham will be fulfilled. The ethno-covenantal mosaic, the "world" of peoples but not every individual, will be "saved" (Jn 3:16–17, 6:33, 12:41, 47; Rom 11:11–32; 2 Cor 5:17ff). The miracle on the day of Pentecost was "tongues," that is clearly languages of the "whole world." The miracle was not of ears: the listeners did not understand a single new unifying language but their own languages and dialects learned in their birth countries. C&S reads into Scripture non-covenantal assumptions.

Second, C&S correctly defines and rejects all racism. Clearly C&S, 95 and 96 (cited above) lead the Synod to some biblical conclusions. These two quotations, along with the following example, rightly rejected all racism: "Whoever in theory or in practice, by attitude and deed implies that one race, nation, or group of nations is inherently superior, and another race, nation, or group of nations is inherently inferior, is guilty of racism."[22]

---

22 C&S, 110.

COVENANT AND PEOPLENESS APPLIED TO C&S

Positive Critique. It is true that mankind in Adam is a genetic unity. There are no genetically superior or inferior races. However, in rejecting group racism, C&S relativizes diversity, that is ethno-covenantal group solidarity. In the relativizing process, it did not absolutely reject it in the organizing of local congregations as C&S, 110–14 made clear.

Negative Critique. However, contrary to C&S, 95, Scripture clearly teaches, first, that fallen mankind was existing in true, ethno-linguistic diversity and a real, rebellious unity. Ethno-linguistic diversity is not merely a relative characterization of humankind. It is part of God's created design and is normative for humanity because of the command to spread abroad across the face of the whole earth stated in the creation account and again immediately after Noah disembarked from the Ark. Second, that unity was a unity-in-rebellion of family-peoples, not a unity of mere individuals. Anderson, Wagner, and others have indeed made a thorough accounting of specific character, context, style, purpose, and historical situation and have come up with conclusions similar to those of DRC scholars of the past. Their exegesis cannot be written off as proof-texting as C&S, 17, cited previously implied.

C&S Rejects Identifying Any People-Group with Church in New Covenant

Furthermore, C&S seemed hesitant to find any identification between a people-group in the Christian new covenant as C&S, 38–9, 65 cited above states. I would reply that this was an implicit denial of real, self-determining diversity. The reason for this seems to be individualistic assumptions, a possible overreaction to the non-biblical excesses of Apartheid and the excessive identification of all aspects of Western culture with Christianity.

To be fair, however, C&S gives a *relative* reality to present ethnic diversity. For example, such as C&S, 38: "With a view to the effective ministry of the Word and in order to minister to the needs of various linguistic and cultural groups, allowance may be made for the church to be indigenous." This relativization was, however, thoroughly explained and contradicted later in C&S, 67 and 68:

> The church, as the one universal people of God, may not be restricted exclusively to one nation or group, nor may it exclude anyone on the basis of origin, national allegiance, language or culture.
> **3.2 The relationship between church, nation and nations**

216   WHEN A THEOLOGICAL SHIFT CHANGED A NATION

3.2.1 By virtue of its universality or catholic nature the church is a church for the nations

The activity of the church has a close relationship with real human life. Through the proclamation of the Gospel to the nations, the church of Christ is formed from believers of different nations. Thereby the church in different countries and within different national and cultural communities will display characteristics which are typical of those communities.

3.2.2 Church and nation may not be identified as one

...

Therefore it must be maintained that the indigenization of the Gospel must never mean that church and nation become so interrelated that the church loses its character as a confessional church and becomes an exclusive church of a particular nation, which serves that nation and chiefly has the function to grant religious sanction to that nation's values, ideals and ambitions.[23]

All of this is certainly true of the universal Church, the New Jerusalem above. However, this again ignores the basic distinction between the Church, invisible and universal, and the church, visible and local. Furthermore, the church of Jesus Christ on earth is not just an abstract Platonic spiritual form (concept). It incarnates (1 Jn 1:1ff) into a very concrete, specific organization that speaks a specific language so that each may hear the praise and word of God in their own tongue as the miracle of Pentecost demonstrated. It must also speak to the specific cultural needs of a particular people-group in that people's own language which the Creator directly made or later providentially divided from all the others. The principles of the one universal church cannot be capriciously applied to local and visible churches that are of necessity linguistically divided from each other.

For example, the church universal and invisible has apostles and prophets. Does this apply to the church visible here and now? The foundation of the apostles and prophets was once and for all laid in the first century and we have built upon their ceased ministry ever since (Eph 2:20, 3:5; 1 Cor 3:10ff; Heb 1:1–3; Jude 3; WCF, 1.1).

Another example is the many hypocrites who are in the church visible. Hypocrites are found in both the pure, "believers'" or "confessing" churches, as well as in the confessional-covenantal Reformed churches. However, none are in the New Jerusalem above, the *ecclesia* invisible. There are several other differences.

Contrary to the implication of C&S, 65–6, the DRC is not "the one universal people of God." It is only one ethno-linguistically and geographically

---

23   C&S, 116–17; bold in original.

COVENANT AND PEOPLENESS APPLIED TO C&S   217

bound manifestation of that one body of Christ that exists in true diversity and unity on earth as well as in heaven. Here again, C&S is much closer to the Radical Reformation than to the more biblical, Magisterial Reformation represented by the earlier, pre-C&S DRC.

In adopting this terminology, C&S implicitly rejects the real, self-controlling indigenization of the gospel that it wants to accept in C&S, 38 as we have seen. While implicitly embracing the Anabaptist-Radical Reformation's individualized holism, it does not seem to comprehend all the implications this view holds for the covenantal understanding of the sacraments and for many other aspects of missiological, ecclesiastical, socio-political, and economic thought.

C. P. Wagner on Church and Culture

C. Peter Wagner in *Our Kind of People* (1979) wrote further on this theme of no real identification of church and culture in a popular version of his Sociology PhD dissertation:

> Therefore, it seems clear that any teaching to the effect that Christianity requires a person to adapt to the culture of another homogeneous unit in order to become an authentic Christian is unethical because it is dehumanizing. Christians, of course, should preserve the right to change homogeneous units if they so desire. To deny that freedom would also be dehumanizing. Consequently, a requirement to change cultures, or to melt in a melting pot, or conversely, a requirement never to change cultures [classic Apartheid] must not be allowed to become part of the Christian gospel . . ..
>
> If such requirements are not to be made, how much ethical content should be included in the presentation of the gospel? . . . Some theologians contend that because an intense feeling of peoplehood can often lead to racism, oppression, or even war, the preaching of the gospel . . . should demand that those who decide to obey it should repent of belonging to a particular people and of participation in a particular culture. Christianity is seen as demanding a new life-style, often described as the "life-style of the Kingdom of God" [and its ethics as "Kingdom ethics"] . . ..
>
> To raise the question in another way: Does an authentic presentation of the Christian gospel insist on a transformation of a person's loyalties in relation to political affiliation, social class, race, and culture? And to go one step further: Is such a transformation, displayed in a tangible way, a necessary characteristic of the testimony of an authentic Christian Church?
>
> Generally speaking, those who follow the *Anabaptist* or so-called radical Christian model for doing theology insist that a change in one's loyalty to culture or society is necessary in order to be an obedient Christian. H. Richard Niebuhr describes this point of view as "Christ against culture."[24]

---

24 Wagner, *Our People*, 99–100; emphasis added.

218   WHEN A THEOLOGICAL SHIFT CHANGED A NATION

Would C&S Agree with René Padilla?

This leads to a sobering question. Would C&S agree with the Radical Reformation influenced, evangelical missiologist René Padilla from Latin America? Padilla, a strong opponent of both McGavran and Wagner in the decade before C&S was published, was often cited with approval by the late, UNISA missiologist David Bosch. Both Bosch and Padilla vehemently rejected the renewed ethnic emphasis of the Church Growth School of Missiology, calling it "cheap grace."[25] Bosch also claims that the deliberate "breaking down of barriers that separate people is an intrinsic part of the gospel. What is more; it is not merely a result of the gospel," it is the gospel! "Evangelism," Bosch immediately adds, "as such itself involves a call to be incorporated into a new community, an alternative community."[26]

Dr. Padilla, wrote in agreement in "The Unity of the Church and the Homogeneous Unit Principle":[27]

> Those who have been baptized "into one body" (1 Cor. 12:13) are members of a community in which the differences that separate people in the world have become *obsolete*. It may be true that "men like to become Christians without crossing barriers" [Donald McGavran], but that is irrelevant. Membership in the body of Christ is not a question of likes or dislikes, but a question of incorporation into a new [holistic] humanity under the lordship of Christ. Whether one likes it or not, the same act that reconciles one to God simultaneously introduces the person into a community where people find their identity in Jesus Christ rather than in their race, culture, social class, or sex and are consequently reconciled to one another.

Padilla immediately added to this: "God's purpose is to bring the universe 'into a unity in Christ' (Eph. 1:10, NEB). That purpose has yet to be consummated." We are in an incomplete "already status." Yet that already state must be a true "anticipation of the end, a new humanity [that] has been created in Jesus Christ, and those who are incorporated in him form a unity." In that he means something quite similar to C&S's Ecumenically influenced teaching on "sign posts" of the end. So already, Christ has joined us to his body in which "all the divisions that separate people in the old humanity are *done away with*." This implies the return to a pristine Edenic egalitarian unity, which is, according to

25   See Wagner's reply (Wagner, *Our People*, 99ff).
26   Bosch, *Alternative*, 258.
27   C. René Padilla, "The Unity of the Church and the Homogeneous Unit Principle [Unity]," in *Mission between the Times: Essays on the Kingdom* (Grand Rapids: Eerdmans, 1985a), 146; emphasis added.

COVENANT AND PEOPLENESS APPLIED TO C&S   219

Padilla, a restored version of "the original unity of the human race," in which "God's purpose of unity in Jesus Christ is thus made historically visible."[28]

Certainly it is true that a person's identity is found in Christ. This is the expression of true unity and the grace of the new creation. However, as Wagner has pointed out, it is also found in one's own ethno-cultural group, gender, age group, respect relationship to parents, and socio-economic class. This is an expression of real diversity and of a renewal of the creation design. A putative return to an original egalitarian unity is a myth, an ancient mythology shared with communalist sects throughout history.

In other words, contrary to this myth, identity for a Christian is a case of *both-and,* not *either-or.* A covenantal view has always emphasized both blood (creational-genetic) and faith (believing, covenantal-family solidarity), not individual faith alone-and-isolated as the Radicals claim the New Testament teaches. Culture and identification of the gospel within a culture is actually included in Christ's command in the Great Commission. He commands us to "disciple the peoples" as ethno-covenantal solidarities. A more accurate, and in this case literal, translation of the word "nations" is peoples or people-groups. Our Lord commands us "to disciple"—a verb, "all the people-groups"—a simple accusative. He does not mandate making disciples *of* the nations, that would need a genitive. Instead, he commands us to "disciple"—an imperative verb— "all the people-groups" of the earth—the direct object of the verb, as I have established in *The Concept of Ethnicity in the Bible: A Theological Analysis.*[29]

In other words, Christ did not say, "Convert inhabitants of earth that are non-Jewish" or "Covert individuals out of the peoples." Hence, the command is not ultimately to destroy God-created ethno-covenantal solidarity, as Padilla and C&S seem to imply, if their mutual logic would be pushed to its extreme. This destruction must always come by extracting individuals out of their ethno-linguistic groups to be rejoined together in a non-ethnic, nonsexist, non-ageist "totally new" creation, as I have shown above. Again Wagner's comments here are poignant: "Theologically, an approach that does not follow this course" of teaching a totally new creation after proclamation that claims all creational "old" group solidarities must be cast aside, "can easily confuse salvation by grace with salvation by works." In other words, he adds: "Introducing an ethical code that demands repentance from 'all forms of sin' is dangerously close to a gospel of salvation by faith plus works." Furthermore, he wrote in support of this from a social science perspective, "Such overloading of

28 Padilla, *Unity,* 145–6.
29 Kreitzer, *The Concept of Ethnicity.*

WHEN A THEOLOGICAL SHIFT CHANGED A NATION

the gospel will ultimately demand a denial of peoplehood." Such anti-ethno-centric rhetoric, because this is what the communalist rhetoric amounts to, is not merely "racism" as our Western social mythology propagates, but anti-high ethnic consciousness or a "high awareness of peoplehood." Wagner continues with a balancing note, which I agree wholeheartedly with:

> Much of the rhetoric concerning racism needs to be balanced by recognizing that what to one group might seem like racism, to another group is simply a high level of peoplehood. This call for balance is not meant in any way to condone the evils of racial discrimination and social injustice wherever they appear, but I submit that issues are frequently more complex than they may appear on the surface. It is important to recognize that Christian communities are communities-in-culture. Thus a condemnation of "culture Christianity" may be misguided. . . .
>
> A high awareness of peoplehood has become very important for ethnic theologians and is a key ingredient of ethnic liberation. Nothing inherent in the Christian gospel requires that the sense of peoplehood be sacrificed.[30]

Perhaps unknowingly, Baptist theologian-missiologist, C. Peter Wagner, adopts a more Reformed, covenantal solution to this problem. Actually, his very theological paradigm shift influenced me in the mid-1980s to adopt covenant theology. The real "out of balance problem" of over-identification of Christianity with any culture should not lead to a rejection of true ethno-covenantal solidarity as C&S did. That paradigm shift lead to its rejection of real self-governing indigenization and real self-contextualizing of the gospel under the Word that each created people-group has an inalienable right to do. C&S tried to find this balance but failed. Its solution should have been to accept the Reformational Trinitarian Principle and the Reformational Sola Scriptura Principle. The Bible is the sole judge of all spheres of life with its Covenant Continuity Principle throughout the whole book. This includes certainly the New Testament but also certainly the principle of using the whole universally valid equity of biblical tôranic wisdom. This wisdom, especially includes the divine wisdom infallibly revealed through Moses and the Prophets, and their covenantal worldview. This leads directly into the next chapter.

30 Wagner, *Our People*, 103.

Conclusion

Biblical Data on Ethnic Solidarities in the Messianic Age

Contrary to C&S, the universal Church is also a covenantal unity of various ethno-covenantal-family groups, exactly as the Abrahamic covenant (Gn 12:3, etc.), the Prophets, and the Psalms prophesied. Paul discusses the relationship of ethnic Israel and the idolatrous peoples especially in Romans (Rom 11). Ethnic Israel was cut out of the covenant (with the exception of the remnant) so that the non-Hebrew peoples can be engrafted into enlarged Israel. Only then, out of jealousy, will all ethnic Israel be saved (except, by analogy, the remnant of unbelievers).[31] In this, Paul is consistent with the Old and New Testament prophesies of the conversion of the peoples (see Rom 15:8ff, 16:25ff, 1:5, 3:29ff, 10:12, et al.).[32]

The Abrahamic Covenant in Both Testaments. Our Father promised that Abraham would be the father of all believers, the heir of the world as Paul explains in Romans 4. He drew from Genesis, which first states this principle: "I will make you into a great nation ... and all the families of the peoples will be blessed through you" (Gn 12:1–3: NASB). Paul interprets this and the other Abrahamic Covenant passages as "the promise that he would be heir of the world" (Rom 4:13), in other words, not every individual but every people, language, and nation.[33] The Davidic Psalm echoes this covenantal

---

31 See, e.g., on Romans 11: (1) Kreitzer, "Chapter 11: ESOL, Paul, and Covenant Theology," in *Theology of Ethnicity*; (2) [Iain] Murray, *Puritan*, 2014; (3) John Murray, *The Epistle to the Romans* (Philadelphia: Westminster Seminary Press, 2022); (4) Douglas Moo, *The Epistle to the Romans*, 2nd ed. (Grand Rapids: Eerdmans, 2018).

32 Examples of OT passages supporting a long-term victorious eschatology that foresees a whole world of people-groups embracing Israel's God and Messianic King: Gn 12:3, 17:5, 18:18, 22:18, 26:4, 28:14–15, 49:10; (see Acts 3:24–6). See 2 Chr 6:32–3; Pss 2:8, 22:27, 47:7–9, 64:9, 65:2, 5; 86:9, 87:4–6, 96:1ff, 102:15, 21–2; Dn 7:14, 27; Hb 2:14; Am 9:11–12 (see Acts 15:16–17); Jl 2:28ff; Zec 2:11, 9:10, 14:16; Mi 4:1–5, 5:3–5, 7:12; Mal 1:11, 14; Is 11:1–10, 19:23–5; the Servants Songs in Isaiah: Is 42:1–11, 45:4–6, 20–5, 49:1–7 (see Acts 13:47–8), 51:4–5; see also Is 60:1–12, 66:18–21; Jer 3:17, 4:2, 12:14–17; 126:19–21; Zep 2:11, 3:9–13.

In the NT: Mt 28:16ff; Acts 3:24–6, 15:16–17; Rom 4:9–25; 11:11–32, 15:7–12; Gal 3:6–14; 2 Cor 5:17–21 ["the world" is every tribe, kindred, tongue and nation, not every single individual: see Jn 3:16–17; 1 Jn 2:1–2; Ps 96:13: "earth," "world," "peoples" in Heb. parallelism]; Eph 2–3: "gentile" = "the peoples"—"ethnic groups"; Rv 5:910, 7:9ff, 22:2.

33 See also Rom 11:11–15: "the peoples" equals "the world." Abrahamic Covenant: Abraham: Gn 12:1–3, 17:5, 18:18, 22:18; Isaac: Gn 26:4; Jacob: Gn 28:14; Judah: Gn 49:10; David: Is 55:3–5.

language: "All the ends of the earth will remember and turn to the LORD, and all the families of the nations will bow down before him, for dominion belongs to the LORD and he rules over the nations" (Ps 22:27–8). Notice the unmistakable reference to the Abrahamic covenant's two types of covenantal solidarities, "families/clans" and "ethno-nations." The Psalmist conflates both of its two forms into one phrase: Abraham will be a blessing to all families of the peoples and all ethno-national solidarities as well.

Isaiah picks up on this Abrahamic-Mosaic covenantal theme as well: "In that day," that is the day of Messiah, "Israel will be the third, along with Egypt and Assyria, a blessing on the earth," again referring to the Abrahamic covenant (Pss 22:27ff, 66:1ff). "The LORD Almighty will bless them, saying, 'Blessed be Egypt my people, Assyria my handiwork, and Israel my inheritance'" (Is 19:19ff). *Covenantal*—not individualistic—terminology, once applied exclusively to Israel, is now equally applied to once pagan nations because they too have become covenantal peoples analogous to Israel. "In that day," the day of Messiah, people-groups not merely individuals have the right to become covenant people-groups. The mono-ethnic emphasis of the old covenant has morphed into an international commonwealth, a pan-ethnic viewpoint in the new covenant in Y'shua, the Anointed King of Israel and all the other ethno-peoples. This is, in sum, the Great Commission.

The New Testament always interprets the present locus of worship, "the holy mountain," not as earthly Jerusalem but heavenly Jerusalem (see Jn 4:21–4; Gal 2:4ff; Heb 11:10, 16; 12:22). So not only will the new covenant become "in Christ" pan-ethnic, but also de-symbolized. The Community (*ekklēsia*) now is the Temple and the sacrifices are now those of praise (Heb 13:15), the physical separation laws of diet and so forth have become realized in staying separate from all moral impurity of body and spirit (2 Cor 6:17), and the curses against those who destroy the physical temple are now fulfilled in curses against those who touch and/or destroy the communities of Christ-followers (1 Cor 3:10–17, 6:19; Eph 2:14–22; 1 Pet 2:4–6). The Old Testament prophesies of centralized Temple worship are fulfilled in Christ in the decentralized Christ-following communities in, eventually, every family, clan, people, and language. The Psalms predict this clearly, the shadows in the OT become real when the shadow-caster, Jesus, comes (Heb 10:1–4; Col 2:17):

> Clap your hands, all you nations . . .. How awesome is the LORD Most High, the great King over all the earth . . .. Sing praises to God . . . For God is the King of all the earth . . .. God reigns over the nations; God is seated on his holy throne. The nobles of the nations assemble as the people of the God of Abraham, for the kings of

the earth belong to God; he is greatly exalted. (Ps 47 NIV, note the reference to the Abrahamic covenant)

He has set his foundation on the holy mountain . . .. Glorious things are said of you, O city of God: "I will record Rahab [Egypt] and Babylon among those who acknowledge me—Philistia too, and Tyre, along with Cush—and I will say, 'This one was born in Zion.'" (Ps 87:4–6)

Ethno-Churches Allowed within Biblical Framework

I conclude, that contrary to C&S, within the unity of the Christ-following Community that is invisible and universal, there can exist multitudes of self-determining, ethno-churches (real diversity). However, the signs of true unity in the Spirit, the bond of peace, listed in a previous chapter must always be followed carefully in those churches. These signs are (1) open baptismal font for children of believers and repentant "of age" believers, (2) open communion table for all believers under oversight of the eldership, and (3) open worship services for all believers and unbelievers.

This is derived from the above discussion plus the following factors.

Voting Requirements. All believers can and must be invited into a church building to hear the Word and partake of the sacraments. However, this does not imply that an ethno-linguistic alien can demand equal voting and leadership rights for himself and his ethnic companions (C&S, 37 is correct but not C&S, 39, 66, or 116).

This implies at least three tiers of membership for *those* ethno-churches that choose to be consequently indigenous: (1) children of at least one baptized believer, are non-communing members of the Christ-following community. (2) Upon a credible and fruit-filled confession of trust in the Lord Jesus alone as Savior and Deliverer, admission to the Lord's Table for children in the first status. (3) Full adult voting membership for those from the ethnos into which the church is indigenized. The biblical analogy would definitely point to age 20 as that age of majority and full participation in the Assembly of YHWH.[34]

Voting and Human Dignity. A last status could very well be added to the three I note above. Honorary membership and counsel privilege analogous to Jethro's relationship with Israel and Moses (Ex 18) could be given to those from an alien ethnie, who learn the language well and have been demonstrating the fruit of maturity. This could include a non-voting membership on the elder board.

---

34 See Nm 1:3, 14:29, 26:2; Ex 30:13–14, 38:26.

224　　WHEN A THEOLOGICAL SHIFT CHANGED A NATION

Again, on the analogy of Israel, grandchildren in the third generation can be admitted to full equal ruling membership in the Assembly of Yehoshua-Jesus (see Dt 23:7–8; 23:1–6 are no longer applicable). Voting membership and eldership, limited and exclusively reserved to one ethno-covenantal group of families, can be and indeed are an expression of true diversity. If the conditions of true unity are carefully followed as outlined again above, then the conditions for true diversity cannot "touch human dignity."

Almost all will agree that children, I believe, should not be given a ruling vote in a church assembly because they do not have the maturity to rule. This does not affect their human dignity nor the image of God in them in the least. If a child is killed, the murderer receives the death penalty for attacking the image of God just as surely as if it were an adult who had been murdered (Gn 10:4–7; Ex 21:21–4). A person's human dignity is not affected by the vote or lack of vote. According to biblical tôranic wisdom, a believing alien could not participate in the legal assembly of Israel's universal God, the *qahal YHWH*, until at least the third generation. That did not affect their human dignity at all. The new covenant universalizes the Body of the Anointed King into an international Commonwealth of King Jesus, but it does not erase creational distinctives such lingual-cultural diversities. As I demonstrate carefully in *The Concept of Ethnicity in the Bible: A Theological Analysis*, Ephesians 2:13–22 does not erase these creational design-norms, but equally welcomes in each people-group in ethno-covenantal solidarity.[35]

Relationship of Exclusivity and Unity. Furthermore, biblical Christians would all agree that protecting sexual exclusiveness with one wife and the exclusiveness of Christian education for one's children in one's own home language, does not destroy Christian unity with other believers. In fact, this exclusiveness is part and parcel of the love commanded in the Law of God (Rom 13:8ff).

According to the Psalms (see Pss 19, 119), God's Law is eternal and totally just. The argument cannot be used that these principles are merely valid for the Old Testament people of God. Therefore, an ethnic alien's dignity is only affected if the universally valid standards of the Word of God are not upheld with respect to him or her. This will prevent the double standards of Jim Crow and apartheid types of caste systems.

35　Kreitzer, *The Concept of Ethnicity.*

Christopher Wright's Concluding Thoughts

A covenantally Christian country and a Christ-following ecclesial community has the right to distinguish between people on the basis of citizen and non-citizen if all are judged by one law. As I mentioned, distinguishing between citizen and alien is explicitly mentioned even in the Tenth Commandments, in the Fourth Command, the one day in seven rest-day injunction (Ex 20:8–11, see 20:10). This is the principle of equal protection of law, as shall be seen more completely in the next chapter. This principle also applies to the church if the principles of unity already mentioned are adhered to.

Holding to this principle of distinguishing between ethnic alien and ethno-citizen in ecclesial and civil orders does not in the least negate the full privilege of an ethnic alien in the kingdom of Christ. In Christ's ecclesial and in a Christian civil order, any ethnic foreigner/alien possesses equal value, importance, dignity, and protection of law because they are created in the image of God. Well-respected, British Old Testament scholar, Christopher J. H. Wright, citing Zephaniah (3:9), agrees that unity does not destroy real ethno-national identity in the kingdom of Christ. Wright is explicit: "This eschatological unity in the worship of God will not mean the dissolving of diverse national identities." Instead, he stated further,

> the glory of the future reign of God will be the influx of the rich variety of all peoples. This is the throbbing joy of Isaiah 60, and the more sober warnings of Zechariah 14:16ff. Furthermore, not just the peoples, but all their achievement, wealth and glory will be brought, purified, into the new Jerusalem of God's reign.

He supports this from Isaiah 60:5–11 and Haggai 2:6–8 and what he terms "in the astonishing conclusion of the oracle against Tyre, Isaiah 23:18,"

> where it is envisaged that all the profits of that archetypal trading empire will be "set apart for the LORD", for the benefit of his people. This is not some kind of Zionist covetousness, but the realization that, since God's ultimate purpose is the creation of a people for himself, a new humanity in a new earth, then all that mankind does and achieves can only, in the end, under God's providential transformation, contribute to the glory of that new order. The same vision is taken up in Revelation when "the kingdom of the world has become the kingdom of our Lord and of his Christ", and "the kings of the earth will bring their splendour into it." (Rev. 11:15; 21:24)[36]

---

36 Wright, *Eye for Eye*, 130.

As intimated earlier, maintaining ethno-national diversity has covenantal implications. In the Spirit's created union with Christ, all peoples will become covenantal peoples analogous to Israel as the fulfillment of the Abrahamic covenant in Christ. Wright continues with this passage from Isaiah that I discussed briefly earlier.

> The final prophetic word must come from Isaiah. There can be few more breathtaking passages in the Old Testament than the conclusion of Isaiah 19. Hard on the heels of the oracle of total judgment on Egypt comes a message of restoration and blessing, in which terms recalling Israel's exodus are applied to Egypt herself, and she turns in repentance to acknowledge God and to find pardon and healing. Before we can recover from the surprise, there is more. Assyria too! Assyria will join Egypt in worshipping God, and on equal terms with Israel! All three will be "a blessing on the earth", God's people, God's handiwork, God's inheritance. Egypt and Assyria—the arch-enemies of Israel, crushing her on both sides, historically and geographically, as hammer and anvil!
>
> No vision could convey more confidence in the infinite power of God's transforming purpose for humanity than this incredible passage.[37]

Conclusion: Danger of Individualistic Holism

Both general and special revelation confront us with the inescapable, created fact of ethno-cultural diversity. C. Peter Wagner provides an excellent summary based upon his theory of the Homogeneous Unit Principle (HUP), something I have modified in the *The Concept of Ethnicity in the Bible: A Theological Analysis*, terming it the ESOP, the Ethnic Solidarity Principle.[38]

> It is the human condition to belong. Humanity is always relational. Strict individualism can never express humanness in any but an inadequate way .... The "we" option is not simply a human option, but part of humanity itself. God said, "It is not good that the man should be alone" (Gen. 2:18), and thus from creation itself human beings have been social creatures. Social psychologists point out that group identity is integral to human personality. It can be argued, therefore, that no one is a whole person who does not participate in the kind of group we are calling a homogeneous unity ....
>
> Belonging to a homogeneous unit that shares a culture and that has a "we" identity, therefore, is not to be regarded as a human deficiency to be overcome by sincere effort or increased piety. It is, rather, a positive human characteristic that should be

---

37 Wright, *Eye for Eye*, 131.
38 Kreitzer, *The Concept of Ethnicity*.

COVENANT AND PEOPLENESS APPLIED TO C&S   227

respected and not destroyed. Cultural integrity is part and parcel of human identity, and any system of thought or behavior that denies cultural integrity is dehumanizing. However, whole cultural integrity needs to be preserved, cultural chauvinism must be avoided. The tendency to think that one's group or culture is superior to all the rest, rather than simply different, leads to arrogance and [sinful] discrimination.[39]

Seeing one's own group or kind as "superior to all the rest" or what social scientists call adopting an ethno-centric perspective is truly arrogant according to Scripture. Our Lord condemns it: "Some people ... trusted in themselves that they were righteous, and viewed others with contempt" (Lk 18:9). What is called "racism" is a sub-set of this sin. It is endemic in every human culture, even those that feel oppressed. The Spanish held the indigenous peoples of Latin American often in contempt. Japanese held the colonial Korean in contempt. The Zulu held the surrounding Nguni nations in contempt in their imperialist years. The Chinese hold the Uighur and the Tibetan in contempt as do the Dutch, British and French-descended colonialists those under their imperial control. Sadly, the British colonialists held the Afrikaner in contempt and the feeling was mutual. It is not merely a "white" European monopoly in Europe, North America, or South Africa.

Any culture's ethno-centric viewpoints and actions can and often do lead to sinful discriminatory judgments. People-groups are different but never superior or inferior in value, importance, and human dignity. True some groups, as a whole, are more Christianized and possess more trusting obedience to God's revealed justice principles. This does not make them superior but only more blessed by our just Creator. Yet even then, each ethno-linguistic group must be respected and given geographical space to flourish so that they can welcome the comprehensive Gospel (see, e.g., Acts 17:26–30). Or they will certainly perish when they do not (e.g., Lv 18:24–8). Wagner concludes: "In final analysis, then, belonging to a community in which the Christian message is contextualized is essential. People are not Christians in isolation from one another."[40]

In other words, in the new covenant to minimize and then to deny the value and existence of covenantally Christian people-groups, as C&S, 118 seems to do, is to accept a sectarian and individualistic form of theological holism. This dogma claims that the one body of Christ is primarily composed

39   Wagner, *Our People*, 97–8
40   Wagner, *Our People*, 97–8.

of believers extracted from created groups. That in turn infects the doctrine of redemption with platonic tendencies that reject the comprehensive, recapitulative work of Christ, who came to restore everything in creation that the First Adam's treason twisted, perverted, and broke.

· 11 ·

WHOLE BIBLE PRINCIPLE: MOSES, LAW, AND CULTURE

Introduction

This brings us to the last principle of classic Reformational theology, the Whole Bible for All of Life Principle or as I termed it in the first chapter, "The Whole Scripture Principle." The whole Bible must impact all spheres of life, as the Kuyperians call them, if the Good News in the long-promised Anointed King, Jesus is to be realized as much as possible in this already-but-not-yet interim period before the Second Coming. In other words, both tables of the Decalogue, the Father's instruction to his children, are to impact family, church and civil governments. All those adopted into Abraham's family by faith and their children (Gal 2:29) are covenantally bound to him in family solidarity as the community of Yahweh.

My basic question in this chapter revolves around whether the social theology explicitly and implicitly propagated in C&S' used a classic biblical, reformation-based paradigm or not. Did C&S find clear and specific transculturally valid principles for social transformation in biblical tôranic wisdom or not? Or does it perhaps use a society changing paradigm more similar to the Radical Reformation's to develop its socio-political and religious blueprints for South Africa?

230 WHEN A THEOLOGICAL SHIFT CHANGED A NATION

In addition, I presuppose that no neutrality exists as our Lord also stated. Either we serve God in Christ or we serve Mammon, human self-esteem, pride, or any other of the myriads of false gods. This implies that every system has an implicit or explicit blueprint for socio-cultural transformation, even if it claims not to. This includes contemporary evangelical Christianity with its imminent great escape doctrine and almost, at times, social antinomianism. In this volume, I choose to base social theology and social ethics upon principles explained in the preceding chapters and the principle of universal valid equity found in "the Law and Prophets" as our Lord did in the Sermon on the Mount.

Definition of Universal Equity

There is no suggestion that the following definition is the only one demanded by either the *Belgic Confession* or *Westminster Confession* but merely that it falls within that which is allowed by their language. The final test of all doctrine, training in justice and righteousness, and moral correction is Scripture, not a human confession (2 Tm 3:16–17). However, the author is convinced the following definition is what Scripture teaches in its entirety, both Old and New Testaments.

Based on Divine Character and Creation Design. Universal equity (old English: "general equity") is that which is moral in every one of the case laws of the Pentateuch. These principles are eternal because they flow out of the eternal nature of God. The morality of the law of God is based on two inescapable characteristics. (1) God's creational design-norms, which remain constant to the end (Jer 33:20–5; Mt 5:17–21), and (2) upon his character, which is unchangeable. Psalm 119, the ode to the Instruction of God, who is the Father of his people says: "Righteous are you, O LORD, and your laws," here *mishpatim*, which according to Exodus 21:1 are cases in which are something like judicial case judgments, "are right. The statutes you have laid down are righteous; they are fully trustworthy" (Ps 119:137–8 NIV). God is eternal; his character never changes; and therefore the tôranic equity of his just case laws (judicial laws) never changes. Well-respected Canadian scholar, Joseph Boot in *The Mission of God: A Manifesto of Hope for Society* adds to this that biblical tôranic instruction expressed in the "biblical law then presents itself to us as a journey into wisdom, in which we are introduced to the essentials of justice and righteousness in a variety of literary forms." This wisdom-teaching literature develops a social order and socio-political leadership that in the end are directly accountable to the Creator of the universe and his Son, as Psalms

WHOLE BIBLE PRINCIPLE: MOSES, LAW, AND CULTURE

2 and 110 unequivocally state.[1] This point is ignored and even rejected by the authors of C&S.

Defined as Moral Law Applied to Concrete Situations. The general (universal) equity of the judicial law is the moral law applied to concrete cases clothed in a changing cultural context or setting. Universal equity consists of the cross-culturally valid principles of charity (love), moral justice, and impartial even-handedness found in every judicial command. These can be discovered by the Spirit using Scripture to enlighten reason but these insights are universally "suppressed" by the unregenerate mind (Rom 1:18–31). For example, observation by humans created in the image of God leads everyone to know that humans are binary, two sexes only, and that it is "against created nature [for] women [to] exchange . . . natural [creational] relations for unnatural ones," and for the males "to abandon . . . natural relations with women and burn with lust for other men" (Rom 1:26–7). But instead, degenerating humanity suppresses that truth in unrighteousness (Rom 1:18) and have become futile in their speculations (Rom 1:21) so that they cannot and will not put into practice what they plainly see. In fact, Paul states that when a human culture reaches the last stage of pushing God out of their reasoning minds (Rom 1:28), they still know what they are doing is evil and deserve the death penalty, "they not only continue to do these very things but also approve of those who practice them" (Rom 1:32 NIV).

Transculturally Valid. Universal equity is transculturally valid, in other words the principles in each of the commands that come from God's wise creation design and his unchanging character are valid in every culture of the earth. The Westminster Assembly used the eight rules of question 99 of the Westminster Larger Catechism to discover this transcultural moral equity. In addition, both the Westminster and Heidelberg catechisms taught that the civil penalties attached to the violations of *at least* the Decalogue (except the Sabbath law) are binding upon all cultures and every magistrate as the ultimate penalty. However, universal equity has built in principles of mercy and compassion for the victim so that many ultimate penalties can be commuted as Numbers implies (Nu 35:31).[2] According to these classic Reformed standards, the

---

1 Boot, *Mission of God*, 257.

2 (1) Kaiser, *OT Ethics*; (2) Kaiser, *OT in New*; (3) Gary North, *Victim's Rights: The Biblical View of Civil Justice* [Victim's Rights] (Tyler, TX: Institute for Christian Economics, 1990). See also, e.g., (4) Joe M. Sprinkle, *Biblical Law and Its Relevance: A Christian Understanding and Ethical Application for Today of the Mosaic Regulations* (Lanham, MD: University Press of America, 2005); (5) Jonathan Burnside, *God, Justice, and Society: Aspects of Law and Legality in the Bible* (Oxford: Oxford University Press, 2010).

232 WHEN A THEOLOGICAL SHIFT CHANGED A NATION

magistrate, church, and family—the three governments ordained by God—are to enforce both tablets of the law with different "tools" for enforcement. For example, the family has the divine right to use the "rod;" and the church is to use the "keys" for church discipline up to and including excommunication. The civil government has the exclusive right of physical coercion, the "steel sword," up to and including capital punishment.[3]

In this wise and gracious enforcement, the *culture-bound* details in which the morality of the judicials were enclothed can be ignored. The culture-bound details are those that cannot be grounded in the creational design and the norms derived from that design and from God's unchanging character as explained throughout the whole Scripture.

Equity Enforced with Wisdom in All Three Divine Institutions. Wisdom and the administration of civil justice are closely connected in Scripture (Dt 1:16–18, 4:6–8; 1 Kgs 3:9–11 and 2 Chr 1:10; Prv 8:12–16; Jas 3:13–18). Wisdom and the "righteous decrees and laws" of Moses are also closely coupled (see Dt 4:5–8; Pss 19:7–9; 119:97–104; Prv 24:23–9, 28:5). Therefore, wise administration of civil justice and the wise application of the universal and eternal in the law are closely intertwined.

Based on Four Levels of Abstraction in Biblical Ethics. According to Walter Kaiser, universal equity is founded upon four levels of abstraction within the biblical ethic's definition of sin *and* criminality.[4]

1. Love is the capsulation of the moral law defining sin and righteousness, which in turn, summarizes the Decalogue (Mt 23:40; 7:12; Rom 13:8ff; Gal 5:14ff; 1 Tm 1:5–11; Jas 2:8ff).
2. The Decalogue summarizes the abiding principles of the moral law's definition of sin. It summarizes and *outlines* what love looks like in thought, word, and deed (Rom 13:9–10).
3. General equity, or the universally applicable principles of justice and equity found in every law of Moses, specifically flesh out the Decalogue's outline. They are thus subpoints under the Ten Categories of moral law.
4. Culturally particular, non-creational cases that still encompass universal principles bound up within the now expired Jewish civil-political order and its culture, "body politick" of the *Westminster Confession.*

---

3 See John Murray, "The Christian World Order," *Westminster Magazine* 1, no. 1 (October 10, 1943), https://wm.wts.edu/content/the-christian-in-the-twentieth-century.

4 See, e.g., James B. Jordan, *The Law of the Covenant* (Tyler, TX: Institute for Christian Economics, 1984); Kaiser, *OT Ethics*, Kaiser, *OT in New.*

WHOLE BIBLE PRINCIPLE: MOSES, LAW, AND CULTURE 233

Certainly, there are also similar culturally exclusive examples found even in the Decalogue such as being enslaved in Egypt, oxen, donkeys that person should not covet and so forth. However, most of the culturally relative aspects of this whole four-level system of ethical summarization are the Hebrew cultural forms found in the fourth level. These parochial cultural details *not* tied to original creation design are, for example, (1) ancient flat-topped versus the modern peaked house construction; (2) threshing with oxen (versus machines); (3) death penalty through stoning versus by the sword (see Rom 13:4); (4) cities of refuge in Israel; and (5) distinctive Hebrew male and female dress customs versus distinctively male and female modern clothing.

On the other hand, tôranic wisdom found in Leviticus 18:22 and Deuteronomy 22:5 certainly treat homosexuality and transvestitism as being universally sinful because, certainly, both violate the original design of the created sexual binary. Original creational design also includes norms for one day in seven rest; the biological male and female one flesh relationship of marriage that God designed to last for a life time and to produce children (Gn 1:26–8, 2:24; Mt 19:1–12; Mk 10:1–12); old and young, parents and children's respect for their parents, and so forth.

In addition, many case laws are also couched in contexts and situations that occur universally within the created order and within now fallen human race. For example, every culture digs wells large enough for someone to fall into, has homes with roofs, possesses property lines even if they are tribal. Clearly every culture has chopping with an axe head that could fly off even in icy Arctic realms. All cultures face lust, fornication and adultery, and so forth. So much of the case laws include cultural universals that are found in every culture and place on the earth where humans live. Hence, they include just principles of love and even-handedness valuable in every culture are of earth. Using this outline of how to derive specific ethical instructions from biblical legal material, we can examine C&S carefully.

C&S and the Law of God

To its credit, C&S did speak about the law of God in several paragraphs. However, upon closer examination, it seems to mean by the law of God only vague, broad guidelines, not the laws as specific models for building the social, political and economic spheres of life. C&S rejects the classic Reformed claim that biblical covenant law gives such models. This would "reduc[e] . . . the Word

234 WHEN A THEOLOGICAL SHIFT CHANGED A NATION

of God to a contemporary recipe book with instant solutions for all human problems."[5]

C&S forthrightly wrote off the clear testimony of the universal equity of the Mosaic judicials and any claim that the biblical norms can give specific blueprints: "The Bible as proclamation of God's Kingdom is not a textbook on, inter alia, sociology, economics or politics."[6] It then continues with an exposition of this paragraph: "The Bible, because of it's [sic] own nature and character may not be used as a manual for solving social, economic or political problems." Because of Scripture's alleged single focus upon individual personal salvation, "all present and previous attempts to deduce a particular social or political policy from the Bible ... must be emphatically rejected."[7]

As I discussed earlier in the chapter about DRC and the Scripture, all this is certainly true, if the meaning is that Scripture is a detailed and systemized anthropological, political or economic textbook. Scripture is not such a text-book and all agree to that proposition. However, that is not, it seems, what is meant here. C&S clearly states that the Bible is merely a spiritual book with a spiritual message for a "kingdom people." This means that the universal equity of biblical law and wisdom cannot provide any paradigm or blueprint for transforming specific political and social problems of this world.

If this is so, C&S' social-ethical theology has moved away from the position of the classic Reformed confessions. Because God's righteousness is unchanging and eternal, his justice and his good law, as a reflection of his character, must be unchanging, and a model for all times and all peoples (see Dt 4:6–8; Pss 111:18, 119:89, 152, 160; Rom 3:31, 7:12, 16). The key is to see that the law for Israel is a contextualized model for all humanity. Our task as modern Christ-followers is to find what the *Westminster Confession* 19.4 calls "the general equity" or translated into modern English, the "universally applicable principles of justice and equity" of each of the judicial laws. These principles are the "truth and substance" and "testimonies taken out of the law and the prophets ... to regulate our lives" as the DRC's standard, the Belgic Confession, also states (BC, step 3 above). These are found within the "culturally particular, non-creational forms bound to the now expired Jewish civil-political order and its culture" (step 4 above).

In summary of this whole-Bible-for-all-of-life principle, Harold G. Cunningham writing in 2007 in the prestigious evangelical British journal, *Tyndale*

5 C&S, 18.
6 C&S, 19.
7 C&S, 21 and 22.

Bulletin, also states that "equity is an abiding principle." He asks, further, the following question to help discover what is a universally applicable principle of "abiding" justice in each law: "[T]o understand 'general equity' in the context of the *Westminster Confession of Faith* is to ask what is the *intention* behind this specific law? Does it have some enduring substance that could possibly render it 'universalisable'?" That which is enduring, then, is what God intends to be generally or universally applicable. Something that is enduring, in turn, "can be applied at all times and in every place." Consequently, that which is "enduring" and "universal," taken "in conjunction with the New Testament 'golden rule'"—finding neighbor-love universals in each command—"provides a way forward "towards appreciating the continuing moral value of the Old Testament."[8] "General equity," then, is a universally valid, enduring principle found in every judicial law of the Torah.

Stephen C. Perks from the Kuyper Foundation in the UK further summarizes:

> The details of the application of the judicial case law are appropriate to the society in which they were originally given, a primitive agricultural society, but the equity of the law is universally valid. Therefore, stoning is not appropriate today, but the equity of the law, the death sentence for murder, is still binding.[9]

Neighbor love, we shall see in the next chapter, provides an important interface with C&S because the "golden rule" is extremely important in developing biblical discernment and judgment against the evil of the many discriminatory aspects of apartheid (separate development), just as C&S claims.

God's Law and the Definition of Key Ethical Concepts in C&S

Too often in history, when segments of the body of Christ or the institutional church as a whole have rejected biblical definitions, they absorb humanistic, cultural definitions of these terms. For example, sectarians, Christian revolutionaries, and especially the Radical Reformers often redefined key biblical

---

8 Harold G. Cunningham, "God's Law, 'General Equity' and the Westminster Confession of Faith," *Tyndale Bulletin* 58, no. 2 (2007): 289–312; emphasis added.

9 Stephen C. Perks, "The Westminster Confession of Faith and the Equity of the Judicial Law," *Kuyper Foundation*, December 13, 2016, https://www.kuyper.org/questions-cont ent/2016/12/13/the-westminster-confession-of-faith-and-the-equity-of-the-judicial-law.

236 WHEN A THEOLOGICAL SHIFT CHANGED A NATION

terms using extra-biblical presuppositions. Reconstructionist David Chilton, writing a year before C&S's first edition, gave a summary of this process and a proposed biblical solution: "Throughout history revolutionaries have demonstrated an almost limitless facility for appropriating as their own the religious terminology of the surrounding culture." He continues by generalizing: "In every revolution of the past, words were revolutionized in meaning, and ordinary people were moved to extraordinary acts, without realizing that the impressive words had been redefined." However, as I have also stated, "the mark of a Christian movement is its willingness to submit to the demands of Scripture," that is not just to abstract principles stripped "from their context and loaded with new content; but rather the actual, concrete, explicit statements of God's Word."[10]

Social Democratic Justice Opposed to Biblical Justice

Unfortunately, C&S also does just this. It uses such terms as "injustice," "righteousness," and "human dignity," but never defines those terms in the light of the specifics of the universal equity of biblical tôranic wisdom.

Holistic Socialist Movements and Social Justice. Igor Shafarevich's monumental volume, *Socialist Phenomenon*, is written by the renowned, former Soviet-Russian Mathematics professor and political dissident. In this then banned volume, he demonstrates how humanists have also consistently redefined the concepts of equity or justice throughout history.[11] This redefinition underlies humanistic definitions of the role of government and its enforcement of just economics and civil rights.

First, socialist movements, whether Christianized or not, as they existed historically throughout the world have a strong tendency to redefine justice as *equality* and not as equal protection of a single legal standard as is found in Scripture and the 14th amendment of the US Constitution. For example, during the writing of C&S, the revolutionary rival to the Afrikaner National Party was the African National Congress, nominally led by Nelson Mandela in prison. One key slogan I experienced in my almost decade living in the RSA during these years of turmoil (1983–92) was: "There shall be no peace without justice and no justice without equality" (ANC slogan).

---

10 David Chilton, *Productive Christians in an Age of Guilt Manipulators: A Biblical Response to Ronald J. Sider* [Productive Christians], 3rd ed. (Tyler, TX: Institute for Christian Economics, 1985), 3–4.

11 Shafarevich, *Socialist Phenomenon*.

As seen in the chapter concerning the Trinitarian key, this means that such justice opts for the right of a collective, the majority whole of a geographically defined community, over any individual right or a smaller ethno-linguistic group within a larger geographic political unit. Implicit in this definition was that nothing should be allowed to divide the unity of the chosen, the semi-sacred social whole. This unity could be variously *"das Volk"* of German National Socialist (Nazi) ideology, "the Italian state" of Mussolini's Italian socialistic Fascism, the international proletariat of Marx's international revolutionary socialism, the social democratic, borderless and nationless ideology of the European Union, or dare I say, *"die Afrikaner volk"* of the National Party from 1948 to 1994. All of these movements could be much more or quite less murderous in their oppressive efforts to maintain the *relative* unity of the Collective. I italicize *relative* because no historical movement has every achieved the ideal of such unity.

Shafarevich summarizes this principle in the following words:[12] "Equality is the basic principle from which other socialist doctrines proceed." The late, former Atheist, Libertarian Philosopher, Antony Flew, agreed with Shafarevich: "Such identification of inequality with injustice and of equality with social justice have become characteristic of 'the socialists of all parties.'" Such individualistic egalitarianism was termed, in the 1980s and still in 2023, "social justice." Flew continues: "The truth, however, is that social justice as customarily conceived is precisely *not* a kind of justice."[13]

It is just the opposite, he adds:

> Such 'social' justice essentially involves what ... must constitute a paradigm case of flagrant injustice; namely, the abstraction under the threat of force (the taxing away) of (some of) the justly acquired property of the better off in order to give it (less, of course, some often substantial service charge) to those whose previous just acquisitions or lack of just acquisitions have left worse off.
>
> It is of the greatest importance to socialists as here conceived thus to maintain that their cherished policies are mandated by a kind of justice. For this enables them to see themselves—and, hopefully, to be seen—as in incontestable occupation of the moral high ground. [14]

---

12 See also, Michael De Golyer, "Marx's Theory of Justice," *Fides et Historia* XVI (Spring–Summer 1984).

13 Antony Flew, "Socialism and 'Social Justice' [Social Justice]," *Journal of Libertarian Studies* 11, no. 2 (Summer 1995): 77–8; emphasis added.

14 Flew, *Social Justice*, 78

238   WHEN A THEOLOGICAL SHIFT CHANGED A NATION

In other words, for more or less radical Christianity, which C&S stealthily adopted, " 'God's justice consists of community and equality' — such a proposition was used to justify," at various times throughout history, "both the abolition of private property and the demand for communal wives" as a form of sexual liberation from the social divisiveness of nuclear families. Having "common wives" and "common children" has always been a communalists ultimate conclusion. Such consequent egalitarianism "can be traced in the medieval heresies and the doctrines of the [revolutionary version of the Radical] Reformation" during Martin Luther's tenure as a Reformer, Shafarevich concludes.[15] This they claim, as Flew pointed out, is "moral high ground." We see this being worked out before our very eyes in South Africa, and certainly also the European Union and the North American states. On the contrary, grievously, it is the broad way to destruction as our Lord and all the Magisterial Reformers agreed.

Social Democratic Justice Examined. The basic assumption of a Social Democratic model of societal justice is that social income inequality is more or less evil and the cause of such social problems as crime and illegitimacy. Evil is thus more or less based in "divisive" socio-economic structures that cause and perpetuate wealth and social inequalities. Society, in socialist ideologies, is composed of oppressor and oppressed groups. Marx merely emphasized the capitalist landowning and industry-owning bourgeoisie classes as the oppressors and everyone else, the proletariat, working class, as the oppressed. However, returning to South Africa, the presently governing one-party state consisting of the African National Congress/South African Communist Party coalition emphasized at the time of C&S's writing and still do emphasize the "supremacist whites" as the South African oppressors, and the "people of color," the LGBTQ+, and other such groups as the oppressed.

In more contemporary times, especially in the USA, the socialist emphasis is upon the sexist Boomer, who is an able, cisgender heterosexual, and part of the "white Christian nationalist" oppressor-group. This group is put into contradistinction with the intersectional coalition of oppressed and shamed groups such as the LGBTQ+, fat-shamed, disabled, young, non-documented immigrant, and people-of-color groups. The solution to this evil is for the democratic socialist or social democratic State to pro-actively tax, confiscate, and redistribute income and social privilege from the oppressor to the oppressed groups. The majority of socialist democrats and social democrats do not yet

---

15 Shafarevich, *Socialist Phenomenon,* 259.

WHOLE BIBLE PRINCIPLE: MOSES, LAW, AND CULTURE 239

advocate the comprehensive totalitarianism of a Marxist state though some do.[16] The binary division of society into oppressor and oppressed groups is essential to any socialist-egalitarian social analysis and does lead to totalitarianism when the core presuppositions of these allied movements are pushed to their logical conclusion.

Scripture Defines Justice According to Universal Equity. First, according to classic continental Reformed theology that the DRC once held tightly to, justice must be normed by the Word alone. Biblical justice and equity can never be separated from the specific principles found in "every word proceeding from the mouth of God" as our Lord quoted from the Pentateuch (Dt 8:3; Mt 4:4). Scripture and the classic Reformed standards thus define "justice" as that good which conforms to the demands of divine moral law and the universal equity of the judicial laws as both the Belgic Confession, 25 and the Heidelberg Catechism, questions 3–5, 92–115 emphasize. So does the *Westminster Confession of Faith* 19, 20.2, 4 and the *Westminster Larger Catechism*, questions 91–152.[17] This definition of justice applies equally both to the magistrate in his official capacity as the wielder of the judicial sword to enforce external conformity to biblical norms of justice and to the individual, including the magistrate, in his personal righteousness and exercise of justice. No person is above the norms of divine law even if such lawbreakers continually accuse their opponents of having such double standards while themselves have double standards for their own partisan group.

Again, both social and personal righteousness/justice standards come from the normative word of the Lord. Hear what Calvin states: "On the other hand, the Lord, in giving the rule of perfect righteousness, has referred all its parts to His will, thereby showing that nothing is more acceptable to him than obedience." This implies, therefore, that "among what are commonly considered good works the commandments of the law are accorded too narrow a place, while that innumerable throng of human precepts occupies almost the whole space." God's Fatherly instructions for the individual and his justly defined social order, when the temporal ceremonial laws are deleted, are relatively very few in comparison to the super-abounding myriads of social democratic laws enforced by bureaucratic socialist states. Such socially pelagian, pharisaical

---

16 See (1) Schlossberg, *Idols*; Nash, *Social Justice*; (2) Chilton, *Productive Christians*; (3) Flew, *Social Justice*; (4) Thomas Sowell, *Social Justice Fallacies* (New York: Basic Books, 2023) for free market and biblical, Christian analyses.

17 Mt 5:19–20; Rom 2:18, 3:23–31, 7:12ff, 8:4, 7; 1 Tm 1:10ff; Dt 4:18, 5:32, 12:32, 6:17–18, 25 "in them is your righteousness"; Pss 19, 119.

240   WHEN A THEOLOGICAL SHIFT CHANGED A NATION

babysitter states destroy human freedom, human dignity created in the image of God, and human value immensely more than a Christian social order based on Abraham Kuyper's spheres correctly understood and applied. Calvin concludes by citing Deuteronomy 12:32: "What I command you, this only you are to do . . . ; you shall not add to it or take from it" (Institutes, 2.8.5). Was C&S's comprehensive paradigm shift a genuine forward step into peace, prosperity, justice and human flourishing? Or was a renewed reformation instead needed based upon returning to a comprehensive sola Scriptura perspective? A renewed reformation would have been and still remains the wiser way forward in a post New South Africa.

Magisterial justice is Restorative, Retributive, and Impartial. First, I would assert that among the several biblical and contextually determined applications of justice, magisterial justice always includes impartiality. Since this is true, the socialist definition of justice and that of Scripture are mutually contradictory. Socialism always opts to turn "justice" to the advantage of the oppressed. This was true in the Afrikaner, oppressed by the British Empire especially since the end of the Anglo-Boer War in 1902. The socialism of the National Party's affirmative action-oriented, apartheid regime took a biased option for the impoverished Afrikaner (with lots trickling down to Anglo-South African) as African American Free Market Economist Walter Williams demonstrated in *South Africa's War on Capitalism.*[18] It is also certainly an accurate description of the socialist, African-centered, affirmative action of the New South African since 1994. It redistributes power, wealth, and privilege to the once oppressed but now elite urban Xhosa-Zulu coalition. The masses of African ethnies are not being uplifted.

American Reformed Philosopher, Professor Ronald Nash agreed at that time as well. He writes that "Justice" was a term "frequently used in classical times as a synonym for personal righteousness. In that universal sense, justice did indeed entail a possession of all the other major virtues including helping the poor." No biblical philosophy can neglect helping the widows, orphans, ethnic alien in the land, and the marginalized. He continued, "Scripture repeatedly mentions justice in contexts that also refer to love, to helping the poor, and to giving food to the hungry." However, he adds, are these "appeals to justice discussions of the kind of universal justice that is synonymous with personal righteousness or are they references to a particular theory of distributive

---

18 Williams, *War against Capitalism.*

WHOLE BIBLE PRINCIPLE: MOSES, LAW, AND CULTURE 241

justice?" This is crucial for discerning a biblical application of justice to a social order such as that of the Republic of South Africa or the United States.

Nash unequivocally states that "They are the former," that is the left appeals to the discussions of personal righteousness but makes these discussions with no applicability to the State or civil government sphere, as Kuyper would call it, actually applicable to the State as an institution. So, just as a crucial text in Job (29:14–17) states "God expects every truly righteous person to care about the poor and to do what is in his power to help them." However, he continues, "it begs the question to maintain that this concern can only be expressed in an endorsement of the coercive and redistributory statism that is so essential to contemporary collectivist approaches to justice."[19]

Second, again in preview, the Decalogue gives mankind five basic covenantal or contractual rights and corresponding responsibilities. These legal duties also give protections against criminal action; thus, they become a legal right to be enforced in a regular court of law. To the basic Decalogue rights and responsibilities, several others can be attached as corollaries (see discussion below). These responsibility-rights are to be zealously guarded by magistrates in courts of law.

The goal of justice is both *restoration* and *retribution*. It is certainly true to Scripture, then, to claim as C&S does that " 'righteousness' means the restoration of 'rights' that have been violated. This restoration of the wronged person's 'rights' is the positive element in 'righteousness'. The negative side is the punishment of those who have deprived someone of his rights."[20] Magisterial righteousness or biblical societal justice in contrast to egalitarian social justice, then, is restorative and retributive. It restores both the wronged and the wrong-doer, who pays restitution. Educator, social ethicist and theologian, R. J. Rushdoony, agrees in his significant collection of essays, *Politics of Guilt and Pity*, part 2, chapter 5, "The meaning of justice." Anything other than this is the "politics of pity"—false compassion that is not based on biblical norms.[21] Well-known British author, C. S. Lewis agrees in *God in the Dock*, "The

19 Ronald H. Nash, *Social Justice and the Christian Church* [Social Justice] (Lima, OH: CSS, 2002), 72–3.

20 C&S, 140.

21 R. J. Rushdoony, *Politics of Guilt and Pity* [Politics] (Vallecito, CA: Ross House, 1995), 116–38, for the retributive and restorative nature of biblical justice. See also, (1) E. Calvin Beisner, "Justice and Poverty: Two Views Contrasted [Two Views]," *Transformation* 10 (January–April 1993); (2) Nash, *Social Justice*, chapter 3, "Justice and Equality," and chapter 6, "Justice and the Bible."

242 WHEN A THEOLOGICAL SHIFT CHANGED A NATION

Humanitarian Theory of Justice" in his discussion of "just deserts," a British expression for impartial justice that is both retributive and rightly restorative.[22]

Furthermore, biblical justice is also *impartial.* Evidently, the universal equity of the Father's tôranic instruction, after all that is what Torah means, commands the civil governmental sphere to be absolutely impartial in its administration of justice, like the God of Scripture is. This is true throughout Scripture (see, e.g., Ex 23:8; Lv 19:15; Dt 1:16–17, 10:17, 16:18–20; Prv 24:23–5; Rom 2:5–11; Col 3:24–4:1). For example, Deuteronomy 1:16–17 (NASB) records the charge that Moses gave to the appointed judges, "'Hear the cases between your fellow-countrymen, and judge righteously between a man and his fellow-countryman, or the alien who is with him. You shall not show partiality in judgment; you shall hear the small and the great alike. You shall not fear man, for the judgment is God's.'" In Leviticus, Moses explains this in similar terms: "You shall do no injustice in judgment; you shall not be partial to the poor nor defer to the great, but you are to judge your neighbor fairly" or better "in righteousness" (ESV) and with impartiality (Lv 19:15 NASB).

In summary, American, Reformed social ethicist, E. Calvin Beisner writes: "The Biblical concept of justice may be summarized as rendering impartially to every one his due in proper proportion according to the norm of God's moral law." He then delineates "four main criteria of [biblical] justice." First, "impartiality," second, "rendering what is due," third, "proportionality," and fourth, "normativity," that is, "conformity with a norm" that is transcendent in origin.[23]

God's Zeal for His Own Justice. God is actually zealous for his glory, which includes impartial justice. When the poor and helpless are unjustly robbed of land and goods, or deprived of God-given legal rights in court through bias, graft, or bribery, or they are robbed of contracted wages, etc., God is justly zealous against such injustice. All of these examples are specifically mentioned in the case laws (see Dt 24:15; Ex 22:21–7; see also Is 10:1–2; Jas 5:4). However, his just wrath also comes against a social democratic State that oppresses even the wealthier when their just rights, land and goods are illegally confiscated through *partial* socialist redistributory taxation and entitlement welfare programs. Though this may sound harsh, remember even the compassion of the ungodly is cruel (Prv 12:19).

Professor Ronald Nash strongly agreed that "the notion of justice appears frequently in the Scriptures." However, he continues, that "'justice' has a

22 C. S. Lewis, *God in the Dock* (Grand Rapids: Eerdmans, 2014), 318–33.
23 Beisner, *Two Views*, 17.

WHOLE BIBLE PRINCIPLE: MOSES, LAW, AND CULTURE 243

variety of meanings." It is quite disconcerting, he believes, when a social justice advocate quotes a Scripture using the word "justice" but rips it out of "context, and simply presume that the verse functions as a proof-text for his position." Any side of the justice issue can do this, I might add, not merely zealous social justice advocates. Some of these passages do not refer to redistributive, or as he terms it, "distributive justice, but to remedial [restorative] justice." For example, "Exodus 23:6 which warns against depriving the poor man of justice but makes it obvious that the justice in view is that found in a court of law. The same chapter (Ex. 23:3) also warns against showing partiality toward the poor in a court of law." He continues: "One recurring error in many attempts to support a particular ideology with biblical texts that mention justice is the failure to distinguish between the interpretation of a verse and its application."

> A good example of this is an article by [a Reformed scholar who] quotes Exodus 22:26–27. [This passage] ... states that if a neighbor has turned over his cloak as collateral for a loan and if that neighbor has no other way to protect himself from the cold, then the person holding the cloak should make it available during times when it is needed.

Now certainly this passage, read in a straight forward manner "poses no special problems," Nash continued. Yet instead of seeing this case law as a paradigm for any similar situation for privatized compassion and neighbor love, the scholar Nash is quoting, jumped "at once to his application: 'A person has a right to the material goods she or he needs for a decent existence.'" This then involves a common, yet still illegitimate exegetical leap from a "general equity" application of privatized interpersonal love of one's neighbor to statist, coercive redistribution of wealth. The scholar continued: "Thus the Bible teaches that there are rights to specific kinds of economic goods, and that these rights bind governments as well as individuals." Nash continues, "Many will conclude, with some justification, that he simply reads his position into the texts."[24]

Neither of these passages cited above claim that the legislator, magistrate, or authoritarian president has any biblical right to make a law, or an executive order compelling redistribution of wealth to his or her chosen class, whether genuinely oppressed or not. It is true that the loving God does good and gives good gifts to evil men. Believers are commanded to do the same, to love their neighbor as themselves (Mt 5:43–8). Yet, at the same time, paradoxically, God and just men hate a covenantal relationship with the person of the wicked (Pss

---

24 Nash, *Social Justice*, 69–71.

5:5–6, 31:6, 119:158, 139:21–2; Rom 9:13). This includes the widow and orphan who despise him and his good and just law. He puts them as well as the wicked and oppressive rich under a curse and destroys them all from his land (see Is 9:17; Ps 1; Prv 2:21–2; Eph 6:2–3; 1 Pt 3:10–12).

No Partial Option for the Poor. Our good and very kind God does not take a partial option on the side of the poor and oppressed merely because they are poor. Isaiah says, "Therefore the Lord will take no pleasure in the young men, nor will he pity the fatherless and widows, for everyone is ungodly and wicked, every mouth speaks vileness" (Is 9:11; see also Dt 27; Pss 5:4–5, 10–12, 10:14–15, 11:5, 37:1ff, 62:22–8; Jn 3:36; Eph 2:1–2). It is absolutely true, on the other hand, that the righteous citizen (see Jb 31:16–40) and especially just magistrates of a righteous civil order must bend over backward to ensure that the powerless receive both *pro-active* yet still *impartial* justice. Scripture teaches that a just magistrate must pro-actively protect the marginalized classes against oppression as defined by Scripture that applies the Decalogue to both the individual and civil realms of a social order (see Jb 29:16–17; Pss 72:1–4, 12–14, 82:1–3).

Furthermore, personal and family wealth does involve a strong moral responsibility to share with the genuinely needy and oppressed. The Bible is full of these types of mandates that are not optional for a God-trusting individual (see Lk 12:13–21, 31–4; Prv 21:13, 14:31, 19:17). However, man does not live by bread (redistributed money) alone but by listening carefully to, trusting in, and then putting into practice every word that proceeds out of the Creator's mouth (Mt 4:4; Dt 8:3). No man has a right to add to the covenantal rights that God has listed in his tôranic instruction. An entitled right to Social Democratic welfare largess is not one of them.

· 1 2 ·

APPLYING THE WHOLE BIBLE
PRINCIPLE TO C&S

Evidence of Social Democratic
Presuppositions in C&S

One key presupposition that Social Democratic and Democratic Socialists take when they attempt to win Christians to their point of view is a powerful claim: God takes a special, biased option for the poor and any other favored groups that feels itself oppressed. This theme applied to the whole social order is transforming of every area of life. However, the God of Scripture reveals himself differently. He is in a special way only the God of his believing and obedient people who call on his name, for whom Christ laid down his life. This is true especially when his trusting and following people are genuinely oppressed by the powerful who hate God and his norms. Our God is "for us" his children, as Paul states. Hence, he is not on the side of any other group or class for any reason other than Christ and those "in him" (Rom 8:28–39). This implies that all humans are under his just wrath except those who are now no longer so. These only have been declared righteous by grace through trusting in Christ alone. This includes those from both the rich and the poor, Jews and idol worshiping ethnies, and male and female groups. All such groups of people are equally condemned yet now in the new covenant "in Christ" can have

246 WHEN A THEOLOGICAL SHIFT CHANGED A NATION

equal access to his throne of grace (Gal 3:26–9). This is standard teaching in the confessional tradition that the DRC of South Africa once held tightly to.

On the other hand, paradoxically, saying this in no way denies the truth that God has a special compassion upon the genuinely oppressed even among unbelievers. The God of Scripture is the God of impartial justice yet also hates any kind of oppression. Consequently, he punishes oppressors with greater wrath than the wrath given to those who have done less oppressive wickedness than others. Both, certainly, well deserve wrath, yet God reserves some mercy for the later (see Rom 2:1–16; Lk 12:48).

However, C&S rejected, it seems, the classic Reformed claim that biblical, covenant law both in the OT and as seen through the eyes of our Royal Lord, provides any kind of model for contemporary social orders. This would "reduc[e] . . . the Word of God to a contemporary recipe book with instant solutions for all human problems."[1] And, "The Bible as proclamation of God's Kingdom is not a textbook on, inter alia, sociology, economics or politics." Would jurisprudence also be included in this list? Perhaps so: "The Bible, because of it's [sic] own nature and character may not be used as a manual for solving social, economic or political problems."[2]

In contrast, as seen previously, C&S' provided at first a definition of justice that seemed on the surface to be biblical. Later, however, another contradictory definition of justice prevailed when C&S stated: "'Righteousness' also involves the structures of human society. It implies that each person receives what is due to him as a member of society, so that he can fulfil his Godgiven [sic] vocation."[3] It seems that C&S fell into the trap that Professor Nash mentioned at the end of the last chapter under the heading, *God's Zeal for His Own Justice*. The above C&S quotation must be understood within the context of the whole document. It seemed to mean economic structures that lead to economic and social inequality must be controlled and/or removed when people do not "receive what is due." Historically, such talk about what "is due" always has led to an entitlement to compassion-less, state-redistributed wealth confiscated by the State's coercive might.

In the place of private Christian and ecclesial compassion, then, C&S envisioned state-controlled "income leveling" structures that must be built into the New South African socio-political system. This paradigm shift away from the total depravity teaching of classic reformed theology, historically, has

1 C&S, 18.
2 C&S, 19.
3 C&S, 140.

always been as revolutionary as Marxist-Leninism has been—but in the long run. The long run summarizes a crucial distinction between Marxian-inspired social democracy and its close cousin, democratic socialism and full-blown revolutionary Marxist-Leninism. Social Democracy chooses to use Fabian or gradual change through manipulating the ballot box instead of rapid catastrophic violence as do classic Marxist-Leninists. And social democrats of all stripes do manipulate by redistributing funds to legally buying the votes of those to whom funds are given. Dependence upon state entitlements provides a loyal following.

In summary, both socialist branches use statist coercion to overturn divisive and oppressive social structures that, the core ideology has always taught, create inequality and oppression. In addition, both types of socialism covet a monopoly of weapons so that the people are not able to resist either the State's wealth redistribution efforts or the privatized criminal elements that also redistribute wealth. The present failing American experiment demonstrates this truism.

Every type of socialism always makes the rich wealthier and the poor poorer. Why? Because the colluding coterie of rich socialists (or better, crony capitalists) who capture control of all parties, along with their generously paid subordinates, always control the money supply of the central bank. This virtual uniparty may include those from multiple nominally independent parties but who walk almost in lock-step on all the core issues. They then redistribute to themselves and their supporters the first fruits of newly created money so that they buy up everything first before money trickles down to the rest, who suffer from the resulting inflation.

For those who would disagree, modern "Capitalism" is merely a crony form of a type of Statism that is owned and ruled by massively wealthy oligarchs with civil government, in effect, under their financial control. This variant type of Fascism, itself a sub-type of Socialism, is totally distinct from a Christian free market system within the bounds of the tôranic wisdom of Scripture that, for example, the USA once more or less had.

The uniparty State must, then, control all property through taxation and regulation. In addition, they have a monopoly control upon foreign policy and the imperial war-making, which creates lucrative profits for the "defense industry." True private property rights and a precious-metal convertible currency are always among the first rights confiscated by these "crony Capitalist," progressive social democrats, democratic socialists, and revolutionary socialists, who end up the actual owners of almost everything.

248   WHEN A THEOLOGICAL SHIFT CHANGED A NATION

This type of biblical social analysis is well stated by Augustine of Hippo in *The City of God* (4.40) and is inseparable from sound Reformed social analysis founded upon the teaching of Absolute Sinfulness or Total Depravity of mankind with its Scripture-founded distrust of centralized states similar to what C&S advocated:

> In the absence of justice, what is sovereignty but organized brigandage? For, what are bands of brigands but petty kingdoms? They also are groups of men, under the rule of a leader, bound together by a common agreement, dividing their booty according to settled principle. If this band of criminals, by recruiting more criminals, acquires enough power to occupy regions, to capture cities, and to subdue whole populations, then it can with fuller right assume the title of kingdom, which in the public estimation is conferred upon it, not by the remuneration of greed, but by the increase in impunity.
>
> The answer which a captured pirate gave to the celebrated Alexander the Great was perfectly accurate and correct. When that kind asked the man what me meant by infesting the sea, he boldly replied: "What you mean by warring on the whole world, I do my fighting on a tiny ship, and they call me a pirate; you do yours with a large fleet, and they call you Commander."[4]

Further Evidence of Social Democratic Presuppositions

In some passages, the C&S, though often ambiguous, implied that a person who is poor has an injustice done to him *because* he is poor. In other words, a poor person has an entitlement to the wealth of society because his or her poverty is caused by the system's evil. If such a person remains poor while society is rich, C&S seemed to imply, he is being unjustly stripped of an entitled right. This is classic Marxian-inspired socialism as discovered by anyone who has read Karl Marx's *Communist Manifesto* and its ten steps to socialize an economy as we shall see.

Saying this, on the other hand, no one denies that oftentimes true oppression occurs when allowed by a corrupt judiciary, legislature, or executive. True oppressive theft, graft, bribery, blackmail, and deception are all par for the course in every human social order, including a true free market order, because human beings are not good. Instead, as Scripture teaches, all but one are born self-centered and self-focused after the fall of Adam. All humans are born self-interested, desiring to please anyone and anything except the Triune Creator to whom belongs all praise and glory (Rom 1:18–32, 3:9–20). A just, Christian

---

4 Augustine of Hippo, *The City of God*, trans. Henry Bettenson (New York: Penguin, 2004), 4.4.

APPLYING THE WHOLE BIBLE PRINCIPLE TO C&S   249

free market system is strictly limited to punishing violations of the Decalogue as expounded in the universal equity of the tôranic wisdom, and nothing else. Socialisms of all stripes, on the other hand, exacerbate such human evil. Evil is rebellion against our Creator and his normative order revealed in Scripture. Evil is not an inescapable aspect of a "divisive" social system, or as the ideology teaches, the "systemic evil" of any socially divisive system. A strictly limited civil government, then, that protects the God-given, inalienable freedom of individuals, families, and ethno-linguistic based people-groups. Only this aids people to flourish *or* wither. Only such a system is strictly limited to impartial justice *alone* as defined by biblical tôranic wisdom. It is the only way forward for the post New South Africa I am advocating.

Again, in summary and in stark contrast, if C&S genuinely used social democratic assumptions, it assumed that a poor man is poor because the rich have unjustly kept back some material good that the poor human person has just right to receive. It covertly seemed to presuppose that a poor man is poor solely because the rich have robbed his wages, his vote, land, rights, and/or just social welfare benefits, etc. This is almost indistinguishable to Marx and Engles' "Labour Theory of Value" for those acquainted with this debunked theory.[5] Let C&S speak for itself concerning whether it possessed a syncretistic social democratic or a biblical tôranic definition of justice, according to what we have previously discovered. First,

> Biblical "justice" and "righteousness" is concerned with the defenseless in the cov-enant community, those lacking the means to maintain themselves: the widow the orphan, the poor, the stranger, the Levite, and so forth. That "justice" be done to these, is for the true Israelite . . . self-evident . . . .
>
> When in this way, God's people intercede for the "rights" of the wronged, they follow the example set by God himself. He is above all, the One who espouses the cause of the destitute and the wronged. This is why the Psalmist avows: "I know that the Lord secures justice for the poor, and upholds the cause of the needy" [Ps 140:13].[6]

If the preceding C&S paragraphs 148–9 were dealing with basic cove-nantal rights equally available to all through open access to regular courts

---

5 For critique of the Marxist labor theory of value underlying Social Democratic economic policy, refer to Presbyterian Theologian and Philosopher, Francis Nigel Lee, *Communist Eschatology: A Christian Philosophical Analysis of Post-Capitalistic View of Marx, Engel, and Lenin* [Communist Eschatology] (Nutley, NJ: Craig, 1974), 204ff. Note also Economic Historian, Gary North, *Marx's Religion of Revolution: Regeneration through Chaos* (Tyler, TX: Institute for Christian Economics, 1989), 113–19, 148–9.

6 C&S, 148–9.

250 WHEN A THEOLOGICAL SHIFT CHANGED A NATION

of law and impartial justice in those courts, the thoughts would be spot on biblically accurate. It seems, however, that C&S is setting the stage for the community represented by the state to exercise compassion defined as "justice." Is C&S' definition of state-sponsored justice for the poor (re)distributive or retributive? Is it a *pro-active*, yet still impartial, application of the universal equity of biblical law as interpreted through the words of our Royal Lord or does it involve a biased/partial statist redistribution of wealth and privilege to favored poor classes? Clearly C&S opts for the second definition in line with a Social Democratic bias. It therefore opts for injustice as defined by Scripture.

C&S, 151–2 and following immediately claim that justice is more than impartial application of the universal equity of biblical law, though it mentions that definition in passing:

> As the poor, the widows, the orphans, and the aliens were usually numbered among the helpless, they in particular could fall prey to exploitation and oppression. Nor were they always fairly treated in the courts of law.
>
> It is important to note that in this context the concern is not with "love" or "compassion" but with the upholding of the "rights" of the destitute. Love, compassion, etc. are assumed here, but are not the prime consideration. The helpless man has own Misjpat [sic: *mishpat*] (rights), of which no one dare deprive him. Created by God and bearing his image, he has the "right" to a decent living. To help him to secure his "rights" is not optional. Like love and compassion, it is also a duty. It is for this reason that the Bible shows such a specific sensitivity concerning those who are oppressed and exploited. This sensitivity for those who are wronged may be regarded as a biblical principle which is valid for all times and for all societies.[7]

In this context the question arises, does every person have "the 'right' to a decent living" merely because he has mishpat-rights and is "[c]reated by God and bear[s] his image" as C&S, 152 boldly claimed? The marginal notes cited several verses (Dt 10:8 [sic: 10:18], Pss 17:2, 26:1, 35:23f, 72:2, 140:12; Lk 1:46–55, 6:19:31). Not a single one of these passages can actually be interpreted to mean God demands that a person has an entitled right to money derived from the state coffers taken from taxpayers with threatened or actual state violence.

The Hebrew word *mishpat* can mean in these contexts either "case or cause presented for judgment" or "a legal right, privilege or due" derived from the equity of divine law. British evangelical Old Testament scholar A. Motyer summarizes the nuances of the word: "From šapat ('to judge/give an authoritative judgment'), the noun ... means 'that which encapsulates/expresses such

7 C&S, 152.

APPLYING THE WHOLE BIBLE PRINCIPLE TO C&S 251

an act', hence 'a legal enactment' (Ex. 21:1), especially a divine 'decision/ordinance' (Ps. 81:4). From this came the meanings, 'decision at law' (Nu. 27:21; Jdg. 4:5), the giving of judgment in a case (Dt. 1:17), the 'case' itself (Nu. 27:5), and so 'right decision' in almost any situation ([Is.] 28:26). The word also means the 'right due to a person [in court]' (Dt. 18:3), 'right conduct' (conforming to norm) of both people (Gn. 18:19; [Jer. 32:7]) and God (Gn. 18:25) and 'justice' in the sense of giving someone his rights ([Is.] 1:17)."[8]

None of these definitions involve state redistribution but always biblical responsibilities and rights springing from the Decalogue, which summarizes the covenant norms. In other words, the passages mean that God or a ruler serves (1) as a sword-armed magistrate, pro-actively defending the oppressed, vulnerable, and marginalized poor (Dt 10:18; Ps(s) 17:2, 140:12); (2) or they serve possibly as a defense attorney (Ps 35:23); or (3) they serve as a chief magistrate who impartially defends the impartial justice due to the helpless in court when someone defrauds them of any of the five basic legal rights of the Decalogue (Ps(s) 26:1, 35:24, 72:2), which I discussed previously. In summary, God's revealed tôranic wisdom is the *sole norm* to which mishpat-justice is bound.

Clearly, instead of man-invented, social democratic "entitlement-rights," the passages speak the opposite. Justice, in Scripture, is all about the king of heaven providing both compassionate love as father of his creatures and impartial justice to those who call upon him as impartial magistrate and judge. This he perfectly did at Christ's cross (Rom 3:24–5) and continues to do in his providential reign over the earth through the Son (Pss 2, 110; Is 42:1–4). God's justice does not result in partial and biased group privilege for the poor merely because they are poor. Some poor are genuinely poor through evil choices. See Moses' beautiful balance:

> For the LORD your God is God of gods and LORD of lords, the great God, mighty and awesome, who shows no partiality and accepts no bribes. He defends the [just] cause [*mishpat*] of the fatherless and the widow, and loves the alien, giving him food and clothing. And you are to love those who are aliens, for you yourselves were aliens in Egypt. (Dt 10:17–18 NIV)

Men, reflecting the dominion image of God when serving as state agents, are to give impartial justice to all and especially the vulnerable and oppressed. However, in their personal capacity as individuals and families, and in the corporate capacity in the church and Christian voluntary organizations, people

---

8 Motyer, *Isaiah*, 318–19, n. 1.

are to give compassion to the genuine, deserving poor who cry out to God for help. But even if they do not cry out to God, part of the preparation for Good News proclamation is to "as we have opportunity, let us do good to everyone, and especially to those who are of the household of faith" (Gal 6:10 ESV).

To make all the poor a new privileged group as C&S does is another sort of racism. This racism, instead of being biased to one ethnic group (the Afrikaner), has instead taken a taken a consequent and *partial* "option for the poor." The whole group of poor individuals especially those of non-European ancestry somehow deserve superior treatment and thus must be benefited by a Social Democratic State through taxpayer financed endowments. In South Africa of 2023, the taxpayer class is overwhelmingly Euro-South African. This partiality is oppressive and unjust from the standards of biblical tôranic wisdom. Therefore, the apartheid system's affirmative action bias for the poor Afrikaner of the old National Party run South Africa was unequivocally oppressive. The same can be said about the ANC-dominated, democratic socialist, affirmative action bias for the non-European poor in the New South Africa. In neither case is there equal and impartial protection of a single legal standard as biblical equity demands. Did C&S create a better and more just paradigm shift?

In addition, if the magistrate, reflecting our Creator's glory, must be an impartial enforcer of one legal standard for all individuals, then it must not take a greater percentage of taxes from one group (the wealthier) and redistribute it to another group (the poor)—except as penalty for genuine oppression in violation of the norms of the Decalogue. The progressive income tax, then, is also anti-biblical because there is no single standard exists for expropriation of income, multiple standards exist. This is exactly equivalent to apartheid's genuinely systemic evil of having multiple legal standards for amenities for each race group. Consequently, when a legislature, court, or executive officer confiscates wealth to enforce anti-biblical, statist forms of wealth redistribution, that individual or collective is and ought to be liable before a just court of law for theft. This is exactly the principle taught by the account of Ahab's coveting and expropriating Naboth's vineyard.

Further Evidence of Social Democratic Justice in C&S

Is the C&S genuinely statist and social democratic in its view of justice? I would think that C&S, 153 verifies this interpretation. It claims rightly that the responsibility for biblical justice is everyone's. However the primary responsibility, it states, is that of the "governing authority in the person of the

APPLYING THE WHOLE BIBLE PRINCIPLE TO C&S   253

king" (that is the State). Couple this with the definition of "justice" as state-sponsored kindness to the poor (alongside of individual kindness), and C&S would support a redistributory ethic.

C&S, 155 and 58–63 explains the State's redistributory role in justice. It further claims that *the church* must cooperate with and encourage the building of such a state, a blatant return to anti-Reformed Erastianism (the State sets the agenda for all other spheres of life including the Christ-following community). First it states that all "injustice and distress must be brought to the attention of the authorities and all parties concerned."[9]

> All this implies that the diaconal services of the church ... must oppose all structures in the community which are contradictory to Scripture and must endeavour to bring about a better society; ... must liaise with the authorities and controlling bodies on all levels to eliminate all causes of distress; ... must take steps to create appropriate organisations to implement care (institutions and welfare services) ... must strive for effective welfare legislation which will ensure that the very best service be given to all people; ... must make all people aware of the fact that they have a personal responsibility to be self-supporting as far as possible.[10]

It seems clear. The several quotes above must mean that every person has entitlement right to coercively taken (i.e., "redistributed") income to help him live a "full life." This violates the fundamental, God-given right of property: "You shall not steal" and "You shall not covet." It also violates Christ's word that we do not live by bread alone but by every word from the mouth of the Father.

Biblical Covenantal Rights Versus Human Rights

Biblical Definition of Civil Rights. The universal equity of biblical law gives mankind five fundamental covenantal (i.e., contractual) rights and corresponding responsibilities. The Commandments are legal duties that also give protections against criminal action. Hence as lawful protection-requirements, they become legal rights for the wronged, to be enforced in a regular court of law. When a commandment is broken (e.g., adultery or theft) God's peace and justice are violated. Justice (mishpat) and a legal restoration of harmony and peace (shalom) are to be sought in court.

---

9   C&S, 155.
10 C&S, 58–63.

254   WHEN A THEOLOGICAL SHIFT CHANGED A NATION

The court adjudicates, pronounces when necessary guilt, then restores the violated peace and justice by enforcing restitution in the case of theft or enforcing the various other penalties such as death, caning, banishment, or imprisonment. Therefore, mishpat-justice or legal rights and duties are inseparably connected to the specific details of the universal equity of biblical legislation (see Lv 26:46; Nm 15:16; Dt 4:8, 17:11; 33:10; 1 Kgs 2:3; 2 Chr 19:10, 33:8; Neh 9:29; Hb 1:4; Mal 4:4).

To these five basic, Decalogue rights and responsibilities, several others are constitutional *corollaries* or logical and necessary deductions. No other rights can justly be added to the rights found in biblical law as the law itself testifies (see Dt 12:32, 5:32).[11]

Examples of these explicit and logically implicit rights and responsibilities include (1) innocence, and therefore no punishment until proven guilty (see Ex 23:6; Prv 17:15, 24:23–5; Acts 23:3); (2) no detention without impartial, speedy trial and speedy execution of sentence (Eccl 8:11); (3) no double jeopardy (Na 1:9);[12] (4) no pardon for unrepentant, convicted criminals (Prv 18:5; Lv 19:15); (5) no judicial fiat on sentencing, therefore the victim's right to negotiate with criminal for monetary ransom in place of capital punishment in most if not all cases except premeditated murder;[13] (6) free association to hear the truth; (7) free press to publish the truth not lies; and so forth.

Responsibility-Rights Enumerated

The following five rights and responsibilities are derived from the Decalogue. Two of the ten commands are attached to each responsibility-right. Notice the

---

11 See, e.g., (1) John Warwick Montgomery, *Human Rights and Human Dignity* [Human Rights] (Grand Rapids: Zondervan, 1986) and (2) J. W. Montgomery, *The Law above the Law* (Irvine, CA: NRP, 2015) [Lutheran Perspective]; (3) T. Robert Ingram, *What Is Wrong with Human Rights?* (Houston: St. Thomas Press, 1978) [American Anglican Perspective]. Note also, Anglo-South African, (4) Derek Morphew, *Kingdom Theology and Human Rights* (Kingdom Theology Series) (Ladysmith, KwaZulu-Natal, RSA: Vineyard International, 2015). I do not agree with everything, this is a noble attempt by a Charismatic evangelical writing from an Anglo-South African, individual rights perspective.

12 See, e.g., Greg Bahnsen, "Double Jeopardy: A Case Study in the Influence of Christian Legislation," *Journal of Christian Reconstruction* II (Winter 1975–6); Montgomery, *Human Rights*, 298, n. 326.

13 See, e.g., (1) Walter Kaiser, *OT Ethics*; (2) Kaiser, *OT in New*; (3) North, *Victim's Rights*; John Murray, "The Sanctity of Life," in *Principles of Conduct: Aspects of Biblical Ethics* (Grand Rapids: Eerdmans, 1957), 107–22.

verbal similarity of these responsibility-rights to those of classic individualistic Liberalism and modern Libertarianism (life, liberty, and property). Take note of the difference of importance and order the biblical list below. The major distinctions between these humanist systems and that of Scripture is the issue of autonomy versus Christonomy: the law of self-made man or the law of God in Jesus the Anointed King of the Father (Ps 2). A second major similarity is that of covenant and contract. "Covenant" in biblical terms is a bond between the Creator, divinely accountable, human governors, and the citizen families ("We the covenanted families"). "Contract," in rights-oriented humanism, is merely a social contract between autonomous individuals ("We the people").

Consequently, though there exist surface verbal similarities, in actual fact, the two systems are ideologically opposed.

1. Liberty under God in whom we trust: The responsibility-right of liberty of individuals and a people who trust in the true God from involuntary servitude so that they may freely worship the one true God and base their law, worship, education, politics, economic system, etc. on his Word (1st and 2nd Commandments).

2. Impartial Justice in truth and contracts: The responsibility-right of impartial justice guaranteed by truth and lack of perjury in regular courts of law, and that of freely entered into contracts, also protected and enforced in regular courts of law (3rd and 9th Commandments).

3. Life from conception to natural death: The responsibility-right of life for all who follow the external constraints of the norms of God, and who do not commit one of the capital crimes specified in it (4th and 6th Commandment).

4. Family: The responsibility-right of family, protected by strict penalties from personal and state interventions except when members of a family break the biblical common law (5th and 7th Commandments).

5. Property: The responsibility-right of private property that is inalienable except in payment of restitution as stipulated in the universal equity of divine law. This is a specific strict limitation on the civil government, which cannot thus confiscate any property except for that taxation which is necessary for the one function of civil government: retributive-restorative justice (Rom 13:4ff; 1 Kgs 21) (8th and 10th Commandments).

Responsibility-rights are Covenantal. Consequently, these five biblical responsibility-rights are covenantal or contractual. In other words, they are not rights *inherent* in humanity as autonomous man. They are derived from the covenantal Creator-creature relationship. The image of God in man is never spoken of as the source of rights in Scripture. Instead the image is the reality of a relationship, broken or unbroken, between God the source of all, king and sovereign law-giver, and man the administrator (technically the vicegerent) or dominion image of God on earth.

Inalienable and Alienable Rights. This mean then that biblical rights are *alienable* with respect to God and his covenant law when a person violates a covenant norm. At the same time, they are *inalienable* with respect to man. Man cannot add to or change the conditions of the covenant obligations and freedoms nor can man change the covenantal sanctions or stipulated punishments (see, e.g., Gal 3:15, 17).

Therefore, human courts, parliaments or executive officers have no moral authority to arbitrarily change these God-stipulated covenantal freedoms/obligations (i.e., rights). On the other hand, because a right is covenantal, that right is abrogated when a person is convicted in a regular court of law of breaking the conditions of the covenant-contract. For example, a thief forfeits the rights of private property and perhaps also freedom (liberty) when convicted in a regular court of law. That individual is then liable to involuntary servitude to work until the debt is paid back. Interestingly enough, the distinction between involuntary servitude as enslavement of a judicially innocent person and involuntary servitude of a criminal is allowed in the 14th Amendment of the USA constitution. Furthermore, a premeditated murderer forfeits his right to life yet the tôranic wisdom does distinguish between premeditated guilt and accidental cause of death. In addition, an adulterer convicted with two or three eyewitnesses forfeits the right of a protected family resulting in at least divorce, if convicted and the victim sues for divorce.

Conclusion: Civil Government and Responsibility-rights. The civil government, therefore, is limited by Scripture to the one task alone: active and impartial retributive-restorative justice (Rom 13:3–5; 1 Pt 2:13ff; Pss 72, 82, Dt 1:16ff, Lv 19:15, etc.). In effect, this means that civil governors must only be involved in praising and protecting the innocent and actively punishing the lawbreakers in regular courts of law. Taxation is authorized for this one *impartial* purpose alone: "This is why you pay taxes, for the authorities are God's servants, who give their full time to governing" that is to govern solely according to the standard of verses 3–4: Romans 13:6 (NIV).

Therefore, a just civil government must not take a partial and biased "option for the poor and the oppressed." Nor must it take the biased option for any other group such as the Afrikaner or the historically oppressed Afro-South

APPLYING THE WHOLE BIBLE PRINCIPLE TO C&S   257

Africans. Such an option always results in oppressive taxation as well as land and wealth redistribution to favored classes and groups.

No specific word in the Scripture nor even a single general principle in Scripture can be correctly interpreted to mean that the state must take care of the poor through coerced, that is stolen taxpayers' money. There are other family, church, and private alternatives for the Scripture's mandatory obligation to aid the elderly, poor, and marginalized.

C&S and the Human Rights Dogma

As discussed in a previous chapter, there was in 1975 to 1994 and still remains to this day a strong bias against the factuality of the creation account of Genesis in DRC theology faculties. Adam and Eve as the historical first pair are ignored. Still to its credit, C&S gives a fairly good summary of the biblical doctrine that every human person is created in the *imago Dei* (image of God).

Therefore, all people possess equal dignity because "he [mankind], and he alone, has been created in God's image." This provides man with his "unique place . . . in God's creation." That image remains even after the Fall because Genesis states that the image "has not been completely lost [Gn 9:6]." "The fact that he bears God's image . . . is precisely the reason for the prohibition concerning the shedding of human blood." The following conclusion is also true: "Outside the circle of the covenant of grace, man remains God's creature and the bearer of His image. His high worth and vocation are obscured by sin, but are not thereby destroyed."[14]

Human Dignity: Unsuitable Basis for C&S's Human Rights Dogma. However, again C&S' application of the principle of human dignity is ambiguous because the document rejects universal equity of biblical law:

This God-given dignity of every human being implies
* that Christians must behave towards all people as befits **one human being** towards other human beings, this is, one bearer of God's image towards other bearers of it. This is genuine humanity. Anyone who regards and treats others as mere objects and not as people with the full spectrum of human needs, desires, fears, aspiration, etc., does not fully respect them as human beings;
* that all regulations and practices;[15] which adversely affect the human dignity of persons or groups in society, are unacceptable to the believer.[16]

---

14 C&S, 165, 173, 174.
15 C&S [1986], 172, reads: "all government or social regulations and practices."
16 C&S, 176–7; bold emphasis in original.

258 WHEN A THEOLOGICAL SHIFT CHANGED A NATION

It is unfortunate that the second section above, though warm-hearted, is so ambiguous. Virtually any humanistic meaning can be read into "human dignity." This ambiguity leads directly to C&S accepting the man-made standards and concepts of the human rights movement in the next major sections. Humanity's "basic rights as a human being" as C&S, 183 states it, is founded upon this ambiguous "human dignity" doctrine. This in turn became the standard for state-coerced "charity," which is not compassionate, flowing from the heart, because it is externally coerced.

Consequently, in developing human rights, C&S first attempts to justify it by the Bible:

3.3.5.2 Man's duties and responsibilities
The gifts God bestows on man placed man under the obligation of using them responsibly to the glory of God. Man is thus called to use all he receives to the best of his ability, with a view to ensuring that he will be able to support himself and to assist others in their need.

In order that he may be able to honour his obligations and also fulfil his destiny as a human being, he possesses certain rights which he may and ought to exercise. These are his basic rights as a human being.
3.3.5.3 The concept "human rights" must be based upon and justified by the Bible.

As I have discussed already and will demonstrate more later, these alleged inherent rights of a human being to have a full life and destiny on earth become a mandate for state entitlements. However, first C&S seems to appeal to biblical specifics to build a rights doctrine.

1. C&S claims that it might deduce "in a derived sense" human rights from "man's various relationships and the mandates and calling he has from God."[17]
2. C&S speaks about general principles that "God [has] determined as conditions essential to the fulfillment of man's 'true destiny.'" These are "the most emphatic general biblical demands" of "love, righteousness, justice, compassion, and truth, referred to and highlighted throughout Scripture—for example, in the Ten Commandments, the preaching of the prophets, Jesus's ethic of his Kingdom, and the apostolic admonition."[18]

17 C&S, 188–9.
18 C&S, 187.

APPLYING THE WHOLE BIBLE PRINCIPLE TO C&S 259

Actually, however, C&S grounds the concept of human rights in a doctrine of the dignity of "man as the image of God." This, it claims, is "especially important" in developing a doctrine of rights. However, there is little exegesis of any of the biblical passages in which the imago Dei concept appears.

Maslowian Psychology Read into Human Rights Dogma. As a result, the concept of the imago Dei is described using Maslowian, psychological terminology, for example, "full realization of his humanity and destiny" and "[human] potentialities and essentials for human existence." To its great credit, C&S correctly observes that man has no rights in himself but that the rights are derived from God and from biblical mandates. Second, it correctly notes that all rights come with corresponding "specific obligations."

Notice C&S's refusal, however, to discuss any specific biblical equity to give concrete content to "general biblical demands":

> Though the concept of "human rights" appears nowhere in the Bible, the topic is very often found in the Bible.
>
> It is true that before God man can only have privileges such as, e.g. that he can live, eat, work or marry. These privileges must be safeguarded and human rights is the way in which God-given privileges can be safeguarded in a sinful world.
>
> In essence it brings the church face to face with a far-reaching question, namely, which matters are peculiar to mankind; that is, what has God determined as conditions essential to the fulfilment of man's true destiny.
>
> In the first place, as far as the believer is concerned, there are the most emphatic general biblical demands for love, righteousness, justice, compassion, and truth, referred to and highlighted throughout Scripture, for example, in the Ten Commandments, the preaching of the prophets, Jesus's [sic] ethic of his Kingdom, and the apostolic admonition.
>
> But, secondly, it is the view of man as the image of God which is very important for the correct understanding and analysis of a biblically-based approach to "human rights." God's intention with man as bearer of his image, with certain responsibilities, potentialities, mandates, vocations, and relationships, is that he must advance to the full realization of his humanity and destiny. These potentialities and essentials for a human existence might in a derived sense be described as "human rights", provided we understand that estranged from God, man himself has no right to anything. The rights of man are rights only because God grants and upholds them, even after the Fall.
>
> The Bible does not provide us with a ready-made model for a bill of human rights. Yet, on the basis of man's various relationships and the mandates he has received for God, we are able to deduce certain essential rights which always include specific obligations. It must, however, be clearly understood that every human right is limited by the will of God.[19]

---

19 C&S, 184–9.

260 WHEN A THEOLOGICAL SHIFT CHANGED A NATION

Significant Deletion. It is very significant that C&S, 179 from the 1986 edition, the exact parallel to C&S, 184, is deleted in the 1990 edition: "The concept 'human rights' is not found anywhere in the Bible. It is a relatively modern concept that is mainly derived from secular philosophy and especially from humanistic sources."[20] University of South Africa law professor, Johan Potgieter was correct in his comment on the above paragraph: "In the same document, [the C&S] declares that for it the Bible is the only valid source of authority and therefore this also applies to human rights." He continues: "This obviously constitutes an inexplicable contradiction." He concludes:

> Human rights cannot have two mothers; they are either born of human philosophy, or of the Bible. A doctrine devised by men does not suddenly change into a biblical doctrine merely because, in the words of . . . [*Church and Society* (1986)] (C&S, 179, and also 182), one "fills it with biblical meaning." Indeed, in such manner, almost any ideology can, so to speak, be "justified" in terms of certain parts of the Bible.[21]

Professor Potgieter was certainly correct. The original C&S was right. Human rights as an ideological concept is completely and thoroughly humanistic. It cannot be reconciled with the Christian belief system. Scripture gives a dynamic alternative as discussed above.

Specific, Universal Equity or "Most Emphatic General Demands." Which is it, then? Certainly, it is true that rights can be biblically derived as C&S admirably claims in a rare support for classic Continental Reformed teaching. However, these can be derived from the specifics of the universal equity of biblical law and not "the most emphatic general biblical demands" of "love, righteousness, justice, compassion, and truth" (C&S, 187). These general demands, of course, are indeed part of the universal equity of God's truth. However, they are only one part of the God-breathed Scripture that is applicable to training in societal justice *and* personal righteousness (2 Tm 3:16–17).

It is also certainly true that a systematic "ready-made model" for a Bill of Rights such as is found in the first ten amendments of the American constitution cannot be directly discovered in Scripture as C&S, 189 claims. However, C&S here seems to be contrasting "emphatic, general principles" with specifics that were and are still classically deduced from the universal equity of biblical law as the Westminster Larger and the Heidelberg Catechism do. This would

---

20 C&S 1986, 179.
21 Johan M Potgieter, *The Future of South Africa Based on the "Freedom Charter" or on Christian Values* [Future] (Cape Town: Gospel Defence League, 1989), 5.

APPLYING THE WHOLE BIBLE PRINCIPLE TO C&S   261

destroy the possibility of any positive, specific biblical blueprint for rights based on careful exegesis, deduction, and application of biblical legal material. This again leaves a vacuum into which rushes a complete statist, Social Democratic, human rights blueprint as Potgieter warns.

When Scripture alone is not the standard for developing covenantal rights for humanity, those rights become human entitlements fulfilled with an idol, the secular social democratic or democratic socialist State, at best. C&S, 190 and following demonstrate that this warning is valid. Equal "human dignity" implies a God-given right to a full and complete life on this physical earth. The only earthly institution with power sufficient to coerce such equality of the means of life is the self-divinized State. In its providential hand, every person's "human rights" are provided for through mandatory and coerced, taxpayer-financed, welfare programs. Scripture, on the other hand, provides kinder and more just alternatives.

For example, a man is to work and earn his living, so he must not depend on personal, state or church welfare: "For even when we were with you we gave you this rule: 'If a man will not work, he shall not eat.' We hear that some among you are idle. They are not busy; they are busy-bodies. Such people we command and urge in the Lord Jesus Christ to settle down and earn the bread they eat" (2 Thes 3:10–12). This passage is within the context of a section dealing with the church's mandatory welfare program for the elderly and deserving poor, supported by mandatory tithes and offerings (see 1 Thes 3:6–14; Acts 2:44–5, 4:32–5; 1 Cor 16:1ff; 2 Cor 8–9; Gal 2:10; Jas 1:27, 2:14ff; 1 Jn 3:16–17; see Dt 15:1–11).

However, according to Scripture, even the church is only a secondary defense against poverty, using mandatory tithe funds in an idealized Christian constitutional order setting up limits and responsibilities of each of the three classical-biblical, governing social spheres: family, ecclesial, and civil governments. The extended family is the first line of support for welfare. In fact, our Lord bases the necessity for the children to take care of their elderly parents upon the Fifth Commandment (Mt 15:1ff; 1 Ti 5:3ff).

When and if a person cannot work, then his extended family must care for him. They will normally treat him with genuine compassion and hold him accountable if necessary. Only then do other aspects of the biblical safety net come in: private charity organizations, corporation grants, and so forth. The civil government sphere, as an impartial administrator of justice, cannot play a redistributive role and remain just.

Paul's letter to Timothy is adamant:

> [Financially support] widows who are widows indeed; but if any widow has children or grandchildren, let them first learn to practice piety in regard to their own family, and to make some return to their parents; for this is acceptable in the sight of God. . . . But if any one does not provide for his own, and especially for those of his household, he has denied the faith, and is worse than an unbeliever. (1 Ti 5:4, 8 NASB)

In direct contradiction to this classic Reformed doctrine of sphere responsibility, C&S implies that any irresponsible or wicked person who refuses to find help in his family and who hates the church, has an entitled right to ask the state to coerce welfare moneys from faithful Christ-followers to support his existence and, at present in 2023, his sexual proclivities. C&S, 190 claims: "As for a man as a created being is concerned, he has the right . . . to a fully human existence: life, food, clothing and protection." Where does that come from? A self-divinized State as Benefactor, Savior, and Lord, the same titles the ancient Caesar's also arrogated to themselves.

Various UN-Recommended Human Rights Supported by C&S

Freedom of Religion. C&S 192–3 states that every Muslim, Hindu, New Ager, and Mormon, every homosexual or Satanist Priest or Wicca witch, and every Goddess Gaia, Allah, and Jah worshiper has the same inherent human right of "freedom of religion" as Christians. C&S states: "As far as the practice of his religion is concerned [man as a created being], . . . has the right to . . . freedom of belief, religion and worship."

This is not the classic Reformed understanding of religious freedom. The Heidelberg Catechism, the Belgic Confession, article 36; chapter 19 and 23 of the *Westminster Confession of Faith*, and other Reformation documents specifically cite the equity of Mosaic judicials and Romans 13 as justification for prosecuting open and practicing anti-Christian idolaters. Though this has not always been done biblically or justly, as discussed, it is still mandatory if two to three cross-examined eyewitnesses are provided for conviction.

To implement this in a Christianizing African continent and in a post New South Africa, a consequent partition of each of the colonially defined nation-states should begin. Such partition should be negotiated, if possible, beginning a radical decentralization and self-partition-secession of these colonial states (Rom 12:17). Later, alliances, confederations, and federations of similar ethno-linguistic groups can form. For example, a confederation between Swazi, Zulu, and Xhosa states. The question, of course, is that of timing. Imposing Christian religion on a largely non-Christian population is the error of the Christian Roman emperors. Neither did the Reformers, who were not always consistent in the application of these principles. Nor did they always follow the full due process principles of universals equity found in Scripture. Nor did they always follow the evidence requirements of biblical tôranic wisdom. Yet, this does not invalidate the principle.

In conclusion, this cited paragraph, C&S is actually speaking about United Nations-defined religious equality, not religious freedom for the various orthodox Christian churches. To advocate total religious equality is to deny and reject the first two commandments of the Decalogue, which state that there is only one God, one faith, and one law (see also Rom 3:21–31). All other law-and-belief systems are hostile to God and therefore actively work to subvert a Christian law-order (Rom 8:7). Tolerance of more than one God is anti-Christian, actually polytheistic. Actually it is a form of the establishment of the State in the form of the uniparty, President or Chairman as the binding god of the society. Rome allowed all kinds of divinities as long as all burned incense to the genius of the Emperor as the apotheosis of Rome.

In a fascinatingly insightful section at the beginning of his magnum opus, *Institutes of Biblical Law*, theonomist R. J. Rushdoony gives the following analysis of religion and the social order. Religious equality and tolerance, he teaches, actually are only a transition between one foundational social religion and another. No religion that maintains its existence, is legally tolerant of other religions as equals. Witness Islamic Iran and Saudi Arabia, Buddhist Myanmar, and Juche and Kim-family worshiping, North Korea. To demonstrate this thesis, he gives the following five points:

1. Law in every culture is religious in origin. A religion is any ultimate authority that gives ultimate value, meaning, and standards in a society. It may, therefore, be totally "secular" in form as, for example, Marxist-Leninism, Secular Humanism, and Nazism.
2. In any culture, the source of law is the "god" of that society.
3. In any society, any change of a legal system is an explicit or implicit change of religion.
4. No disestablishment of religion as such is possible in any society because when one church or religion is disestablished, another must be established in its place. There can be no philosophical, spiritual or moral neutrality in this life. "Since the foundation of law is inescapably

religious, no society exists without a religious foundation or without a law system which codifies the morality of its religion."[22]

5. There can be no tolerance in a legal system for another religion. Toleration is a strategy used to introduce a new law system as a prelude to a new intolerance. "Every law-system must maintain its existence by hostility to every other law-system and to alien religious foundations, or else it commits suicide."[23] I would add, there is no neutrality in any area of life just as Abraham Kuyper has been famously cited as saying: "There is not a square inch in the whole domain of our human existence over which Christ, who is Sovereign over all, does not cry, 'Mine!'"[24]

While I distance myself from several aspects of the late R. J. Rushdoony's theonomy, however, he can still be extremely insightful in his analysis of Western culture and especially education, the area of his doctoral research. In the section summarized above, I agree with him wholeheartedly.

State-Provided Education. C&S 197 stated that every person, because he or she is created in the image of God, has a state-guaranteed entitlement-right to taxpayer-financed school, education and other training. However, state-financed public education is thoroughly socialist and humanistic in concept, financed by coerced funds, and ultimately anti-Christian because the State, not the Triune Creator, is the center of the system. At present in the RSA and the USA, the goal of humanist equal education is to create a new secular/social man, who has broken from the exclusivist, sexist, *cis*-gendered, racist, parochial-ethnic ("white"), and creedally bound past. This process, inspired by Karl Marx's false prophecy, seeks to form a totally new Humanity not bound by any divisive social structure based upon the past.

In Scripture, thoroughly Christian education based on creational and covenantal grounds, however, is the sole right of the parents and (now) Christian organizations (with the church). Christian education under the apartheid-oriented, National Party, nonetheless, was nationalized. Its monopoly is now dominated by the secular-atheistic state that now dominates RSA. Thoroughly Christian education remains standard fare among

---

22 R. J. Rushdoony, *Institutes of Biblical Law. A Chalcedon Study*, vol. 1, The Institutes of Biblical Law Series [Institutes] (Vallecito, CA: Chalcedon/Ross House, 2020), 4–5.

23 Rushdoony, *Institutes*, 6.

24 Abraham Kuyper, "Sphere Sovereignty," in James D. Bratt, ed., *Abraham Kuyper: A Centennial Reader* (Grand Rapids: Eerdmans, 1998), 461.

APPLYING THE WHOLE BIBLE PRINCIPLE TO C&S 265

especially continental Reformed background communities like the DRC of South Africa. This is true as well among North American Presbyterianism among many others groups, as for example, Richard Edlin, R. J. Rushdoony, and Samuel Blumenfeld demonstrate. As a Libertarian-oriented, Jewish follower of Jesus, Samuel Blumenfeld defends privatized and home education by providing a history of the deliberate and systematic subversion of American private Christian education by New England, anti-Calvinist Unitarians who introduced nationalized schools. Rushdoony demonstrates its anti-Christian foundation, and R. Edlin provides profound biblical reasons why Christian parents should not send their children to socialist, taxpayer-financed schools.[25]

Freedom of Speech and Movement. C&S states that every person has the right to "freedom of movement and speech."[26] Unfortunately this is not biblically limited. There is absolutely no justification in the Scripture for the unqualified freedom of speech. That would include pornography, Muslim anti-Christian blasphemy, slander, and so forth.

Slander causing financial injury and perjury in court are prohibited by the third and ninth commandments as well as the judicials that apply them (see Ps 50:19–20). The Scripture states that a man who looks at a woman with lustful intent has committed adultery. A woman or man selling her/his body photographically is the etymological meaning of pornography (i.e., pictured or written prostitution). This principle has led Christian states to prohibit pornography because it is a form of prostitution.

There are again no biblical qualifications or limits to the "right" of freedom of movement as it is stated in the C&S, only a repetition of humanist human rights dogma. When no in context Scriptural input is *a priori* allowed, humanist input floods in. As the right is now written, the RSA could not impose immigration controls against AIDS-infected Malawians or impose any influx controls against internal migration in the subcontinent (including Mozambique, Botswana, Lesotho, Zimbabwe, Namibia, and Nigeria).

---

25 See, e.g., (1) Samuel Blumenfeld, *Is Public Education Necessary?* (Powder Springs, GA: American Vision, 2011); (2) Richard Edlin, *The Cause of Christian Education*, 4th ed. (Sioux Center, IA: Dordt, 2014); (3) R. J. Rushdoony, *The Messianic Character of American Education: Studies in the History of the Philosophy of Education* (Vallecito, CA: Ross House, 1995); (4) R. J. Rushdoony, *Intellectual Schizophrenia: Culture, Crisis, and Education*, 2nd ed. (Chalcedon/Vallecito, CA: Ross House, 2002b).

26 C&S, 201.

266   WHEN A THEOLOGICAL SHIFT CHANGED A NATION

Freedom of Association. C&S states that every person has the right to "free association and participation in cultural and labour contexts."[27] In the United States, the courts have interpreted this right to mean that no club or association can be ethnically exclusive and that every group must be open for women. Even showers and toilets are not legally off-limits to American males, who identify as female. The same goes for female sports activities. Homosexuals are now testing the laws to see if the courts will give them a right to work for any church or Christian school.

The Christian basis for the common law right to free association is the responsibility-right of liberty under God. The logical corollary of this right is the liberty to freely gather to hear the truth. Humanism, however, has reinterpreted this common law right to mean that no association can be gender, ethnic, age, sexual orientation, or social class exclusive.

This interpretation, however, not only violates the right of liberty under God but also violates the right of property. Property rights also grant the right of freedom of association with its logical corollary, the freedom of disassociation. The property owner has the right to exclude whomever he wishes from his property. "Public interest"—the will of the State's rulers, cannot over rule a property owner's responsibility and right of property. However, and this caveat is extremely important, he or she will have to suffer the economic consequences of rejecting certain clientele through formal and informal consumer boycotts and so forth if the owner discriminates on the basis of color, gender, etc. The power of the people to boycott is more powerful than the State.

The eighth and tenth commandments, therefore, protect property, contract, and commercial rights absolutely (see WLC, A. 141). The only exception is where property rights are used as a cover for evil purposes defined by the other four basic rights cited above. For example, houses of prostitution violate the right to civil government protection of the exclusive sexual bond between a male-husband and his single, biologically female, wife. In addition, air, water, and even noise pollution violate the right of private property of others; the golden rule is an expression of the two Great Commandments, and specific case law equity (see Ex 22:5–6).[28] In that case, "restitution of goods unlawfully detained from the right owners thereof" is enjoined (WLC, ans. 141, citing Lv

---

27 C&S, 203.

28 Gary North, "Pollution, Ownership and Responsibility (Ex. 22:5–6)," in *Authority and Dominion: An Economic Commentary on Exodus*, vol. 3. Part 3, Tools of Dominion (Dallas, GA: Point Five Press, 2020a), 776–843.

APPLYING THE WHOLE BIBLE PRINCIPLE TO C&S 267

6:2–5; Lk 19:8; see WCF, 26.3; BC, 36). Significantly, property rights are not cited by C&S. That is one of the five basic foundation stones of political and economic freedom according to biblical wisdom.

Right to a Just Socio-Economic System. C&S states that every person has a right to "the fruits of his labour, amongst others, in the way of fair compensation" and "to an equitable socio-economic order." These are described in vague terms, opening the door to oppressive state taxation and regulations denying the basic biblical rights to have private oaths and contracts and private property enforced in regular courts of law. This understanding would certainly allow for state expropriation of property, contrary to the clear teaching of Scripture and both the Apartheid State and the New South Africa's practice (see 1 Kgs 21: Ahab's theft of Naboth's property; Is 5:8–10; Ez 45:9ff).[29]

Examples of this type of law are closed-shop labor union regulations oppressing unemployed "scabs" willing to work for less than the union dictates. These regulations unjustly benefit union members with partial, state-created monopoly privileges. Another example is state-created minimum wage laws, which oppress the able poor who wish to work but cannot find work at the set minimum wage. These laws are cases of the state taking a biased option for one group over another instead of enforcing one impartial law, equally protecting all groups and individuals. These laws always lead to higher unemployment in the long run because employers lay off workers they cannot afford at the minimum wage or at least refuse to hire new workers at the unprofitable union or state-mandated wage.

Furthermore, there is no biblical right for the state to arbitrarily determine what is "fair compensation" and "an equitable socio-economic order." State intervention destroys both the biblical responsibility-right of property (eighth and tenth commandments), the responsibility-right to contract by written or verbal oath-promise (third commandment), and the responsibility-right of liberty. These responsibility-rights protect employers and employees from involuntary servitude to the state and unions. It grants freedom to employers to freely negotiated contracts between themselves and individuals and/or themselves and non-coercive, non-closed-shop labor unions.

The state instead must pro-actively protect these responsibility-rights in the market place, especially by protecting the weak, the marginalized, and the alien. Only in such a private property based, free economic system can compensation be mutually agreeable to both the employer and employee.

---

29 C&S, 204, 205.

268   WHEN A THEOLOGICAL SHIFT CHANGED A NATION

Therefore, C&S, 204–5 can only be interpreted to mean coercive state redistribution of wealth to provide "free" schools and universities, amenities, very likely housing, but also, certainly basic welfare such as food and clothing.[30]

Lovingkindness and Compassion

Lastly, C&S' definition of lovingkindness and compassion must be addressed. C&S, 156–9 gives a generally excellent definition of compassion. However, because it does not discuss compassion in the context of discipline, purity, responsibility, and discernment as Paul carefully does (see 1 Thes 4; 2 Thes 3; Phil 1:9–11), it leaves the door open for more Social Democratic, state-coerced compassion.

In Scripture, love and compassion can never be divorced from the specifics of the universal equity of biblical tôranic wisdom. Jesus and the Apostles say that the Great Commandment and its compassion are merely the summary of the "law and the prophets." The summary cannot destroy that which it summarizes.

Without biblical righteousness as the integral part of love, compassion becomes cruel: "The compassion of the wicked is cruel" (Prv 12:10 NASB). Why? Because godless, statist compassion gives someone else's money away to chosen recipients without coupling that gift with accountability and personal responsibility. This leads to inevitable slave-dependence upon the self-divinized State for the welfare recipients. They receive without having to work or be morally responsible.

This also leads to an attitude of paternalistic and classist noblesse oblige on the part of the givers. They are forced to give through the state and therefore, can say or feel: "My duty for the inferior is satisfied." Note that the sin of Sodom was arrogant riches but no real, personal compassionate care for the poor (Ez 16:49). The welfare state ultimately destroys the function of family and church as defined in Scripture. It also destroys much long-term private initiative and compassion.

Therefore, an equalitarian and undisciplined compassion is not equal to God's just and righteous love. Love does not treat or make everyone equal. Love respect God-created diversity but not the diversity created by man. The Canons of Dort teach the opposite. Christ's common grace is for all men (see Rom 2:4; Mt 5:43ff), but certainly his special love is very partial and discriminating.

---

30 C&S, 196 and 190.

He preferred (i.e., loved), therefore He chose a distinct nation (now multiethnic); died for them (not everyone), called, justified and glorified them alone (a definitive and particular redemption). God does not handle everyone exactly "equally" but he does impartially judge all with a single standard based on his character and creation design-norms. Absolutely, God's "justice" is impartial, which can be established by many passages. All are to be judged by one law and one gospel (see Lv 19:15; Dt 1:16ff, Rom 2). However, God's compassionate love is not impartial (Christian welfare program: Lv 25:35–8; Dt 15:1–11; Is 58; Acts 4:32–35; 2 Cor 8–9; 2 Thes 3:6–13; 1 Tm 5:3–16; Jas 2; 1 Jn 3:16–17).

· 13 ·

THE WHOLE BIBLE PRINCIPLE: C&S AND SOCIAL ANTINOMIAN TENDENCIES

C&S Moves Away from Divine Wisdom

I propose, then, that *Church and Society* (1990) strongly tends to moves its authority foundation away from God's tôranic wisdom. This is the wisdom of the "Law and the Prophets" as fulfilled in and interpreted through the eyes of King Jesus and his apostolic and prophetic messengers (Mt 5:17–20; Eph 2:20). Instead, C&S leads Christians to build socio-economic and political structures upon humanistic law enclothed in Christian terminology redefined. In essence this is a non-consistent form of "social antinomianism" because its authority tends to listen to the always varying human perspective and resulting law. Certainly, this is not personal antinomianism nor is it a consistent social antinomianism. Some remnant of the biblical word remains.[1] Yet nevertheless it has certainly trended in the direction of social antinomianism, becoming ever more consistent over the last four decades since the paradigm shift of 1986–94 that rocked the South African nation as we have seen.

---

1 See A. Troost, "A Plea for a Christian Creation Ethic," *International Reformed Bulletin* 31 (October 1967): 52–6. An updated version of a Christian free market response is: Gary North, *Authority and Dominion: An Economic Commentary on Exodus*, vol. 6: Appendixes (Dallas, GA: Point Five Press, 2020b).

272   WHEN A THEOLOGICAL SHIFT CHANGED A NATION

This social-ethical position is, in essence, similar to that of the Radical Reformers of Calvin's day. Instead of God's glory and holy will as revealed in his whole Word, and especially with Israel as a model Republic (e.g., Dt 4:5–8), the transforming model for ethical personal and social behavior is "personal and group relations as viewed from the perspective of the Kingdom." "The Kingdom" tends to be seen as a purely new covenant creation read through the eyes of an egalitarian ideal.

The two following passages in C&S subtly tend in this direction when seen in the whole context. Notice how these paragraphs move from the nation and people of Israel as a group of families, that is as a covenantal whole who are together glorify the Creator to a virtual aggregation of individuals who do something similar in the new covenant.

> Under the old covenant, he made Israel his very own people with a calling to glorify him and to be a blessing to all the nations. The new covenant proclaims that through Jesus Christ, God has reconciled the world to himself. Furthermore, that he has brought together in his church all those who believe in him and have accepted the message, giving them the vocation to serve him as king in all spheres of life, and to be a blessing to the world until that day when he brings all things to consummation.[2]
>
> [This means] ... that the new relation in which the citizens of the Kingdom were placed with regard to God, to each other and the world, causes them to have a solemn calling which must be practised in all walks of life. They must exercise this calling in such a manner that in obedience to His Word and in accordance with their own conscience, they can at all times justify their actions before God and all other people. For this reason attention is given firstly to the nature and calling of the church and the relationships which result therefrom, and secondly to personal and group relationships as viewed from the perspective of the Kingdom.[3]

Dispensational Distinction between Old and New Covenants?

Certainly, the paragraphs above correctly state that God's new covenant children are "to serve him as king in all spheres of life," and "to have a solemn calling which must be practised in all walks of life," echoing older Kuyperian themes. However, that "service" is ambiguously general. The "relational" emphasis in these and the surrounding paragraphs, along with the rejection of the specific equity of biblical tôranic wisdom, severely dilutes the meaning of covenantal service to the king.

2   C&S, 21.
3   C&S, 23.

THE WHOLE BIBLE PRINCIPLE   273

C&S provides no specific, unchanging tôranic wisdom of the King of Kings with which to transform society in the power of the Spirit. Instead, C&S provides three nonspecific ones: (1) general rules for more or less inclusive "personal and group relationships," (2) a non-model-giving Scripture ("his Word" in general with many passages arbitrarily excised), and (3) one's "own conscience." This "service" that individual believers are to give God and society is not biblically covenantal nor always normative but relative to circumstance and culture. However, the New Testament disagrees. The ethic of the Scripture's old and new covenants is the same in the words of our Lord and of his Apostles (Mt 5:17–21; 1 Cor 10:1–10; 2 Tm 3:16–17; Rom 3:31, 7:12, 8:4, 15:4; 1 Tm 1:7–11) because both are firmly founded on the never-changing character, wisdom, and creation design of our Triune Creator.

Certainly, many of the external forms are changed because we are not now part of the Israelite community with the Temple, Cities of Refuge, and flat-topped homes. Yet still the inner core—"the truth and substance"—of justice, mercy, and humble reliance upon God "regulate our lives" and hence remain the same (BC, 25). Our God says repeatedly, "Be holy because I am holy" in both testaments. Instead, C&S apparently contrasts the two testaments' ethics and communities.

An implication of these C&S citations, further, is that the uniquely biblical and specific transforming message seems to be categorized as "old covenant." The new covenant brings a new ethic. Thus, C&S would seem to imply, the old ethic was relevant to an archaic age when God dealt with and uniquely transformed only *one* people. In the new covenant age, however, God has "reconciled the world to himself" and "has brought together in his church all those who believe in him and have accepted the message." This new message brings about a "new relationship with regard to God, to each other and the world" so that *individual* believers must now "at all times justify their actions before God and all other people."

However, was this not true also of the old covenant people of God? On the other hand, is this not a dispensational, Radical Reformation-like distinction between covenants not found in Scripture nor in the Three Forms of Unity that the DRC still nominally upholds as their doctrinal standards?

Further Radical Reformation-like Discontinuities?

As the chapters on eschatology and the covenant demonstrated, C&S tended to believe that the new covenant draws all individual believers from throughout

274 WHEN A THEOLOGICAL SHIFT CHANGED A NATION

the world into one totally new kingdom-church (nova creatio). In other words, the implication seems again to be that God moves historically from one type of social ethic in the old covenant to a radically different type of ethic in the new. In the old, YHWH is busy making a unique culture for one distinct people. In the new, God does not seem to make separate, distinct, unique cultures for each ethno-cultural group based upon their applying the universal equity of the former, Mosaic law.

Instead, the implication seems to be, that God is now taking individuals from all peoples unifying them into one new unifying kingdom-humanity. In this new humanity, God's old covenant law, culturally separating his people from all other peoples, is no longer the standard by which to judge actions. In other words, in the new covenant God neither uses the ceremonial holiness laws, nor the universal equity of the moral and judicial laws to create a uniquely Christian culture.

Therefore, the implication seems to be, that this *totally new* relationship *itself* must serve as an existential standard for judging human associations in the socio-political and economic spheres. Despite the disclaimers that Scripture does not teach either segregation or integration, C&S had an implicit model for social unity in Southern Africa after all. C&S's implicit social model is based upon groupless individuals instead of color-based race as apartheid did or upon ethno-covenantal solidarity as the Scripture does.

In addition, the holist-individualist church implicitly and explicitly taught by C&S is to model *now* what *then* will be in the consummation kingdom. This will be a system without divisions between classes, genders, and ethnic groups as discussed in previous chapters. According to C&S, it seems that separate cultures and separate peoples maintaining their uniqueness using biblical tôranic wisdom, are anachronistic. This is exactly what the Boers of old did, albeit quite imperfectly, using an understanding of the biblical covenant theology and application of whole Bible norms.

To summarize, then, individuals who come *out of* ethno-cultural solidarities, working together toward a greater world oneness, in one new kingdom "organism," are then "new covenantal." In the coming, eternal, non-divided "kingdom," all forms of discrimination (e.g., preference for one's own language group and culture) are sinful by definition. Yet this itself clearly is a social blueprint, but not a biblical one. Again it is clear that no one can escape social blueprints. Even when C&S denies to God's Word its normative, blueprint-giving capability, it substitutes an implicitly covenant-denying alternative. This "new covenant ethic" will not result in a society different from any other

THE WHOLE BIBLE PRINCIPLE   275

which would occur by applying the various modern humanistic theories of the present day. Even C&S' inconsequent social antinomianism ultimately opens the door to humanistic legalism or "anthroponomianism," that is the millions of human created laws.

Examples of Specific Blueprints Denied by C&S

The Law of God, Apartheid and Inter-Ethnic Relations. In contradiction to what C&S, 123 (below) claims, Scripture does contain specific, "direct prescriptions regarding the regulation of relationships among peoples." These are found in the very much neglected stranger or alien (*ger*) laws of the Pentateuch. They are transculturally valid with universal equity throughout because these kinds of contexts are found throughout the earth. We will always have the Other (as well as the poor) in our midst the Lord directly taught in the Parable of the Good Samaritan and other contexts. Actually to order all forms of human behavior is certainly "the particular nature" Scripture as Paul tells Timothy: "All Scripture is God-breathed and is useful for teaching, rebuking, correcting and training in righteousness" (2 Tm 3:16–17). Hear C&S, 123 to 129:

> It is clear that by virtue of its particular nature God's Word contains no direct prescription regarding the regulation of relationships among peoples. This does not mean that the Bible has no message concerning group relationships. However we have to look for it in the biblical guidelines for interpersonal behaviour. God has indeed given his people clear instructions regarding their attitudes and actions relating to their fellow-men. Although these commands deal mainly with person-to-person relationships, we must accept their importance with respect to group relationships. Moreover group relationships is [*sic*] mainly concerned with the quality of our person to person human conduct.
>
> The guidelines for inter-personal behaviour in group relationships must be derived from consistent ethical directives to be found throughout the Bible. They are
>
> * Christian love for one's neighbour
> * righteousness and justice
> * compassion
> * truth
> * respect for the God-given dignity of man.[4]

C&S and Exclusivism. Note carefully also the implicit Radical Reformation doctrine of a redemptive-historical shift from group to individual. C&S, 112 connects "discrimination" with "sinful absolutising of one's own nation and

---

4 C&S, 123–9.

276   WHEN A THEOLOGICAL SHIFT CHANGED A NATION

race" and "contempt." To its credit, C&S, 111 says that the previous condemnation of racism and discrimination must be "clearly distinguished from" "a sincere love for one's own people, aimed at creating and preserving one's own culture." However, the whole tenor of the argument would imply that this must be done within inclusive, democratic and holistic, political <u>and</u> ecclesiastical structures. Ultimately this logic leads to a one-world unitary State contrary to the clear message of the Babel account as we have seen.

The question must be pressed. Are all forms of exclusive clubs sinful? Are male-only, Xhosa or Afrikaner-only, children-only, or binary female-exclusive clubs sinful? Are they "sexist" perhaps (male-only organizations such as a golf club), or "ageist" (children-only), "cis-gendered" (binary female swim clubs), or "racist" (exclusive Indian South African club), or "classist" (involving a membership fee for a golf club). Do all of these types of exclusivity involve by definition "contempt for others?" What about an exclusive, mono-ethnic country like Swaziland? Is that sinful? What about a Christians-only church, excluding adulterers, sexually immoral, practicing liars, swindlers, incestuous, homosexuals, and idolaters (1 Cor 5–6)?

However, as already discussed, God has created certain revealed distinctions and diversities, hence he created also a "discrimination" based upon his God-created diversity. A *sinful* discrimination is a prejudicial distinction that is not in conformity with the universal equity of God's tôranic wisdom in the whole of Scripture. For example, excluding a faithful confessing Christ-follower from the Lord's Table merely because she is dark-skinned. Then and only then can discrimination be connected to "sin" and "contempt." However, C&S appears to reject this and hence appears to be importing an extra-biblical, holistic-equalitarian presupposition into its hermeneutic. (Could Ruth have been excluded from Passover after marrying Boaz and taking her oath of loyalty to Naomi's God and people? No according to Nm 9:14; cf. Ex 12:48 for males who have been circumcised or baptized in the name of King Jesus in the new covenant)?

A further example of this extra-biblical presupposition is C&S' recommendation that the state give to all the unqualified right to "free association and participation in cultural and labour contexts" (C&S, 203). Why is this? Could it not be that preference for one's own kind (age, gender, language) is suspect and possibly evil? "Love for one's own must never be exclusive and prejudice the values and culture of others."[5]

5 C&S, 269.

THE WHOLE BIBLE PRINCIPLE   277

However, again this is not logical nor biblical. A husband's love for his wife, the heavenly father's love for his children, and a person's love for his God are exclusive. "Being exclusive" does not define "sin" or "evil." God's law does. The implication of C&S, 269, thus, seems to be that anything exclusive (i.e., divided) always leads to the rejecting of an appreciation for others' values and culture. In other words, this leads to discrimination, and—the implication seems clear—divisive discrimination and exclusivity are *always* evil. Is this not explicit anthroponomianism with an appearance of holiness (2 Cor 11:13–15)?

Universal Equity, not Exclusivism, Defines Discriminatory Law. In other words, in summary, most forms of legal discrimination and race separation are indeed evil because they violate the universal equity of specific biblical laws, *not* because they are exclusivistic. Biblical equity mandates that one legal standard must apply to every citizen and alien dwelling in a land, and especially for those that covenant to follow the God of Scripture. From this came the "equal protection of law" doctrine found in both Anglo-American and Roman-Dutch common law systems.

C&S gives a beautiful summary of what neighbor love means in a general sense without mentioning that the "golden rule" summarizes the essence of the "law and the prophets," and is not a Scripture autonomous form of new covenant only law (Mt 7:14, 22:20; cf. Mt 5:17).

> This command to genuine love for our neighbour includes amongst others the following implications for us: ... that ... as the heart of God's will for our interpersonal conduct, [love] must always be central in the church's message concerning all group relationships; This is indeed a precious love, for it embraces those who might threaten or oppress or persecute or humiliate or hate us. It builds a bridge of goodwill cross all the chasms that separate people from one another .... However, salvation in Christ is more than [proclaiming the good news of salvation and reconciliation in Jesus Christ]. Christ's love included the healing of the sick, the feeding of the hungry, and reached out to all those in real need. Hence Christian neighbourly love is also a love expressed in deeds. It is a love which seeks the complete well-being, not only of our brothers and sisters, but of all people. A serious responsibility rests upon all privileged Christians to practise this all-embracing neighbourly love. We express this love whenever we apply Christ's golden rule: in that we are not only willing to grant to other people what we ourselves want, but that we do to others what we would have them do to us.[6]

Notwithstanding an excellent rhetorical expression of neighbor love here in C&S, 133–8 that, I agree, all should emulate, C&S still equates something

---

6 C&S, 133–8.

278 WHEN A THEOLOGICAL SHIFT CHANGED A NATION

socially exclusive with "evil." C&S' critique of "racism" a few paragraphs earlier demonstrates this. However, putting an excellent summary of the golden rule together with anything socially exclusive destroys Christ's own ethical worldview as we have seen. It is certainly accurate to state that racism is "an earnest sin that no person or church may defend or practise [*sic*]."[7] The old apartheid system of racial-color-based separation in major social spheres *is* desperately evil. The former Synod document, HRLS, does not treat one ethnic group as "inherently superior" because it teaches that all living humans are descendants from the first Adam and his wife, Eve. But in practice, many on the street held to that doctrine both in conversation and practice. I lived in the RSA from 1983 to 1994. C&S, 96 also correctly mentioned this fact, though ironically most C&S writers would probably not believe the creation account was literal history (see the chapter on DRC and the Scripture).

It is also very true that "racism" is a sin that absolutizes one's own above all others. C&S, 273 agrees:

> Absolutising of one's own leads to discrimination against others, especially in a country where a diversity of communities, each with their own cultural heritage and values, have to live together. This can lead to injustice. All people must have the freedom of self-expression within their own cultural milieu, this must not take place at the expense of others. Of special significance here are the words of Christ [in the Golden Rule] . . . (Matt. 7:12).[8]

However, in correctly rejecting the idolization of one's own cultural values, does C&S here imply that inclusivistic, value-pluralism is God's norm? Does the Golden Rule actually teach "live and let live" and "do not hurt someone else, so that all imperial boundaries must be upheld?" Again I must ask, who defines "hurt" (see Rom 13:8ff)? Certainly this would not be the Synod's true opinion if the logical implications of such inclusivism were clearly spelled out. Therefore, the appeal here to a soft cultural relativism is not biblically legitimate.

Furthermore, does this passage imply that anything "exclusive" breaks the Golden Rule? Did not Christ say that the Golden Rule is designed to sum up the law and the prophets, not bring in a new law, "Thou shalt not be exclusive." This all leads to a great dilemma. Once again, I must ask. Are exclusive women's toilets, exclusive women's clothing, sinful? God specifically prohibited transvestitism (Dt 22:5; see 1 Cor 11:12–16). Or was this "Old Testament"

---

7 C&S, 110.
8 C&S, 273.

THE WHOLE BIBLE PRINCIPLE   279

exclusivity abolished in a new covenant, in which men and women, Barbarian and Jew, homosexual and heterosexual are now exactly equal and interchangeable at will? Certainly not. This was the perspective of Gnosticism and of the most radical of the libertine sects.

Furthermore, the implication of C&S, 273 also seems to be that social exclusivity in anything including age, gender, language, culture, impartial enforcement of a biblical law upon all alike and so forth is an absolutizing one's own. This, it claims, leads to injustice and is always at the expense of others. Therefore, the Afrikaner's enforcement of Sabbath closing laws until about 1990, the banning of soft pornography magazines and all abortions until 1975, the enforcement of English and Afrikaans only in Parliament must be a basic injustice. Again, why does the DRC synod accept the imperial boundaries?

C&S's tendency to define exclusivity as sinful is easily deduced from C&S's definition of the relationship between unity and diversity (see the chapter on the Trinitarian key). C&S's conclusion clearly seemed to be that since unity is primary and diversity secondary, then, logically, any exclusivity must absolutize that which must *not* be absolutized. Logically, C&S teaches that only unity is absolute and thus must be made a social norm. Therefore, "exclusivity," which always divides, is imperfect, yes sinful, unjust, and must always be "at the expense of others." The reason is simply that all must have the right to participate in all areas of life within any geographic area. That area is expanded now to include the whole planet.

In other words, the right of free association mentioned in C&S, 203 is holistic and non-exclusivistic. (Does man have the right to participate in God's exclusive prerogatives, as Satan claimed he must, to be truly free?) In addition, C&S read into the Scriptures an alien philosophy that demands voting rights for all inhabitants in a geographically and imperialistically defined nation-state. This is a corollary of its holistic and anti-biblical ethic. C&S, 199 claimed that every person has the right based upon the image of God to "political say, participation, and activities" within RSA. Again, as the boundaries of unity are expanded it ends up with no nations, no borders, and no more deportations—the modern globalist ideal.

Furthermore, I must ask whether C&S's dogma ultimately would mean that teenagers or even pre-teens should vote? What should be the voting limit? The Children's Rights Movement was at that time, and probably still does demand, a drastic lowering of the voting age based on this alleged right. This certainly was used to demand voting rights in the past for every person, male and female, landowner, or pauper. However, is it biblically just? It seems that

280   WHEN A THEOLOGICAL SHIFT CHANGED A NATION

no one has an inherent personal right to vote as C&S implies. (In Scripture, a good deductive case can be made for the age of 20 to become a full "voting" member of the legal assembly).

Biblical Norms Protect the Ethnic Alien Residents. The problem of unkind ethnic and cultural (as well as gender and age) discrimination was, therefore, not solved by the statist removal of all politico-economic boundaries and inequalities in the RSA in 1994. Nor was it removed in the USA with similar legislation in the 1960s. And it will certainly not solve the problems of massive immigration into the South Africa welfare state—nor for the North America states either. Giving every individual totally equal, *individual* human rights, with an absolutely equal vote, equal opportunity, and equal final condition is not a biblical solution. God desires community based on a common God, creed and values along with people of the same language and by extension, culture and geography. This community will intermarry (endogamy). This is a biblical definition of ethnicity that is not co-extensive with "race" or color.[9] Non-biblical discrimination must be solved by careful exegesis and application of the *specific*, universal equity of God's tôranic wisdom concerning the stranger in the land.

The stranger laws of the Mosaic legislation are similar to the equal protection doctrine of both the Roman-Dutch and English common laws. Equal protection, however, does not remove the barrier or the distinction between the ethno-covenantal citizen and the ethnic alien. The Fourth Commandment itself makes the distinction between citizen and alien.

Compare the following list of specific legal protections for the foreigner, the *gêr*, also translated sometimes as "stranger" or "alien." In Scripture, the terms specifically refer to a believing, ethnic alien or at least a permanent resident foreigner:[10]

---

9 See, e.g., (1) Kreitzer, "Mosaic-Prophetic Social-Ethical Principles for ESOL [Ethnic Solidarity]," in *Theology of Ethnicity*, 234–71, see also, 115–22, 170; (2) Richard De Ridder, *Discipling the Nations* (Grand Rapids: Baker, 1975), 41–8; (3) R. J. Rushdoony, *Law and Society*, vol. 2, *The Institutes of Biblical Law* (Vallecito, CA: Chalcedon/Ross House, 2010), 198–201; (4) Derek Kidner, "The Resident Alien," in *Hard Sayings: The Challenge of Old Testament Morals* (London: IVP, 1972), 29–30.

10 See (1) Andy Bowling, "Legal Provisions for Gentile Converts in the Law of Moses" (paper presented to the Evangelical Theological Society, ETS Microfiche, 1989); (2) Christiana de Groot Van Houten, "The Alien in Israelite Law," *Journal for the Study of the Old Testament* (Sheffield: JSOT Press, 1991).

THE WHOLE BIBLE PRINCIPLE

1. Love the stranger who is living in the land as oneself. This means to treat them as native-born, to provide them with food and clothing if indigent (Ex 22:21; Lv 19:33, 23:9; Dt 10:18–19). This was especially poignant for the Jews who had been mistreated in Egypt for so long because they were ethno-covenantal aliens: "When an alien lives with you in your land, do not ill-treat him. The alien living with you must be treated as one of your native-born. Love him as yourself, for you were aliens in Egypt. I am the LORD your God" (Lv 19:33–4).

2. There is to be only one law for the stranger and for the ethno-citizen, thus destroying the justification for most if not all petty apartheid legislation (Lv 24:22; Nm 15:15ff).

3. The stranger was understood to have come as an immigrant with Ruth's attitude respecting the God, law ("your God shall be my God"), and language ("your people shall be my people") of the ethno-covenantally defined citizen group. Basil Rebera insightfully writes: "This utterance by Ruth is not a piece of emotional rhetoric. It is not a simple declaration. It is an oath of allegiance. Each of the verbs has the force of swearing an oath. We can identify this declaration as an oath because of the [self-maledictory, self-cursing] formula with which it concludes."[11]

4. The stranger was allowed to assimilate, yet at the same time, each individual "stranger" comes from different peoples and God told Israel to treat each as members of distinct ethno-cultural groups (see Dt 23:3–7). (In the New Testament, Paul considered himself an ethnic Hebrew Christian (e.g., Rom 9:3–4, 11:1ff; Phil 3:4–6); he instructed Titus to mark out the ethnic Cretan Christians for special rebuke (Ti 1:12ff); and the General Council in Acts 15, all recognized customs can be people specific).

5. Biblical law states that a people can be born and live in a land for generations without being admitted to the decision–making processes of the land. Compare Israel's four generations as aliens in Egypt and the heathen peoples as aliens in Israel (Gn 15:13–16; Ex 22:21, 23:9; Lv 19:34; Dt 10:18–19; Ps 105:23).

These laws protected the ger from exploitation. Even so, according to biblical law, citizenship, and "voting rights/ legal political participation rights" ("political say, participation, and activities . . ." [C&S, 199]) are ethno-covenantally

---

11 Basil A. Rebera, "Translating a Text to be Spoken and Heard: A Study of Ruth 1," *Bible Translator* 43 (April 1992): 236.

282 WHEN A THEOLOGICAL SHIFT CHANGED A NATION

determined. They are not based upon one's "humanity," a U.N.-determined human right, nor upon birth within an arbitrarily defined geographic boundary. If so, then any immigrant could claim the automatic right to vote. For example, the Gibeonites, Jebusites and others born within Israelite boundaries would have voting rights in the pre-monarchical republic and would have had "power sharing" rights to anoint the king in the monarchy.

There are clear implications of stranger legislation for apartheid. Disobedience to the specifics of God's tôranic wisdom and word is the sin of apartheid, not refusal to extend voting rights, nor ethnic distinction, nor partition. Again, C&S' critique of apartheid seems deeply flawed with non-biblical presuppositions.

"Praxis" and the Rejection of Universal Equity. As discussed already, this rejection of the equity in the specifics of the Instruction (Torah) of God leads C&S, 274 to reject specific political models because the Bible is "not a political manual from which specific political models can be deduced," as we have discussed. A further implication of this is that Scripture can give only general, nonspecific principles that must be interpreted subjectively, according to personal experience of a total socio-legal system and according to the value system of the ethno-worldview in which an interpreter lives. The church must see and judge a whole socio-legal system from a holistic perspective, that is from the viewpoint of "how it serves the interests of the entire society." Yet again, in the context of South Africa's "entire [multi-ethnic] society, this means acquiescing to the boundaries set by the European powers exercising divine-like powers contrary to the explicit teaching of Scripture that only the Creator has that right, as we have seen."

The following spells this out:

> Scripture proclaims norms and principles such as love, justice, human dignity and peace which must be embodied in society. Therefore the church may not prescribe political models to the government, but by virtue of its prophetic function the church will continue to test every existing and proposed political model against the Biblical principles and norms. When evaluating political models there is always a strong subjective factor present. That is why churches and Christians often differ in their evaluation of a specific model. Often it also depends on their different experiences thereof, and in particular by the way their personal and group interests are affected. In order to judge a political model as objectively as possible, the church must not only consider it theoretically, but also question the practical manner in which it will serve the interests of the entire society.[12]

12 C&S, 275–6.

THE WHOLE BIBLE PRINCIPLE   283

Logically this means that Scripture provides no transculturally valid, truly *objective*, that is detailed, rational-deductive model to judge any socio-political system whatsoever, let alone apartheid. Why? If all peoples can take the text of Scripture and not find any common principles for evaluation cross-culturally, then there is only pure subjectivity, not a mere "strong objective factor."

C&S continues by teaching "that is why churches and Christians often differ in their evaluation of a specific model. Often it also depends on their different experiences thereof."[13] C&S states that one must judge a system from the *praxis*, that is how it affects the whole society ("practical manner in which it will serve the interests of the entire society"). Praxis, as a philosophical concept, is actually a Marxian concept taken from liberation theology. This judgment from praxis and from subjective experience must include the judgment of other churches, even if they are deep into apostasy, it seemed at the time, and still is a very valid interpretation. This must include especially those churches that were negatively affected by the political system of apartheid (in other words, the SACC churches).[14]

Furthermore, this experiential judgment must include the judgment of multitudes of individual true and nominal Christians, including the majority of inhabitants of the old RSA, who saw apartheid as racist and oppressive, that is

> a racist and oppressive system which protects and promotes the interests of the white minority to the detriment of the majority of the population. Consequently numerous churches condemn it as unchristian and sinful. Apartheid is condemned by states and political institutions worldwide as a form of racism and a transgression against humanity.[15]

This judgment must also include "states and political institutions" throughout the world who judge apartheid "as a form of racism and a transgression against humanity."[16] In other words, sinful and humanistic man, not the specific, universally valid equity of God's judgment in his present ("this age") and future ("the age to come"), is of major importance in ethical judgment (see, e.g., 1 Cor 1–3).

---

13 C&S, 276.
14 C&S, 273. See, e.g., (1) Emilio A. Núñez, *Liberation Theology*, trans. Paul E. Sywulka (Chicago: Moody, 1985), 136–7; (2) Michael Novak, *Will It Liberate? Questions about Liberation Theology* (Lanham, MD: Madison Books, 1991).
15 C&S, 278.
16 C&S, 276.

284   WHEN A THEOLOGICAL SHIFT CHANGED A NATION

Holistic Presuppositions and the Rejection of Equity. The use of experience-based praxis was consistent with the holistic bias of C&S (see the chapter on the Trinity Principle). The holistic-experiential bias was the real basis of C&S' social ethic as clearly observed in the following:

1. C&S virtually, though not totally, ignored the various ethno-covenantally bound peoples in South Africa and virtually, though not consequently, adopts the imperialist and global humanist vision of South Africa as one country made up of individuals. This is the perspective of both individualistic, classic Liberalism and globalist Marxism in all its various permutations.
2. C&S adopts the humanistic criterion of the SACC and World Council of Churches, who in turn are influenced by the French Revolution's and the United Nation's perspectives on human rights such as the International Declaration of Human Rights.
3. C&S, 278, for example, welcomed the criticism of humanistic, Social Democratic and/or Marxist-dominated states.
4. C&S saw the subjective experience of the majority as having ethical validity in judgment contrary to Scripture.
5. C&S rejected the specific universal equity of biblical laws dealing with inter-ethnic relations and thus read humanistic ethical standards into the general principles of the Word, which it claimed to find in the Word.

The *classical* biblical magisterial-oriented biblical faith, coming out of Geneva especially, has the exact opposite perspective—antithetical, in Kuyperian terms:

1. Sees people in ethno-covenantal solidarity (see chapter on covenant and ethnicity).
2. Rejects any humanistic ethic as the commandments of men (Mt 15:1ff; Col 2:20–4).
3. Rejects the criticism of the values and norms of the anti-Christian, world-system which is in the hands of the Slanderer (see 1 Jn 2:15–17, 4:1ff; Jas 4:4).
4. Rejects majoritarianism: "Do not follow the crowd in doing wrong. When you give testimony in a lawsuit, do not pervert justice by siding with the crowd" (Ex 23:2 NIV).
5. Rejects the subjective feelings of men who twist the truth in ungodliness and whose consciences have often times been seared by lying

THE WHOLE BIBLE PRINCIPLE   285

spirits: "The Spirit clearly says that in later times some will abandon the faith and follow deceiving spirits and things taught by demons. Such teachings come through hypocritical liars, whose consciences have been seared as with a hot iron" (1 Tm 4:1–4 NIV; see 1 Jn 4:1–8).

Having said this, it is absolutely accurate that the DRC should have indeed listened carefully to the insights of true brothers and sisters in Christ from other cultures. However, should not the DRC have listened primarily to the voice of the Spirit *in the Scripture* through whomever, wherever, and whenever he speaks. The multicultural body of Christ is indeed one, and the Spirit does indeed indwell it, giving unique biblical insight to every group and culture in which there are Christians, just as he chooses. Therefore, every culture group is important. However, he still speaks infallibly only through Scripture alone, not through the rebellious nations and feelings of sinful man (Ps(s) 2, 110).

The Law, Prophets, and Gospel of God Gives Blueprints for the Economy. Lastly, the law of God does give a blueprint for the economy in the eighth and tenth commandments and the equity of various case laws that specify and apply the Decalogue to the social and political arena.[17] A biblical economy will bring blessing to the righteous in the long run: "The wealth of the wicked is laid up for the righteous," and a comprehensive cursing for the wicked in the long run.[18] "The righteous will inherit the earth/the land" (Mt 5:5; Rom 4:13; Ps 37; Prv 2:21ff; Dt 27–8; Lv 26), "but the wicked will be cut off from it," as Calvin also emphasized in both his *Sermons on Deuteronomy* and his Institutes (2.8.4).[19] Therefore, the righteous can be patient. God's justice will prevail in the long run as the universal principles of divine equity of even the Psalms teaches:

17 For excellent material on biblical economics, see, e.g., (1) E. L. Hebdon-Taylor, *Economics, Money and Banking: Christian Principles* (Nutley, NJ: Craig, 1978); (2) Rushdoony, *Politics*; (3) Wright, *Eye for Eye*; (4) Chilton, *Productive Christians*; (5) Gary North, *Honest Money: Biblical Blueprint for Money and Banking*, 2nd ed. (Auburn, AL: Mises Institute, 2015); (6) Gary North, *Christian Economics in One Lesson*, 2nd ed. (Dallas, GA: Point Five Press, 2020c). There may be a flaw in most of these works. They are perhaps too deeply influenced by Austrian, individualist philosophy and economic policy, though there are very many points of agreement between biblical and Austrian economics.

18 See, e.g., (1) Gary North *Dominion and Common Grace: The Biblical Basis of Progress* (Tyler, TX: Institute for Christian Economics, 1987b); (2) North, *Millennialism and Social Theory*.

19 James Jordan, *The Covenant Enforced: [Calvin's] Sermons on Deuteronomy 27 and 28* (Tyler, TX: Institute for Christian Economics, 1990).

286   WHEN A THEOLOGICAL SHIFT CHANGED A NATION

> The scepter of the wicked will not remain over the land allotted to the righteous, for then the righteous might use their hands to do evil. Do good, O LORD, to those who are good, to those who are upright in heart. But those who turn to crooked ways the LORD will banish with the evildoers. Peace be upon Israel. (Ps 125:3 NIV; see Dt 28; Lv 26; Prv 2:21–2; Ps 37)

A godly and just economic policy does not assume that a huge gap between rich and poor is per definition evil. It may very well be because of genuine oppression as has occurred in South Africa, Latin America, and now in the USA, for example, but not necessarily. Oppression must be defined by Scripture alone and its worldview that establishes the basic framework of justice in the Decalogue.

According to Scripture, neither absolute nor even relative socio-economic equality is per definition good and just. Truly earned socio-economic distinction is not the cause of revolution by the unjustly oppressed. However, stirring up murderous envy and covetousness are (Jas 4:1–6). That violation of the tenth commandment is the evil passion to confiscate and redistribute wealth to the rich who control the political and legal system. Among the poor it is the lust to use the state to do the same for themselves through redistribution schemes.

Social class distinction is only evil if the rich are rich because they have deceived, enslaved, raped, stolen, coerced, empowered covetousness, and plundered the poor for their own lawless benefit. This is mentioned throughout Scripture and has occurred throughout all recorded history. However, in a Scripture-based economic system based upon an enforced ethical framework of biblical covenantal equity, this type of exploitation and theft by the rich and powerful is consistently and impartially punished. There are several foundational principles to biblical justice some of which I have mentioned previously. For example, biblical justice enforces first, the five basic rights-and-responsibilities of the Decalogue, namely legal protection only for married binary families, truth and contract protected in courts, private property, limited government under impartial laws, etc. Second, extended family must be enforced as the basic welfare organization (1 Tm 5:3–16).

Third, citizenship is not a human right but a covenantal responsibility given to families that remain at least externally faithful to an agreed-upon written social constitution. Fourth, strictly limited taxation of citizen and permanent resident aliens must pay for the work of exercising impartial justice alone (Rom 13:1–7). This, alongside of a mandatory tithe for all citizens, should go to Christian organizations that care for the Word (eldership) and the poor

THE WHOLE BIBLE PRINCIPLE   287

(diaconate). Fifth, private charities and structural workfare charity such as the equity of the gleaning system would bring. Sixth, inflation cannot ruin the poor and elderly because a 100% precious metal-backed currency standard will be enforced as the Heidelberg and Westminster Larger Catechism mandate (HC, A. 110 forbids "counterfeiting coins and false weights [of silver]," citing Prv 11:1, 16:11, Ez 45:9, 10; Dt 25:13. WLC, A. 142 forbids "false weights [of coins] and measures," citing Prv 11:1, 20:10).

Seventh, property taxes are banned as violating landowner's property rights. Such taxes, in actual effect, are rent to the State, which actually owns the land. In other words, when a citizen (or alien) fails to pay such tax-rent to the State, the State claims it has a legal right to expropriate the land. Eighth, no income tax must ever be allowed whether it is the oppressive progressive income tax or a flat income tax. Both violates either the equal protection of one law principle (progressive) or give too much centralizing power to provincial and central governmental entities. Last, free exchange in a market system devoid of anti-biblical state regulations. The only *just* regulations are those that forbid theft in its many facets especially confiscating family inheritance justly gained. Biblical justice also socially controls sexuality outside of binary marriages (e.g., adultery, fornication and homosexual unions), and totally rejects enslavement of the citizen in a civil order (trafficking of children, and laws that violate the responsibility and right of liberty except for just conviction of crime). Such enslavement implies controlling and/or limiting free contract and property.

In summary, this type of social order was what occurred in just social-constitutional orders such as the American and Swiss civil orders before the rise of socialism. These social orders, ideally at least, saw all social class-oriented theft ideologies as springing from covetousness. Whether such an ideology (e.g., humanist globalism) is propounded and acted upon by wealthy individuals so often working in collusion with their social class members or by well-to-do state officials acting in the name of being "Benefactors of the people" of the poor (e.g., socialism) (Lk 22:25 NIV, NLV), both class actions are evil and ultimately revolutionary. The poor, on the other hand, claim that wealth equality and social or communal ownership of wealth is true justice. On the other hand, the rich claim they are better endowed to own all property and to rule as a de facto oligarchy (often with democratic externals). However, an income gap in itself is not inevitably revolutionary when accompanied with biblical contentment and strict enforcement. Such biblical enforcement must

288 WHEN A THEOLOGICAL SHIFT CHANGED A NATION

be against both the wealthy controlling the institutions of the State for their benefit and against the insurrections of the poor.

Ironically, the ideology of a centralized, "democratized" economy that both forms of Marxian economic theory espouse (i.e., revolutionary Marxist-Leninism and Fabian Social Democracy) actually fit the biblical description of an oppressive and plundering economy. Both types of socialism actually benefit only the rich, whether the rich are upper-class "investors" or merely Party apparatchiks both are wealthy by plebian-proletarian standards. Only an economy built on the universal equity of biblical law can be just because God alone defines justice.

C&S Denies Many Basic Principles of Biblical Economic Law

This principle is denied by C&S (see C&S, 19, 21) and the 1990 Synod. It ultimately backs a pragmatic and hence, almost inevitably, a humanistic social market or Social Democratic system. Such a system is, unrecognized by most, built on Marx's ten planks or steps to bring socialism into a land, described in the *Communist Manifesto*.[20] All ten are contrary to the law of God.

1. Abolition of private property in land and application of all rents of land to public purpose (Violates right of private property).
2. A heavy progressive or graduated income tax (Violates equal protection of law and the stipulation that there must be a single standard uniformly enforced).
3. Abolition of all rights of inheritance (Theft that violates the right of private property)
4. Confiscation of the property of all emigrants and rebels (Theft).
5. Centralization of credit in the hands of the state, by means of a national bank with state capital and an exclusive monopoly (Theft. Gold and silver in the hands of the people were the currency of the biblical worldview).
6. Centralization of the means of communication and transportation in the hands of the state (Theft).
7. Extension of factories and instruments of production owned by the state; the bringing into cultivation of waste lands, and the improvement of the soil generally in accordance with a common plan (Violates the right of property).

---

20 Karl Marx and Frederick Engels, *The Communist Manifesto*, trans. Samuel Moore (New York: Penguin Classics, 1888/1967), 104–5.

THE WHOLE BIBLE PRINCIPLE   289

8. Equal obligation of all to work. Establishment of Industrial armies, especially for agriculture (Involves kidnapping and forced labor violating the right of liberty under God).
9. Combination of agriculture with manufacturing industries; gradual abolition of the distinction between town and country by a more equable distribution of the population over the country (Theft and violation of the right of property).
10. Free education for all children in government schools. Abolition of children's factory labor in its present form. Combination of education with industrial production, etc. (Kidnapping of children and violating the right and responsibility of two parent, binary family).

The DRC's official mouthpiece, *Kerkbode*, in an article in the October 26, 1990 edition, sums up the economic policy of C&S. This is a policy that leans heavily toward Social Democratic rhetoric, emphasizing a "mixed economy" combining State and private ownership in a unified new South Africa:

> The General Synod decided that the expansion of a free market economy can be morally justified in so far as it furthers the maintenance of high economic growth that is so vital for the betterment, on a broad scale, of the economic position of lesser privileged South Africans . . ..
> The Synod also warned against an over-hasty and uncontrolled introduction of a free market economy because this would hold several real dangers. It can lead to the removal of legislation protecting workers, the reduction and even cancellation of social services from the State (such as education and housing), neglect of the care by the State for those suffering emergencies, the increasing of the income gap between rich and poor in South Africa, the further concentration of economic power in the hands of a small number of private enterprises, the general increase of the cost of education and health care, and the sharpening of the conflict between white and black in South Africa, [especially] if the impression is gained that the growth of a free market system serves in the first place to further the economic interests of whites.

Conclusion

The biblical model, then, for an equitable economic system demands that the family and Christian organizations, along with Christ-following local communities, lovingly and personally care for the aged, poor, and marginalized. Paul implies that those who trust in the state or make any other arrangements for the care of elderly parents have "fallen from the faith and are worse than an unbeliever" (1 Tm 5:3–8).

Anything more or less than this biblical standard is anti-Christian. Actually it is revolutionary and is contrary to the *Belgic Confession* (BC, 36) and *Westminster Confession* (WCF, 27.3). Both forbid the communalist heresy of the most consequent of the radical reformers, the radical Anabaptists. To turn social welfare over to an irresponsible and impersonal Social Democratic or revolutionary socialist state is a form of idolatry, trusting in a false messiah. This type of state has an operating mythology derived from Marxism, which in turn depended on the ancient medieval (actually Stoic and Platonic) myth of original communal property.

Jeremiah spoke about this type of wisdom:

> Even the stork in the sky knows her appointed seasons, and the dove, the swift and the thrush observe the time of their migration. But my people do not know the requirements of the LORD. How can you say, "We are wise, for we have the law of the LORD," when actually the lying pen of the scribes has handled it falsely? The wise will be put to shame; they will be dismayed and trapped. Since they have rejected the word of the LORD, what kind of wisdom do they have? (Jer 8:7–8)

When the New South Africa collapses—and even much before that time—Christians in every ethno-cultural group in that African subcontinental area should begin building parallel structures that will provide for their people's welfare when the inevitable collapse occurs. This applies certainly for the rest of Africa, Latin American, and North America as well. The rest of the earth can watch to see how biblical Christian social orders arise out of the ashes of the old.

· 1 4 ·

SUMMARY AND A NEW WAY FORWARD

C&S' new social theology sometimes uses the rhetoric of a classic Reformed culture transformation worldview. However, it adopts much of the futurist eschatology and individual-based social ethics shared by the Radical Reformation and contemporary socialist social theologies. Like these theologies, C&S' church-centered ecclesiology and a future vision (eschatology) that is cut off from a literal creation are influenced by a non-covenantal and non-Trinitarian dualism. This it shares with medieval, neo-orthodox, and Radical Reformation theologies. C&S, lastly, rejects biblical inerrancy and a biblical tôranic wisdom-based view of justice. Instead it adopts a humanist philosophy of rights. It is not as if this has not happened before. The USA, UK, Germany and the other once mighty Christianized nations have undergone the same downward spiral.[1]

The result is a covert radicalism seeking to realize a postulated future holistic kingdom in today's social structures. A covenantal perspective based on biblical tôranic wisdom and the presuppositions which C&S shares with

---

1 For an example in the USA, see Gary North, *Crossed Fingers: How the [Progressive] Liberals Captured the Presbyterian Church* [USA] (Tyler, TX: Institute for Christian Economics, 1996), https://www.garynorth.com/freebooks/docs/pdf/crossed_fingers.pdf.

dualist theologies cannot be fused. Any such syncretism is unstable in the long run and ultimately futile.

While rejecting apartheid, the social theology I propose acknowledges a covenantal worldview—shared with the Orthodox Kuyperians—founded on literal creation design-norms and a long-term future hope both in this age and the age to come. This is true wholism (implying a total or comprehensive redemption in the vocabulary of Kuperianism) is the biblical and reformational alternative to C&S' form of statist holism. Such comprehensive wholism allows for self-determining ethno-cultures under God in family, church and civil governments yet holds to the ideal of visible structures of unity, modeled on the Trinity. It also provides for non-statist, God-mandated social compassion and impartial justice for all, including unbelievers, aliens and the poor (see, e.g., Gal 3:10).

A Proposed Model for Church Unity of DRC Family

A Trinitarian model maintains visible unity and true diversity, giving an alternative to C&S' holistic union of churches.

Mandatory Biblical Stipulations for Ethnic Churches

Open Community. Fellowship between individuals, families, and congregations; the proclamation of the word, the Eucharist, and the baptismal font must be open to all believers.

One Confession. All accept one common confession and the one common gospel, which establishes the one law of God.

Mutual Recognition of Church Discipline. All are under the same church discipline, and therefore the jurisdiction of each unit's *just* church discipline or discipline gatherings is respected by all others.

Concentric-Circle-Shaped Federal Gatherings

The unity of church discipline is expressed in a series of gatherings structured as concentric circles. Each presbytery or classis would be a compact geographic area with several congregations whose elders consider themselves one (con) federation. Regional synods are not the Church but a (con)federation of congregational communities (presbyteries, classes). This holds also for other larger gatherings.

Second, the progressively larger gatherings only have appellate jurisdiction over the circle immediately next to and smaller than it. The larger gatherings do not have direct authority over all smaller courts nor over all individuals. Thus all levels of synods would serve with appellate function alone.

Ethnic Diversity at All Levels

Regional and/or national synods could consist of self-financing, self-propagating, self-governing, self-theologizing ethnic churches *and* those churches that claim not to be ethnic-based. Such federalism rejects the idealized Roman Catholic model of one congregation for each area.

Conclusion

Table 2. Two Models for Culture Transformation

Classic Reformed	Neo-Radical
Sola Scriptura	Scripture plus other premises
Optimistic, restorative eschatology: True unity and real diversity in all of creation. Goal: all divinely created institutions restored to mature form of Edenic design.	Pessimistic eschatology: Fundamental assumption is eschatological dualism, i.e., the divisive old order totally passes away; new order is a totally new creation (*nova creatio*).
Trinitarian, totally sovereign Creator God.	Implicit: social unitarianism plus contingent god.
Trinitarian, covenantal order. Family is foundational building block of social order.	Individual-collective, bi-polarity in society. Individual is sole building block.
Universal equity of a biblical tôranic wisdom order that gives design-norms for every social and individual sphere of life.	Social ethics borrowed from holistic socialist, secular ideology. Personal ethics derived from New Testament.

These exact same principles can and should be applied to the partitioning and to the (con)federating of the partitioned parts into larger units within the social and political orders with, ideally, peaceful negotiations (Rom 12:17). The same applies throughout Africa and all other areas that have been oppressed by imperial imposition of boundaries. North America, Mexico, the British

Isles, France, Italy, or Spain, for example, come readily to mind. China and Russia could learn from these principles as well. This is the biblical renewal wave of the future, how long, no one can predict, however.

Positive and Negative Tendencies of C&S

Positive Tendencies

There were several excellent tendencies in the DRC of South Africa's *Church and Society* (1990) document. C&S rightly condemned racism and points out that race and color play no role in the Scripture. Furthermore, C&S was right in opening worship services for all to hear the Word proclaimed.

C&S showed a commendable desire to find a biblical church unity and to seek some sort of biblical justice so as to right the wrongs of the past perpetuated in the name of apartheid.

C&S still claimed, at least nominally, that the Scripture is the final authority for all questions of faith. Even to the present time, the DRC thus has not yet officially denied Christ's divinity and the theological doctrine of the Trinity, though its de facto social theology is implicitly anti-Trinitarian.

Furthermore, C&S has not totally withdrawn from the prophetic function of teaching biblical norms for all of life. This is good. Yet, the paradigm shift that C&S introduced has radically changed the now even more radically centralized State called the Republic of South Africa, which has been ruled as a virtual one-party State from 1994 to the present under the ANC-SACP alliance.

Negative Tendencies

However, negatively, C&S was theologically closer to the Radical Reformation's social thought than that of the Genevan Reformation. C&S implicitly rejected the classic Reformational view of Scripture. Therefore, it gave little allowance for legitimate deductions from biblical data for socio-political and economic issues. In this regard, the document was contradictory. It claimed that Scripture did not give models to solve the complex ethnic problems in South Africa, but then gave an explicit blueprint for a humanist, human rights solution.

C&S implicitly rejected the concept that the creation design is good in itself. It seems to believe that the structures of created reality are not revelatory.

They are mere givens. This includes the Creator's creation, development, and destruction of various ethno-covenantal solidarities throughout history. C&S implicitly accepted the very radical concept that redemption progressively removes all of humankind's social or group divisions. I agree but only if these divisions are sinful as defined by Scripture alone. However, no social divisions built on the Creator's design and design-norms are evil or sinful. Clear examples are the created sexual binary, created and providentially upheld ethno-linguistic diversity, and to a certain extent social class distinction, if they are based on Scripture-defined character, created skill differences, talents, and gifts, and if within a truly free market system upheld by a strictly limited civil government elected by the families of a people-group.

As can be seen, I often take an antithetical perspective to that of C&S based on Scripture. Redemptive history restores covenant fidelity to the Creator's original design, in matured form in every people of the earth. The Garden will become a City in a Garden-earth. The Lord, as the possessor of all authority in heaven and earth, promised he would remain with his multiethnic people until all peoples learn and put into practice all that he instructs from Genesis to Revelation (Mt 28:17–20). This certainly applies to family, ecclesial, and ethno-national civil governments (e.g., Rom 5:12, 18, 21 NASB; Pss 2, 96). His promise and command to disciple every people-group of earth definitely applies to every other voluntary organization human can develop. From the beginning, our God gave mankind stewardship to cultivate, protect, and advance God's providential creation of languages, geographic areas, and culture groups on earth so that all would seek and come to know the LORD (Acts 17:24–31).

God-fearing mankind, including individuals, families, the church, and socio-political entities, is obligated to protect each language and created culture under biblical *norms*. For example, the Cultural Mandate and the Great Commission give authority to preserve distinctly Zulu, Xhosa, and Afrikaner or any other ethno-culture and language group in the RSA, USA, Nigeria or Peoples Republic of China. Such preservation, therefore, is right in itself *if* truly directed by biblical norms. This includes planting churches in each ethno-covenantal solidarity but not in race-color groups. That concept, then, is not equal to race-based churches.

C&S accepted a concept of unity that denied the equal value and eternal ultimacy of unity and diversity. C&S seemed to reject the Trinitarian hermeneutical key in defining the relationship of unity to diversity. C&S, therefore, possessed strong prejudice against applying that key to church, social, and political structures. C&S possessed a bias toward over-emphasizing church unity above inerrant biblical truth and created diversity. Instead of seeing structural church unity in (con)federal forms, it tends to see it in unitarian, centralized forms in both ecclesial and social-political orders. Only a relatively small concession is given to linguistic and cultural diversity in that model.

C&S also implicitly rejected a key theological concept possibly because it implicitly rejects the social and institutional implications of the Trinitarian presupposition. This concept is the distinction between the invisible and visible church. The invisible church is the New Jerusalem above. The visible church is an institutional social sphere in a specific time, place and lingual-cultural context.

C&S had anti-covenantal and individualistic tendencies causing it to lean toward anti-creational, equalitarian individualism. C&S, therefore, *tended* toward seeing the local church as a confessing fellowship made up of individuals, irrespective of family or ethno-covenantal group. Lastly, C&S had strong social antinomian and Social Democratic tendencies leading it to accept the human rights dogma of modern humanism with its resulting globalism and the slow-rolling revolution against God.

Social Theological and Ethical Issues Neglected

C&S correctly desired to be socially relevant. That is commendable. However, so did the authors of apartheid theology. Both saw themselves, perhaps, as an example of the "city on the hill." Both, however, while seeking to be socially prophetic became horribly syncretistic. Just as the apartheid system collapsed, so will the New South Africa collapse from moral degeneration and anti-Christian presuppositions. My conclusion, then, is that C&S did not prophetically speak to the many burning issues of South African church and society that should have been addressed. For example, in its discussion of societal justice and human rights, C&S did not address the following pertinent issues:

1. The rapid growth of pornography, homosexuality, and abortion.
2. The rapid impoverishment of the middle and lower classes by inflation caused by a debased currency and heavy progressive income taxes. The DRC's own Heidelberg Catechism addresses this directly. Both the Kuyperians and the DRC progressives ignored sound classic economic theory based on Scripture. The Heidelberg Catechism is

unequivocal: "Unjust weights, . . . false coins," result in debased coinage. When that occurs, the continuing growth of paper money created by a central bank creates inflation because 100% backing of currency with precious metals as required by biblical principles is defiantly and directly rejected (HC, ans. 110; citing Prv 11:1, 16:11; Ez 45:9, 10; Dt 25:13).

3. Unjust, state-created monopolies. For example, it neglected to address the virtual monopoly on large gold ownership, monopoly on money creation by a private, elite-owned Reserve bank, the monopoly, now very corrupt and inefficient ESCOM/ESKOM (Electricity Supply Commission), and the South African Broadcasting Corporation (SABC), which remains still today a virtual, though not complete, State controlled broadcasting monopoly.

4. The oppression of interest-demanding loans for drought-stricken farmers.

5. The massive breakdown of families caused by the Apartheid system of only allowing males to work in the major cities. This breakdown also includes very high illegitimacy rate and of divorce rate caused in large part by anti-biblical divorce laws. C&S did not address the family issue except to rightly accept that mixed marriages cannot always be forbidden. However, it ignores the most important concept affecting that issue: parental approval.

6. The burgeoning transvestite and homosexual movements, now constitutionally protected.

7. The issue of developing a truly free, parent-controlled and financed, consequently Christian school system.

8. The rapid increase in crime and violence due in part to the releasing of and negotiations with sworn enemies of God and the banning of the mandatory death penalty for premeditated murder.

9. C&S failed to deal with the comprehensive worldview issues that the apartheid theologians attempted to, again more or less in a syncretistic manner, depending on the theologians and philosophers addressed.

For example, the outstanding Afrikaner Reformed Philosopher, H. G. Stoker, whom I had the privilege to meet in the early 1990s while he was in his early 90s, made an excellent contribution to understanding a comprehensive and transformational biblical worldview. His volume *Die Stryd om die Ordes* [The Battle of the Social Orders] (1941) is an outstanding example of developing the socio-political ramifications of the biblical worldview.[2] Unfortunately, he supported the Afrikaner National Party's vision of Separate Development (Apartheid), which weakened his international impact.

At the present moment (2023), however, Stoker's grandson, Dr. Henk G. Stoker, Professor of Apologetics and Ethics at North-West University in South Africa, an expert in the biblical worldview in Calvinist perspective, is translating this excellent work into English and updating it. *The Battle of Social Orders* compared the socio-political impact of the worldviews of individualist-oriented Classic Liberalism, collective-oriented Communism (Bolshevism), National Socialism, Fascism, and Calvinism.[3] Updated, it should be quite relevant both for South Africa but also for the English-speaking world as well since all of these ideologies in contemporary form still exist and are making a major impact upon Western cultures.

Lastly, C&S interacted primarily with one syncretistic, Christo-humanist ideology: apartheid. It did not address two other even more dangerous ideologies affecting DRC members. For example, first Secular and New Age Humanism is rapidly infiltrating into church, school and state circles. Second, Atheistic Evolutionism and its virtual monopoly in the media, and in taxpayer-financed schools, museums and universities is endemic in the RSA. It failed, third, to deal with the French Revolutionary spirit that keeps spawning neo-Marxian ideologies that are very much alive in the RSA, the West, and which Abraham Kuyper and his predecessors such as Guillaume Groen Van Prinsterer wrote extensively about.

Conclusion: Anti-Reformational Paradigm Shift

In conclusion, the DRC actually embarked on the long process of falling away from a biblical view of the relationship of Scripture and church in the late 1950s and 1960s. The fruit of not disciplining these errant viewpoints and

---

2   Hendrik Gerhardus Stoker, *Die Stryd om die Ordes* [The Struggle of the Social Orders] (Pretoria: Calvyn Jubileum Boekefonds, 1941), https://archive.org/details/HendrikGerhardusStokerDieStrydOmDieOrdes/page/n3/mode/2up.

3   What he means by Liberalism is the classic (nineteenth and early twentieth century, pre-Libertarian) social-economic Liberalism based upon the free individual and particularly emphasized in the English-speaking world. The book was written before the Austrian School, now termed Libertarianism, had fully developed. This Austrian school was built upon many insights of classical Liberalism, and developed by scholars such as Ludwig von Mises, Murray Rothbard, Friedrich Hayek.

scholars bore dreadful fruit with the publication of C&S 1986 and 1990 that changed the South Africa nation. This consequent paradigm shift changed South Africa for the worse though certainly it brought several positive tendencies that I have mentioned above. However, just as an angle begins with a tiny departure from the base (i.e., norm), but later is an infinite distance away from that base, so in time a small theological deviation begun with the rejection of full biblical infallibility becomes a full-blown anti-Christian heresy. The DRC has undergone a far-reaching paradigm shift not only away from the classic, Reformed biblical perspective but also away from biblical Christianity. That change, if not checked and reversed, will destroy both the Afrikaner people, their church, and the New South African nation it helped spawn.

A New Way Forward

What is the way forward? First and foremost must be a return to consequent biblical, Mission and Gospel-centered, Spirit-led Christianity. This Faith is based on infallibility—Scripture is incapable of speaking error instead Scripture always speaks solid truth without deception in every area that it addresses, and inerrancy—the Bible does not ever err on anything it addresses with truth claims. To do this would be a reuniting of the missional, warm piety of the Andrew Murray and the wholistic, transformationist Abraham Kuyper wings of the old DRC.

This, then, is the Sola Scriptura Principle that holds as its absolute *sine qua non* the resurrection of Christian cultures for, in the beginning, all of Africa. The Trinitarian principle that diversity and unity are equally valuable and ultimate is a logical deduction from the Scriptural authority and is both inescapable and unmistakable in Scripture. Second, *at least* the Zulu, Xhosa, and Tswana nations must develop a biblical, comprehensive worldview. This includes completely turning away from flirting with the spirit world, yet still maintaining an open-eyed experience of the power of the Holy Spirit to stand against the dark domain of the Accuser and his demonic subordinates. This will take decades of hard work in the power of the Spirit of the living Christ to bring to some measure of success. And it can, as actually occurred especially in Northern Europe after the Reformation.

Each of these ethno-nations, including now the Afrikaans-speaking and English-speaking South Africans, need to develop a healthy *distrust* in the goodness of humankind including that of their own religious, political, and

300   WHEN A THEOLOGICAL SHIFT CHANGED A NATION

social leaders. A centralized State always sinks as low as its rapacious leaders take it generation after generation (Rom 1:18–32). The biblical teaching of the Total Sinfulness of Man (Total Depravity) is as relevant now as it always has been and must impact social-cultural structures. This confession of the faith will lead in the long run to decentralization movements and much more emphasis upon local rule. It will lead to the development of family (not tax-payer) financed home and Christian schools for every child up to the tertiary level. It should in the long run lead to secession movements as the eyes of Africa open to the still pervasive Western control-imperialism in their home territories and countries. This is the Creation Restoration Principle in Christ, the cosmic Lord.

Certainly, neocolonialism—now also being introduced by the Chinese—is not as direct and blatant now as in the open colonial years. Yet on reflection, it is still extant through, for example, Western control of central banking, use of Keynesian (actually social democratic/democratic socialist) economics, and printing of masses of paper currency as what notoriously occurred in Zimbabwe over the last two or more decades. The infiltration of Western-developed evolutionary ideology throughout African educational systems is also blatantly pervasive. French, British, and now American direct and covert manipulation of political processes that are ongoing at present in, for example, the resource-rich Sahel regions are cases in point. Their economic and military manipulation of the independence forces in Southern Africa (Angola, Malawi, Mozambique, Zimbabwe, Namibia, and South Africa) is also well documented.

Again, secession through negotiation, on the other hand, is the way forward in all of Africa as well as other geographic areas of the earth, I might add. True human unity and real ethno-covenantal diversity need to be balanced in confederal and/or federal structures in ecclesial and civil governments (the Trinitarian Principle). As to the social and political arenas, some ethnies may have to fight and sometimes lose, such as what happened in the Nigerian-Biafran War in the late 1960s. The Union of South Africa, an artificial country, born out of the loss of one-third of the Afrikaner people in the Anglo-Boer War (1898–1902) should be broken up by the people of what is now the Republic of South Africa. When I say "the people," I actually mean the many people-groups including the developing English-speaking urban, neo-ethnic conglomerations such as Johannesburg and Port Elizabeth. The Xhosa and especially the Zulu have a contiguous land area, the most fertile in all of the subcontinent, I am told. Why are they not independent or confederated together? After all Lesotho, in the middle of the Southern African map, eSwatini (Swaziland), and Botswana are almost ethnically homogenous and independent, set free by the British Empire. The Tswana of South Africa could also consolidate their territory, (con)federate, and/or secede from the RSA. Or they could even federate with Botswana. This is the Covenant Principle.

When this process has matured over the next half-century to century, could the Afrikaners not also secede and/or confederate as well, after having developed a core territory perhaps along the Orange River and in the pre-1994 boundaries of Pretoria? The same applies for the other smaller ethnies in the Republic such as the Griqua and the Venda. The future is in the Triune Creator's hands and he alone is the God of love and justice, unity and diversity because that is who he is. He will succeed with his plans to fill the earth with his glory as the waters cover the seas (Hb 2:14). To accomplish this goal, he will be leading South Africa to rethink its radical individualist theologies exemplified by *Church and Society* of the Dutch Reformed Church of South Africa.

All the peoples of the Southern African subcontinental region need the whole Word of God for all of life—especially now Afrikanerdom and their University elite, most of whom are deep into apostasy. This, now rejected, Kuyperian-oriented, culture transformation project, must be restored. However, this time around the restoration must come with a sound biblical ethic based on the whole tôranic wisdom and equity of the Law and Prophets and a long-term optimistic, missional eschatology. However, this time God's vision also needs to be fulfilled in the power of the resurrected Lord as the King and Lord of heaven and earth, with Scripture being interpreted through the grid of the new covenant in ethical continuity with the old covenant in consultation with all the people-groups in the subcontinent. This Whole Scripture Principle, its long-term realistic yet also optimistic eschatology, furthermore, along with the Covenant Principle provide hope in this age and the age to come. However, the Prophet Isaiah gives us a final sobering word of covenant warning and of future blessing for those individuals and groups who come to our loving and just Father in repentant rest and trust. After all, our Lord's blessing is wholistic (comprehensive) but not holistic.

> This is what the Sovereign LORD, the Holy One of Israel, says: "In repentance and rest is your salvation, in quietness and trust is your strength, but you would have none of it. You said, 'No, we will flee on horses.' Therefore you will flee! You said, 'We will ride off on swift horses.' Therefore your pursuers will be swift! A thousand will flee at the threat of one; at the threat of five you will all flee away, till you are left like a flagstaff on a mountaintop, like a banner on a hill."

Yet the LORD longs to be gracious to you; therefore he will rise up to show you compassion. For the LORD is a God of justice. Blessed are all who wait for him! (Is 30:15–18 NIV)

BIBLIOGRAPHY

Adonis, J. C. *Die Afgebreekte Skeidsmuur weer Opgebou. Die Verstrengeling van die Sending Beleid van die Nederduitse Gereformeerde Kerk in Suid-Afrika met die Praktyk en Ideologie van die Apartheid in Historiese Perspektief* [The Broken-down Dividing Wall Rebuilt: The Intertwining of the Mission Policy of the DRC in South Africa with the Practice and Ideology of Apartheid in Historical Perspective]. Amsterdam: Rodopi, 1982.

Alberts, Louw, and Frank Chikane, ed. *Road to Rustenburg: The Church Looking Forward to a New South Africa.* Cape Town: Struik Christian Books, 1991.

Algemene Sinodale Kommissie. *Kerk en Samelewing: 'n Getuienis van die Ned[erduitse] Geref[ormeerde] Kerk soos aanvaar deur die Algemene Sinode van die Ned[erduitse] Geref[ormeerde] Kerk. Oktober 1986* [Church and Society: A Testimony of the Dutch Reformed Church as Approved by the General Synod of the Ned Geref Kerk. October 1986]. Bloemfontein: Pro Christo-Publikasies, 1987.

———. *Antwoord van Ned. Geref. Kerk op Geloof en Protes* [Answer of the DRC to *Faith and Protest*]. N.p.: Algemene Sinodale Kommissie, 1988.

———. *Kerk en Samelewing 1990: 'n Getuienis van die Nederduitse Gereformeerde Kerk soos aanvaar deur die Algemene Sinode van die Ned[erduitse] Geref[ormeerde] Kerk. Oktober 1990* [Church and society 1990: A Testimony of the Dutch Reformed Church as Approved by the General Synod of the Ned Geref Kerk. October 1990]. Bloemfontein: Pro Christo-Publikasies, 1991.

Algemene Sinode [General Synod]. *Skrifgesag en Skrifgebruik: Beleidstuk van die Nederduitse Gereformeerde Kerk, soos Goedgekeur deur die Algemene Sinode, 1986* [The Authority and Use of Scripture: Policy Document of the Dutch Reformed Church, as Approved by the

General Synod]. In *Skrif, Dogma en Verkondiging*, edited by Pieter Potgieter, 59–67. Kaapstad: Lux Verbi, 1986.

Akenson, Donald H. *God's Peoples: Covenant and Land in South Africa, Israel, and Ulster*. Ithaca and London: Cornell University Press, 1992.

Anderson, Bernhard. "The Babel Story: Paradigm of Human Unity and Diversity." In *Ethnicity*, edited by Andrew M. Greenley, and Gregory Baum, 63–70. New York: The Seabury, 1977.

Augustine of Hippo. *The City of God*. Penguin Classics. Translated by Henry Bettenson. New York: Penguin, 2004.

Bahnsen, Greg. "Double Jeopardy: A Case Study in the Influence of Christian Legislation." *Journal of Christian Reconstruction II* (Winter 1975–6): 40–54.

Balke, Willem. *Calvin and the Anabaptist Radicals*. Translated by William Heynen. Eugene, OR: Wipf and Stock, 1999.

Bavinck, Herman. "The Catholicity of Christianity and the Church." Translated by John Bolt. *Calvin Theological Journal* 27 (1992), 220–51.

Beale, Gregory K. *The Erosion of Inerrancy in Evangelicalism: Responding to New Challenges to Biblical Authority*. Wheaton, IL: Crossway, 2008.

———. "Introduction." In *The Temple and the Church's Mission: A Biblical Theology of the Dwelling Place of God*. New Studies in Biblical Theology. Downers Grove, IL: IVP Academic, 2004.

———, and Mitchell Kim. *God Dwells Among Us: A Biblical Theology of the Temple*. Essential Studies in Biblical Theology. Downers Grove, IL: IVP, 2021.

Beisner, E. Calvin. "Justice and Poverty: Two Views Contrasted." *Transformation* 10 (January–April 1993): 16–22.

Berkhof, Hendrikus. Foreword to *Here Am I!: A Christian Reflection upon God*, by Adrio König, i–xi. Grand Rapids: Eerdmans, 1982.

Berkhof, Louis. *Systematic Theology*. Grand Rapids: Eerdmans, 1941.

Berkouwer, G. P. *Het Probleem der Skriftkritiek* [The Problem with Higher Criticism]. Kampen: Kok, 1938.

———. *The Holy Scripture*. Translated and edited by Jack B. Rogers. Grand Rapids: Eerdmans 1975.

Beukes, Piet. *The Holistic Smuts: A Study in Personality*. Foreword by H. F. Oppenheimer. Cape Town: Human and Rousseau, 1989.

Beyerhaus, Peter. *Die Selbstständigkeit der Jungen Kirchen als Missionarisches Problem* [The Independence of the Younger Churches as Missiological Problem]. Wuppertal-Barmen: Verlag der Rheinishchen Missions Gesellschaft, 1956.

———. *The Responsible Church and the Foreign Mission*. London: World Dominion, 1964.

Blumenfeld, Samuel. *Is Public Education Necessary?* Powder Springs, GA: American Vision, 2011.

Boesak, Alan. *Black and Reformed: Apartheid, Calvinism, and the Calvinist Tradition*. Eugene, OR: Wipf and Stock, 2015.

Bolt, John, ed. *Orthodoxy and Orthopraxis in the Reformed Community Today*. Jordan Station, ON: Paideia, 1986.

Bolt, John. "Eschatological Hermeneutics, Women's Ordination, and the Reformed Tradition." *Calvin Theological Journal* 26 (1991): 370–88.

BIBLIOGRAPHY

Boot, Joseph. "In Understanding be Men: The Crisis of our Age and the Recovery of the Gospel." In *The Mission of God: A Manifesto of Hope for Society*. 2nd ed., 43–76. London: Wilberforce Publications, 2016.

Bosch, David J., Adrio König, and Willem Nicol. *Perspektief op die Ope Brief* [Perspective on the Open Letter]. Cape Town: Human & Rousseau, 1982.

Bosch, David J. *The Church as Alternative Community*. Wetenskaplike bydraes van die PU vir CHO. Reeks F: Instituut vir Reformatoriese Studie. Reeks F1:IBC-Studiestukke. Studiestuk no. 170. Potchefstroom, RSA: Instituut vir Reformatoriese Studie, 1982.

———. *Transforming Mission: Paradigm Shifts in Theology of Mission*. 20th Anniversary Edition. American Society of Missiology Series, No. 16. Foreword by William R. Burrows. With a new concluding chapter by Darrell L. Guder and Martin Repenhagen. Maryknoll, NY: Orbis, 2011.

Boshoff, Carel W. H. *Kerk en Samelewing in Oënskou: Kommentaar en Kritiek* [Church and Society in Review: Commentary and Critique]. Pretoria: Suid-Afrikaanse Calvinistiese Uitgewersmaatskappy Beperk, 1987.

Botman, H. Russel. "The Decisions of the Dutch Reformed Church." In *Farewell to Apartheid? Church Relations in South Africa. The WARC Consultation in South Africa March 1–5, 1993. Koinonia Centre. Judith's Pearl, Johannesburg*, edited by Páraic Réamonn, 42–7. Geneva: World Alliance of Reformed Churches, 1994.

Bowling, Andy. "Legal Provisions for Gentile Converts in the Law of Moses." Paper presented to the Evangelical Theological Society. ETS Microfiche, 1989.

Braaten, Carl E. *Eschatology and Ethics: Essays on the Theology and Ethics of the Kingdom of God*. Eugene, OR: Wipf and Stock, 2017.

Bratt, James D, ed. *Abraham Kuyper: A Centennial Reader*. Grand Rapids: Eerdmans, 1998.

Breckinridge, Robert J. *Presbyterian Government: Not a Hierarchy, but a Commonwealth*. Edited, with Introductory essay, Biblical Presbyterianism, by Kevin Reed. Dallas: Presbyterian Heritage Publications, 1843/1988.

Britannica. "Afrikaner-Broederbond." Accessed August 3, 2023. https://www.britannica.com/topic/Afrikaner-Broederbond.

Bromiley, Geoffrey W. *Children of Promise: The Case for Baptizing Infants*. Grand Rapids: Eerdmans, 1979.

Burnside, Jonathan. *God, Justice, and Society: Aspects of Law and Legality in the Bible*. Oxford: Oxford University Press, 2010.

Chilton, David. *Productive Christians in an Age of Guilt Manipulators: A Biblical Response to Ronald J. Sider*. 3rd ed. Tyler, TX: Institute for Christian Economics, 1985. https://www.garynorth.com/freebooks/docs/pdf/productive_christians.pdf.

———. *Days of Vengeance: An Exposition of the Book of Revelation*. Tyler, TX: Institute for Christian Economics, 1987a. https://www.garynorth.com/freebooks/docs/pdf/days_of_vengeance.pdf.

Christian Century. "Membership Denied." *Christian Century* 109 (June 3–10, 1992): 579.

Cimmino, Jeffrey, and Matthew Kroenig. "Strategic Context: The Rules-Based International System." *Atlantic Council*. Atlantic Council Strategy Paper Series (December 16, 2020).

Cloete, G. D., and D. J. Smit. *A Moment of Truth: The Confession of the Dutch Reformed Mission Church, 1982*. Grand Rapids: Eerdmans, 1984.

Cohn, Norman. *The Pursuit of the Millennium: Revolutionary Millenarians and Mystical Anarchists of the Middle Ages*. London: Paladin, 1970.

Colwell, John E. "A Radical Church? A Reappraisal of Anabaptist Ecclesiology." *Tyndale Bulletin* 38 (1987): 119–42. https://docslib.org/doc/9555934/a-radical-church-a-reappraisal-of-anabaptist-ecclesiology.

Crafford, Dionne, and Gustav Gous, ed., *Een Liggaam—Baie Lede: Die Kerk se Ekumeniese Roeping Wêreldwyd en in Suid-Afrika* [One Body—Many Members: The Church's Ecumenical Calling Worldwide and in South Africa]. 'n Projek van die Instiuut vir Sendingwetenskaplike Navorsing. Pretoria: Verba Vitae, 1993.

CRCNA [Christian Reformed Church of North America]. "World News: Allan Boesak Quits Church Posts over Homosexuality Policy, Belhar." *The Banner*, January 18, 2011. https://www.thebanner.org/news/2011/01/world-news-allan-boesak-quits-church-posts-over-homosexuality-policy-belhar/.

Cunningham, Harold G. "God's Law, 'General Equity' and the Westminster Confession Of Faith." *Tyndale Bulletin* 58, no. 2 (2007): 289–312.

Dahl, N. A. "Christ, Creation and the Church." In *The Background of the New Testament and Its Eschatology: In Honour of Charles Harold Dodd*, edited by W. D. Davies and D. Daube, 422–43. Reprint ed. Cambridge: At the University Press, 1964.

Dayton, Edward, and David A. Fraser. *Planning Strategies for World Evangelization*. Grand Rapids: Eerdmans, 1980.

———. *Planning Strategies for World Evangelization*. Rev. ed. Eugene, OR: Wipf and Stock, 2003.

De Barros, Luiz, "Dutch Reformed Church Agrees (Again) to Allow Same-Sex Unions." October 9, 2019. http://www.Mambaonline.com.

De Golyer, Michael. "Marx's Theory of Justice." *Fides et Historia* XVI (Spring–Summer 1984): 18–37.

De Gruchy, John, and Charles Villa-Vicencio, eds., *Apartheid Is a Heresy*. With a Foreword by Allan Boesak. Cape Town: David Phillip; Guildford, England: Lutterworth, 1983.

De Gruchy, John W. *Bonhoeffer and South Africa: Theology in dialogue*. Grand Rapids: Eerdmans, 1984.

———. *Liberating Reformed Theology: A South African Contribution to an Ecumenical Debate*. Grand Rapids: Eerdmans and Cape Town: David Philip, 1991a.

De Gruchy, John W., and Steve de Gruchy. 3rd ed. *Church Struggle in South Africa: 25th Anniversary Edition*. With a Foreword by Desmond Tutu. Minneapolis: Fortress, 2005.

De Jong, J. A. *As the Waters Cover the Sea: Millennial Expectations in the Rise of Anglo-American Missions 1640–1810*. Laurel, MS: Audubon, 2006.

De Ridder, Richard R. *Discipling the Nations*. Grand Rapids: Baker, 1975.

De Ridder, Richard R., ed. *The Church Orders of the Sixteenth Century Reformed Churches of the Netherlands Together with Their Social, Political, and Ecclesiastical Context*. Translated by Richard R. DeRidder with the assistance of Peter H. Jonker and Rev. Leonard Verduin (Calvin Theological Seminary, 1987), 546–57. Translated from C. Hoijer, *Oude*

BIBLIOGRAPHY

307

Kerkordeningen der Nederlandsche Gemeente (1563–1638). Zalt-Bommel: Joh. Noman en Zoon, n.d.

De Wet, C. J. H. "Bybelgeloof—Bybelkritiek—Bybelfoute" [Biblical Faith — Biblical [Higher] Criticism—Biblical Errors]. In *Koers in die Krisis*. [Course in the Crisis], ed. H. G. Stoker and F. J. M. Potgieter, 1:89ff. Stellenbosch: Pro Ecclesia, 1935.

Deist, Ferdinand. *Sê God So?* [Does God Say So?]. Cape Town: Tafelberg, 1982.

———. *Kan Ons die Bybel Dan Nog Glo: Onderweg na 'n Gereformeerde Skrifbeskouing* [Can We Then Still Believe the Bible? Towards a Reformed View of Scripture]. Pretoria: J. L. van Schaik, 1986.

———. *Ervaring, Rede en Metode in Skrifuitleg* [Experience, Reason, and Methodology in Scripture Exposition]. Pretoria: Raad vir Geesteswetenskaplike Navorsing, 1994.

Dooyeweerd, Herman. *Roots of Western Culture: Pagan, Secular, and Christian Options*. Translated by John Kraay. Edited by Mark Vander Vennen and Bernard Zylstra. Toronto: Wedge Publishing Foundation, 1979.

———. *Roots of Western Culture: Pagan, Secular, and Christian Options*. Jordan Station, ON: Paideia Press/Reformational Publishing Project, 2012.

Du Toit, Andrie B. *Fundamentalisme: Konsep van Onfeilbaarheid op Bybel Afgedruk* [Fundamentalism: Concept of Infallibility Forced upon the Bible]. Johannesburg, RSA: *Beeld*, 26 November 1991, 12.

Duewel, Wesley L. "Christian Unity: The Biblical Basis and Practical Outgrowth." In *New Horizons in World Mission: Evangelicals and the Christian Mission in the 1980's—Papers Given at Trinity Consultation No. 2*, edited by David J. Hesselgrave. Grand Rapids: Baker, 1979.

Dulles, Avery Cardinal. *Models of the Church*. Image Classics. New York: Image, 2002.

Durand, J. J. F. "Church and State in South Africa: Karl Barth vs. Abraham Kuyper." In *On Reading Karl Barth in South Africa*, edited by Charles Villa-Vicencio, 121–38. Grand Rapids: Eerdmans, 1988.

Durand, J. J. F., and D. J. Smit, ed. *Teks Binne Konteks 1: Versamelde Opstelle oor Kerk en Politiek* [Texts within Contexts 1: Collected Essays on Church and Politics]. Cape Town: University of the Western Cape, n.d.

Edlin, Richard. *The Cause of Christian Education*. 4th ed. Sioux Center, IA: Dordt, 2014.

Engles, Friedrich. *The Peasant War in Germany*. Routledge Revivals. Translated by Moissaye J. Olgin. New York: Rouledge, 2017.

Eglinton, James. "From Babel to Pentecost Via Paris and Amsterdam: Multi-Lingualism in Neo-Calvinist and [French] Revolutionary Thought." In *Neo-Calvinism and the French Revolution*, edited by James Eglington and George Harinck, 31–60. London: Bloomsbury T&T Clark Theology, 2014.

Eliade, Mircea. *The Myth of the Eternal Return: Or, Cosmos and History*. Mythos: The Princeton/Bollingen Series in World Mythology, 122. Translated by Willard R. Trask. Introduction by Jonathan Z. Smith. 2nd ed. Princeton, NJ: Princeton University Press, 2018.

Estep, William R. *The Anabaptist Story: An Introduction of Sixteenth Century Anabaptism*. Grand Rapids: Eerdmans, 1995.

Feinberg, Paul. "The Meaning of Inerrancy." In *Inerrancy*, edited by Norman L. Geisler, 263–304. Grand Rapids: Zondervan, 1980.

BIBLIOGRAPHY

———. "Truth: Relationship of Theories of Truth to Hermeneutics." In *Hermeneutics, Inerrancy, and the Bible: Papers from ICBI Summit II*, edited by Earl Radmacher and Robert Preus, 3–50. Grand Rapids: Zondervan, Academie Books, 1984.

Flew, Antony. "Socialism and 'Social Justice.'" *Journal of Libertarian Studies* 11, no. 2 (Summer 1995): 76–93.

Fuller, Daniel P. *Gospel and Law: Contrast or Continuum? The Hermeneutics of Dispensationalism and Covenant Theology.* Grand Rapids: Eerdmans, 1980.

Gaffin, Richard. *God's Word in Servant-Form: Abraham Kuyper and Herman Bavinck and the Doctrine of Scripture*, Foreword by Peter Lillback. Jackson, MS: Reformed Academic, 2008.

Gage, Warren Austin. *The Gospel of Genesis: Studies in Protology and Eschatology.* With a Foreword by Bruce K. Waltke. Winona Lake, IN: Carpenter, 1984.

Gassmann, Günther. "The Church as Sacrament, Sign and Instrument." In *Church Kingdom World: The Church as Mystery and Prophetic Sign*, edited by Gennadios Limouris, 1–17. Faith and Order Paper No. 130. Geneva: World Council of Churches, 1986.

Geisler, Norman, ed. *Inerrancy.* Grand Rapids: Zondervan, 1980.

Geisler, Norman L., and William C. Roach, with a Foreword by J. I. Packer. *Defending Inerrancy: Affirming the Accuracy of Scripture for a New Generation.* Grand Rapids: Baker, 2012.

Geldenhuys, F. E. O'Brien. *In die Stroomversnellings* [In the Rapids]. Cape Town: Tafelberg, 1982.

General Synod of the Dutch Reformed Church. *Human Relations and the South African Scene in the Light of Scripture: Official Translation of the Report* Ras, Volk en Nasie en Volkereverhoudinge in die Lig van die Skrif, *Approved and Accepted by the General Synod of the Dutch Reformed Church October 1974.* Cape Town and Pretoria: Dutch Reformed Church Publications, 1976.

General Synodical Commission. *Church and Society: A Testimony Approved by the Synod of the Dutch Reformed Church as Translated from the Original Afrikaans Manuscript. October 1986.* Bloemfontein: Pro Christo, 1987.

———. *Church and Society 1990: A Testimony of the Dutch Reformed Church* (Ned Geref Kerk) *as Translated from the Original Afrikaans Manuscript. Approved by the General Synod of the Dutch Reformed Church. October 1990.* Bloemfontein: General Synodical Commission, 1991.

Gentry, Kenneth L., Jr. *He Shall Have Dominion: A Postmillennial Eschatology.* 3rd ed. Chesnee, SC: Victorious Hope, 2021.

Gerber, Schalk. "On the Political Theology of Apartheid: A Philosophical Investigation." *Social Dynamics: A Journal of African Studies* 48, no. 3 (2022): 442–56. https://doi.org/10.1080/02533952.2022.2154561.

Gerstner, Jonathan Neil. *The Thousand Generation Covenant: Dutch Reformed Covenant Theology and Group Identity In Colonial South Africa, 1652–1814.* Leiden: Brill, 1991.

Glasser, Arthur, and Donald McGavran. *Contemporary Theologies of Mission.* Grand Rapids: Baker, 1983.

Greenley, Andrew M. "Notes on a Theology of Pluralism." *Christian Century* (3–10 July 1974): 697. Quoted in C. Peter Wagner. *Our Kind of People: The Ethical Dimensions of Church Growth in America*, 111. Atlanta: John Knox Press.

Greenley, Andrew M., and Gregory Baum, ed. *Ethnicity.* New York: The Seabury, 1977.

BIBLIOGRAPHY

Hannah, John, ed. *Inerrancy and the Church*. Chicago: Moody Press, 1984.

Hebdon-Taylor, E. L. *Economics, Money and Banking: Christian Principles*. Nutley, NJ: Craig, 1978.

Heideman, Eugene P. "Old Confessions and New Testimony." *Reformed Journal* 38 (1988): 7–10.

Hershberger, Guy F., ed. *The Recovery of the Anabaptist Vision: A Sixtieth Anniversary Tribute to Harold S. Bender*. Scottdale, PA: Herald, 1957.

Hexham, Irving. *The Irony of Apartheid: The Struggle for National Independence of Afrikaner Calvinism against British Imperialism*. New York: Edwin Mellen, 1981.

Heyns, Johan A. "Bible, Church and Proclamation." In *Scripture and its Authority: Conference papers, RES Conference on Scripture, Sydney 1972. International Reformed Bulletin* 54 (1973): 36–55.

———. *Brug Tussen God en Mens: Oor die Bybel* [Bridge between God and Mankind: Concerning the Bible]. Pretoria: N.G. Kerkboekhandel, 1976.

———. *Dogmatiek* [Dogmatics]. Pretoria: N.G. Kerkboekhandel Transvaal, 1978.

———. *The Church*. Translated by D. Roy Briggs. Pretoria: N.G. Kerkboekhandel Transvaal, 1980.

Hoekendijk, Johannes Christiaan. "*Kerk en Volk in de Duitse Zendingwetenschap*" [Church and People in German Missiology]. D.Th. diss., Rijksuniversiteit van Utrecht, 1948.

Horn, Nico. "The Belhar Confession—29 Years On." NGTT [*Niederduitse Gereformeerde Teologiese Tydskrif*], 54, nos. 3–4 (September–December 2013): 1–11. https://hdl.handle.net/10520/EJC146118.

House, H. Wayne. "Creation and Redemption: A Study of Kingdom Interplay." *Journal of the Evangelical Theological Society* 35 (March 1992): 3–17.

Hughes, Dewi A. *Ethnic Identity from the Margins: A Christian Perspective*. Pasadena, CA: William Carey Library, 2012.

Hurley, James. *Man and Woman in Biblical Perspective: A Study in Roles*. Eugene, OR: Wipf and Stock, 2002.

ICBI. "The Chicago Statement on Biblical Inerrancy." *Evangelical Review of Theology* 4, no. 1 (April 1980): 8ff.

ICWE. *Let the Earth Hear His Voice: Official Reference Volume, Papers, and Responses. International Congress of World Evangelization, Lausanne, Switzerland*. Edited by J. D. Douglas. Minneapolis: World Wide, 1974. https://archive.org/details/letearthhearhisv0000inte.

Ingram, T. Robert. *What Is Wrong with Human Rights?*. Houston: St. Thomas Press, 1978.

Jones, Peter. *The Gnostic Empire Strikes Back*. Phillipsburg, NJ: P&R, 1992.

———. *One or Two: Seeing a World of Difference*. Escondido, CA: Main Entry Editions, 2010.

———. *The Other Worldview: Exposing Christianity's Greatest Threat*. Bellingham, WA: Kirkdale, 2015.

Jordaan, C. L., and M. R. Kreitzer. *'n Manifes vir Christene in Suiderlike Afrika* [A Manifesto for Christian in Southern Africa]. Pretoria: Christian Action Africa, 1991.

Jordan, James B. *The Law of the Covenant*. Tyler, TX: Institute for Christian Economics, 1984.

———. *The Covenant Enforced: [Calvin's] Sermons on Deuteronomy 27 and 28*. Tyler, TX: Institute for Christian Economics, 1990.

Joustra, Robert J. "Abraham Kuyper among the Nations." *Politics and Religion* 11, no. 1 (March 2018): 146–68. https://doi.org/10.1017/S1755048317000554.

310 BIBLIOGRAPHY

Kaiser, Walter, Jr. *Toward Old Testament Ethics*. Reprint ed. Grand Rapids: Zondervan, Academie, 1991.

———. *The Uses of the Old Testament in the New*. Eugene, OR: Wipf and Stock, 2001.

Kelly, Douglas F. *The Emergence of Liberty in the Modern World: The Influence of Calvin on Five Governments from the 16th Through 18th Centuries*. Phillipsburg, NJ: P&R, 1992.

Kidner, Derek. *Hard Sayings: The Challenge of Old Testament Morals*. London: IVP, 1972.

Kistler, Don ed. *Sola Scriptura: The Protestant Position on the Bible*. 2nd ed. Orlando, FL: Ligonier Ministries, 2009.

Kinghorn, Johann, ed. *Die NG Kerk en Apartheid* [The DRC and Apartheid]. Johannesburg: Macmillan, 1986a.

———. "Die Groei van 'n Teologie—van Sendingbeleid tot Verskeidenheidsteologie" [The Growth of a Theology—from Missions Policy to a Theology of Diversity]. In *Die NG Kerk en Apartheid* [The DRC and Apartheid], edited by Johann Kinghorn. Johannesburg: Macmillan, 1986b.

———. "'n Rondte Meer" [A Round Sea]. In *Kommentaar op Kerk en Samelewing*. [Commentary on Church and Society], 29–43. Potchefstroom, RSA: Instituut vir Reformatoriese Studie, 1989.

———. On the Theology of *Church and Society* in the DRC. *Journal of Theology for Southern Africa* 70 (1990a): 21–36.

———. "The Theology of Separate Equality: A Critical Outline of the DRC's Position on Apartheid." In *Christianity amidst Apartheid*, edited by M. Prozesky, 57–80. New York: St. Martin's Press, 1990b.

———. *'n Tuiste vir Almal: 'n Sosiaal-teologiese Studie oor 'n Gesamentlike Demokrasie in Suid-Afrika* [A Home for Everyone: A Social Theological Study on a Common Democracy in South Africa]. With a foreword by Bernard Lategan. Stellenbosch, South Africa: Sentrum vir Kontekstuele Hermeneutiek, Universiteit van Stellenbosch, 1990c.

Kleynhans, E. P. J. *Gereformeerde Kerkreg* [Reformed Church Law]. Vol. 1, *Inleiding* [Introduction]. Pretoria: N.G. Kerkboekhandel Transvaal, 1982.

KLAS-WK [Western Cape Regional Synod]. *Die Reformatoriese Sola Scriptura en die Skrifberoep in Etiese Vrae* [*The Reformational Sola Scriptura and the Appeal to Scripture in Ethical Questions*]. Cape Town: Kommissie van Leer- en Aktuele Sake, Weskaapland. [The Commission on Doctrine and Contemporary Affairs of the Western Cape regional synod]/NG Kerk-Uitgewers, 1980. https://williejonker.co.za/20110901-2/.

Kloppers, F. "Skrifgebruik in die Beoordeling van Uitsprake oor die Doodstraf [The Use of Scripture and the Judgment of Sayings Concerning the Death Penalty]." *Skrif en Kerk* 11, no. 2 (1990): 174–86.

König, Adrio. *Here Am I! A Christian Reflection upon God*. Grand Rapids: Eerdmans, 1982.

———. *New and Greater Things: Re-evaluating the Biblical Message on Creation*. Pretoria: University of South Africa, 1988.

Krabbendam, Henry. "B. B. Warfield versus G. C. Berkouwer on Scripture." In *Inerrancy*, edited by Norman L. Geisler, 413–46. Zondervan, Academie Books, 1980.

———. "The Functional Theology of G. C. Berkouwer." In *Challenges to Inerrancy: A Theological Response*, edited by Gordon R. Lewis and Bruce Demarest, 285–316. Chicago: Moody, 1984.

BIBLIOGRAPHY

Kreitzer, Mark R. Review of *The Thousand Generation Covenant: Dutch Reformed Covenant Theology and Group Identity in Colonial South Africa, 1652–1814*, by Jonathan Gerstner. In *Contra Mundum: A Reformed Cultural Review* 13 (Fall 1994): 64–8.

———. "Toward a Biblical Philosophy of Science." *Christianity and Society: The Biannual Journal of the Kuyper Foundation* XVII, no. 2 (Winter 2007): 6–19.

———. *The Concept of Ethnicity in the Bible: A Theological Analysis*. Lewiston, NY: Mellen, 2008.

———. "Ethnic Solidarity, Babel-Pentecost Relationship, and the New Covenant." *Global Missiology English* (10 April 2010). https://www.academia.edu/es/65046607/Ethnic_Solidarity_Babel_Pentecost_Relationship_and_the_New_Covenant.

Kritzinger, J. J. (Dons). "The Witness of the Reformed Churches in South Africa: A Certain Past and an Uncertain Future." *International Review of Mission* LXXXIII, no. 328 (January 1994): 179–83.

Kruse, Martin. "Duitse Kerke se Mening oor 'Kerk en Samelewing' [German Churches' Opinion on 'Church and Society']." *Kerkbode* (16 December 1988): 8–9.

Kuhn, Thomas S. *The Structure of Scientific Revolutions: 50th Anniversary Edition*. 4th ed. With an introduction by Ian Hacking. Chicago: University of Chicago Press, 2012.

Kuyper, Abraham. *Eenvormigheid, de Vloek van het Moderne Leven: Lesing, Gehouden in het Odéon te Amsterdam, 22 April 1869* [Uniformity, the Curse of Modern Life: Lecture held in the Odéon in Amsterdam, 22 April 1869]. Amsterdam: H. De Hoogh, 1870. Reprinted in James D. Bratt, *Abraham Kuyper: A Centennial Reader*. Grand Rapids: Eerdmans, 1998.

Kuyper, Abraham. "Calvinism: Source and Stronghold of Our Constitutional Liberties." In *Abraham Kuyper: A Centennial Reader* [Kuyper's Uniformity], edited by James D. Bratt, 279–322. Grand Rapids: Eerdmans, 1998.

———. "Sphere Sovereignty." In *Abraham Kuyper: A Centennial Reader*, edited by James D. Bratt, 461–90. Grand Rapids: Eerdmans, 1998.

———. "The South African Crisis." In *Abraham Kuyper: A Centennial Reader*, edited by James D. Bratt, 323–60. Grand Rapids: Eerdmans, 1998.

———. "Uniformity, the Curse of Modern Life: Lecture held in the Odéon in Amsterdam [1869]." In *Abraham Kuyper: A Centennial Reader* [Kuyper's Uniformity], edited by James D. Bratt, 19–44. Grand Rapids: Eerdmans, 1998.

———. *Lecture on Calvinism: Six Lectures Delivered at Princeton University under Auspices of the L. P. Stone Foundations*. Grand Rapids: Eerdmans, 1943.

———. "The Tower of Babel." In *Common Grace*, vol. 1, edited by Jordan Ballor and Stephen Grabill, 357–64. Bellingham, Washington: Lexham, 2016.

Lamola, M. John. "D9.2 Alliance of Reformed Christians in South Africa, 1981, ABRESCA Charter [Chapter 53]." In *Sowing in Tears: A Documentary History of the Church Struggle against Apartheid 1960–90*. Grant Park, RSA: African Perspectives, 2021. https://zoboko.com/text/156rd9g4/sowing-in-tears-a-documentary-history-of-the-church-struggle-against-apartheid-1960-1990/53.

Landman, W. A. *A Plea for Understanding: A Reply to the Reformed Church in America*. Cape Town: Nederduitse Gereformeerde Kerk-Uitgewers, 1967.

BIBLIOGRAPHY

Lane, Anthony N. S. "Sola Scriptura? Making Sense of a Post-Reformation Slogan." In *A Pathway into the Holy Scripture*, edited by Philip E. Satterthwaite and David F. Wright, 297–327. Grand Rapids: Eerdmans.

Larkin, William J., Jr., *Culture and Biblical Hermeneutics: Interpreting and Applying the Authoritative Word in a Relativistic Age*. Eugene, OR: Wipf and Stock, 2003.

Lee, Philip J. *Against the Protestant Gnostics*. Oxford: Oxford University Press, 1987.

Lee, Francis Nigel. *Communist Eschatology: A Christian Philosophical Analysis of Post-Capitalistic View of Marx, Engel, and Lenin*. Nutley, NJ: Craig, 1974.

Lewis, Clive Staples. *God in the Dock*. Grand Rapids: Eerdmans, 2014.

Limouris, Gennadios, ed. *Church Kingdom World: The Church as Mystery and Prophetic Sign*. Faith and Order Paper No. 130. Geneva: World Council of Churches, 1986.

Lochman, Jan Milic. "Church and World in the Light of the Kingdom of God." In *Church Kingdom World: The Church as Mystery and Prophetic Sign*. Faith and Order Paper No. 130, edited by Gennadios Limouris, 58–72. Geneva: World Council of Churches, 1986.

Loubser, J. A. *The Apartheid Bible: A Critical Review of Racial Theology in South Africa*. Cape Town: Maskew, Miller, Longman, 1987.

Loubser, J. A. "Apartheid Theology: A 'Contextual' Theology Gone Wrong?" *Journal of Church and State* 38, no. 2 (1996): 321–37. http://www.jstor.org/stable/23921177.

Louw, Leon, and Frances Kendall. *After Apartheid: The Solution for South Africa*. 3rd ed. Bisho, Ciskei: Amagi, 1989. https://www.sahistory.org.za/archive/after-apartheid-solution-south-africa-leon-louw-and-frances-kendall-foreword-clem-sunter.

Lückhoff, A. H. *Cottesloe*. Cape Town: Tafelberg, 1978.

Malan, F. S. *Ons Kerk en Prof. Du Plessis* [Our Church and Prof. Du Plessis]. Cape Town: Nasionale Pers, 1933.

Manavhela, Gwashi Freddy. *Theological Justification of Apartheid in South African Churches: Did Churches in South Africa Justify Apartheid?* London: Lambert Academic Publishing, 2012.

Marx, Karl, and Frederick Engels. *The Communist Manifesto*. Translated by Samuel Moore. New York: Penguin Classics, 1888/1967.

McGavran, Donald A. *The Bridges of God: A Study in the Strategy of Missions*. Eugene, OR: Wipf and Stock, 1955/2005.

———. *Ethnic Realities and the Church: Lessons From India*. Pasadena, CA: Wm. Carey, 1979.

———. *Understanding Church Growth*. 2nd ed. Grand Rapids: Eerdmans, 1980.

McIlhenny, Ryan C., ed. *Kingdoms Apart: Engaging the Two Kingdoms Perspective*. Phillipsburg, NJ: P&R Publishing, 2012.

Meiring, Pieter G. J. "The Churches' Contribution to Change in South Africa." In *Change in South Africa*, edited by D. J. Van Vuuren, N. E. Wiehahn, J. A. Lombard, and N. J. Rhoodie. Durban: Butterworths, 1983.

Mennonite World Conference. "Mennonite and Reformed Reconciliation in a Global Perspective." Accessed August 17, 2023. https://mwc-cmm.org/en/stories/mennonite-and-reformed-reconciliation-global-perspective.

Moltmann, Jürgen. *The Future of Creation: Collected Essays*. Philadephia: Fortress, 1979.

Montgomery, John Warwick. *Human Rights and Human Dignity*. Grand Rapids: Zondervan; Dallas: Probe Ministries International, 1986.

BIBLIOGRAPHY

———. *The Law above the Law*. Irvine, CA: NRP, 2015.

Moo, Douglas. *The Epistle to the Romans*. The New International Commentary on the New Testament. 2nd ed. Grand Rapids: Eerdmans, 2018.

Moodie, T. D. "Confessing Responsibility for the Evils of Apartheid: The Dutch Reformed Church in the 1980s." *South African Historical Journal* 72, no. 4 (2020): 627–50. http://dx.doi.org/10.1080/02582473.2020.1839542.

Morphew, Derek. *Kingdom Theology and Human Rights*. Kingdom Theology Series. Ladysmith, Kwa-Zulu Natal, RSA: Vineyard International, 2015.

Motyer, J. Alec. *The Prophecy of Isaiah: An Introduction and Commentary*. Downers Grove, IL: InterVarsity, 1993.

Mouw, Richard J. "Abandoning the Typology: A Reformed Assist." *Theological Students Fellowship Bulletin* 8 (May–June 1985): 7–10.

Mouw, Richard J., and John H. Yoder. "Evangelical Ethics and the Anabaptist-Reformed Dialogue." *Journal of Religious Ethics* 17 (Fall 1989): 121–37.

Müller-Fahrenholz, Geiko. *Unity in Today's World*. The Faith and Order Studies on "Unity of the Church—Unity of Humankind." Geneva: World Council of Churches, 1978.

Murray, Iain. *The Puritan Hope: Revival and the Interpretation of Prophecy*. Edinburgh: Banner of Truth, 2014.

Murray, John. "The Christian World Order," *Westminster Magazine* 1, no. 1 (October 10, 1943). https://wm.wts.edu/content/the-christian-in-the-twentieth-century.

———. "The Sanctity of Life." In *Principles of Conduct: Aspects of Biblical Ethics*, 107–22. Grand Rapids: Eerdmans, 1957.

———. *The Epistle to the Romans*. Introduction by Sinclair Ferguson. Philadelphia: Westminster Seminary Press, 2022.

Nash, Ronald H. *Social Justice and the Christian Church*. Lima, OH: CSS, 2002.

Naudé, Beyers. "Support in Word and Deed." In *Farewell to Apartheid? Church Relations in South Africa. The WARC Consultation in South Africa March 1–5, 1993. Koinonia Centre. Judith's Pearl, Johannesburg*, edited by Páraic Réamonn, 67–74. Geneva: World Alliance of Reformed Churches, 1994.

Naylor, Ann. *Apartheid is a Heresy*. Toronto: South African Education Project, United Church of Canada, n.d.

Nisbet, Robert. *The History of the Idea of Progress*. 2nd ed. New York: Routledge, 2017.

North, Gary. "Publisher's Preface." In *Days of Vengeance*, by David Chilton, xv–xxxiii. Tyler, TX: Institute for Christian Economics, 1987a. https://www.garynorth.com/freebooks/docs/pdf/days_of_vengeance.pdf

———. *Dominion and Common Grace: The Biblical Basis of Progress*. Tyler, TX: Institute for Christian Economics, 1987b. https://www.garynorth.com/freebooks/docs/pdf/dominion_and_common_grace.pdf.

———. *Marx's Religion of Revolution: Regeneration through Chaos*. Tyler, TX: Institute for Christian Economics, 1989. https://www.garynorth.com/freebooks/docs/pdf/marx_religion_of_revolution.pdf.

———. *Victim's Rights: The Biblical View of Civil Justice*. Tyler, TX: Institute for Christian Economics, 1990. https://www.garynorth.com/freebooks/docs/pdf/victims_rights.pdf.

314 BIBLIOGRAPHY

———. *Millennialism and Social Theory*. Tyler, TX: Institute for Christian Economics, 1991. https://www.garynorth.com/freebooks/docs/pdf/millennialism_and_social_theory.pdf.

———. *Crossed Fingers: How the Liberals Captured the Presbyterian Church*. Tyler, TX: Institute for Christian Economics, 1996. https://www.garynorth.com/freebooks/docs/pdf/crossed_fingers.pdf.

———. *Honest Money: Biblical Blueprint for Money and Banking*. 2nd ed. Auburn, AL: Mises Institute, 2015. https://cdn.mises.org/Honest%20Money%20second%20edition%202015.pdf.

———. *Authority and Dominion: An Economic Commentary on Exodus*. Vol. 3. Part 3: Tools of Dominion. Dallas, GA: Point Five Press, 2020a. https://www.garynorth.com/Exodus3.pdf.

———. *Authority and Dominion: An Economic Commentary on Exodus*. Vol. 6: Appendixes. Dallas, GA: Point Five Press, 2020b. https://www.garynorth.com/Exodus6.pdf.

———. *Christian Economics in One Lesson*. 2nd ed. Dallas, GA: Point Five Press, 2020c. https://www.garynorth.com/OneLesson2020.pdf.

———. *Sovereignty and Dominion: An Economic Commentary on Genesis*. Vol. 1. 2nd ed. Dallas, GA: Point Five Press, 2020d. https://www.garynorth.com/SovereigntyAndDominion1.pdf.

North, Gary, and David Chilton. "Apologetics and Strategy." In *Christianity and Civilization: A Symposium*, edited by Gary North. Vol. 3, *Tactics of Christian Resistance*, 100–41. Tyler, TX: Geneva Divinity School Press, 1983. https://www.garynorth.com/freebooks/docs/pdf/tactics_of_christian_resistance.pdf.

Novak, Michael. *Will It Liberate? Questions About Liberation Theology*. Lanham, MD: Madison Books, 1991.

Núñez, Emilio A. *Liberation Theology*. Translated by Paul E. Sywulka. Chicago: Moody, 1985.

Ong, Andrew. "Neo-Calvinism and Ethnic Church in Multiethnic Contexts." *Journal of Reformed Theology* 12 (2018), 296–320.

———. "Toward a Chinese American Evangelical Theology: The Promise of Neo-Calvinism." PhD Thesis, New College, The University of Edinburgh, 2019. https://era.ed.ac.uk/bitstream/handle/1842/36711/Ong2020.pdf?sequence=1.

Olthuis, James H., Hendrik Hart, John Van Dyk, Arnold De Graaff, Calvin Seerveld, Bernard Zylstra, and John A. Olthuis. *Will All the King's Men Out of Concern for the Church Phase II*. With an Introduction by Robert Lee Carvill. Toronto: Wedge Publishing Foundation, 1972.

Ouweneel, Willem J. *The World is Christ's: A Critique of Two Kingdoms Theology*. Toronto: Ezra Press, 2018.

Padilla, C. René. "The Unity of the Church and the Homogeneous Unit Principle." In *Mission between the Times: Essays on the Kingdom*. Grand Rapids: Eerdmans, 1985a.

———. *Mission between the Times: Essays on the Kingdom*. Grand Rapids: Eerdmans, 1985b.

Peikoff, Leonard. *The Ominous Parallels: The End of Freedom in America*. Foreword by Ayn Rand. New York: Meridian/Penguin, 1983.

Perks, Stephen C. "The Westminster Confession of Faith and the Equity of the Judicial Law." *Kuyper Foundation*. Accessed December 13, 2016. https://www.kuyper.org/questions-content/2016/12/13/the-westminster-confession-of-faith-and-the-equity-of-the-judicial-law.

Plato. *The Republic*. Translated by H. D. P. Lee. Baltimore: Penguin, 2007.

BIBLIOGRAPHY

Potgieter, F. J. M. *Kerk en Samelewing—'n Wesenskou* [Church and Society—A Look at its Essence]. Cape Town: NG Kerk-Uitgewers, 1990.

Potgieter, Johan M. *The Future of South Africa Based on the "Freedom Charter" or on Christian Values.* Cape Town: Gospel Defence League, 1989.

Potgieter, Pieter C. *Skrif, Dogma en Verkondiging.* Cape Town: Lux Verbi, 1990.

Potter, Philip. "The Task Ahead." In *A Long Struggle: The Involvement of the World Council of Churches in South Africa,* edited by Pauline Webb, 116–26. Geneva: WCC Publications, World Council of Churches, 1994.

Preus, Robert. "The View of the Bible Held by the Church: The Early Church through Luther." In *Inerrancy,* edited by Norman L. Geisler, 357–84. Grand Rapids: Zondervan, 1980.

Quigley, Carroll. *Tragedy and Hope: The History of the World of our Time.* New York: MacMillan/Dauphin, 2014.

———. *The Anglo-American Establishment.* San Pedro, CA: GSG, 1981.

Radmacher, Earl, and Robert Preus, ed. *Hermeneutics, Inerrancy, and the Bible: Papers from ICBI Summit II.* Grand Rapids: Zondervan, Academie Books, 1984.

Réamonn, Páraic, ed. *Farewell to Apartheid? Church Relations in South Africa. The WARC consultation in South Africa March 1–5, 1993. Koinonia Centre. Judith's Pearl, Johannesburg.* Geneva: World Alliance of Reformed Churches, 1994.

Rebera, Basil A. "Translating a Text to be Spoken and Heard: A Study of Ruth 1." *Bible Translator* 43 (April 1992): 230–6.

Redaelli, Simone. "The Psychology of Shame: What Happens When We Feel Ashamed of Ourselves in Public." *Psychology Today.* September 27, 2020. https://www.psychologytoday.com/us/blog/sonnet-freud/202009/the-psychology-shame.

Richardson, Neville. *The World Council of Churches and Race Relations, 1960 to 1969.* Frankfurt am Main: Lang, 1977.

———. "Apartheid, Heresy, and the Church in South Africa." *The Journal of Religious Ethics* 14 (Spring 1986): 1–21.

Ridderbos, Herman N. *When the Time had Fully Come: Studies in New Testament Theology.* Jordan Station, ON: Paideia Press, 1982.

Robertson, O. Palmer. *The Christ of the Covenants.* Phillipsburg, NJ: P&R, 2017.

Runia, Klaas. *Karl Barth's Doctrine of Holy Scripture.* Eugene, OR: Wipf and Stock, 2018.

Rushdoony, Rousas J. "The Society of Satan." *Christian Economics* (August 1964). Quoted in *Genesis: The Dominion Covenant.* 2nd ed., 151. Tyler, TX: Institute for Christian Economics, 1987.

———. *Messianic Character of American Education: Studies in the History of the Philosophy of Education.* Vallecito, CA: Ross House, 1995.

———. *Politics of Guilt and Pity.* Vallecito, CA: Ross House, 1995.

———. *Institutes of Biblical Law. A Chalcedon Study,* vol. 1. The Institutes of Biblical Law Series. Vallecito, CA: Ross House, 2020.

———. *Law and Society,* vol. 2, *The Institutes of Biblical Law.* The Institutes of Biblical Law Series. Vallecito, CA: Ross House, 2010.

———. *Infallibility: An Inescapable Concept.* Vallecito, CA: Ross House, 1978.

316 BIBLIOGRAPHY

———. *This Independent Republic: Studies In The Nature And Meaning Of American History.* Vallecito, CA: Ross House, 2002a.

———. *Intellectual Schizophrenia: Culture, Crisis, and Education.* 2nd ed. Vallecito, CA: Ross House, 2002b.

———. *The One and the Many: Studies in the Philosophy of Order and Ultimacy.* New ed. Vallecito: Ross House, 2007.

———. "The One and Many Problem—The Contribution of Van Til." In *Jerusalem and Athens: Critical Discussions on the Philosophy and Apologetics of Cornelius Van Til,* edited by E. R. Geehan, 339–48. Philipsburg, NJ: Presbyterian and Reformed, 2023.

Schlossberg, Herbert. *Idols for Destruction: Christian Faith and Its Confrontation with American Society.* Preface by Robert H. Bork. Foreword by Charles Colson. Nashville, TN: Thomas Nelson, 1993.

Schrotenboer, Paul G. "Turning the Tide?" *The Reformed Journal* (January 1987): 1–11, 31–2.

Schuurman, Douglas. *Creation, Eschaton, and Ethics: The Ethical Significance of the Creation-Eschaton Relation in the Thought of Emil Brunner and Jürgen Moltmann.* New York: Peter Lang, 1991.

Serfontein, Hennie. *Apartheid, Change and the DRC.* Emmarentia, Johannesburg: Taurus, 1982.

Setiloane, Gariel M., and Ivan H. M. Peden, ed. *Pangs of Growth: A Dialogue on Church Growth in Southern Africa.* Braamfontein, Johannesburg: Skotaville, 1988.

Sowell, Thomas. *Social Justice Fallacies.* New York: Basic Books, 2023.

Shafarevich, Igor. *The Socialist Phenomenon: A Historical Survey of Socialist Policies and Ideals.* Translated by William Tjalsma. Foreword by Alexander Solzhenitsyn. Shawnee, KS: Gideon House, 2019.

Shenk, Wilbert R., ed. *Exploring Church Growth.* Grand Rapids: Eerdmans, 1983.

Smith, Nico, Frans E. O'Brien Geldenhuys, and Piet Meiring. *Storm-kompas: Opstelle op Soek na 'n Suiwer Koers in die Suid-Afrikaanse Konteks van die Jare Tagtig* [Storm-Compass: In the Search of a True Direction in the South African Context of the Eighties]. Kaapstad: Tafelberg, 1981.

Smuts, Jan Christiaan. *Holism and Evolution.* Cape Town: N & S Press, 1987.

Smyth, Thomas. *Complete Works of Rev. Thomas Smyth, D.D.* 2nd ed. Edited by J. W. Flinn. Vol. III, *Ecclesiastical Republicanism or the Republicanism, Liberality and Catholicity of Presbytery in Contrast with prelacy and Popery.* Columbia, SC: R. L. Bryan, 1908.

Snyder, C. Arnold. *Anabaptist History and Theology: An Introduction.* Kitchener, ON: Pandora, 2022.

Snyman, P. G. W. "Die Barthiaanse Teologie (Dialektiese Teologie) [The Barthian Theology (Dialectical Theology]." In *Koers in die Krisis II,* edited by H. G. Stoker, J. D. Vorster, 106ff. Stellenbosch: Pro Ecclesia, 1940.

Sprinkle, Joe M. *Biblical Law and Its Relevance: A Christian Understanding and Ethical Application for Today of the Mosaic Regulations.* Lanham, MD: University Press of America, 2005.

Sproul, R. C. "Sola Scriptura: Crucial to Evangelicalism." In *The Foundation of Biblical Authority,* edited by James M. Boice, 103–19. Grand Rapids: Zondervan, 1978.

BIBLIOGRAPHY

Sproul, R. C., and Norman L. Geisler, *Explaining Biblical Inerrancy: The Chicago Statement on Biblical Inerrancy, Hermeneutics and Application with Official ICBI Commentary.* Arlington, TX: The International Council on Biblical Inerrancy/Bastion, 2013.

Sproul, R. C. *Scripture Alone: The Evangelical Doctrine.* Phillipsburg, NJ: P&R, 2013.

Spykman, Gordon, *Reformational Theology: A New Paradigm for Doing Dogmatics.* Grand Rapids: Eerdmans, 1992.

Stendahl, Krister. *The Bible and the Role of Women: A Case Study in Hermeneutics.* Facet books, Biblical series, edited by John Henry Paul Reumann, no. 15. Translated by Emilie T. Sander. Philadelphia: Fortress, 1966.

Stoker, H. G. *Die Stryd om die Ordes* [The Battle of the Social Orders]. Pretoria: Calvyn Jubileum Boekefonds, 1941. https://archive.org/details/HendrikGerhardusStokerDieStrydOmDieOrdes/page/n3/mode/2up.

Stoker, Hendrik Gerhardus (H. G.), and F. J. M. Potgieter, eds. *Koers in die Krisis.* Stellenbosch: Pro Ecclesia, 1935.

Stoker, H. G., and J. D. Vorster, eds. *Koers in die Krisis II* [Course in the Crisis]. Stellenbosch: Pro Ecclesia, 1940.

Strauss, P. J., "Abraham Kuyper, Apartheid and the Reformed Church in South Africa in their Support of Apartheid." *Theological Forum* XXIII (March 1995): 4–27.

Sonshine, Glenn S. *Slaying Leviathan: Limited Government and Resistance in the Christian Tradition.* Moscow, ID: Canon, 2020.

Sutton, Lodewyk, and Walter Sutton. "The Legal Consequences of Decisions Made without Complying with Procedures Prescribed in the Church Order with Respect to the Decisions by the General Synod of the Dutch Reformed Church [Regsgevolge volgens die *Gaum*-saak vir Nienakoming van Kerkordelike Prosedures ten opsigte van Besluite deur Die Algemene Sinode van die Nederduitse Gereformeerde Kerk]." *Sabinet: African Journals* 4 (November 2019). https://hdl.handle.net/10520/EJC-192d0dd06b. https://journals.co.za/doi/abs/10.10520/EJC-192d0dd06b.

Tingle, Rachel. *Revolution or Reconciliation: The Struggle in the Church in South Africa.* London: Christian Studies Centre, 1992.

Treurnicht, A. P. "Apartheidsbesluit Gee Probleme [Decision on Apartheid Is Problematic]." *Kerkbode,* November 29, 1991a.

———. Insertion in the OMSENDBRIEF (November 28, 1991b). [From the *Voorsettingskomitee: NG Kerk* (committee of dissenters to the C&S) headed by former General Synod moderator, Kobus Potgieter].

Troost, A. "A Plea for a Christian Creation Ethic." *International Reformed Bulletin* 31 (October 1967): 52–6.

Van der Merwe, Gerdrie. "Aktueel, In Memory: Adrio König." *Die Kerkbode.* July 25, 2022. https://kerkbode.christians.co.za/2022/07/25/gerekende-akademikus-en-teoloog-vir-almal-sterf/.

Van der Riet, Louis R., and Cobus G. J. Van Wyngaard. "The Other Side of Whiteness: the Dutch Reformed Church And the Search For a Theology of Racial Reconciliation in the Afterlife of Apartheid." *Stellenbosch Theological Journal* 7, no. 1 (2021), 1–25. http://dx.doi.org/10.17570/stj.2021.v7n1.t2.

318 BIBLIOGRAPHY

Van der Watt, P. B. *Die Nederduitse Gereformeerde Kerk: 1825–1905* [The DRC: 1982–1905]. Pretoria: N.G. Kerkboekhandel, 1980.

Van der Watt, P. B. *Die Nederduitse Gereformeerde Kerk: 1905–75* [The DRC: 1905–75]. Pretoria: N.G. Kerkboekhandel, 1987.

Van Houten, Christiana de Groot. "The Alien in Israelite law." *Journal for the Study of the Old Testament.* Supplement series; 107, 1989 under title: "The Legal Status of the Alien: A Study of the Pentateuchal Laws Pertaining to the Alien." Sheffield: JSOT Press, 1991.

Van Til, C. A. *In Defense of the Faith: The Protestant Doctrine of Scripture.* Vol. 1. In *Defense of Biblical Christianity.* Phillipsburg, NJ: P&R, 1967.

———. *Introduction to Systematic Theology: Prolegomena and the Doctrines of Revelation, Scripture, and God.* Edited by William Edgar. 2nd ed. Phillipsburg, NJ: P&R, 2007.

———. *Common Grace and the Gospel,* edited by K. Scott Oliphint. 2nd ed. Phillipsburg, NJ: P&R, 2015.

Veenhof, Jan, ed. *Nature and Grace in Herman Bavinck.* Translated by Albert M. Wolters. Orange City, IA: Dordt College Press, 2006.

Venema, Cornelis P. *The Promise of the Future.* Foreword by Sinclair Ferguson. Edinburgh: Banner of Truth, 2000.

Verduin, Leonard. *The Reformers and their Stepchildren.* The Dissent and Nonconformity Series, 14. Foreword by Franklin H. Littell. Grand Rapids: The Baptist Standard Bearer, 2001.

Verhoef, Pieter A. *Bybellig op Verhoudings. "Kerk en Samelewing" vir die Gewone Lidmaat. Uitgegee op Versoek van en in Samewerking met die Algemene Kommissie vir die Lidmaattoerusting Program en die Algemene Sinodale Sending Kommissie van die Ned. Geref. Kerk* [Biblical Light upon Relationships. "Church And Society" For the Normal Member. Distributed upon the Request of and the Cooperation with the General Synodical Commission for Equipping of Members and the General Synod Missions Commission of the DRC]. Wellington: Bybelkor, 1987.

Verkuyl, Johannes. *Break Down the Walls: A Christian Cry for Racial Justice.* Edited and translated by Lewis B. Smedes. Grand Rapids: Eerdmans, 1973.

———. *Contemporary Missiology: An Introduction.* Grand Rapids: Eerdmans, 1978.

Villa-Vicencio, Charles. "Report from a Safe Synod [Safe Synod]." *Reformed Journal* 36 (November 1986): 9–12.

Voegelin, Eric. *Science, Politics, and Gnosticism: Two Essays.* Washington, DC: Regnery Gateway, 1990.

Vom Berg, Hans Georg, Henk Kossen, Larry Miller, and Lukas Vischer. *Mennonites and Reformed in Dialogue.* Geneva: World Alliance of Reformed Churches, 1986.

Von Allman, Daniel. *Theology—Advocate or Critic of Apartheid: A Critical Study of the "Landman Report" (1974) of the Dutch Reformed Church (South Africa).* Berne: Swiss Federation of Protestant Churches, 1977.

Von Rad, Gerhard. *Genesis: A Commentary.* 2nd ed. Philadelphia: Westminster, 2016.

Voortsettingskomitee. *Geloof en Protes: 'n Antwoord Namens Beswaarde Lidmate op Sekere Aspekte van "Kerk en Samelewing"* [Faith and Protest: An Answer in the Name of Dissenting Members to Various Aspects of "Church and Society"]. Pretoria: Die Voortsettingskomitee, 1987.

BIBLIOGRAPHY

Wagner, C. Peter. *Our Kind of People: The Ethical Dimensions of Church Growth in America.* Atlanta: John Knox Press, 1979.

———. *Church Growth and the Whole Gospel: A Biblical Mandate.* San Francisco: Harper and Row, 1981.

Webb, Pauline, ed., *A Long Struggle: The Involvement of the World Council of Churches in South Africa.* Geneva: WCC Publications, World Council of Churches, 1994.

Weisse, Wolfram, and Carel Anthonissen, eds. *Maintaining Apartheid or Promoting Change? The Role of the Dutch Reformed Church in a Phase of Increasing Conflict in South Africa.* Religion and Society in Transition, no. 5. New York: Waxman Münster, 2004.

Westminster Confession of Faith. Glasgow: Free Presbyterian Publications, 1647/1985.

Williams, George H. *The Radical Reformation.* 3rd ed. Kirksville, MO: Truman State University, 1995.

Williams, Walter, *South Africa's War against Capitalism.* Cape Town, Kenwyn-Johannesburg: Juta, 1990.

Wingren, Gustaf. *Man and the Incarnation: A Study in the Biblical Theology of Irenaeus.* Translated by Ross Mackenzie. Edinburgh: Oliver & Boyd, 1959.

———. *The Flight from Creation.* Minneapolis, MN: Augsburg, 1971.

———. *Creation and Gospel: The New Situation in European Theology.* With an Introduction and Bibliography by Henry VanderGoot. Eugene, OR: Wipf and Stock, 1979/2019.

Winter, Ralph D., and Steven C. Hawthorne, eds. *Perspective on the World Christian Movement: A Reader.* 4th ed. Pasadena, CA: Wm. Carey Library, 2009.

Witherow, Thomas. "The Apostolic Church: Which Is It?" In *I Will Build My Church: Selected Writings on Church Polity, Baptism, and the Sabbath.* Edited by Jonathan Gibson. With a Foreword by Sinclair B. Ferguson. Philadelphia: Westminster Seminary Press, 2022.

Wolters, Albert M., *Creation Regained: Biblical Basics for a Reformational Worldview,* with a Postscript co-authored by Michael W. Goheen. Grand Rapids: Eerdmans, 2005.

World Council of Churches [WCC]. *World Conference on Church and Society: Christians in the Technical and Social Revolutions of our Time.* With a Description of the conference by M. M. Thomas and Paul Abrecht. Geneva: World Council of Churches, 1967.

Wright, Christoper J. H. *An Eye for an Eye: The Place of Old Testament Ethics Today.* Downers Grove: IVP, 1983.

Yoder, John Howard. "The Social Shape of the Gospel." In *Exploring Church Growth,* edited by Wilbert R. Shenk, 277–84. Grand Rapids: Eerdmans, 1983.

Yoder, John Howard. "Reformed Versus Anabaptist Social Strategies: An Inadequate Typology." *Theological Students Fellowship* 8 (May–June 1985): 2–7.

Yoder, Perry B. *Shalom: The Bible's Word for Salvation, Justice, & Peace.* Eugene, OR: Wipf and Stock, 2017.

INDEX

Abrahamic Covenant 45, 66, 186, 187, 189,
    191, 192, 193, 214, 221, 222
abortion 70, 177, 279, 296
ABRESCA *see* Alliance of Black
    Reformed Christians in South Africa
Adam 9-10, 51–2, 72, 83, 98, 102, 117, 132,
    136, 138, 152, 162, 179, 204, 213, 214–5,
    248, 257, 278
Adam, Second teaching on 9, 10, 52, 83,
    126, 136, 138, 152, 160, 162, 183, 213–4
    New Man/Mankind in Christ 183
    see also Christology
Adonis, J. C. 1, 16, 17, 18
African National Congress 146, 169,
    236, 238
    ANC/SACP Alliance 146, 169
Afrikaner 1, 3, 6, 14, 15, 18, 21, 22, 23, 24,
    25, 28, 32, 33, 35, 41, 43, 44, 49, 53, 54,
    59, 63, 66, 69, 73, 77, 79, 80, 82, 87, 90,
    93, 106, 111, 122, 147, 149, 152, 170, 176,
    182, 196, 185, 197, 198, 199, 200, 201,

202, 205, 209, 212, 214, 227, 236, 256,
    276, 279, 295, 297, 298, 299, 300, 301
Afrikaans Protestante Kerk 90
Afrikaner apartheid 18, 87
    Afrikaner, black 54
    Afrikaner, brown 54
    Afrikaner churches 209
    Afrikanerdom 301
    Afrikaner-English alliance 146
    Afrikaner inclusivists 19
    Afrikaner-dominated State 205
    Afrikaner National Party *see*
      National Party
    Afrikaner theologians 23, 106, 122, 197,
      198, 212
    Afrikanervolk 177, 237
*After Apartheid: The Solution for South
    Africa* 23
alien laws 21, 22, 86, 183, 201, 224, 267, 275,
    280, 287
    alien, love 44

322   INDEX

alien-citizen distinction 74, 225, 242, 251, 280
  believing alien 224, 280
  biblical laws 121, 277, 284
  ethnic alien 22, 44, 183, 201, 223, 225, 240, 280
  linguistic alien 86, 223
  one legal standard for citizen and alien 277, 280, 287
  permanent resident alien (ger) 21
  see also stranger (ger) laws
Alliance of Black Reformed Christians in South Africa (ABRECSA) 71, 72
already-but-not-yet tension 7, 131, 141, 143, 165, 229
amillennial view 126, 141
Anabaptist *see* Radical Reformation
ANC/SACP alliance 146, 169, 236, 238, 294
Anglicization process *see* English
Anderson, Bernhard 208, 209, 210, 211, 215
Anglo-American 121, 122, 126, 198, 199, 200
Anglo-Boer War 22, 196, 240, 300
Anglo-Saxon imperialism 197
Anglo-South African 29, 33, 43, 72, 79, 90, 240, 254, 277
Anti-apartheid movement 67
Anti-apartheid theologian 80
Apartheid 1, 2, 3, 4, 5, 14–24, 25, 26–8, 30–6, 40, 41, 50, 52, 53, 59, 69, 70, 72–5, 77, 82, 83, 107, 108, 117, 123, 124, 130, 145, 152, 158, 161, 162, 166, 169, 170, 171, 182, 190, 195, 198, 200, 203, 205, 209, 215, 217, 224, 235, 240, 252, 264, 267, 274, 275, 278, 281–3, 292, 294, 296, 297
  Apartheid alternative 170
  Apartheid caste system 224
  Apartheid churches 58, 161
  Apartheid evil 82
  "Apartheid is a heresy" 2, 25, 26, 35
  Apartheid ideology 166, 298
  Apartheid Imperial Colonialism 52

Apartheid justification 166
Apartheid legislation 57, 120, 196
Apartheid politician 116
Apartheid regime 198, 240
Apartheid South Africa 145
Apartheid state 43, 85, 87, 202, 267
Apartheid social theology 35
Apartheid system 44, 76, 122, 252, 297
Apartheid theologian 118, 132, 161, 297
Apartheid theology 6, 14, 24, 25, 26, 31, 69, 72, 84, 108, 124, 169, 170
Apartheid verses .190
  see also Separate Development
Apostles' Creed 127, 188
  First Article doctrine 127, 128, 154, 166
  Second Article doctrine 66, 127, 151, 154, 155, 157, 166, 167, 169
  Third Article doctrine 128, 151, 166
Augustine, St. of Hippo 248

Babel 39, 102, 167–8, 195, 201, 203–7, 207–12, 276
  Babel-Pentecost Relationship 66, 83–4
  C&S Reverses HRLS on Babel 203
Barth, Karl 3-4, 19, 23, 24–5, 26, 39, 49, 66, 67, 70, 77, 99, 100, 101, 106, 118, 119, 127, 139, 158, 163, 167, 170, 179, 180, 189
  Barthian-influenced (oriented) 24, 39, 71, 99, 103, 106, 107, 111, 118, 128, 139, 204, 214
  Barth and the believers' church 158, 163
  Barth and the Radical Reformation 163, 179–80
  Barth and "peopleness" 167-8
  Barth (doctrine of Scripture) 99, 106, 107, 109, 111, 112, 114
  Neo-orthodox 23, 66, 99, 106–7, 112, 114, 116, 118, 119, 128, 139, 142, 158, 167, 169, 179, 291
Bavinck, Herman 5, 70, 84, 115, 132, 134, 168, 185, 213

INDEX

Bavinck on a biblical third way 84, 95, 115
Bavinck's doctrine of Scripture 5, 70, 95
Bavinck on nature and grace 70, 134, 161, 168
Bavinck on Radical [Anabaptistic] Reformation 132
Beisner, E. Calvin 241–2
Belgic Confession see *Three Forms of Unity*
Belhar Confession 13, 17, 19, 27–31
    see also Dutch Reformed Mission Church
Berkouwer, G. C. 4, 99, 100, 101, 102, 111
    Holy Scripture 95, 99, 100, 118
biblical errancy 114
biblical law *see* tôranic wisdom
Blumenfeld, Samuel 265
Boer 49, 87, 199
    Boer Republics 198, 199
    see also Anglo-Boer War
Bonhoeffer, Dietrich 26, 72, 73
Bosch, David 5, 18, 19, 24, 80, 81, 84, 165, 176, 179, 218
Boshoff, Carel 14, 15
boundaries 201,278, 279, 282
    cause oppression and injustice in philosophical theories 70-1,
    church
        parish boundaries 76, 88
        classis/presbytery 88
        General synod 88
    ethics of maintaining 278, 279
    importance of in Scripture 11, 74, 201–2, 282
    imperially imposed boundaries 43, 278, 279, 282, 293
    in ancient Israel 282
    of language and culture 47
    of race in Apartheid 69
    overstepping of defines tyranny 74
    politico-economic 280
    post-New South Africa Afrikaner, proposal 301
Braaten, Carl E. 127, 137, 139, 143

British Empire 87, 199
    Annexed Xhosa territories 87
    brutal oppression of Afrikaners in Anglo-Boer War 196, 198, 199, 240
    brutally crushed Zulu kingdom 199
    unifying and homogenizing intention 199
    mono-ethnic Swaziland and Botswana given independence by 301
Bromiley, G. W. 190-1
Brunner, Emil 128, 134, 180

Calvin, John 10, 62, 65, 104, 127, 133, 211, 214, 239, 240, 272, 285
    Anti-Calvinist 265
    Calvinism 15, 31, 172, 298
    Neo-Calvinism 82-3, 104, 122, 160, 207
Canons of Dort see *Three Forms of Unity*
Cape-Afrikaans 16, 185
Capitalism 23, 240, 247
case laws *see* Pentateuch
CERCOS (Centre for Reformed and Contemporary Studies) 110, 111
Chicago Statement on Biblical Inerrancy and Hermeneutics 96
Chilton, David 6, 7, 236, 239, 285
Christian Reformed Church of North America (CRCNA) 26
Christology 162, 168, 169
    Second Adam Christology 83, 136, 152, 167
    Second Article Christology 167
    see also Adam
C&S
    Church and Society: A Testimony of the Dutch Reformed Church (Ned Geref Kerk)(1986, 1990 [2d ed.]) 3
    C&S 1986 3, 5, 6, 27, 33, 34, 39, 57, 101, 121, 153, 260, 299
    C&S 1990 3, 4, 6, 13, 14–15, 21, 25, 28, 30–4, 36, 37–57, 59–60, 61–72, 75–86, 88–89, 93, 97, 99, 101, 103, 105, 109, 111, 113–24, 125, 127, 132, 139, 144, 145–8, 151–70, 171–85, 187–8, 190–6,

198–202, 203–4, 207, 211–12, 213–21, 223, 227, 229, 231, 233–6, 238, 240–1, 245, 248–50, 252–3, 255, 257–68, 271–84, 288–89, 291–2, 294–99

Church Growth School of Missiology
  (Fuller) 18, 72, 78, 80, 82, 207, 208, 209, 218
  Extractionist missiology 174, 174, 175, 180

Church
  holist-individualist church 274
  covenantal church 7, 9, 16, 28, 48, 64, 66, 67, 75, 87, 142, 159, 163, 171–2, 173, 183, 189, 193
  ethno-covenantal solidarity in 28, 64, 87, 174, 177, 183, 187, 188, 189, 190, 192, 221, 300
  ethno-covenantal diversity in 75, 195, 212, 300
  Federal/covenantal unity 85, 90, 180, 187, 189

Church Order, Synod of Dort see Synod of Dort Church Order

Cohn, Norman 55, 73, 132–3, 163, 165

colonialism 52, 53, 122, 199, 227
  decolonize 122
  decolonize the decolonizers 52, 199

Communist Manifesto, The see Marx, Karl

Concept of Ethnicity in the Bible: A Theological Analysis see Kreitzer, Mark

confederation of Churches see federation of Churches

Covenant Principle 7, 9, 16, 48, 66
  Covenantal rights 249, 253, 255
  Orthodox Dutch Reformed covenantalism 7, 9, 16, 48, 66, 138, 142, 154, 159, 163, 168, 171, 172, 173, 180, 181, 183, 184, 187, 188, 189, 193, 195, 208, 213, 214, 216, 217, 219, 220, 221, 222, 226, 241, 243, 244, 249, 253, 255, 256, 261, 264, 272, 273, 286, 291–2, 292, 293
  Covenant education 264
  Covenant equity 286

Creatio ex nihilo 125, 132

Creation account 102, 155, 161, 176, 215, 257, 278

Creation Restoration Principle 7, 70, 125, 151, 300

crony Capitalism 247

Cultural Mandate 7, 126, 142, 167–8, 295

Cunningham, Harold G. 234

Dahl, N. H. 135

Dayton, Edward and David Fraser 195–6, 208

Decolonize see colonialism

De Gruchy, John 1, 2, 20, 25–7, 28–9, 33, 36, 72–3

Deist, Ferdinand 35–6, 97, 98, 105, 106

Deuteronomy 22:5 233

Dialogical inspiration see Heyns, Johan

Dominion Covenant 9, 123, 126, 138, 142, 206, 208, 251, 256, 266, 271, 285

DRC see Dutch Reformed Church of South Africa

DRMC see Dutch Reformed Mission Church

Du Plessis, Johannes 97-9, 107

Du Toit, A. B. 114–5

Duewel,Wesley L. 65

Dumas, André 163

Durand, J. J. F. 4, 106, 107, 108
  "Church and State in South Africa: Karl Barth vs. Abraham Kuyper" 106

Dutch Reformed covenantalism see Covenant Principle

Dutch Reformed Church in Africa, multi-lingual, "black" 53

Dutch Reformed Church of South Africa (DRC) 1, 3, 5, 16, 20, 29, 36, 53, 95, 108, 182, 301
  General Synod as concept or term 54, 76, 88, 89, 156
  General Synod of the Dutch Reformed Church in the Cape 16
  General Synod 1974 1, 13, 14
  General Synod 1982 3

INDEX

General Synod 1986 3, 13, 31, 59, 101–2, 103, 111
General Synod 1990 3, 13, 29, 34, 37, 49, 59, 109, 151, 156, 157, 289
General Synod 1994 29
General Synod Commission 1988 161–2
Dutch Reformed Mission Church(DRMC) General Synod 1982 27
   see also Belhar Confession

ecclesiology
   Anabaptist 172
   "Church centered" 158, 191
Edlin, Richard 265
egalitarianism 237, 238
Eglinton, James 207
Engles, Friedrich 165, 166, 167, 249
   Peasant War in Germany,The 166
English 2, 14, 24, 40, 53, 59, 61, 79, 87, 89, 90, 122, 146, 158, 184, 199, 202, 230, 234, 279, 298, 300
   Common Law 280
   language of Anglo-South Africans 19, 299
   lingua franca 90, 146, 202
   Anglicization process 41
   imperial language 158, 185, 199
   imperialism of 52, 87, 122, 158
Equity 236, 252, 274, 282, 283, 286, 287, 288, 301
   and biblical covenantal rights and responsibilities 253, 254, 255, 286
   and culture transformation 293
   and *Discriminatory Law* 277
   and the South African economy 288
   and the C&S 1990 257, 259, 284
   and Mosaic judicials 262, 266, 274, 275, 285
   and restitution 255
   and stranger laws 275, 276
   Four Levels of Abstraction in 232, 234
   definition of and justice 235, 239, 252, 257, 260

"general [or universal] equity" of biblical law 11, 140, 220, 230, 231, 232, 242, 243, 263, 277
tôranic equity 230, 236, 239, 249, 250, 252, 268, 272, 280, 301
   see also universal equity
Ethnicity 212
   ethno-covenantal exegesis of HRLS 207
   ethno-covenantal family groups 221
   ethno-covenantal groups or solidarities 2125, 219, 222, 295–6
   ethno-covenantal mosaic 214
   Ethnic Solidarity Principle (ESOP) 274, 284
equalultimacy (of unity and diversity) *see* Trinitarian Principle
equity *see* universal equity
Eschatology 130, 137, 139, 273, 291
   already-but-not-yet 131, 165
   anachronistic 143
   and ethics 127
   classic, reformed eschatology 126
   Communist eschatology 249
   eschatology of victory 141
   futurist [revolutionary-]egalitarian eschatology 128, 129, 146, 291
   optimistic yet restorative and missional eschatology 126, 172, 293, 301
   of hope *see* Moltmann, Jürgen
   pessimistic 293
   Proleptic Eschatology 143, 145, 146
      WCC and 144
   protology-eschatology relationship 130–3, 135, 137
   Puritan Hope 140
   realistic, long-term victorious 137, 139, 221
   recapitulative 148
   Third-Article [futurist] 167
ethnic alien 22
   see ethno-linguistic alien
   see alien laws
   see stranger laws

326 INDEX

ethno-covenantal alien *see* ethno-linguistic alien
ethno-covenantally defined citizen *see* ethno-citizen
ethnic bonds (*volksverband*) 46
Ethno-covenantal solidarity *see* Ethnicity
Ethno-centric perspective 227
ethno-church (*volskerk*) 57, 61, 63, 72, 76, 86, 90, 223
ethno-cultural group, diversity, or distinction 65, 67, 69, 70, 75, 80, 85, 98, 149, 162, 166, 168, 176, 177, 193, 212, 215, 216–7, 219, 226, 227, 281, 295
ethno-linguistic alien 223, 280, 281
ethno-citizen or ethno-covenantally defined citizen 225, 280, 281, 281
ethno-linguistic group, diversity, or identity 49, 51, 53, 54, 55, 56, 57, 61, 63, 65, 66, 67, 69, 71, 76, 80, 81, 85, 86, 87, 122, 161, 183, 184, 191, 193, 195, 203, 207, 209, 212–3, 219, 237, 249, 274, 290, 292
ethno-linguistic based social order 87
ethno-linguistic uniformity [ideal] 209
ethno-nations 48, 191, 192, 193, 196–7, 198, 222, 299
ethno-national solidarity or diversity 222, 226, 295
ethno-peoples 222
ethno-racial churches (of apartheid) 63, 67, 212
ethno-states 91
ethno-linguistic people-groups 126, 141
ethno-national civil government 295
ethno-worldview 282

Fascism 177, 237, 247, 298
   see also Statism and crony Capitalism
Faith and Protest 32, 33, 161–2
Farewell to Apartheid? Church Relations in South Africa 27, 32, 35, 182
federation (or confederation) of churches 86, 89, 292

Lutheran World Federation 2, 25
Swiss Federation of Protestant Churches 20, 26
First Article doctrine *see* Apostles' Creed
Flew, Antony 237, 238, 239
free market 239, 271, 289
economics 22
economist 240
system or order 247, 248, 249, 295
Free University of Amsterdam 23, 38, 70
Freedom of
Association and/or Disassociation 266
Expression 278
Religion 262
Speech and Movement 265
Fuller, Daniel 190, 191, 192, 193
Fuller School of World Mission 5, 18, 208
Fundamentalism or fundamentalist 114, 115, 190
Fundamentalist approach to Scripture (or mechanical view) 4, 99, 204
Fundamentalist majority in DRC 98
Kuyperian 98
sectarian 110

Gaffin, Richard 95
Gage,Warren 137
Galatians 3:28 (Gal 3:28) 18, 26, 49, 78, 123, 152, 163, 165, 193
Gassmann, Günther 144, 145, 146
Gay marriage 102
General equity *see* universal equity
Genevan Reformation 122, 133, 294
Ger laws *see* stranger laws and alien laws
German Christians 23, 129, 134
Gnosticism 55, 73, 74, 279
Golden Rule (and social ethics) 235, 266, 277, 278
Great Commandment(s) 266, 268
Great Commission 6, 7, 51, 58, 75, 126, 141, 149, 219, 222, 295
Greenley, Andrew 208, 210
Gunton, Colin 37

INDEX

Heidelberg Catechism see *Three Forms of Unity*

Heyns, Johan Adam 14, 101, 111, 112, 113, 114, 115, 117, 145
  dialogical inspiration 101, 112, 113, 119
  relationship to G. C. Berkouwer 111

Hoekendijk, J. C. 18, 80

Hexham, Irving 22
  The Irony of Apartheid: The Struggle for National Independence of Afrikaner Calvinism against British Imperialism 22

Holism 4, 11, 49, 50, 176, 200, 217
  individualist holism 200, 217, 226
  monistic concept of 176
  one-world holism 200
  social holism 4
  statist holism 292
  theological holism 227
  see also wholism
  see also Jan Smuts

Holism and Evolution 11, 49, 176

Homogeneous Unit Principle (HUP) 72, 217, 218, 226

Homogeneous nature of French Revolution and Imperialism (A. Kuyper) 198

Homosexual(s) 57, 124, 132, 266, 276
  homosexuality 31, 233, 296
  see LGBTQ+

HRLS see *Human Relations and the South African Scene in the Light of Scripture*

Hughes, Dewi A. 196, 197

human dignity 67, 108, 119, 223, 227, 236, 240, 254, 257, 258, 261, 282
  and people-group identity 227
  and voting 223–4

HRLS see *Human Relations and the South African Scene in the Light of Scripture*

Human Relations and the South African Scene in the Light of Scripture 13, 14, 25, 166
  Landman Commission 14, 20
  Landman Report 20

Ras, Volk en Nasie en Volkereverhouding in die Lig van die Skrif 14

HUP *see* Homogeneous Unit Principle

Human rights (especially in C&S) 147, 253, 257–62, 262–4
  Biblical definition of 253–7, 263–4
  UN guaranteed 148
  Universal Declaration of Human Rights 147

Hurley, James 190, 193, 194, 195

image of God 8, 26, 52, 149, 224, 225, 231, 240, 250, 251, 256, 257, 259, 264, 279
  imago Dei 257

imago Dei see image of God

Imperialism 79, 196, 201, 227, 300
  African indigenous imperialism 43, 227
  Afrikaner people, ironic imperialism of 198–9
  Afrikaner resistance to 122
  Anglo-Saxon 197
  British, imperialism of 22
  condemned by Prophets 201
  homogenizing result of 43, 52
  imperial imposed boundaries *see* boundaries
  imperial language 52, 158, 227
  Western in Africa 300
  see also Hexham, Irving

Inerrancy 94, 96
  see also Scripture Alone Principle

Infallibility 90–8, 99, 103, 104, 106
  as sectarian fundamentalism accusation 110–1
  anti-infallibility in DRC 98, 106, 113
  bibliolatry of 99
  classic Kuyperian view 111
  danger of rejecting 124, 299
  definition of 94, 95, 109
  form-content distinction 100, 104
  mechanical theory accusation 109, 115
  way forward 299
  see also Scripture Alone Principle

328 INDEX

International Socialism *see* Marxism

Irenaeus, St. 133, 135, 136

   recapitulative eschatology *see*
     eschatology

irruption of Kingdom 129, 131, 132

Israelvisie [Israel Vision] 185

John, Apostle

   Apocalypse of 141, 178

   John 17 62, 63, 64, 65, 123, 185

Jones, Peter 73, 74

Jonker, Willem Daniël Jonker
   ("Willie") 103

Jordaan, Christiaan L. 111

Justice 28, 29, 52, 118, 162, 227, 230–1,
   232, 234, 236–8, 240–4, 248, 273, 284,
   286, 294

   biblical wisdom based 291

   collectivist approaches to 241, 287

   definition of in Scripture 242, 248, 250–
     1, 286, 287, 288, 291, 301–2

   impartial and unchanging justice 11, 22,
     52, 162, 232, 234, 235, 238, 240, 242,
     246, 250, 251, 269, 286, 292

   linguistic justice 44, 87, 212, 220

   oppression and 286

   option for the poor and oppressed 29

   pro-active justice 250

   racial justice 18, 278

   redistributionary justice 147, 150

   retributive and restorative
     justice 139, 240–4

   versus K. Marx 288

   see Social Justice

Kik, J. Marcellus 141

   Puritan Hope 141

Kinghorn, Johann 3, 15, 16, 17, 25, 31, 32,
   36, 118, 158, 161

King Jesus 7, 8, 9, 10, 126, 133, 171, 172, 173,
   271, 276

   Anointed King 133, 191, 229, 271

   Kingdom of God in 10

   Lord of heaven and earth 195, 301

   Messiah-King 161

   Most holy Imperial Majesty 43

   of Nazareth 9, 43

   Universal Church of 48

Kloppers, F. 114

König, Adrio 4, 24, 30, 135

Korea, South 227

   Korean classis in CRCNA 40

   Korean Presbytery in PCA 40

Korea, North 263

Kreitzer, Mark 15, 83, 84, 221, 280

   "Ethnic Solidarity, Babel-Pentecost
     Relationship, and the New
     Covenant" 66

   *'n Manifes vir Christene in Suiderlike
     Afrika* [A Manifesto for Christian in
     SouthernAfrica] 111

   *The Concept of Ethnicity in the Bible: A
     Theological Analysis* 21, 48, 74, 84, 108,
     167, 177, 187, 189, 195, 206, 219, 221,
     224, 226, 280

   "Toward a Biblical Philosophy of
     Science" 38

Kruger, Paul 87

Kulaks 71, 177

Kuyper, Abraham 2, 4, 5, 23, 24, 28, 38, 65,
   69, 70, 83, 84, 85, 95, 99, 100, 106, 107,
   115, 118, 123, 128, 132, 137, 161, 168,
   184, 197, 198, 200, 206, 207, 235, 240,
   241, 264, 298, 299

   Dutch-Kuyperian 139

   Kuyperian 2, 23, 25, 37, 43, 77, 82, 107,
     110, 116, 139, 160, 169, 199, 200, 206,
     213, 272, 283, 301

   Kuyperian construct 32

   Kuyperian fundamentalism 99, 111

   Kuyperianism 81, 106, 107, 120

   Kuyperianized apartheid social
     theology 25

   Kuyperian Neo-Calvinist 160

   Kuyperian one-kingdom perspective
     139

   Kuyperian resistance 106, 107

   Kuyperian social analysis 106

INDEX 329

Kuyperian theology 2, 3, 38, 107, 124, 143, 167
Kuyperian transformationalist view 301
Kuyperian versus Barthian 107
Kuyperian view of Scripture 24, 25, 99, 100, 101, 106, 114, 116, 143
Non-Kuyperian 24, 204

Landman Commission see *Human Relations and the South African Scene in the Light of Scripture*
Landman, W. A. 20, 22
Leviticus, book of 22, 242
  18:22 233
  18:26-30 201
  19:15 242
  19:33-4 22, 281
Lewis, C. S. 241, 242
  God in the Dock 241, 242
LGBTQ+ 5, 19, 30, 31, 45, 98, 108, 154, 166, 169, 238
  see homosexuality
  see transvestitism
Liberation Theologian 14, 165
Liberation, ethnic 82, 220
Liberation 130, 144
  movements 93, 146
  sentiment (anti-colonial) 17
  sexual 238
Liberation Theology 28, 29, 67, 96, 131, 283
Louw, Leon and Francis Kendall 23, 34
  see *After Apartheid: The Solution for South Africa*
Lückhoff, A. H. 20
Lutheran World Federation *see* federation of churches

Mandela, Nelson 71, 85, 97, 236
Mattheos, Juan 165
Marx, Karl 73, 166, 176, 177, 238, 249, 288
  Communist Manifesto, The 248, 288
  ten planks/steps to socialism 288
Marxian 106, 165, 247, 248, 283, 288
  Neo-Marxian 23, 29, 67, 96, 166, 298

social analysis 106, 239
Marxism 127, 143, 146, 177, 284
  Antifa and 166
  globalism and 284
  Labor Theory of Value 249
  Marxism-Leninism 131, 247, 263, 288
  myth of original communal property 290
  pre-Marxist 166
  revolution and 200, 288
  totalitarian state and 239
Marxist *see* Marxism
McGavran, Donald 5, 18, 77, 78, 80, 174, 208, 218
  conglomerate churches and 77, 78, 174
  important works of 78
Mennonite Central Committee *see* Radical Reformation
Missiology 1, 5, 6, 14, 15, 16, 17, 18, 19, 24, 31, 66, 72, 81, 84
  apartheid missiology 20, 21, 35
  biblical missiology 114
  Church Growth Missiology 72, 80, 208, 218
  extractionist missiology 174
  HRLS missiology 204
  Warneck school of missiology 81
Moltmann, Jürgen 128, 129, 131, 134, 143, 145
  already-but-not-yet consensus 143
  Eschatology of Hope 134
  inspiration for ecclesia based revolutionary movements 130–1
  later moderating aspect of 131
  nova creationist (radically new) 131
  radically futurist 130, 131, 139, 143, 144
  rejects creation-based ethic 133
monopoly 227, 247
  central banking monopoly 288, 297
  economic 267
  media 298
  political 264
  unjust nature of 297
Motyer, J. Alex 189, 190, 250, 251
Müntzer, Thomas *see* Radical Reformation

330 INDEX

Murray, Andrew 24, 53, 299
 missional and warm piety wing of
  DRC 24, 299
 opposed to Kuyperian transformationist
  wing of DRC 299
Murray, Iain 126, 140, 221
 Puritan Hope 126, 140, 221
Murray, John 221, 232, 254

Nash, Ronald 239, 240, 241, 242, 243,
 246
National Party, Afrikaner 20, 34, 170, 199,
 236, 237, 252
 socialism of 240
 apartheid vision 264, 298
National Socialism 18, 23, 177, 298
 Nazi 26, 129, 134
 Nazism 26, 177, 263
Naudé, Beyers 35
Nazi *see* National Socialism
Nederduitse Gereformeerde Kerk see Dutch
 Reformed Church
Nederduitse Gereformeerde Sending
 Kerk *see* Dutch Reformed
 Mission Church
Neo-Calvinism *see* Calvinism
Neo-Marxian *see* Marxian
Neo-Orthodox *see* Barth, Karl
New South Africa *see* South Africa
Nova Creatio (totally-new creation) 130–3,
 157, 161, 166, 173, 274, 293
 Church as 157
North, Gary 6, 7, 141, 208, 231, 249, 254,
 266, 271, 285, 291

Ong, Andrew 82, 83, 84
Optimillennialism 141, 142
Orthodox Dutch Reformed covenantalism
 see Covenant Principle
Orthodox Movement 41, 44, 59
 Eastern Orthodox communion of
  churches 44, 59, 144

Padilla, Rene 218, 219

paradigm 8, 85, 121, 123, 124, 153, 210, 211,
 220, 234, 237, 243
 paradigm shift (DRC) 1–5, 6, 19, 25, 33,
  35, 36, 45, 84, 85, 93, 95, 97, 101, 103,
  105, 106, 109, 111, 115, 145, 148, 156,
  196, 199, 271
 anti-Reformational paradigm shift 298
 Barthian background 168, 169
 Berkouwer, G.C. paradigm shift 99
 biblical paradigm shift 46, 155, 167, 168,
  199, 229, 246
 caused centralizing tendency 294
 changed the nation 145, 148, 158, 240
 individualizing paradigm shift 189
 in DRC ecclesiology 158
 paradigm shift not for the good 121, 123,
  252, 299
 possible motive for 153, 154, 155
 in social theology 6, 35, 124
Paul, Apostle 136
Pentateuch 21, 75, 102, 107, 169, 201, 208,
 230, 239
 Mosaic authorship of 98, 107, 155, 156
 case laws in 230
 see also stranger laws
Pentecost 39, 40, 187, 195, 201, 210, 214, 216
 Babel-Pentecost relationship 66, 84,
  201, 207
 Creation and 201
 does not reverse linguistic
  diversity 195, 207
 fulfilled Abrahamic covenant 187
 miracle of 66, 84, 216
Peoples' Republic of China, The 79, 295
Perks, Stephen C. 235
Planning Strategies for World Evangelization
 (E. Dayton and D. Fraser) 195, 196
Plato 54, 73
 anti-Christian Platonic assumptions 185
 idealist-platonic 141
 infects doctrine of redemption 228
 Platonic myth 290
 Platonic concepts 69
 platonic-gnostic 84

INDEX

spiritual-platonic form 121, 216
Post New South Africa *see* South Africa
postmillennial view 126
Puritan Hope see Murray, Iain
Potgieter, F. J. M. 37, 61, 69, 109, 110, 132, 162, 179
Potgieter, Johan 260, 261
Potgieter, Pieter 34, 101, 109, 110, 111, 115
Preus, Robert 95
Protology 126, 130, 137
  matured 126
  protology-eschatology 130, 132, 133, 135
Puritan Hope see Murray, Iain

qahal Yahweh 160, 183, 224

Race Groups 1, 205, 252
  C&S rightly rejects 63
  only Scripture on (Sg 1:6; Jer 13:23) 57, 162, 294
  race-color not co-extensive with ethnicity 280, 295
  race-color and property/association rights 266
  race-color basis as ethnic demarcation indicator 16, 17, 21
  race-color in Scripture descriptive not prescriptive 57
  race-color basis for separation is evil and oppressive 57-8
  race-color basis for denomination 16, 20, 28, 57, 58, 63, 72, 89, 122
  race-color basis for denomination versus linguistic basis 90
  race-color basis for mission 17
  race-color basis of separate political orders 16, 28, 57, 122, 161, 205, 206
  failed miserably and evil 161, 278
  race-color and ethnic identity equated in HRLS 205
  race-color grouped with LGBTQ+ and other groups 238, 238
  race-color versus groupless individual, false dilemma 274

Ras, Volk en Nasie en Volkereverhouding in die Lig van die Skrif see *Human Relations and the South African Scene in the Light of Scripture*
Radical Reformation 217
  Anabaptist 24, 54, 62, 72, 132, 138, 139, 162, 164, 171, 172, 175, 179, 217, 290
  Anabaptist-Radical individualized holism 217
  Anabaptist social strategies versus Reformed 171, 179, 217
  Christ against culture (Niebuhr) 217
  Biblical Anabaptist 164
  Mennonite-Anabaptist 72
  Mennonite Central Committee 164
  Müntzer,Thomas 54, 164, 166
  non-covenantal 172, 179, 217
  Peasant War in Germany,The see Engles, Friedrich
Radical Anabaptists 54, 62, 132, 162, 290
  van Leyden, Jan 54, 164, 165, 166
Rainbow Nation, South Africa 43, 79, 85, 169, 200
recapitulation *(Recapitulatio)* 125-6, 130-4, 135, 136, 137, 138, 139, 140
  and Irenaeus 135-6
  and Kuyperian one-kingdom view 139
  and union with Christ 140
  conservative and transformative 140
  continuity with covenants 138
  continuity with creation order 137
  implications for social theology 138, 140
  meaning of 135
  rejected by C&S 161, 169
  renovatio or renovation, equivalent to 133
  restoration, equivalent to 125
Reformed Theology 26, 39, 60, 66, 83, 139, 155, 159, 239, 247
  and the Universal Assembly 160
  orthodox or classic, Dutch/Continental Reformed 39, 66, 119, 139, 155, 159, 239, 247
  almost completely abandoned by DRC 60

332 INDEX

reformational theology 229
renovatio or renovation *see* recapitulation
restoration *see* recapitulation
Report of the Landman Commission see
    Human Relations and the South African
    Scene in the Light of Scripture
Repristination 55, 131, 132, 133
  and recapitulation 133
Republic of South Africa (RSA) *see*
  South Africa
Ridderbos, H. [Herman] 4, 99, 139
rights 86-7, 117, 169
  and responsibilities, C&S 258, 259
  and responsibilities, biblical 8, 225, 232,
    241, 243, 244, 249, 253, 254, 256, 261,
    266, 276, 280, 282
  alienable 256
  entitlement-rights 87, 244, 248, 250, 251,
    253, 262, 264
  entitlement to, State-granted 242, 246,
    247, 248, 258, 261
  responsibility-rights, Decalogue based 241,
    251, 253, 254, 286
  inalienable 17, 87, 122, 220, 249, 255, 256
  right to just system (income, health care,
    vote, etc.), C&S 182, 243, 244, 249,
    250, 253, 259, 261, 262, 264, 265, 266,
    276, 279, 280, 282, 287
  rights, human *see* human rights
Robertson, O. Palmer 7, 8
Rules Based International System 198,
  200, 201
Rushdoony, R. J. 37, 38, 94, 178, 208, 241,
  263, 264, 265, 280, 285

SACC *see* South African Council of
  Churches
SACP *see* South African Communist Party
Sacraments, Lord's Table, Baptismal
  font 28, 57
  Sign, sacrament and instrument, Church
    is 143, 144, 145, 146
  Word and Sacrament 56, 143, 144
Schöpfungsordnungen [creation orders] 129,
  149

Schuurman, Douglas 128, 129, 130, 131,
  134, 140
Scripture Alone Principle 7, 36, 93, 96, 104,
  105, 108, 109, 118, 148, 173, 200, 261,
  285, 286, 295
  higher-critical view and 97, 99, 100, 101,
    103, 107, 111, 113, 114, 122, 149, 154,
    155, 156, 167, 200, 202
  sola Scriptura 93, 95–6, 97, 103, 104, 105,
    108, 109, 116, 121–3, 124, 173, 190,
    220, 240, 293, 299
Second Adam *see* Adam
Second Article doctrine *see*
  Apostles' Creed
Second Adam Christology *see* Christology
Second Coming 7, 8, 131, 136, 141, 229
Semper Reformanda 94
Separate development (separateness) 1, 14,
  123, 200, 203, 235, 298
  and C&S 4, 44, 174, 273–4, 277
  and HRLS 10, 14, 15, 206
  and Afrikaner, National Party 298
  and Radical Reformation critics 218
  and WARC 182
  coerced vs. voluntary 81, 123
  meaning of Apartheid 14, 27, 123, 235
  of race-based denominations 1, 15, 16,
    20, 45, 47, 80, 81
  of volk-groups 21, 22
  syncretistic 205
Shafarevich, Igor 163, 165, 236–8
Smuts, Jan 11, 49, 50, 176
  and UN Charter 49
  coined term "holism" 11, 176
  pantheist 49
  The Holistic Smuts 11, 49
Social analysis 106, 239, 248
  biblical 248, 259, 263, 264
  Reformed 248
    see Kuyperian social analysis
    see Marxian social analysis
social theology 1, 229, 230, 294
  and covenantal worldview 292
  and DRC 1, 6, 13, 14, 20, 24, 25, 32, 38,
    99, 106, 128. 138, 196, 291

INDEX

333

and missiology 6
and SACC 33
and WCC 5, 6
definition of 11
Protestant versions of 171
Reformation-based 6, 114, 153, 158, 167
syncretistic version 29, 167, 294
see also Apartheid social theology
Social Gospel 6
Social Justice (especially in C&S) 6, 24, 26, 28, 67, 96, 129, 145, 147, 236–8, 248, 249, 252–3, 275, 282–3, 287, 296
Socialism 240, 247, 248, 249, 287, 287, 288
and Afrikaner, National Party 240
and Communism 298
and social justice 237
benefit the rich 288
democratic socialist ideology 247
International 177, 248
Marx's ten planks 288
social democratic ideology 236, 237, 238, 239, 242, 244, 245
Soviet 22, 71, 236
revolutionary socialism (Marxist-Leninism) 237
see also Fascism
see also National Socialism
sola Scriptura *see* Scripture Alone Principle
South Africa, country of 1, 2, 5, 18, 19, 23, 26, 43, 53, 82, 94, 98, 99, 119, 145, 146, 147, 152, 196, 198, 199, 207, 209, 227, 229, 238, 286, 298, 299, 300
and Afrikaner Apartheid 198, 252
and English imperialism 199
and English language 41, 158
and Xhosa-Zulu rule 199
as welfare state 280
ethnic problems in 294
New South Africa (1994 to present) 16, 30, 59, 71, 85, 86, 87, 110, 145, 162, 169, 200, 252, 289, 290, 296
oppression of Euro-South African 252
paradigm shift in 111

Post New South Africa (author postulated) 88–9, 94, 240, 249, 262, 290, 299–301
Republic of 19, 67, 85, 170, 241, 294, 300
Union of South Africa 87, 300
United States and 50, 79, 241
South African Council of Churches (SACC) 2, 6, 31, 33
South African Communist Party 146, 169, 238
SACP 294
Sproul, R. C. 96, 109, 111
Spykman, Gordon 8, 9, 125, 127, 128, 133, 137, 138
Statism, coercive and redistributory 241, 247
and crony Capitalism 247
statist 243, 247, 250, 252, 261, 268, 280, 292
status confessionis 25, 26, 27
Stendahl, Krister 163, 165
stranger laws (*ger* laws) 169, 201, 249, 275, 280, 281, 282
similar to equal protection principle 280, 281
see also Alien Laws
Stoker, H. G. 77, 111, 297, 298
Stoker, Henk G. 298
Synod of Dort Church Order 41, 44, 61, 76
allowed for linguistic diversity 41, 76
synodocracy of DRC General Synod 124, 156
institutional infallibility 124
replaces biblical infallibility 124

The Holistic Smuts see Smuts, Jan
Three Forms of Unity 27, 29, 51, 95, 273
Belgic Confession 51, 62, 64, 95, 96, 98, 102, 138, 156, 230, 234, 239, 262, 290
Heidelberg Catechism 51, 239, 262
Canons of the Synod of Dort 29, 51, 268
Third Article doctrine *see* Apostles' Creed
three governments (family, civil, and ecclesial) 10, 232

INDEX

tôranic wisdom 75, 115, 208, 220, 223, 256,
  271, 274, 276, 280, 282
  and Pentateuch 208, 271, 301
  sin of apartheid 282
  and sound biblical ethic 301
  biblical 220, 223, 224, 229, 236, 247,
    249, 251, 252, 263, 268, 272, 273, 274,
    291, 293
  of the Law and Prophets 271, 301
  unchanging 273
  view of justice 291
Transvestitism 233, 278
  see also LGBTQ+
transformatio mundi (transformation of the
  world) 130, 133
Treurnicht, A. P. 116, 117, 118
Trinitarian Principle 7, 36, 37, 40, 45,
  53, 62, 64, 65, 84, 90, 153, 212, 220,
  299, 300
Tswana people and language 53, 73, 79,
  122, 149, 185, 299, 301

United States 50, 79, 148, 241, 266
Uniting Reformed Church 29, 30, 53, 59,
  66, 78, 80, 185
Universal Declaration of Human Rights see
  human rights
Universal equity 230, 231, 232, 234, 236,
  239, 242, 249, 250, 253, 254, 255, 257,
  260, 268, 274, 275, 276, 277, 280, 282,
  288, 293
  and culture transformation 293
  and divine character and creation
    design 230
  and trans-culturally validity 231
  C&S rejects 234, 284
  definition of justice and 239, 288
  definition 11, 230–2
  general equity, synonym of 231
  and moral law 239
  of biblical law 260
  of judicial laws 239
University of Cape Town (UCT) 2,
  14, 32, 33

University of Pretoria (UP) 14, 24, 111, 114
University of South Africa (UNISA) 113,
  135, 260
University of Stellenbosch (US) 14, 35, 105

van Leyden, Jan see Radical Reformation
Van Til, Cornelius A. 37, 38, 83, 84, 109
Veenhof, Jan 70, 132
Verenigende Gereformeerde Kerk see
    Uniting Reformed Church (of South
    Africa)
Verhoef, P. A. 14, 156, 161, 162
Verkuyl, J. (Johannes) 18, 19, 122
Villa-Vicencio, Charles 2, 4, 14, 25, 26, 32,
  33, 36, 107, 118
Voegelin, Eric 55, 73
Volkskerk see ethno-church
Volksverband see ethnic bonds
Von Allman, Daniel 20, 21
von Rad, Gerhard 207, 318

Wagner, C. Peter 18, 82, 208, 209, 210, 215,
  217, 218, 219, 220, 226, 227
  see also Homogeneous Unit Principle
WARC see World Alliance of Reformed
    Churches
Warneck, Gustav 18, 81
WCRC see World Communion of
    Reformed Churches
Western Cape Regional Synod, DRC 103
Westminster Confession of Faith 235,
  239, 262
Westminster Larger Catechism 231, 239,
  260, 287
WCC see World Council of Churches
Whole Scripture Principle 7, 69, 75, 229,
  232, 301
wholism 11, 292
  definition 11
  in contrast to holism 11
Williams, Walter 22, 23, 172, 240
Wingren, Gustaf 129, 135, 136, 137,
  168, 170
Wolters, Albert 10, 125, 134

World Council of Churches (WCC) 2, 5, 6, 18, 29, 33, 34, 69, 103, 144, 145, 146, 147, 154, 200, 284

World Alliance of Reformed Churches (now WCRC) 2, 14, 25, 27, 35, 72, 182

World Communion of Reformed Churches (WCRC) *see* World Alliance of Reformed Churches

Wright, Christopher J. H. 211, 212, 225, 226, 285, 255

Xhosa 27, 43, 53, 59, 73, 79, 87, 90, 122, 146, 149, 184, 200, 276, 295, 299, 300
  abandoned to Anglo-American world hegemony 122
  ANC Xhosa dominated 43
  as ethnic Other 79
  confederal state with Zulu and Swazi 262
  culture 73
  heartland 27
  independent political unit 59
  language 53, 149, 184, 185, 198
  Xhosa-Zulu alliance 146, 199, 240
Xhosa-Zulu coalition *see* Xhosa

Yoder, John Howard 72, 83
  Mennonite-Anabaptist author 72, 83, 84, 164, 171

Zulu 27, 43, 53, 54, 59, 79, 87, 120, 146, 149, 177, 182, 185, 199, 227, 299, 300
  abandoned to English dominated world hegemony 122
  and apartheid laws 120, 198
  annexation of Zulu Kingdom 87, 199, 200
  as ethnic Other 79
  colonial shame 199
  Kwa-Zulu Natal province 27, 59, 300
  culture 73, 149
  ethno-nation 43, 54
  indigenous denomination 59
  independent Kwa-Zulu Natal 59
  language, love of 53, 79, 185, 295
  Xhosa-Zulu alliance/coalition *see* Xhosa
  Zulu imperialism 227
  Zulu, Xhosa, Swazi confederation (postulated) 262